'Wise portrayals of romantic nationalists are much rarer now as 21st-century Western academia and the publishing world start to extol enemies of gradualism and peaceful change. This is a probing and detached appraisal of the seven revolutionaries who placed Ireland on a fateful course in 1916.

It seeks to explore and explain rather than condemn or disparage. Connolly, Pearse, Clarke and the others obtain more sympathetic treatment from Ruth Dudley Edwards than many of their hagiographers are likely to provide. This book will give succour to moderate citizens in Ireland at an emotive time when the island looks back. It warns of the damage and futility ensuing when the politics of grievance are channelled into violence. It is a lesson applicable for many Western countries where cultural and educational shifts mean there may be plenty of 'rebels' yearning to perform their own 'purifying' 1916 act.'

Tom Gallagher – Emeritus Professor in Peace Studies, University of Bradford, author and commentator

'Ruth Dudley Edwards brings a unique perspective to bear on the leaders of the Easter Rising: empathetic, interrogative, and highly conscious of the questions raised and left unanswered by their sacrificial gesture of rebellion. With this book she completes the analysis begun with her path-breaking study of Patrick Pearse nearly forty years ago, providing a group biography of the disparate revolutionary leaders and a clear-eyed consideration of the legacy they left. It should be required reading.'

R. F. Foster, Carroll Professor of Irish History, University of Oxford

'The leaders of the 1916 Rising are generally regarded by Irish nationalists as heroes and they are honoured as the founding fathers of the Irish Republic. A minority take the view that the Rising was unnecessary and undemocratic. In a timely re-assessment, the respected historian Ruth Dudley Edwards looks at the legacy of seven leaders of the Rising, including the legacy of violence which has blighted Ireland in the century since. Her book deserves a wide readership both by traditional nationalists and by those who believe it is time to reassess the legacy of the Rising.'

Seán Donlon, former Head of the Irish Diplomatic Service

THE SEVEN

*The Lives and Legacies of
the Founding Fathers of the Irish Republic*

RUTH DUDLEY EDWARDS

ONEWORLD

A Oneworld Book

First published in North America, Great Britain and
Australia by Oneworld Publications, 2016
Reprinted, 2016

Copyright © Ruth Dudley Edwards 2016
Map copyright © Laura McFarlane 2016

The moral right of Ruth Dudley Edwards to be identified as the Author of this work has
been asserted by her in accordance with the Copyright, Designs, and Patents Act 1988

ISBN 978-1-78074-865-8
eISBN 978-1-78074-872-6

Typeset by Hewer Text UK Ltd, Edinburgh
Printed and bound by Clays Ltd, St Ives plc

Oneworld Publications
10 Bloomsbury Street
London WC1B 3SR
England

To Owen, my brother

CONTENTS

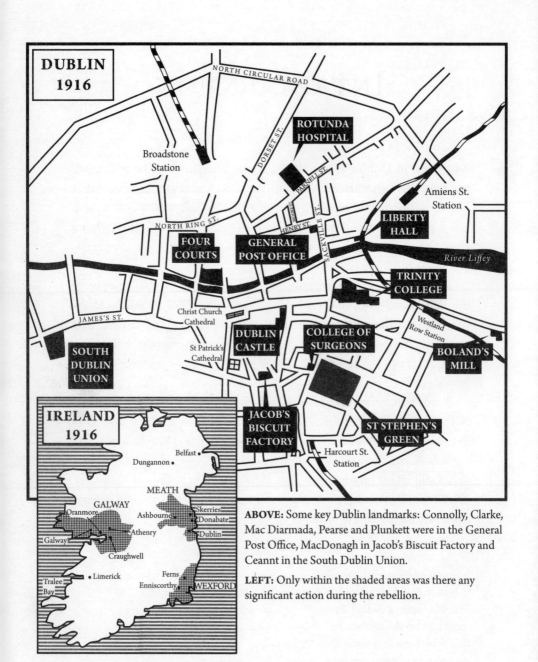

ABOVE: Some key Dublin landmarks: Connolly, Clarke, Mac Diarmada, Pearse and Plunkett were in the General Post Office, MacDonagh in Jacob's Biscuit Factory and Ceannt in the South Dublin Union.

LEFT: Only within the shaded areas was there any significant action during the rebellion.

INTRODUCTION

As a child in Dublin in the 1950s, I was fascinated by the enormous picture over the fireplace in the bedroom occupied by my Grandmother Edwards, the devout republican in the family. Called *The Last Stand*, it was a portrait in the heroic style of a scene of carnage in the General Post Office during the last desperate hours of what was popularly known as the 1916 Easter Rising.[*]

In the picture, Grandmother pointed out to me five signatories of the Proclamation of the Irish Republic who had been 'murdered' by the British. (She never minced her words.) There in the centre, lying on a stretcher, was Commandant General James Connolly, the spokesman of the poor who led the Irish Citizen Army, bravely bearing the terrible pain of his shattered ankle.

Beside him, gazing into the middle distance, was the visionary President of the Provisional Republic, Patrick Pearse; he was standing beside his devoted brother, Willie, who was not a signatory but who was executed anyway. Racing towards Connolly was the poet Joseph Plunkett, seriously ill but still intent on freeing Ireland. At the bottom of the stretcher knelt Seán Mac Diarmada, Connolly's adjutant, and peeping self-effacingly from behind the Pearse brothers was the moustachioed Thomas Clarke.[†]

---

[*] The term Easter Rising, with its religious overtones, is the one long favoured in nationalist Ireland and is seen by critics as loaded. When in 1992 David Trimble, later a Nobel Prize winner for his part in making peace, wrote a pamphlet on the subject, he called it *The Easter Rebellion of 1916*. Sometimes in this book I use that term, as I also use insurrection or rebellion, without worrying too much about precise meanings or theological or legalistic implications.

[†] Scholars disagree about some of these identifications, but I think Grandmother got them right.

(Thomas MacDonagh and Éamonn Ceannt, the other two signatories, were fighting elsewhere, but posters showing the Proclamation headed or surrounded by headshots of seven men were ubiquitous.)

Occasionally, Grandmother would arrive home in late afternoon and announce portentously: 'I have had tea with Mrs Tom Clarke and she says the Pearses think they own 1916.' I did not really follow what this was about – it would take a while for me to grasp that men I had been told were heroes and martyrs were not mythical beings but real people with living relatives who were not always in harmony.

In my primary school, where teaching was through Irish and the ethos was intensely patriotic, there were reverential references to *Éirí Amach na Cásca* (the up-rising at Easter) or *Aiséirí na Cásca* (literally, the resurrection at Easter) as the heroic climax of 800 years of nationalist struggle. We were told that afterwards there was a war of independence against the British, which we won. History seemingly came to an end in 1921.

We were told nothing at school about the casualties of 1916 or the subsequent war: the dead who mattered were those executed by the British, particularly Patrick Pearse. Nor were we told about the bitter civil war following the Anglo-Irish treaty, or the seventy-seven men executed by Free State forces. And if Northern Ireland was ever mentioned, it was as a bit of Ireland that was ours, and we would get it back some day. No one ever seemed to go there or know anything about it.

I was better informed than most because my parents talked at home about such inconvenient facts as civil war fatalities, sundered families and vicious political divisions, the involvement of many Irishmen in the British Army in the two world wars, and their view that Protestant unionists deserved our respect. Unlike the IRA and fellow-travellers like my fascist grandmother, they had also been unequivocally anti-Nazi.

It was Patrick Pearse who most fascinated me, because we were told he was the noblest man in Irish history and that he could be canonized someday, yet no one seemed to know anything about him. One friend was taught in her middle-class convent school that Jesus and Pearse were the only two men in the history of the world who were exactly six feet tall. That kind of nonsense made me want to find the real man. I wrote a student paper about Pearse as an educationalist and in 1964 I tried and failed to find enough material to write a master's thesis about him. The following year, a new cathedral consecrated in Galway city had a side chapel where the image of the risen Christ was flanked by mosaic representations of Patrick Pearse and John F. Kennedy praying to him. Both of them, along with favourite popes and saints, were on many an Irish nationalist mantelpiece.

Then came 1966 and a raft of commemorations that caused some thoughtful people to question discreetly why we had embraced the Easter Rising lock, stock and barrel and why we sang songs praising people who had later killed in its name. The Irish proclamation that was our nationalist bible told us that 'the Irish Republic is entitled to, and hereby claims, the allegiance of every Irishman and Irishwoman'. Yet those who had written and signed it were unelected and claimed their justification from God and 'the dead generations' rather than a living electorate. So did those who followed their example.

After 1969, with the eruption of full-scale terrorism, everything became much more relevant and some new historical material became available. Although I was living and working in England, I jumped at a request from a publisher to write a biography of Patrick Pearse.

Published in 1977, the book was a critical success, though denounced by IRA apologists as revisionist, a term of abuse levelled at anyone critically examining the nationalist narrative. However, as Marxism became fashionable, Pearse began to recede slightly into the background and his socialist comrade-in-arms James Connolly moved into the foreground. I wrote a short book about him too. As a biographer, I don't have to agree with my subjects: I was not hostile to either Pearse or Connolly, though I concluded they had opened a Pandora's box.

Although I've written a lot about non-Irish subjects, the Troubles kept me close to Ireland not least, from 1993, as a journalist. I was fascinated by the nationalist preoccupation with a seamless lineage of heroes and martyrs, particularly over the past two centuries, who have been used to inspire generation after generation to kill and die for Ireland without any regard to the wishes of the people.

Coming up to the centenary of 1916, a flood of books has emerged. Many now try to paint a complex picture – most Irish people have moved beyond the stage of thinking that the nationalist narrative is the only one that deserves a civil hearing.

It is significant how fairly the National Library in Dublin, in its introduction to its 1916 Exhibition, pointed out that initially the insurrection had been widely condemned as 'foolhardy in the extreme and downright criminal', but that within two years 'a substantial sector of the nationalist electorate now pledged allegiance to the Irish Republic and honoured the Proclamation as virtually constituting the national constitution':

> The morality and political legacy of the 1916 Rising have long been matters of debate. Some maintain that the Rising was unnecessary and that a republic could have been achieved by purely democratic means, claiming that the limited form of Home Rule already enacted (but suspended for the duration of the war) was a basis for further advance in an evolving process. They deplore the loss of life and national trauma resulting from the Rising, from the ensuing War of Independence (1919–21) and from the Civil War (1922–23), and further argue that the Rising made the Ulster unionists more averse to sharing power with nationalists, thus making the partition of the country in 1921 all the more inevitable. Others, however, believe that the 1916 Rising was the catalyst that inspired the country to abandon Home Rule as a worthless half-measure and to strive for complete independence from Britain. These accord the 1916 leaders iconic status as the founding fathers of the present Irish Republic.

I became obsessed with the subject again, particularly the founding fathers. There were good new biographies, but each concentrated on one subject, making the others bit parts in each other's lives. I became ever more curious about why and how such an apparently ill-matched group should have teamed up and done what they did, what the chemistry was like between them, and who led whom into what and how.

And so I wrote this book . . .

Chapter One

THOMAS J. CLARKE[1]

Tom Clarke himself wrote that the horrors of his convict
cell had burned ineffaceable memories into his soul.
What had burned into his soul was something akin
to the Miltonic hate, unconquerable will and study of
revenge, and most certainly a courage never to submit or
yield until the flame of insurrection and a flash of rifles
rounded off the tragic glory and intensity of his life.[2]

Desmond Ryan, 1959

Able, vengeful, focused, selfless and implacable, Tom Clarke was the
spider at the centre of the conspiratorial web. Although he was better
known to the police and intelligence services in Dublin than he ever
was to the public, he was the primary, consistent driving force behind
the Rising. From the age of twenty-one, when he committed himself
to the cause of Irish independence, until his death forty years later,
Clarke never wavered in his dedication to rebellion, whatever its
terrible cost in suffering to him, his wife, his family or the people of
Ireland.

It was a life that would have horrified his father.

In 1847, a month short of his eighteenth birthday, in Ballyshannon,
County Donegal, Clarke's father James joined the Royal Artillery as a
cavalry soldier. He had been brought up on a four-acre farm shared by
his father and uncle in Carrigallen, Leitrim, which was by now in the
second year of the devastating famine that through death and emigration would reduce the population of the county by a quarter. A
member of the Church of Ireland and loyal to the crown, Clarke
would survive dreadful conditions fighting against Russia in the
Crimean War.[3]

Now a bombardier, he was garrisoned in 1856 with his regiment in Clonmel, County Tipperary, when he met Mary Palmer, an illiterate Roman Catholic servant from Clogheen whose father worked in the Bridewell jail; they married in an Anglican church in her village two months after she bore their son, Thomas James, on 11 March 1857.[4] James agreed that their children would follow her religion.

James Clarke was stationed on the Isle of Wight at this time, but when Tom was two he and his mother accompanied the regiment to South Africa. Augmented by daughter Maria Jane, the family returned to Ireland in 1865 when Tom was eight, by which time the boy, who had been to school in Natal, was already sympathetic to the Boers, seeing them as victims of British oppression, and would embrace their cause passionately. As boy and man, Tom Clarke was of fixed views: he would never seem aware that, while the Boers had legitimate griev-ances, much of their quarrel with their colonial governors had to do with enlightened British actions in abolishing slavery and imposing legal equality between races.

James Clarke – who had risen through the non-commissioned officer ranks – transferred on return to the Ulster Militia as a sergeant and set up home in Dungannon, in Tyrone.[*] He would remain in the army until 1886 when, at fifty-six, he was discharged on the grounds of age.

Dungannon was a bitter town in an angry county: the inhabitants of Tyrone were mired in tribal and sectarian hatred. From a Gaelic Catholic perspective, it was part of a vast area of land that was forcibly seized and colonised by the crown after clan chief Hugh O'Neill, 2nd Earl of Tyrone, had been forced into exile in 1607, along with many other native leaders. From the perspective of the English and Scottish Anglican and Presbyterian settlers, internecine warfare between native clans had made proper cultivation of land impossible and the constant backdoor threat from continental Catholic enemies made confiscation and reallocation of land justifiable. To them, the Ulster Plantation was a force for peace and prosperity. The town was evenly split between Catholics and the generally more prosperous

---

* In 1868, after twenty-one years of service, he was honourably discharged and given a pension, but immediately appointed a sergeant on the permanent staff.

Protestants; vicious sectarian rioting was frequent, particularly when there were parades on their respective high days by the Orange Order, founded in 1795 to uphold the Protestant Faith, or the Catholic Ancient Order of Hibernians (AOH), set up in opposition several decades later.

Tom Clarke was educated at St Patrick's National School. His wife would later say that his character had been formed by 'the ruin and desolation, the evictions and injustices he saw all around him [that] drove him mad'.[5] He was ten at the time of the abortive Fenian* upris- ing of 1867, which further polarised the population, not least because police and soldiers kept a close eye on republican sympathisers.

The normal school-leaving age was about thirteen, but, though shy, Clarke was clever and industrious and was appointed a monitor, an assistant to his teacher, Cornelius Collins. The job was that of a badly paid dogsbody. In the 1890s (while trying to help get him released from jail), Collins would describe Clarke as having been 'a quiet, harmless, good boy, regular in his attendance to school duty, and respectful and attentive in the discharge of the work laid off for him by me'.[6]

Yet Clarke was instinctively rebellious and the loathing he had developed in South Africa for the British was honed and intensified in his school years in Dungannon. His school friend Billy Kelly said that even in his early teens he was obsessed with driving out the British and 'found no pleasure in the companionship of anyone who acquiesced in the existing regime'.[7]

Nor did Clarke find any pleasure in learning about views that chal- lenged his own. He read Irish history for confirmation of English villainy and of Irish suffering interspersed with derring-do and heroism. He was particularly stirred by the story of the United Irishmen, educated liberal Protestants inspired by the ideals of the French Revolution to form in 1791 in Belfast – then a cauldron of reformist political ideas – a society dedicated to the achievement of religious equality and a radical

---

* The secret oath-bound Irish Revolutionary (later Republican) Brotherhood, otherwise known as 'the organisation' or the Fenians, was set up in 1858 with the objective of establishing an Irish republic through physical force; it was based in Britain, Ireland and America.

extension of the franchise. He loved their leader, the effervescent utopian Dubliner Theobald Wolfe Tone.*

Radicalised by the unresponsiveness of the Dublin parliament and by the outbreak in 1793 of war between Britain and revolutionary France, the United Irishmen embraced violent republicanism and sought and obtained French support. Their anti-sectarian ethos was fatally undermined when they were joined by large numbers of Defenders, members of an oath-bound Catholic agrarian secret society with a history of cruelty. Yet Tone was sanguine about revolution: if there was a strong enough invading French force, he believed, it would be supported by the Presbyterians, who were 'the most enlightened body of the nation . . . are steady republicans, devoted to liberty and through all the stages of the French revolution have been enthusiastically attached to it'. The vast majority of Catholics would support it too, for they 'are in the lowest degree of ignorance and are ready for any change because no change can make them worse'.

As well as stirring rhetoric, there was plenty of romance in the Tone story, which culminated in a dramatic last few years, to stir the imagination of the young Clarke. To avoid prosecution for his association with a French spy, in 1795 Tone agreed to go with his family to live in America, but he hated it, not least because the American government

---

* Tone was born in 1763 in Dublin, the eldest of sixteen children, of whom six survived infancy. His Church of Ireland father was a coachbuilder descended from sixteenth-century French religious refugees: his Catholic mother converted to Protestantism when Wolfe was eight. Though he wanted to join the army, he was sent to Trinity College in 1791; suspended for a year after a fatal duel, he returned as an outstanding student and debater. Given to passionate attachments, he eloped in 1785 with a sixteen-year-old, with whom he had four children. Impulsive, curious and easily distracted, he qualified as a lawyer, but was utterly bored. After the outbreak of the French Revolution in 1789, he became a pamphleteer, denying that Ireland had any obligations to be involved in Britain's foreign wars. In 1791 in the brilliantly written, passionate and influential *An argument on behalf of the Catholics of Ireland*, he echoed other advanced reformers by calling for unity of all denominations in pursuit of parliamentary reform. He ignored the evidence that there were many Presbyterians who doubted that Catholics were fit for liberty and many Catholics who trusted the government more than they did Presbyterians.

refused to back the French revolutionary government against the British. He yearned to be part of the action back home. The following year he left to become a revolutionary ambassador to France. Later that year, in his new role as a French brigadier general, he sailed from Brest to Cork with more than 14,000 troops, but disastrous weather sent the fleet back to France without landing a single soldier.* Enraged at this treason in wartime, the government's savagely repressive measures, implemented by yeomen and militia, escalated to the imposition of harsh martial law and executions of suspects.

The United Irishmen continued to plan a rebellion, believing that they could count on about 250,000 supporters, with 100,000 from Ulster. Well-meaning, but ignorant and naïve about both the French revolutionaries and his fellow-Irishmen, as Thomas Bartlett puts it, Tone 'was utterly blind to the havoc wreaked by the French war machine on Europe (and on France); he had only a hazy idea of the furies that lurked beneath the surface of Irish life and which would have undoubtedly emerged after a successful French invasion.'[8]

Back in Paris, he had some inconclusive meetings with Napoleon Bonaparte, the rising military star, who sounded positive but was occupied elsewhere. Tone was surprised to learn of the rebellion in Ireland that had begun in May 1798: already doomed because government spies had led to the arrest of most of the leadership, the outbreaks of violence were scattered, incoherent and mostly aborted. A supportive French invasion in August had short-lived success and its successor, in September, with Tone on board again, was another fiasco that led to his capture.

In the dock, Tone cut a romantic figure in full French uniform: 'A large and fiercely cocked hat with broad gold lace and the tricoloured

* Such setbacks did not silence the balladeers. The *Shan Van Vocht* (a corruption of Sean Bhean Bhocht – 'poor old woman' – a poetic representation of Ireland) assures the listener that 'the French are on the sea', 'the Orange will decay', the yeomen will 'throw off the red and blue' and green will be ubiquitous. It ends:
And will Ireland then be free?
Says the Shan Van Vocht
Yes! Ireland shall be free,
From the centre to the sea;
Then hurrah for Liberty!
Says the Shan Van Vocht

cockade, a blue uniform coat with gold and embroidered collar and two large gold epaulets, blue pantaloons with gold laced garters at the knees and short boots bound at the top with gold lace.' He pleaded guilty, though denied he was a traitor, explaining in his fine speech from the dock that he had fought under the French flag 'to save and liberate my own country'. For that aim, he had 'repeatedly braved the terrors of the ocean' and had 'courted poverty; I have left a beloved wife, unprotected, and children whom I adored, fatherless. After such sacrifices, in a cause which I have always conscientiously considered as the cause of justice and freedom – it is no great effort, at this day, to add the sacrifice of my life.' He was denied his request to be shot rather than hanged and committed suicide.

The authorities were interested in crimes, not motives. About 30,000 people had died and there were terrible atrocities on both sides: the massacres of Protestants by priest-led rebels in Wexford ended Presbyterian flirtations with rebellion.* As well as striking a heavy blow against notions of fraternity and equality, another unintended consequence was the end of the Irish parliament, for in 1801 the government introduced the Act of Union to bind the two kingdoms firmly into the United Kingdom of Great Britain and Ireland.

His aspirations, life and death made Wolfe Tone the patron saint of Irish republican separatism and the life-long hero of Tom Clarke. 'To subvert the tyranny of our execrable government,' Tone had said in words that would be echoed down the generations,

> to break the connection with England, the never failing source of all our political evils, and to assert the independence of my country – these were my objects. To unite the whole people of Ireland, to abolish the memory of all past dissentions, and to substitute the common name of

---

* In the ballad 'Father Murphy', a priest from Boolavogue, who had proved a daring and effective rebel leader, was compared to his advantage with Julius Caesar, Alexander and King Arthur. The last verse of the much more rousing and still popular 'Boolavogue', written for the centenary of 1798, is: 'God grant you glory, brave Father Murphy, / And open Heaven to all your men, / The cause that called you may call tomorrow / In another fight for the Green again.'

Irishman, in the place of the denominations of Protestant, Catholic, and Dissenter – these were my means.

These were also to be the aims and means of Thomas James Clarke.

In viewing Tone and his legacy uncritically, Clarke was part of a long Irish tradition of worshipping unexamined heroes because of their good intentions and tragic ends. Most people blamed the authorities for the terrible events caused by the revolution and more songs and stories of rebel martyrs were added to the long oral history of Ireland's wrongs. Ireland's is a singing culture full of potent songs about valour and sacrifice and suffering that fuel nationalism, with ballads so rousing and memorable as to be enjoyed even by those of different political persuasions. Many of the songs extolling the United Irishmen and subsequent anti-sectarian revolutionaries would be sung into the twenty-first century by a band called the Wolfe Tones, which specialised in celebrating the Provisional IRA and its squalid sectarian war on Irish Protestants. In his prison diary, the hunger striker Bobby Sands referred to 'The Rising of the Moon', possibly the most famous of all songs commemorating 1798. It ends: 'And a thousand pikes* were flashing at the rising of the moon / At the rising of the moon, at the rising of the moon. / And a thousand pikes were flashing at the rising of the moon.'

Yet there was nothing sectarian about Clarke. His consciousness that both Protestant idealism and Catholic bigotry featured in 1798, combined with the Catholic Church's condemnation of oath-bound organisations like the Fenians, helped make him lukewarm about his religion and inclined towards anti-clericalism. He would have no prejudices against Protestants as long as they shared his politics.

Tom Clarke's parents had eight children, of whom four survived. Theirs was an affectionate home: family harmony survived Tom's teenage rejection of his father's loyalties and his refusal to contemplate acquiescing with his wish that he follow him into the British army, as

---

* The pike remains a metaphor for arms. The IRA reluctance to decommission in the early part of this century, for instance, is still referred to as wishing to 'keep the pike in the thatch'.

Alfred, thirteen years Tom's junior, later did. Tom would tell his wife that in discussion of his politics his father assured him that the British Empire was unassailable. Defying it, he said, would be akin to banging his head against a wall, to which Tom said he replied that he would just keep going however long it took. In that, as in so much else, he was a man of his word.

In 1878, when he was twenty-one, Clarke's instinctive pull towards physical-force nationalism found its validation when he heard a rousing speech by John Daly, a separatist zealot from Limerick who would dictate the course of Clarke's life and become one of his most intimate friends and co-conspirators.

From an ardently republican family, Daly had joined the secret Irish Republic Brotherhood (IRB) in 1865 at the age of eighteen. His niece Kathleen would record that he had imbibed his passionate republicanism from his mother, who led night-time family prayers that always began with a supplication for Irish freedom. Mothers, aunts and grandmothers who told children tales of Irish suffering and nationalist heroism were a potent force in inspiring generations of men to kill and die for Ireland. It was, as Conor Cruise O'Brien once said, a mutant gene transmitted through the female line.

Arrested and tried for treason-felony* in March 1867 and released on sureties of good behaviour, Daly took part the following month in an IRB attack on a Limerick police barracks and had to flee to America. He returned home in 1869 and in 1872 was appointed travelling organiser of the IRB in Ulster and joined its supreme council. Implacably opposed to the Home Rule movement, he disrupted its public meetings at every opportunity.

The oratory of this charismatic, uncompromising man convinced Clarke he should devote himself to the overthrow of British authority in Ireland. Not long afterwards, in Dublin, Daly formally set Clarke on his life-long revolutionary path by having the young man and his best

---

* Treason, which covered deeds, carried an aggravated death penalty disliked by juries. The 1848 Treason Felony Act covered threats and conspiracies and imposed penalties of transportation or imprisonment. It infuriated those Fenians who regarded themselves as political prisoners rather than common criminals.

friend Billy Kelly swear a solemn oath to do their 'utmost to establish the independence of Ireland' and 'bear true allegiance to the Supreme Council of the Irish Republican Brotherhood and the Government of the Irish Republic and implicitly obey the constitution of the Irish Republican Brotherhood' and all their superior officers, and 'preserve inviolable the secrets of the organisation'.

The pair had travelled to Dublin under the improbable auspices of the Dungannon Catholic and Total Abstinence Reading Rooms and Dramatic Club, in which Clarke was a prominent actor. Such was his success in the role of the crippled, homicidal, doomed servant Danny in Dion Boucicault's melodrama *Colleen Bawn* that he was invited to join the Irish National Company. Instead, Clarke accepted Daly's instruction to be the centre, or leader, of the Dungannon District Circle* of the IRB, a cell that operated under the cover of the club. His acting ability would, however, prove useful throughout a life of concealment, conspiracy and deceit. Like Daly, he was implacably opposed to constitutional nationalism and loathed the Home Rule[†] movement, and as a leader he was 'a strong disciplinarian, with no mercy for slackers'.[9]

Clarke met his mentor again when Daly came to address the IRB members on the need to be armed and trained for action when required, especially against the Royal Irish Constabulary (RIC). On 15 August 1880, a parade celebrating the Feast of the Assumption was attacked by Protestants, and in the ensuing savage riot the police fired on the crowd; one died, many were injured, and Clarke and Kelly were among those firing back. The following night, according to Kelly, they and the rest of the circle fired on several members of the RIC and, though there were no casualties, with Clarke under suspicion from the

* Organised on continental lines, and designed to reduce the impact of inform-ers, assuming there were enough recruits, a centre (A) appointed nine captains (B), who each selected nine sergeants (C), who each appointed nine men (D), with rigid hierarchical restrictions on who knew what.

† The opposition to the Act of Union gradually developed into a succession of popular and parliamentary campaigns for a return to parliamentary independ-ence that in the mid-nineteenth century became known in all their constitu-tional manifestations as the Home Rule movement.

authorities, he, Kelly and some others decided to abandon Dungannon and head for America. Falling school rolls had cost Clarke his monitor's job and he had nothing to lose. He left without telling his family.

They reached New York in October and headed straight to the house of Pat O'Connor, from Dungannon, who was a member of the IRB's sister organisation, Clan na Gael.* He gave them jobs in his shoe shop for a few months, after which Clarke became a night porter in a Brooklyn hotel and Kelly a boilerman.

O'Connor introduced them to Clan na Gael's Napper Tandy Club,[†] where they were sworn in. Clarke – described long afterwards by its president as a 'bright, earnest, wiry, alert young fellow' – soon became recording secretary. The Clan provided a political and social outlet for its members as it sought money to finance the armed campaign back home: the young men had neither need nor inclination to look for company or inspiration beyond its virulently Anglophobic boundaries.

In 1871 Prime Minister William Gladstone had released and exiled to America several IRB prisoners, who immediately set about revitalising Irish-American revolutionary politics before falling out over policy. John Devoy, who for most of Tom Clarke's life would be the dominant figure in the Clan, had lost support from the more militant wing in 1879 when he put the organisation's weight and resources behind what became known as the 'New Departure', an alliance in Ireland of the IRB, the National Land League and Charles Stewart Parnell's parliamentary party.

What Tom Clarke had learned about hate in Dungannon was mild compared to what he would encounter in Irish America, which lived

---

* When the IRB's American sister organisation, the Fenian Brotherhood, split rancorously after a decade, the IRB sided with those who formed in 1867 the new Irish–American secret society known as Clan na Gael. It recognised the authority of the IRB Supreme Council.
† Napper Tandy had an inglorious career as a revolutionary leader in 1798, ended up living self-indulgently in France, and was immortalised in the famous lament 'The Wearing of the Green':
    I met with Napper Tandy, and he took me by the hand
    And he said, 'How's poor old Ireland, and how does she stand?'
    'She's the most distressful country that ever yet was seen
    For they're hanging men and women there for the Wearin' o' the Green.'

off an ever more wildly embellished narrative about past grievances and heroic struggles. None of the stories and songs of persecution and resistance was distinguished for understatement. There was, for instance, no one in nationalist circles challenging the belief that the famine had been genocide. The gifted and incendiary propagandist John Mitchel, the Young Irelanders'* greatest hater, explained it thus: 'The Almighty indeed sent the potato blight but the English created the famine . . . a million and half men, women and children were carefully, prudently and peacefully slain by the English government.'

Popular mythology added such memorable twists as the story invented in the late nineteenth century and cherished in republican circles that Queen Victoria – who became vilified as the 'Famine Queen' – had contemptuously donated just £5 for famine relief. She had in fact given £2000,[†] the largest individual donation in the kingdom.

Irish Americans would take the narrative of exceptional Irish victimhood to extreme levels of narcissism, self-pity and absurdity and feed it back to republicans in Ireland in what became a malign circle. For decades, old exiled Fenians ruled the roost in New York, Boston and Chicago, collecting dimes and dollars to incite, fund and control revolution back home. Many of them did well in business, politics and the law. Revered for having suffered when transported or imprisoned, they enlisted for their cause younger men who would meet such fates, or worse.

---

* The Young Irelanders were a group of idealists that included cultural, political and social nationalists who became radicalised after the outbreak of a terrible famine in 1845 and inspired by Europe-wide insurrections would launch a rebellion in July 1848 that was farcically ineffective and derided in the press as the rebellion of 'the Widow McCormack's cabbage patch'. John Mitchel, from a Londonderry Presbyterian family, was a lawyer who became a brilliant and openly seditious journalist and who in May 1848, despite the efforts of Robert Emmet's brother-in-law, his defence counsel, was sentenced to transportation. After Bermuda and Australia, he ended up in America, where as an enthusiast for slavery he sent his three sons to join the Confederate Army.

† Calculated in today's money as being worth anything from £150,000 to over £2 million.

Jeremiah O'Donovan Rossa, who had been released with Devoy, was a legendary hater. His family had been impoverished and separated by the famine, which his reading of John Mitchel had convinced him was genocide, and set him on the Fenian path that would land him in jail. His account of the 'severest of sufferings and indignities' he endured 'in the British dungeons', said Henri Le Caron (a successful British spy in Irish America), won him much sympathy, 'and as both in public and in private he lost no opportunity of dilating upon his grievance, the sentiment was in no sense allowed to waver or grow weak'.[10] Rossa had indeed had terrible times in his first three years in jail, exacerbated by his persistent breaking of the rules and sometimes violent aggression, but Edmund Du Cane, the new chief director of convict prisons, proposed a fresh start in 1868, after which conditions improved considerably. Not that Rossa gave him any such credit.

Self-aggrandising, alcoholic, wildly indiscreet and prone to helping himself to funds, Rossa was set on sending waves of 'skirmishers' to England to slaughter, cause widespread panic and set the English against the Irish in their midst. His plans included the assassination of Queen Victoria, the poisoning of the entire House of Commons and the indiscriminate bombing of civilians. Fenians who believed in a military code of honour and in not alienating public opinion found their voices drowned out by those who embraced terrorism and set out to spread carnage, destruction and panic among the most vulnerable. Devoy was displaced by a triumvirate known as the 'Triangle', led by Alexander Sullivan, a Chicago machine boss, who wished to compete with Rossa by replacing gunpowder with the new-fangled dynamite whose infinite possibilities had seized the imaginations of the bloodthirsty.

Where previous republican militants had been prepared to accept civilian casualties as an unintended consequence, these believed in a terror campaign that would seek them out. The instruments of terror were single young men whose lives their superiors were happy to lay down for Ireland. Le Caron, who was close to many of the Clan na Gael leadership, wrote in 1892 of his profound contempt for the 'modern Irish political agitator in America'. In a description that would be true of elements of Irish America for more than a century, he wrote:

Brave and blustering in speech, he advocates, in the safety of his American city, three thousand miles from the seat of danger, the most desperate of enterprises; and without the slightest pang of compunction or twinge of conscience he rushes his poor dupes across the water to their fate on the scaffold or the living death of penal servitude.[11]

As the historian Carla King has reminded us, Michael Davitt, who transformed Irish politics and society with the foundation in 1879 of the Irish National Land League, habitually referred to Rossa as 'O'Donovan Assa', describing him as 'the buffoon in Irish revolution-ary politics with no advantage to himself but with terrible consequences to the many poor wretches who acted the Sancho Panza to his more than idiotic Don Quixote'.[12]

Rossa's skirmishers began their work in England in 1881. Sullivan was paranoid about infiltration and his preparations took longer, but under him the Clan was set on an 'unsparing and unceasing' course. The executive committee's policy, Clan branches were told in a secret memorandum, 'would be to make assaults in all directions, so that the suffering, bitterness and desolation which followed active measures should be felt in every place'. A memorandum went out seeking 'men best fitted for private work of a confidential and dangerous character': Clarke and Kelly volunteered and, after vetting, were accepted.

Being set on fighting for Ireland one way or another, and being by nature secretive, Clarke had maintained no contact with his family for their and his sake, and he had formed no attachments in New York. That Kelly was less dedicated was clear when he dropped out because his job took him to Long Island.

Clarke's dynamite mentor was Dr Thomas Gallagher, a Glaswegian of Irish parentage who had trained at a New York medical school and had a successful practice. His hatred of Britain was matched by his enthusiasm for explosives. The classes he ran in the Napper Tandy Club lasted for about two years: on one occasion Gallagher took Clarke to Staten Island to blast rocks with nitroglycerine.

In late 1882 Sullivan sent Gallagher to England to plan a civilian bombing campaign and he returned bullish and full of purpose. But, as one of Clarke's biographers put it, 'Tom's fate now rested in the hands of an amateur who was about to give a master class in ineptitude.'[13] Not only had Gallagher little idea of what he was doing, but the spy Henri Le Caron was a trusted confidant.

Gallagher dispatched Alfred George Whitehead to Birmingham to rent premises for a bomb-making factory and two months later others began the journey separately. Clarke, who was now twenty-six, was about to take up a job managing a large hotel near Coney Island, but he answered the skirmishing call instantly and left America under the alias Henry Hammond Wilson. He was so disciplined that he left without telling his friend Billy Kelly, something he said later had been one of the hardest things he ever did. Kelly didn't know he had gone until another Dungannon exile delivered Clarke's trunk to him for safe keeping, along with a note telling him to stonewall any enquiries from the Clarke family.

Le Caron distinguished between 'miserable dupes' and those, like Gallagher and John Daly, who were 'men inspired with fanatical hatred of all things English, and ready at all times to risk freedom and life in working out their designs'.[14] Tom Clarke, whose hatred would rival that of Mitchel and Rossa, would prove to be the most effective of all their recruits.

In 1859, the ship taking the toddler Tom and his parents to South Africa had been involved in a serious collision with a coal ship. In 1883, Clarke almost drowned for the second time when his ship hit an iceberg and sank. The passengers were rescued and taken to Newfoundland, but, given new clothes and £5, Clarke pressed on to Liverpool. By now, as well as knowing from Le Caron that the Clan were planning to bomb London, Special Branch had already responded to a tip-off from a supplier about the paint and wallpaper shop in which Whitehead was industriously manufacturing dynamite, and were watching the building and reading his mail. Conveniently for the police, Clarke, who was en route to London, stopped off in Birmingham, where he met Whitehead, who was being visited by Gallagher.

Elementary errors by several of the conspirators helped put the whole scheme at risk almost immediately. Clarke's contribution to the disaster included a letter to Whitehead with his London address, declaring his intention of calling on him to collect explosives. On 3 April, in Birmingham, Clarke packed a case containing 80lbs of nitroglycerine in rubber bags and returned to London. Gallagher was thinking big: his plan was to blow up the Houses of Parliament and Scotland Yard.[15]

On 4 April, nine days after his arrival in England, the police had Clarke, Gallagher, Whitehead and others in custody along with 500lbs of explosives – enough to destroy large swathes of London. Since January 1881 there had been explosions in Manchester, Chester, Liverpool and Glasgow, and in March 1883 bombs in Whitehall and at *The Times* office. Londoners were terrified by the activities of the Fenian dynamitards and by the feverish rumours of what they were planning next, so in June what was called the 'Dynamite Conspiracy' trial – presided over by the Lord Chief Justice and two other senior judges – was a ticket-only event of great public interest.

They were charged with treason-felony, which, *The Times* explained loftily, had been introduced in 1848 'to clear up uncertainties, and to substitute in certain instances a milder sentence for offenders who were deemed too contemptible to be executed'.[16] Events were followed closely in the United States too, where most of the press were viciously condemnatory of the Irishmen in their midst who were taking advantage of their legal immunity to plan death and destruction in Britain. 'There is not a right-thinking man in this country who does not detest the principles and practices of O'Donovan Rossa and his fellow-Fenians,' said the *New York Times* a few days before Clarke landed in England. 'Who is responsible for their existence, and why do they come over here to try our patience with this violence and make the name of Irish–American fairly hateful to us?' The revelations in court when the six men were charged caused the *New York Herald*, in a philippic against O'Donovan Rossa 'and his gang of dupes, fools and rascals', to declare that it would be 'the first to adjust the noose and pull the rope, were it lawful to hang O'Donovan Rossa and his fellow cowards and blatherskites as the worst enemies Ireland has'.[17]

The six men went on trial at the Old Bailey in June on charges that included levying war and conspiracy to murder. To their horror, the main prosecution witness was one of Gallagher's team who had turned Queen's Evidence. 'It seems to be a law of nature that when three or four partners in an ignoble conspiracy are gathered together an informer is present,' observed *The Times* mordantly.[18]

Sticking to his alias of Henry Hammond Wilson, giving his age as twenty-two and his occupation as clerk (apparently a pun), like his co-defendants, Clarke pleaded not guilty. Never short of self-confidence, he decided, unlike them, to conduct his own defence during the four days of the trial, arguing that there was no proof that he would have committed any crime. He cross-examined witnesses with some success, but made an important mistake by correcting a lawyer about the composition of the explosive found in his room, which brought the response 'So, you know all about it.' That foolish error would help make this already secretive man obsessively so. He never again, wrote one of his biographers, 'said a word too much about anything'.[19]

Clarke refused to address the jury, but received a back-handed compliment from one of the three judges, who regretted 'such ability was misused'. Two defendants were acquitted; the others were sentenced to penal servitude for life. *The Times* reported that Clarke shouted at the judge 'Good-bye, we shall meet in Heaven.'[20]

Thirty years later, Clarke would recall that after the Lord Chief Justice passed the sentence of penal servitude for life on him and three others

> we were hustled out of the dock into the prison van, surrounded by a troop of mounted police, and driven away at a furious pace through the howling mobs that thronged the streets from the Courthouse to Millbank Prison. London was panic-stricken at the time, and the hooting and yelling with which the street mobs used to assail us, going to and from the Courthouse whilst the trial lasted, need not be further noticed. A few hours later saw us in · prison dress, with close-cropped heads.[21]

He had experienced solitary confinement while on remand in Millbank prison, but that had been a temporary privation. What horrified him among the rules and regulations now read to them was that strict silence at all times was obligatory. Prisoners were never to speak to one another and no one would be considered for release for twenty years. Having 'remembered with what relentless savagery the English Government has always dealt with the Irishmen it gets into its clutches, the future appeared as black and appalling as my imagination could then picture it'.

No one except three of the perpetrators was killed by the bombs planted by agents of the Clan and O'Donovan Rossa in a campaign that lasted from 1881 until 1887, four years after Clarke's incarceration, but many others had been hurt, maimed and traumatised, and twenty-five of the dynamitards had been sentenced to penal servitude. By the end, the Clan had split, political Irish America was reeling from the terrible publicity and even hardliners had grasped that violence had been a total failure at a time when Parnell – like Daniel O'Connell before him with Catholic Emancipation – was achieving a great deal for Ireland through the skilful use of a mixture of popular agitation and aggressive tactics at Westminster.

For now, Clarke and the other dynamitards were on their own, 'men with precious few friends on either side of the Irish Sea or the Atlantic'.[22] This time, there was no chance of Gladstone riding to the rescue and once more releasing Fenian prisoners. As would happen to Clarke towards the end of 1883, most Fenians were sent to Chatham, the toughest of the public works prisons.

By 1870, transportation had been replaced by penal servitude in British prisons, with a centralised system laid down by Rossa's saviour, Edmund Du Cane, who became more arrogant over the years and brooked no opposition to his belief in prison as a deterrent and his scepticism about reform or rehabilitation. Conditions were terrible, labour was heavy, the dreary diet was barely adequate and punishments for the infringement of any rules severe. Du Cane believed that silence and isolation improved a prisoner's character. Visitors were limited to two a year for the first four years, and only the exceptionally tough-minded survived mentally intact. The policy was similar but rather less brutal in application to that in operation in the often overcrowded American penitentiaries, where prisoners often went hungry, diseases were rampant, whippings frequent and prisoners were confined to dark cells for weeks on end.

Clarke would write contemptuously that at the time of his conviction 'all England was panic-stricken. The English imagination got rattled and started to work overtime . . . the prison gates did not close out from us the spirit of vengeance that was holding sway throughout

England.' There was some truth in that. Rossa, a hate figure for the British public, was still uttering apocalyptic threats from his American refuge.

The violence unleashed on Britain by the Fenians and threatened from overseas was a new phenomenon that a liberal state struggled to deal with. What they saw as the emotionalism and contrariness of the Irish drove British politicians wild. As they saw it, if you hanged the traitors/revolutionaries, the Irish regarded them as martyrs, made a terrific fuss and inspired the young to emulate them. If you showed leniency by treating them as common criminals despite their murderous conspiracies, they took offence, made a terrific fuss and fomented public protests demanding their release. And if, then, you released them into exile (since you could not allow them the opportunity to re-offend), from wherever they went they would finance more revolution and spread anti-British propaganda in their new homes. This was poisonous in both domestic and foreign policy terms and in the long term caused even more fuss.

While the system did not dictate that Irish prisoners should be treated worse than others – and indeed as political prisoners they were exempt from flogging – it was inevitable that as the dynamite campaign went on outside some warders were especially hostile towards people whom they believed would have rightly been hanged in a previous generation.

To confuse the issue further, from the time largely middle-class Young Irelanders found themselves in jail, Irish political prisoners looked down on ordinary convicts, and indeed on prison warders, and saw themselves as a superior caste.* A.M. Sullivan, the populist nationalist historian and moralist, expressed this floridly in the 1860s:

> Condemned to associate with the vilest of the scoundrels
> bred by the immorality and godlessness of England –
> exposed, without possibility of redress, to the persecutions
> of brutal, coarse-minded men, accustomed to deal only

---

* An exception was Michael Davitt. Having grown up in an English mill town, when he was in prison for IRB activities between 1870 and 1877 he had some sympathy for its working class and his fellow prisoners.

with ruffians than whom beasts are less ferocious and unre-
claimable – restricted to a course of discipline which blasts
the vigour of the body, and under whose influence reason
herself totters upon her throne – the Irish rebel against
whom the doom of penal servitude has been pronounced
is condemned to the most hideous and agonizing punishments to which men of their class could be exposed.[23]

(This attitude would become a permanent feature of Irish republicanism, culminating in the 1980s in hunger strikes to the death over political status, a demand challenged by one irrepressible old Irish communist, Peadar O'Donnell: 'The hunger-strikers are a pack of snobs! They
say they object to being treated as members of the criminal classes.
What's wrong with the criminal classes, I'd like to know? A very decent
crowd I've always found them.'[24] In a similar spirit of indignation, the
term 'Ordinary Decent Criminals' was adopted in Northern Ireland by
those offenders who wished it known that they mostly did less harm
than the paramilitaries, and by the prison warders who found them
much easier to deal with.)

Along with this sense of moral superiority went a passionate if
usually unfounded belief that Irish prisoners were treated particularly
badly by the prison authorities. These twin perceptions enhanced their
sense of singularity and commonality and 'an attitude of repulsion and
raw contempt'[25] towards their fellow prisoners. O'Donovan Rossa had
excelled himself when he complained that being tried under the
Treason-Felony Act had reduced his status to that of 'the garrotters and
Sodomites of England'.[26] Clarke was no exception: 'with all her power
this great England could not force me – one of the mere units of the
Irish rank and file – to regard myself as one of the criminal class any
more than I could ever be forced to regard myself as English'.

The outside world felt differently. A denunciation in the *Saturday
Review* in January 1885 spoke of the 'ridiculous and disastrous leniency' that had the dynamitards, who might have murdered and injured
scores, 'treated with the same indulgence as the luckless clerk who in
dread of ruin forged his employer's name'.[27]

While the regime was harsh and unforgiving for everyone, and the
staff knew they would suffer themselves if they showed leniency, it was

worse for the treason-felony prisoners, who were known as 'the Special Men' because they were kept in penal cells. From Clarke's perspective, this was 'so that we could be the more conveniently persecuted' by a 'scientific system of perpetual and persistent harassing' day or night. It was also true that unlike many poor prisoners or those who had experienced the army or the workhouse, the political prisoners usually were used to much better conditions outside, and therefore suffered far more from deprivation, confinement and the sordidness of an unhygienic world where, for instance, lavatory paper was meanly rationed and filthy language made them flinch.

From the perspective of the authorities, tight security made the separation of the Special Men as imperative as were frequent searches, bi-monthly body examinations* and constant surveillance, which included hourly inspections at night that caused sleep deprivation. Fenians had plenty of form when it came to escape plots. Very much on any prison governor's mind, for instance, would have been the attempt in 1867 to free an IRB prisoner on remand at Clerkenwell Prison by planting a bomb that killed 12 and injured 120 in nearby houses.

Governor Harris, a former army officer and a stickler for discipline, believed in keeping control by following Du Cane's enforcement of 'unremitting, unreserved and manifest submission'.[28] And there is no doubt that some officials were unnecessarily 'officious, assiduous and unrelenting in enforcing the discipline'.[29] Clarke took his loathing, learned via the Boers, the IRB, the very air of Dungannon and the toxic world of Clan na Gael, to new levels in prison. He became a champion hater who was fixated on the idea that the prison was 'a battleground in a Manichean struggle between good and evil, one with Harris as its satanic face'.[30]

* As would all future republicans, Fenian prisoners found strip-searching indecent, humiliating and a particular affront, yet warders knew all too well that concealment was the norm for many prisoners. From Rossa right through to Bobby Sands and beyond, Irish republicans used their body cavities to hide contraband, yet took the high moral ground about being searched and used the experience for propaganda. To Clarke, it was all part of the government determination 'to degrade the Irish political prisoner to the level of the ordinary criminal . . . [and] to try and debase his mind and sap his self-respect'.

Yet Harris and his largely ex-servicemen staff had every reason to be wary of the Special Men. 'These were determined and ingenious men', wrote an historian of prisons, 'with resources in the outside world and comrades more than willing to aid their escape.' Clarke, he concluded 'was perhaps the most resolute and astute of all'.[31]

On remand in Millbank, Clarke and his co-defendants had found a method of communicating with the help of lead from the cell gates' pivots and scraps of lavatory paper. Despite the heavy security surrounding the Special Men, only a couple of months after he arrived in Chatham he devised a telegraph system based on his own version of Morse code that enabled six or seven cells to communicate. He was constantly on the alert for further means of escaping the isolation that drove men mad.

With 1,700 convicts, Chatham had a wide range of workshops. The system was that as convicts mastered a trade they were required to take on another, all the while without being given formal instruction or allowed to communicate with their fellow workers. Wrote Clarke,

> From the *cleaners' party* I was moved off to the foundry, where after four or five years I learnt *iron moulding*; out of that away to learn *stereotyping*, then on to learn *japanning* and *stencilling*, from that to *carpentering* and *joinery*; mastering that shifted off to learn *tinsmithing*; from the tinsmiths' shop to learn *wood turning*; after mastering that set at *pattern-making* – continuous performance for almost sixteen years.[32]

These activities required different levels of brawn and brain. The work in the foundry, for instance – where Henry Hammond Wilson, Prisoner Number J464, laboured for three years – was particularly hard, since it involved heaving heavy metal castings about in terrible heat, while joinery required mathematical knowledge and dexterity. Clarke was young, healthy, clever and practical, so even though prisoners mostly had to learn the job simply by watching what others did, he acquired an impressive range of skills.

He would put some of these to use in finding ways of circumventing the ban on communication. From August 1884, he had the active help of his old mentor, the ebullient John Daly, whom he had last seen in America just before he embarked for England, and who arrived in Chatham with his friend James Egan. They had been sentenced respectively to penal servitude for life and twenty years for explosives offences. Le Caron insisted that Daly was 'the most dangerous and desperate criminal' of all the dynamitards and that letters proved he had visited the Strangers' Gallery of the House of Commons twice with the intention of throwing bombs on the table in front of the Speaker that were so powerful they would have blown up the MPs and the building.[33] While Daly would deny some of the charges made against him, in his effort to exonerate Egan, who though an IRB man may well have been innocent, he admitted responsibility for the nitroglycerine and cartridges buried in Egan's garden.

While Clarke was too suspicious to have become close to any of the other prisoners,

> before long we were fast friends, and more loyal or kinder friends, or more manly, self-reliant men I could not wish to have by my side in a fight with the English foe inside these walls, or outside them either . . . Yes, when your own hearts were wrung with anguish under the torture you were suffering, no weak cry, no coward's whine fell from you.

Ingenious, defiant and with shared humour at a time when many other dynamitards were beginning to show signs of mental disturbance, Clarke, Daly and Egan saved each other. They invented just for the three of them a signalling code and tapping system and a method of circulating thousands of notes, each of which was chewed to a pulp before being dropped into the airshafts. When Clarke was working in the printers' shop he even managed to create a treasonable newspaper, 'The Irish Felon, Published at Her Majesty's Convict Prison Chatham by Henry Hammond Wilson'. In their notes, they derided their captors, Daly recounted what the tame spider for which his friends provided moths was up to, Egan provided comic sketches, and at Christmas they wrote each other verse.

In his prison reminiscences, Clarke would say that prison life had two sides: 'the dismal, dark side, full of wretchedness and misery, that even now I cannot think of without shuddering, and, strange as it may seem, the bright side too, the side which I can now look back upon with some degree of pleasure and pride'. The pleasure was in the intensity of the comradeship; the pride in their audacious subversion of authority.

Taking such risks often had severe consequences. Clarke was put in round-the-clock solitary confinement on a bread-and-water diet several times for talking, writing or signalling to fellow prisoners. Two or three days of punishment was the norm, but in January 1885 he was given twenty-three days ('having a piece of newspaper in his possession and dropping it in the passage leading to the RC church') and, in March, thirteen ('having a piece of lead secreted in his cell broom').[34]

It was an exceptionally cold winter, he later recalled, and he was put in what was known as the Arctic cell. To allay hunger pangs, he frequently chewed the rags with which he cleaned his tin plate. John Daly later told his family that after the twenty-three-day spell Clarke was sent into the exercise yard. 'He marched around the ring with us. His eye was bright although he tottered and fell.' After his second period in that cell, Clarke said, he was utterly exhausted, was unable to straighten himself or stand upright, staggered like a drunk, and yet had to return to hard labour.

Yet though the three of them continued their clandestine communication, most of their time was spent in silent work or solitary confinement. Clarke's small cell with its stone floor was cheerless, containing only a plank bed, a chamber pot, a bowl of water, a broom, a copy of prison regulations and, for a stool, a wooden stump fastened to the floor. 'Day after day all alike', wrote Clarke – 'no change, maddening silence'. His survival mechanism was mathematical. He counted all the bricks in his walls, the bolts in the ironclad doors and the perforations in the iron ventilators, and he calculated the number and weight of the bricks used in the whole prison and the total number of buttons and arrows on the clothing of the entire prison population. Restricted to two randomly provided books a year, a dreadful deprivation for a voracious reader, Clarke taught himself shorthand from *Cassell's Popular Educator*, used it to translate the entire Bible twice and worked out a way of calculating his shorthand speed with the aid of the peals from the prison church bells. Otherwise, he claimed, for the first few years 'I never got any but girls' and boys' trashy story books.' When he complained to Governor Harris 'and asked to be given some kind of books that would be adapted to my educational rating, he ordered the escort to take me away, and next time I became due for a library book they gave me a volume of nursery rhymes'.[35] It's hard not to conclude that it was a petty punishment for what would have been seen as arrogance. The very occasional censored letters Clarke was allowed were a joy, as were the even more infrequent visitors. Clarke had retained the name of Wilson and revealed his true identity to no one, but his friend Billy Kelly, who saw photographs in an American newspapers of those arrested in the 'Dynamite Conspiracy', had recognised him immediately. Having returned to Ireland a few months later, Kelly sent Clarke's trunk to his younger sister, Hannah. He found that even the near-moribund Dungannon IRB didn't know Wilson was Clarke. Having heard that the Clan was arranging a job in America for Clarke's other sister, Maria, Kelly went to see her in Cork, where she worked as a dressmaker, and told her about her brother.

Posing as a relative of Henry Hammond Wilson, Kelly asked to visit, but this took nine months to arrange.[36] In October 1885, he was Clarke's first visitor. He saw him again eighteen months later. Because Clarke's real name wasn't disclosed for some years, he saw no relatives until 1889, when Hannah came twice, followed later by Maria.

The outside world occasionally impinged. In March 1887, at a febrile time in Anglo-Irish politics, The Times published a series of articles under the title 'Parnellism and crime'. This culminated in a facsimile of a letter in Parnell's name implicating him in the sensational Phoenix Park murders of five years earlier, in which the Chief Secretary for Ireland and the Permanent Undersecretary had been stabbed to death by the Irish National Invincibles, an IRB splinter group.

Since this crude forgery was enthusiastically accepted as genuine by many of Parnell's enemies – particularly those who believed him hand-in-glove with the Fenians – he demanded the appointment of a select committee. The Conservative government instead proposed a judicial commission to investigate Parnellite complicity in political and agrarian crime.

Chief Inspector Littlechild, who had arrested Clarke almost six years previously, was sent to Chatham to interview Clarke, Daly and six other dynamitards whom it was hoped might implicate Parnell. Explaining that there were allegations that the Irish Parliamentary Party was connected with 'the Irish Revolutionary Party in America', Littlechild asked Clarke if he would be a witness before the Commission. 'I am ready to take down anything you'd wish to say,' he said. Clarke's pithy answer was: 'Look here, Mr Inspector, if a single word of information would get me out of here tomorrow, sooner than give it to you, I'd prefer to remain here till the day of judgement. Please take that as final.'

Littlechild reminded Clarke how much better his life would be as a free man rather than

> cooped up there with the blackguardism and ruffianism of the country and . . . subject to all the misery and degrada-tion of convict life, denied God's free air and the love and sympathy of friends and everything else that goes to make life worth living . . . He gave me to understand that if I would only be 'sensible' (as he phrased it) not only would it mean release for me but also a job in the Civil Service.

Clarke wrote two furious letters to friends denouncing the authorities for compelling him to see Littlechild. When both were suppressed, he asked Governor Harris if it was because they didn't want his friends to have the information about Littlechild's offer. 'After a short pause the Governor said: "No; it is not." I then wrote the third letter, telling about the visit and my reply to Mr. Littlechild, but avoiding anything in the nature of blaming the authorities. That letter was despatched all right.' This was another important lesson in knowing your way around the system.

Unlike Clarke, who mostly took refuge in his head, John Daly's method of coping with boredom was to complain incessantly, because, brutal though the prison regime was, it prided itself on having proper procedures to handle complaints, and interviews with chaplains, doctors, official Visitors and other representatives of authority were better than silence. And like the contents of Clarke's letter, news leak-ing to the outside world helped build up indignation about the fate of Irish prisoners in British jails. This was intensified when Daly was poisoned.

In late 1889, Daly had been given medicine to treat sores on his feet; among the side-effects that lasted for three days were 'rapid heart rate, rashes and mental confusion'. He was fine afterwards, but refused to accept the explanation that the prison compounder (who was subsequently demoted) had accidentally put too much belladonna in the mixture and insisted it was an attempt to murder him in revenge for his refusal to help Littlechild.

The Inhuman Treatment of John Daly and Other Political Prisoners in English Jails, a pamphlet that came out in January 1890, received plenty of publicity in Irish newspapers. In February, at a meeting supervised by Governor Harris, Daly told his sister Ellen that he had been poisoned 'either by accident or intent' and had been 'lying at death's door . . . near the brink of the grave'. Irish Parliamentary Party MPs, who were grateful for Clarke's and Daly's dismissal of Littlechild, began constantly raising the issue of prisoner welfare in the Commons. Urged to campaign for a full investigation, Ellen was able to tell Daly that his local MP was already pressing for it.

There was pressure from Dublin Castle too, so the Home Office gave the Chatham Visitors the job of conducting an inquiry under the chairmanship of a county court judge. Daly had contributed thirty pages of written testimony, Clarke fifteen and Egan ten, and all were cross-examined during March and April. Although Clarke's evidence was less exaggerated than that of Daly or Egan, like them he was antagonistic, seemed unable to understand that prison life was inevitably hard, and listed innumerable grievances big and small. Additionally, flagrant lies from Daly undermined their evidence. 'I never telegraphed a word to a single prisoner. I declare it upon my word,' he said, yet he had been found with the telegraphic code they used written on his slate.

Institutions' default position is self-defence, and the Chatham Visitors were no exception. Not only did they have 'a strong reflexive middle-class English tendency to believe the authorities',[37] but since it was they who were supposed to monitor the conduct of the prison they were hardly likely to judge themselves ineffective. The inquiry ruled that, apart from some minor transgressions by junior officers, there was no ill-treatment. Other than its recommending that the cells' fixed stumps be replaced by movable stools, there was little joy from the final report.

All the witness testimony was published, complete with a revealing comment from a chaplain asked his opinion of Clarke: 'I think he feels it very much . . . those are a different class to the others, and naturally they would feel their imprisonment more . . . their sentences are longer, and they have not been in prison before, and they feel it more acutely.'[38] It was Clarke, however, who would point out that an educated man with a mind 'well stocked with healthy ideas' had a better chance of surviving the imposed silence than an illiterate. An observer would have to add that whatever the 'health' of his ideas, his brains, his skills and his toughness gave him a better chance than most.

The publication of the Visitors' report offered ammunition both to those who believed the prisoners were being treated properly and those who thought them persecuted. Public sympathy for the dynamitards was a new phenomenon: shadowy figures who left bombs in busy places and injured ordinary people had few supporters. By contrast, the Fenians imprisoned in the 1860s had been plotters so unsuccessful that most got no chance to kill or injure anyone, so they could be represented as having been spoiling for a fair fight and therefore having about them a certain nobility.

O'Donovan Rossa, for instance, was sentenced to life imprisonment essentially because he was manager of a subversive newspaper, a recruiter for the IRB and a separatist agitator. At his trial in 1865 he had conducted his own defence to maximum dramatic effect and with the instincts of a natural propagandist. In jail, his energetic defiance had brought brutal and sometimes illegal reaction, but his success in smuggling out letters detailing his punishments made him notorious.

In Rossa's case, when a commission of inquiry confirmed that he and other Fenian prisoners had been mistreated, there was public condemnation. In 1867 there was initially shock at the killing of a policeman when Fenians tried to rescue two prisoners in England, but when three of them were publicly hanged, as far as the Irish were concerned they became heroes, there were enormous funeral processions in Manchester, Cork, Dublin, Limerick and Kerry, and they entered the nationalist pantheon as the Manchester Martyrs. A.M. Sullivan's brother and business partner, T.D. Sullivan, wrote 'God Save

Ireland', the ballad in their honour that became so popular as to have been the unofficial national anthem.

> High upon the gallows tree swung the noble-hearted
>   three.
> By the vengeful tyrant stricken in their bloom;
> But they met him face to face, with the courage of their
>   race,
> And they went with hearts undaunted to their doom.

Even now, the refrain is so catchy and the words so memorable that it is sung at football matches in the same spirit as the English at rugby matches sing 'Jerusalem', and still features in pub sing-alongs.

> 'God save Ireland!' said the heroes;
> 'God save Ireland' said they all.
> 'Whether on the scaffold high
> Or the battlefield we die,
> Oh, what matter when for Erin dear we fall!'*

Up to 1890, there was no such public embracing of the imprisoned dynamitards, not least because – apart from John Daly – they had been living in America and were unknown in Ireland. But the campaign was beginning. The highly successful Amnesty Association that had been formed in 1869 had succeeded in obtaining early release for the Fenians: Rossa was released after six years. It became moribund, but by 1890, when it was revived, it was five years since the end of the dynamite campaign and memories of injury and destruction had

---

* That I sang this in the Felons' Club in the Falls Road more than a century later during a West Belfast Festival deeply annoyed some republicans present who thought it an affront that a 'revisionist' (an insult I tell my critics is a compliment, in that it is a poor historian who does not change her mind if the evidence requires it) should think herself entitled to sing a rebel song. The best joke about revisionists is that we believe that the cause of the deaths during the Great Famine was anorexia nervosa.

faded. Although there were no martyrs to inspire stories and songs, there was a growing sense that they had been punished enough. By 1890, the Amnesty Association claimed 200,000 members in Ireland and parts of urban Britain with a high level of Irish immigration. Gradually, Irish MPs began to press for their release or, at least, a move from Chatham.

The British Conservative government were in no mood to release prisoners but were anxious to move them. Sir Edward Du Cane resisted, explaining that these 'most difficult prisoners have been well managed at Chatham and with all their ingenuity, unscrupulousness and their irritability they have not been able to substantiate any griev- ance, nor have they been able to carry on surreptitious communication with their friends outside'.[39] However, the Admiralty's decision to build a new naval base on the site of the prison provided a get-out, and in January 1891 the inmates were moved to Portland Prison, which was on a peninsula off the Dorset coast and so inaccessible that the prison regime was less repressive.

At the end of 1891, the South Tyrone MP, Thomas Russell, a Presbyterian and anti-sectarian liberal unionist, intensified his efforts on Clarke's behalf by organising a petition to Queen Victoria asking for clemency for 'Mr Thomas J. Clarke (alias H.H. Wilson)'. Clarke's iden- tity came as a surprise to the prison authorities, but since they assumed Clarke, not Wilson, was the alias, his name in jail remained unchanged. Much was made in the petition of the loyal service to the crown of his father James and his twenty-one-year-old brother Alfred, now in the Royal Artillery.

Clarke had led a blameless life as a young man in Dungannon, the petition claimed, but while in New York 'he unfortunately became acquainted with certain men', was ensnared into their 'diabolical conspiracy' and persuaded 'to join a secret organisation representing to him that it had for its object the destruction of public buildings in England without causing loss of life'.[40] The Clarkes were a popular local family, so those signing included Viscount Avonmore, who had been a major in the Royal Artillery, three officers from the Mid Ulster Artillery, local professional men and twenty-seven 'leading merchants'.

The petition was rejected by the Home Secretary, but the agitation became more and more political, with nationalist politicians now in the foreground, caught up in the catastrophic aftermath of the fall and death of Parnell and the ensuing party civil war and looking for electoral support wherever they might find it.

When in 1885, after the combined votes of the Conservatives and Parnell's party had brought down Gladstone's government and he was converted to Home Rule for Ireland, it became the defining issue between the two great parties. After a further election in 1886 made the Irish Party, with eighty-six seats, the king-makers, Gladstone was again elected Prime Minister for long enough to bring in a Home Rule Bill that split his party, and brought about the end of his government and the return of Lord Salisbury as Prime Minister.

The scandal surrounding the *Times* letter had ended with the discrediting and suicide of the forger in 1889, but Parnell's private life was soon to bring his extraordinary career to a close. At the end of 1890, when it emerged in the divorce court that Parnell had had three children with Katherine O'Shea, the wife of one of his MPs, Gladstone let it be known publicly that Parnell was now anathema, and the Irish Party and all nationalist Ireland split. After a torrid period fighting vainly for his political life, Parnell died in October 1891.

The Parnellite faction won only nine seats to their opponents' seventy-two in the 1892 general election that returned Gladstone with a minority government. For their leader, John Redmond, who had a sneaking regard for the Fenians, flirting with them as Parnell had been wont to do and helping resolve the prisoners' grievances was the logical way to pursue popularity at home.

For some time Redmond had been demanding an inquiry into what he said were the 'unsafe convictions' of Daly and Egan, for whom he was now legal adviser. In August 1892 he repeated those demands in the *Fortnightly Review*, appealing also for an amnesty for all the treason-felony prisoners. Motives mattered, he wrote, and someone who had committed a criminal offence 'not from any selfish sordid unworthy, or depraved motive, but . . . to advance the cause of popular freedom or national right, no matter how culpable, dangerous or stupid his methods may be, he is, and must be, a political offender as distinguished from an ordinary criminal'. Bobby Sands and his companions were to starve themselves to death ninety years later over this very issue.[41]

Early in 1893, the government released Egan, whom Daly had always claimed knew nothing about the illegal materials hidden in his garden, but insisted the other dynamitards must see their sentences out. Gladstone's second Home Rule bill got through the Commons and died in the Lords shortly before he retired from politics. The Liberals lost power in 1895, Ireland had dropped off the public radar and the Conservatives, from whom no one expected clemency, quietly set about finding excuses for releasing prisoners.

Clarke was better informed than usual about some of these developments, since in Portland he had pulled off his greatest prison coup. Given the job of packing tinware for dispatch to Woolwich Arsenal for use in English warships, he took a thin piece of wood smuggled from the carpenter's shop by Daly, and – using the black paint and chalk he needed for numbering tins and packing cases – wrote on it: 'For God's sake throw in a piece of newspaper – any old newspaper – and earn the gratitude of a long term convict.'[42]

Case number twenty-four returned full of newspapers and they kept coming. By dint of elaborate arrangements that involved among other things smuggling bits of newspaper in his boot and sewing them into his mattress, he and Daly managed to catch up with what was happening in the world, including the small print of Gladstone's bill. His Woolwich friend also acted as a conduit between Clarke and Egan, who provided him with a £5 reward and gave him a steady supply of news-clippings to send to Portland. Clarke was using the intermediary to arrange with Egan by shorthand a plan of escape when he was moved to another kind of work and the whole arrangement collapsed.

There was a lifeline with regular visits to the prisoners from Redmond. Many years later, in 1913, as Clarke was striving single-mindedly to destroy the Home Rule movement to which Redmond had given his political life, he wrote publicly that he would never forget his kindness on his many visits to Portland.

Quite apart from wanting their own release, Clarke and Daly were genuinely desperate to convince the authorities that some of their fellow-prisoners were going mad. In the case of one of them, Herbert Asquith, the Liberal Home Secretary, assured the Commons that 'one of our most eminent authorities in mental disease' had agreed with previous medical reports that 'the convict exhibits no symptoms of mental unsoundness'.[43] Medical inquiries kept finding what they wanted to find – that people other prisoners claimed were gibbering lunatics were merely malingering – and when Governor Harris was drafted into Portland for a few months to fill a temporary vacancy he reinforced that assumption. One unfortunate consequence for the Irish political prisoners of stressing their superiority to the common prisoner was that the authorities often overestimated their guile and mendacity. Another was that their denials of past wrong-doing even when they were patently guilty, plus their aggression and the exaggerations by them and their supporters, made the authorities disinclined to believe them.

Clarke did what he could for his fellows. In 1895, after a particularly distressing episode with Alfred George Whitehead, he asked the Catholic chaplain to intervene, but Father Matthews said that while he knew Whitehead was out of his mind, he wouldn't tell the authorities in case they sent him 'back to his bishop'. Furious at this cowardice, Clarke wrote a detailed letter to Redmond about finding Whitehead, with his 'pitiful, dazed stare', trying to eat crushed glass, which Clarke threw out the window.

He railed that, had he been found helping Whitehead, he would have been punished. 'The truth is that as far as a refined system of cruelty is concerned there is nothing on God's earth to-day to compare with the treatment which we Irish prisoners have been receiving at the hands of the English Government.'[44] It was a paragraph that helped ensure the letter was suppressed.

The previous year, 1894, Clarke had heard of the death of his father, whom he had not seen for fourteen years. 'Since I was a schoolboy,' Clarke would later confess, 'I can only recollect tears flowing from me once – that was when I heard of my father's death in Portland.'[45] Since this ended the army pension, Mary Clarke was in difficulties and in need of help from the Amnesty Association, and this spurred another attempt to obtain clemency. Maud Gonne, the muse of W.B. Yeats, an Englishwoman turned extreme Irish nationalist, had become involved in the campaign in 1893, had given Mrs Clarke money and now made another attempt to have her son released, submitting in November 1895 an appeal that included numerous testimonials attesting to

Clarke's virtues in his youth.* Never one to downplay a case, she claimed that his mother had become unhinged and was committed when she learned of his incarceration: 'Since then she has been able to return but her heart is broken.' A letter to Gonne from Mary Clarke thanked her for several cheques and for giving her hope that 'my poor boy will be home with me for Christmas . . . It is so lonely since the death of my dear husband . . . We have all ready for him when he comes. I have his own cup and teapot waiting for him and his room prepared.'[46] She was, Clarke said once, 'as simple-minded and guileless as a child'.

Daly helped the agitation along in suitably flamboyant style when through the machinations of Limerick's Amnesty Association he was elected as an MP for Limerick City in July 1895, although subsequently disqualified on the grounds of being a felon. When that didn't work, he went on hunger strike, and when force-fed regurgitated the food. He was released in August 1896 and went home to Limerick, Irish papers writing indignantly of his enfeebled condition without mentioning the reason why he was in jail in the first place. That was par for the course, for, as Seán McConville mordantly puts it, the campaign involved 'vigorous appeals for clemency, as well as a contribution to the dynamitards' book of amnesiac self-justification'.[47]

Pressure from the USA on behalf of their citizen, Dr Thomas Gallagher, also helped to have him and Whitehead released that same month, but – disastrously for Clarke and the four other remaining treason-felony prisoners – just at this time the British government heard rumours of another dynamite expedition from New York, to be headed by the man who had led the Invincibles when they had murdered Chief

---

* In 1898, in a Commons debate, a Liberal MP spoke of the testimony from the Dungannon parish priest and schoolmaster that at the time Clarke was dismissed because of the falling school roll 'he was a boy of the highest possible character, and was engaged at that time as a leader in temperance work'. He had got into trouble in America, when 'he joined, as many young men do, without realising the gravity of the step, one of the secret societies of America. The leaders of the society would not risk their own lives, but they singled out this young man, who foolishly had taken their oath, and sent him to England, with the result that he found himself, against his own judgment, mixed up in this business, and has suffered fifteen years' penal servitude.'

Secretary Lord Frederick Cavendish and Under-Secretary Thomas Burke in Phoenix Park in 1882. It came to nothing, but even the Amnesty Association admitted this had done serious damage.

Daly, who had made a very rapid recovery, worked hard for his friend in Ireland and on a lecture tour in America: 'Uncle John never forgot for one moment his fellow prisoner, Tom Clarke,' wrote his niece Kathleen. 'He talked about him continually at home, and elsewhere, and spoke about him in every speech or lecture he delivered. He fretted all the time about him and worked in every possible way to bring about his release.' So did Egan, assuring a Boston audience that the political prisoners were in chains in English dungeons.[48]

Gallagher and Whitehead had gone to America, where they were declared insane: Gallagher would spend twenty-nine years in a private asylum, paid for by the Clan. The widespread horror at their condition would help get the amnesty campaign going again in the face of a newly implacable government. Parnellites, anti-Parnellites and some Liberal MPs were indefatigable in raising their case in parliament. Redmond asked the Secretary for the Colonies if he had heard from the Legislative Council of Cape Colony of a resolution 'calling upon the Government of the Colony to approach the Imperial Government in order to ask them to extend to the Irish political prisoners similar clemency to that extended by President Kruger to the Reform leaders'.[49] And although Redmond had consistently claimed that Daly had been innocent, his brother Willie, also an MP, insisted that Daly had been a ringleader and the remaining five prisoners were his innocent victims.

Bereft of his friends, Clarke was in increasingly low spirits, and this was affecting his health. His sister Hannah told the Amnesty Association that he had become 'a complete wreck' and had had more medicines in the previous few months than in all the rest of his time in jail.[50] A medical examination in May 1897 described him as being in 'fair general health' despite an 'irritable heart' and, although 'fidgety', showing no signs of mental instability.[51] But loneliness and disappointments were getting him down: 'the slow going days and hours of it never seemed to drag along as slowly as now', he wrote in December 1897.[52]

The parliamentary pressure intensified and in June 1898 Redmond was told that Clarke would have five years remitted, be removed to

Pentonville and be released on licence in September. In a letter to his young brother Alfie, Clarke mentioned his amusement that a female correspondent had compared his life to that of 'a Carthusian'* saint or a 'Rapt Culdee.'† 'Bless the woman's soul,' he added.

Clarke might have been shy and reserved, but believing absolutely in his own rectitude helped him guard against the perils of self-examination. He told Alfie:

> When a moral man feels in all his bitterness what it is to have the delicate curves and tender angels of his human nature rubbed up and currycombed against the grain, then is not the time to rub salt from within by interior nig-nag and self-inflicted worry. Why, man alive, had I set to work on those lines, endeavouring to cultivate a lackadaisical tone of mind, my wits would have been gone years ago. No. Clinch your teeth hard and never say die.

His prescription was straightforward:

> Keep your thoughts off yourself all you can.
> No mooning or brown studies.
> Guard your self-respect (if you lost that you'd lose the backbone of your manhood).
> Keep your eyes wide open and don't bang your head against the wall.
> These and a few others, which the deferential regard my prison pen has for The Rules prevent me from mentioning here, are 'The Golden Rules of Life for a Long Sentence Prisoner,' that might be found hung up in my cell had I any say in the furnishing of it.[53]

When he walked out of Pentonville to a welcome from intimates, Clarke took only his letters, refused the £3 he had earned, and wore a

* Carthusian monasteries are communities of hermits.
† Rapt Culdees were Celtic monks living in reclusion in a state of spiritual rapture.

smart blue serge suit provided by a friend. Slightly stooped and haggard, he looked old for forty-one, but he had been plied for months, he said, with cod liver oil and malt 'to fatten me up for public view' and had been declared by the doctor in 'fair good health'. Knowing that none of the other dynamitards had served such a long sentence and emerged so strong in mind and body had added to the exceptional self-belief and self-confidence that lay under his unassuming exterior and ensured he would suffer no doubts along the path that lay ahead. In jail, as he had dreamed of his release, he had thought long and hard about how past Fenian failures had been a result of informers, unreliable conspirators, careless talk and cavalier planning. Dreaming about how he would get it right were he in control gave him hope and purpose. Driven by a desire for vengeance, an all-pervading hatred for the British, an implacable ambition to get them out of Ireland, a steely determination to do whatever it took and exceptional strength of character, he was readying himself to start a revolution.

Clarke went to Dublin to stay with his mother and Alfie and find a way of earning a living and mobilising the IRB. His friends seemed in a position to help: Egan now occupied the influential sinecure of sword-bearer in the Dublin Corporation and Daly had a successful bakery in Limerick, financed by a highly successful American lecture tour. Under the aegis of the Amnesty Association, they took him to several Irish locations on a martyr's tour, which raised money for him and gave valuable publicity to the republican cause.

Unlike Clan na Gael, the IRB had had no truck with the dynamite campaign, and had always stuck to its ambition to have another attempt at the armed rising that had failed in 1867. Clarke was pragmatic enough now to go along with that, but he was no more minded than he had ever been to pay attention to a provision added to the IRB constitution in 1873 forbidding a war against Britain without the support of the majority of the Irish people. However, for now all this was a theoretical matter, since – as Clarke quickly ascertained on his travels – as things stood there was little chance of rousing the IRB from its stupor. Even Daly seemed to him lacking in properly directed purpose. A watching policeman paid Clarke the compliment of reporting he anticipated 'trouble from this man' and another declared him 'really clever, very bitter in disposition and holds views about promoting outrages that are intelligible'. But, for now, he was thwarted.

Being on licence, Clarke had to be careful not to break the law, but he didn't stint on the rhetoric. A few weeks after his release, there was a vast celebration in his honour in Dungannon, the town of his youth, where the address of welcome hailed him as having been delivered from 'a living tomb after undergoing nearly sixteen years' imprisonment for a crime of which we still believe and know you were not guilty'. In his response, Clarke spoke of his pride in having been with Daly and Egan, felons 'for Ireland's sake. The head and front of our sins has been honest-souled service for Ireland and hatred of her enemies. Our crime has been the same for which so many sons of old Ireland, generation after generation, trod the dark path or mounted the scaffold or filled the felon's grave.' This being the centenary of 1798, he spoke of his pride in following in the footsteps of such illustrious martyrs as Wolfe Tone, who had 'kept alive the loving flame that glows in Irish hearts'. He quoted the lines 'They rose in dark and evil days, / To free their native land' from another famous ballad, 'Who fears to speak of "Ninety-eight"?' It began:

> Who blushes at the name?
> When cowards mock the patriot's fate
> Who hangs his head for shame?
> He's all a knave or half a slave
> Who slights his country thus,
> But a true man, like you, man,
> Will fill your glass with us.*

* Also known as 'The Memory of the Dead', this ballad was written in 1843 by Trinity student John Kells Ingram, a Church of Ireland rector's son, after an evening discussing with friends the sectarian nature of contemporary nationalism and how in 1798 Catholics and Presbyterians had briefly united to fight the Anglican ascendancy from which they were excluded. It was set to music two years later and became one of the most popular nationalist songs, yet Ingram, a distinguished economist who became Vice-Provost of Trinity, was an anti-sectarian radical who was never a nationalist because he thought Ireland then incapable of self-government.

As for the savage treatment meted out in English prisons, 'better fall into the hands of the American Red Indian or the African Ashantee'.[54]

Clarke had no experience as a public speaker and was too self-effacing to enjoy being lionised, but there were several more such events, culminating in his becoming under duress in March 1899 a Freeman of the City of Limerick, of which John Daly had become mayor. Clarke's nervous delivery would embarrass him, but he was very clear in his stumbling speech about his principles: he was dedicated to the cause of saving Ireland's identity from the British boa constrictor that was threatening to squeeze the life out of it.

The occasion, however, was life-changing for Clarke, for he went to stay with the Dalys. The unmarried John Daly was paterfamilias to his widowed sister-in-law and her large family. Clarke revelled in domestic life, feeling 'just as much at home in your home as I do here in our own'.[55] This was an environment that more than most would have understood his difficulties of adjustment after jail, which in his case included using cutlery, dining at a table and sitting in an easy chair.

The third daughter, the strong-minded twenty-year-old Kathleen, had long nourished romantic ideas about Clarke based on her uncle's stories featuring 'a noble, courageous, unselfish character, one who had showed unwonted sweetness and restraint under the most terrible provocation during his imprisonment'.[56] She was disappointed that his appearance lacked the 'kingly, heroic qualities' she had expected, but within a short time she and Clarke became friendly enough to correspond.

Kathleen's Fenian pedigree was impeccable. Raised in a republican stronghold of bitter revolutionary Anglophobia, as a small child she had stuck stamps on envelopes for the amnesty campaign to help 'free Uncle John and of course Ireland'. When a letter arrived from Uncle John, it would be read to the whole family:

> My grandmother cried bitterly on these occasions. Poor grandmother, he was her favourite son, suffering through loving his country, a love she had instilled in him. She was a grand woman, whose sorrow for her son's sufferings was deep, but whose pride in the fact that he could suffer and, if necessary, die for Ireland's freedom was greater.

She could, recalled Kathleen, 'see good in everyone and everything but England'.[57]

Grandmother would live to the age of ninety-seven, 'a rebel against England to her last breath', as was her son Edward, Kathleen's father, who predeceased her in 1890 at the age of forty-one. Imprisoned briefly at seventeen in 1865 because of his Fenian connections, he campaigned in his last years to get his brother out of jail, but died six years before his release, leaving nine daughters. His posthumous son Ned would be executed in 1916.

Edward Daly's early death was blamed on his youthful imprisonment. Every shop and factory closed and his funeral was the largest ever known in Limerick: 'several thousand mourners marched "to show they believed with the dead man in his brother's innocence"'.[58] The position of the Dalys as republican royalty was beyond challenge.

Kathleen might have been in bred into an ideological straitjacket, but she was otherwise independent-minded and capable. By the time she met Clarke, she had her own successful dressmaking company, and had greatly annoyed Uncle John when she refused to join his bakery business. She needed all her strength of character after she and Tom Clarke fell in love in the summer of 1899. The young man who, according to his sister Maria, 'used to hate the girls', was now a susceptible middle-aged man. After he had joined the Daly family holiday in County Clare, and he and Kathleen had explored their mutual enjoyment of reading, politics and long walks in the country, they became unofficially engaged. This horrified her mother and disconcerted John Daly. He loved Tom Clarke – indeed he used to speak of him as dearer to him than a brother – but at more than twice Kathleen's age and without any money or job prospects, Clarke did not seem like a good match, and Daly was self-centred and as paternalistic and bourgeois as he was revolutionary. 'He ought to remember the centre of the universe is not at all times himself,'[59] railed Clarke to Kathleen after enduring months of opposition and delaying tactics.

Clarke had believed that his friends could get him work, but they turned out to be less influential than he or they thought. The Amnesty Association had assured him that he was a shoo-in to be elected clerk to the Rathdown Board of Guardians that ran south Dublin workhouses. Among his testimonials was one from John Redmond that said he had developed for him 'feelings of the greatest respect and good-will', but though Clarke fought hard for votes, he lost decisively, blaming it on the 'unprincipled so-called nationalists' on the board.[60]

The next port of call was John Devoy, now back at the helm of a Clan na Gael united after many years of vicious splits, to whom Clarke proposed a lecture tour about his prison experiences. The response in August was negative and curt: in Daly's angry words, 'It's about as cold-blooded an epistle as ever I read.' But, he added, 'Tom, never say die. We lived through a bloody sight worse than the cold indifference of Mr. Devoy and his friends.'[61]

It was an ironic moment in the history of Tom Clarke and John Devoy. Desmond Ryan, a republican socialist and a participant in the 1916 Rising as well as an acute historian of physical force nationalism, judged later:

> Three men, James Stephens, John Devoy and Thomas Clarke, concentrated in their several life-times not only three great phases of Fenianism, but all that need be known of Fenianism. Stephens founded Fenianism and stamped his spirit upon it; Devoy, three times in fifty years, brought it within sight of victory; and when Clarke, strong in will and endurance, went, as first signatory of the 1916 Proclamation, into insurrection, sixty years of Fenianism ended in the realisation of a hope long deferred, of a hope that nothing could kill in the hearts of these three men.[62]

By an odd coincidence, the month after his disappointment with Devoy, Clarke met James Stephens, who was nearing the end of his life and whose reputation was at a low ebb since his ousting from Fenian and IRB leadership in 1866. Yet Ryan's assessment was the truth: even if he had been lacking in follow-through, Stephens had the vision that created the Fenians.

A twenty-three-year-old railway worker who escaped arrest after his involvement in the 1848 revolutionary fiasco by fleeing to Paris, Stephens earned a poor living teaching English, while observing from there in 1849 another failed revolutionary conspiracy in Ireland, a failed French republican attempt to seize power and in 1851 Louis

Napoleon's successful *coup d'état* and his defeat and suppression of radical republicans.

Back in Ireland from 1855 and reunited with old comrades, after two years Stephens had linked up with two American exiles, the friends who had founded in New York the Emmet Monument Association. It was named after Robert Emmet, leader of a hopeless rebellion in 1803 who had been hanged and beheaded. Emmet was much admired by republicans because of his stirring speech from the dock, which he had concluded with a demand that no man should write his epitaph until Ireland had taken its place among the nations of the world. The title Emmet Monument was therefore a demand for Irish independence.

Inspired by the United Kingdom's preoccupation with first the Crimean War (in which James Clarke was fighting) and then the Indian Mutiny of 1857, the intention was that there should be a Fenian invasion of Ireland when the British were otherwise engaged. 'England's difficulty was Ireland's opportunity' was becoming the mantra of Irish physical-force nationalism.

No military activity materialised then, but an envoy was sent to Stephens, who was now back in Dublin, to propose he prepare for the arrival of a military expedition. In exchange for money and absolute authority, Stephens agreed. On Saint Patrick's Day in 1858 he and his associates set up the oath-bound, cellular secret society dedicated to making Ireland 'an independent democratic republic' that became known as the IRB. Stephens was known as the 'head centre'. Obsessive, egotistical, autocratic and single-minded, he made republicanism a force in Irish political life.

When further funds failed to materialise, Stephens visited America, established a partnership with New York separatists and inspired his friend John O'Mahony, another refugee from 1848, to establish the IRB's American equivalent. Based on the Emmet Monument Association, it was named the Fenian Brotherhood after the mythical Celtic warrior bands of the Fianna who were led by the equally myth- ical Fionn MacCumhaill. Stephens had now succeeded in making Irish America a potent force in Irish nationalism.

While members of both organisations were known as Fenians, there were differences: free to say what they liked, the American Fenians did not need to adopt the obsessive secrecy of the Irish, and, to avoid censure from Catholic clergy, they eschewed oaths. There were also tensions, for while O'Mahony thought the American and Irish organisations were equal, Stephens insisted the Americans were merely suppliers of money and arms for the IRB and wrested control of the organisation 'at home and abroad'.

Transatlantic disputation followed, and the factionalism of the American Fenians was intensified by the American civil war. When afterwards, in 1865, demobilised Fenian soldiers travelled to Ireland, the government arrested Stephens, O'Donovan Rossa and other close associates. Stephens escaped and reached America in time to find the organisation split between those who wanted to attack British military targets in Canada and those still intent on targeting Ireland.

Fenian raids on Canada from 1866 to 1871 would serve mainly to help unite Canada into Confederation. And in Ireland, as the government continued the suppression of the IRB, the order Stephens sent from America to the Supreme Council to postpone the rebellion planned for 1866 led to his deposition by lieutenants. They went ahead in 1867, with disastrous consequences, but were nonetheless celebrated in a ballad written fifty years later by a participant* in the 1916 Rising, who was, of course, making a contemporary point.

Thereafter, Stephens was again exiled in poverty on the Continent, vainly trying to regain control of the IRB from his enemies as the divided Fenian Brotherhood lost ground in America to Clan na Gael, which had been set up in disgust at the feuding.

In 1874, three years after his arrival in America, thirty-two-year-old John Devoy, now a journalist, was at the Clan's head. As obsessive as Stephens, at the age of nineteen Devoy had joined the IRB and then the French Foreign Legion to experience military life. Back in Ireland from 1862, he had worked as an IRB organiser and written anonymously for the *Irish People*, a radical nationalist paper founded by

---

* Peadar Kearney, the author in 1913 of the 'Soldier's Song', which became the national anthem.

    Some died on the glenside, some died mid the stranger,
    And wise men have told us their cause was a failure,
    But they rose for old Ireland and never feared danger,
    Glory O, Glory O, to the bold Fenian men.

Stephens that was suppressed in 1865. While on the run, he was charged with recruiting Fenians from soldiers serving in the British army.

Having been one of those helping Stephens to escape, and believing that that serving soldiers included tens of thousands of Fenians, Devoy was furious that Stephens refused the call from the IRB for a revolution the month he was arrested. After a year on remand, he pleaded guilty,* was held on remand for a year until his trial on 19 February 1867 and sentenced to fifteen years' hard labour. Like Clarke, he experienced Millbank, Chatham and Portland prisons, but unlike him he was lucky enough to be released under amnesty with the stipulation that he stay away from British territories until the fifteen years were up.

Much more an action-man than Stephens, Devoy's first priority was to rescue Fenian prisoners in Australia. He dispatched two capable Clan agents to Australia and bought *Catalpa*, a three-masted whaling ship, which left Massachusetts in April 1875. After a round trip of more than twenty-thousand miles, she docked in New York in August 1876 with the six prisoners and a stirring story to tell.† The propaganda value in Ireland and America ensured that Clan na Gael rather than the Fenian Brotherhood was henceforward seen as the voice of Irish America, although Fenian remained a catch-all term to describe militant separatists.

Annually, the IRB sent envoys to Clan conventions, but Devoy was not prepared to take orders. Against their wishes, from 1877 he sought an alliance with Parnell, then the rising parliamentary Irish star of the Home Rule party, and the ex-prisoner Michael Davitt, whom he had met in 1878 as he embarked on his first American lecture tour. It was Devoy who introduced Davitt to the beliefs of the land agitator James

---

* There was heavy criticism of him for this within the movement, where there were two schools of thought about the propriety of pleading guilty: for those who did, it was often a matter of pride.
† The *Catalpa* songs were poor stuff. An example:

> A noble whale ship and commander
> Called the *Catalpa*, they say,
> Came out to Western Australia,
> And took six poor Fenians away.

Fintan Lalor, who had died shortly after his failed 1849 revolution, and who had urged a general rent strike to secure 'The soil of Ireland for the people of Ireland.'

In 1879, at the time when Tom Clarke was being drawn into the IRB, Devoy breached the terms of his amnesty to travel around the British Isles inspecting the IRB, 'a compact body of 35,000 men',[63] and have meetings with Davitt and Parnell. Davitt would found the Land League with Parnell as president, and Devoy would help fund it with the American Land League. Fenianism would be wrong-footed by Gladstone's land reforms, which strengthened constitu-tionalism, weakened the IRB and enabled Devoy's enemies, the dynamitards, to take control of the Clan. Devoy would spend the first decade of the twentieth century rebuilding the organisation in his own image.

Clarke still had a worm's eye view of this complicated history when he met Stephens, who following a plea from Parnell had been allowed to live in Ireland after 1891. It was clear from Clarke's account of their meeting that he knew little of the old man's significance. With his sister Maria he had spent 'a nice day out at James Stephens yesterday,' he reported to Kathleen.

> This is Stephens, the old Fenian Chief Centre. We started out from Dublin two brakes full of friends to pick up Stephens and his family at Blackrock and go off pic-nicking but it kept steadily raining all morning and so we changed our plans . . . we all (upwards of twenty) remained for the greater part of the day, eating and singing and drinking and reciting during the remainder of the day . . . I . . . whiled away a good portion of the time talking politics or rubbish to one or two old frail gents who interested or amused me.[64]

If Clarke knew little of the reality rather than the mythology of the Fenian past, he was at the time equally poorly acquainted with its present. He had not realised that Daly was famous in Irish America and a reliable crowd-puller, but Tom Clarke was just another Fenian ex-prisoner. Nor did he appreciate that Devoy hated the very people whose leadership had dispatched Clarke to London and jail. 'Oh Kattie,' he wrote,

> I never anticipated such a decision on the part of the 'Bosses' on the other side. I was living in a fool's paradise all the while for I took it for granted those people would willingly, enthusiastically co-operate as they co-operated with John . . . I built everything upon that tour . . . but alas hopes and plans and fairy castles and myself are knocked smash in a moment.

He had to be dissuaded, apparently, from going to South Africa to join the Boers in their second war against the British. Aware that he was going to America to get a job at the bottom of the heap, in great distress he told her she was not bound to him.

She dismissed his scruples: 'I have all I care about, your love and so long as I have that I'm all right.'[65] With Maria, he sailed to New York in October 1899 to get a job and find a home where Kathleen could join him.

Initially, the Clarkes stayed at a Manhattan hotel owned by a Clan member who kept open house for anti-British revolutionaries, where Clarke caught up with Irish American gossip and realised there was no basis for his hopes that when on the spot he might have a chance of a lecture tour. 'The Boer War* is occupying every one's thoughts around here,' he wrote to Kathleen. It was the same story in Limerick: 'What do you think of the War,' wrote Kathleen. 'Isn't it grand the slating the

---

* The second Boer War, from 11 October 1899 to 31 May 1902, was between Britain and the South African Republic, aka ZAR or the Transvaal, and the Orange Free State, independent Boer Republics. To the British it was about securing fair treatment for the British minority; to fervently pro-Boer Irish nationalists it was about British colonial thuggery. To them, President Paul Kruger, the face of Afrikanerdom, was a hero whom John Daly made a Freeman of Limerick. The later news about the concentration camps where conditions were so bad that more than 4,000 Afrikaner women and 22,000 children died would reinforce beliefs about British cruelty. The Boers lost, but acquired limited self-government within the British Empire as – from 1910 onwards – the Union of South Africa.

English are getting? There's great excitement over it. You hear nothing on all sides from morning till night but war. Uncle John is threatening us he'll go off to the Transvaal.'[66]

Clarke was optimistic about opening a shoe shop by selling shares to Clan members, which would have 'nothing of the "begging hat" about it', but though the Clan had just united, there was no lack of poisonous politics. Suspicious as ever, Clarke feared 'hostility on the quiet from "Friends" who are not satisfied unless I become a "party man" and allow myself to become a tool of by such friends'.[67]

Instead he drew on one of his prison-acquired skills by getting a job as a patternmaker in a foundry courtesy of a foreman who employed only fellow-members of the Clan. With an evening job doing clerical work at Clan headquarters, he had enough money to send for his brother Alfie, whom he feared might be called up to fight the Boers, though he told Kathleen he was sure that if he were sent to South Africa Alfie wouldn't be fighting 'for the English'.[68] Clarke took his responsibilities as head of his family very seriously: he also declared his intention of sending for his mother and sister Hannah and of setting his sisters up in some sort of business. In the event, the three stayed in Dublin, where Alfie now had a corporation job.

When he wasn't working or writing to Kathleen, Clarke was talking politics among Clan members, attending pro-Boer rallies, being honoured by Tyrone associations or going to such events as a concert commemorating the birthday of Robert Emmet. Among its stars was the Dublin-born baritone William Ludwig who the previous year had moved Clarke to tears for only the second time in his adult life with the 'pathos' he put into 'General Monroe'.[69] Honouring a Presbyterian United Irishman from Lisburn – about thirty miles from Dungannon – who ended up on the gallows, its last verse was: 'All ye good men who listen, just think of the fate / Of the brave men who died in the year Ninety Eight. / For poor old Ireland would be free long ago / If her sons were all rebels like Henry Munro.' 'I am taking Maria and a couple of other friends to it', he told Kathleen, 'and I am sure it will be thoroughly Irish.'

Everything in Clarke's life was thoroughly Irish. He lived from choice in an Irish republican bubble. 'There are any amount of niggers living hereabouts and we Irish as a rule don't care for coming too much into contact with those absurd folks,' he told Kathleen, when explaining why he and Maria had moved apartments again.[70] She sympathised: 'I thought you were quite satisfied where you were but I suppose those niggers were too much for you. I must say I've an objection to them myself.'[71]

There had been great turf-wars in mid-nineteenth-century New York between the blacks and the Irish and the memories lingered on in Irish America, but what this comment illustrates more is Clarke's total lack of interest in any culture other than his own except in its capacity to damage the English. Had the prison authorities had the wit to give their political prisoners ample reading matter about other countries and peoples, that narrowness might have been challenged. As it was, starving them of intellectual stimulation left them relying on whatever songs and stories they retained in their memories, and this helped, as with Clarke, to feed a sense of racial superiority and Irish exceptionalism and feed a myth-laden grievance culture.

Working so hard and doing so well, and playing with entrepreneurial ideas, he waited with increasing impatience for Kathleen to join him, furious at the delaying tactics employed by Uncle John and a hold-up occasioned by her being caught up as a witness in a court case involving an accident suffered by James Egan's wife. And though he still loved his old friends, this disciplined, focused teetotaller was maddened by their dilatoriness when it came to letter-writing, their general inefficiency and their fondness for the bottle: it was Daly's niece Madge who made the bakery a success.

Another farcical experience with local government in Dublin had put him off job-hunting in Ireland for good, for at considerable expense and trouble he had travelled back home in the autumn of 1900 to discover that once again he was a victim of Egan's over-confidence. Despite a ringing endorsement by Maud Gonne at a public meeting, Tom Clarke was not elected Superintendent of the Dublin Abattoirs. The police reported pandemonium among Tom's supporters, with 'a great outburst of groans, boos and cries of "To Hell with you", three cheers for Clarke, Egan and Maud Gonne and the singing of "Who fears to speak of 98".'[72] The only bright spot was that when he met Daly in Limerick he finally persuaded him to agree to Kathleen going to America in 1901 to marry him.

Maria Clarke was excited about this, and, Clarke told Kathleen, 'has great hopes that you will make me a kind of a saintly Holy Roman Catholic and influence me to be more regular at Mass than she can'. Reservations about Catholicism were something else he and Kathleen shared: 'It was kind of her to think of it,' she replied. 'You can tell Maria from me that I'm afraid 'twill be all the other way. That instead of I making you a good Catholic you'll make me a bad one. I can't boast of ever being a very good one.'[73] (A few years later, when Kathleen was recuperating from illness in an institution run by New Jersey nuns, Clarke sent her a positively skittish letter: 'You have me all in a "tremor" at the thought of finding you suffering from a stroke of piety when you get home,' he wrote. 'The picture of my demure girl hands and fingers correctly folded up in front of your breast and the uplifted holy and nun-like eyes – with a heavenward gaze is the picture that has me sitting here in fear and trembling. However I'll wait till I see you and then I'll investigate for myself as to what manner of change has taken place.'[74])

Kathleen was just as anxious as Clarke that they should be reunited, although she would be leaving her family, her home and her very successful business. Indeed, when she was getting nowhere with Uncle John, she threatened to leave without his permission. Expecting her arrival imminently, in March 1901 Clarke told her he had invited as chief witnesses to their wedding John MacBride, who had been on the lecture circuit telling of his adventures fighting in South Africa with his Irish Transvaal Brigade, and Maud Gonne, who had been the figure-head of anti-Boer agitation in Ireland. In the event, Kathleen was held up once again and didn't arrive until July, so they had MacBride, but not Gonne, and John Devoy was also in attendance. MacBride was a great admirer: 'plucky Tom Clarke' he called him in a letter to Devoy the following year, emphasising his ability.[75]

They were married immediately in a Catholic church, and, difficult though the transition was for Kathleen, they settled very happily. Clarke gave up his clerical work at the Clan in order to spend more time with her, yet he stayed involved with the Clan through becoming president of one of its clubs, promoting Irish music, dancing and language, founding a journal called The Clansman that declared itself for 'Total Separation: Ireland as Independent Republic', organising lectures for the Brooklyn Gaelic Society and in 1902 the celebration of Robert Emmet's birthday. Although neither he nor Kathleen spoke Irish, they had been influenced by the passionate cultural nationalism of the Gaelic League that had been founded in Dublin in 1893; Kathleen recalled an article he wrote at that time saying 'that a free Ireland without its language was inconceivable' and that all Irish men and women should join the League.[76]

Though the Clarkes shared their political passions and had a trusting and loving relationship, it was not without its problems. Kathleen was used to a noisy, open family, but now she was living 'with a very silent man. Those terrible years developed the habit of repressing every sign of emotion and made him suspicious of every stranger.'[77]

Their first son, John Daly, was born in June 1902: 'Tom's joy over the little boy was great. The idea of having a son to follow him to carry on the fight for Ireland's freedom was almost too good to be true.'[78] Clarke lost his job the following year when the Clan foreman was fired along with all the men he had hired, but Kathleen had enough money to buy a candy and ice-cream store that kept them going. Clarke was reduced to looking for a job as a street-sweeper, and told his wife that at least in Portland prison he had not had to beg for work.[79] But his earlier attendance at Clan na Gael was about to bear fruit, for through acting as a secretary for Devoy he had earned his liking and respect.

'Forbidding of aspect, with a perpetual scowl upon his face,' commented Le Caron, 'Devoy . . . immediately conveyed the idea of being a quarrelsome man, an idea sustained and strengthened by both his manner of speech and gruffness of voice.' The image, said Le Caron, was that of the reality. 'Quarrelsome and discontented, ambitious and unscrupulous, his friendships were few and far between,' but his 'undoubted ability' propelled him to the top.[80] Yet to Kathleen Clarke Devoy had seemed 'gruff and unsociable', but finding him in private sociable, simple and kind, she came to conclude his manner was a pose to cover his intense shyness.[81]

To Clarke he was a life-saver, giving him in 1903 a job for which he was exceptionally well suited. Devoy was setting up the *Gaelic American*, a weekly republican newspaper. He was editor and Clarke his assistant as well as general manager. The paper had been founded as part of the war between the parliamentarians and the revolutionaries that polarised American–Irish politics.

The Clan and an increasing proportion of the AOH were bitterly opposed to the United Irish League (UIL) of America, the organ of John Redmond's Irish Parliamentary Party, which was scoring successes on the land-reform front. In July 1902 the Clan tried to get the AOH formally to condemn the UIL and was denounced by Redmondites for creating 'malignant factionalism' among Irish American nationalists.

Clarke threw himself into one skirmish in the battle for the hearts and minds of Irish Americans – the row over *McFadden's Row of Flats*. A popular musical farce first produced in 1897, this concerned two saloon keepers, a green-whiskered Irishman and a German who talks about his 'gut beer', competing to be elected alderman. It attracted no comment until in October 1902 it was condemned by the Gaelic League and the AOH in Denver. In New York, in March the following year, the Clan decided to get in on the act.

Kathleen remembers an argument with Clarke when she was ill and he was refusing to leave her even though he had been organising a protest that night over the play, 'which was defaming the Irish'. She insisted that if he did not go, 'I would get worse with the worry of it, the worry of knowing his comrades would think he had let them down. They intended using rotten eggs and tomatoes in their protest, and were likely to be arrested.'[82]

Five were, though not Clarke,

> after they threw eggs and vegetables on to the stage. They complained about green whiskers on the Stage Irishman, the appearance of Mrs. Murphy drunk in a wheelbarrow, and pigs in McFadden's flat. Protesters announced their support for the Clan na Gael, a secret, revolutionary Irish organization devoted to driving the British out of Ireland by force.

Whiskers, drunken woman and pigs were removed from future productions and the protestors of New York, Philadelphia and Denver were triumphant. 'The theater riots were manly dares, defiant displays, and recruiting tools not only in the battles between Irish nationalists and Anglo-Saxon authority,' wrote Alison Kibler, 'but also in the fiery debates between Irish nationalists themselves. Practical censorship was practical politics.'[83] The Clan was intent on broadening its base and the Irish involved in disrupting *McFadden's Row of Flats* were actually 'immigrant, lower-class backers of aggressive Irish ethnocentrism.'[84] It was censorship by the bully-boys.

There would be more of these shows of force outside and in theatres over the next decade, including those in Dublin and New York between 1907 and 1912 directed at Synge's *The Playboy of the Western World*. Clarke was indeed angered by any apparent slights on the Irish, but he had more serious reasons for getting involved in demonstrations: he was a serious operator who was learning lessons he would put to excellent use later about the value of stunts performed for political reasons. That the Irish–American press, by now largely a supporter of constitutional nationalism and integration into American society, disapproved of the violence was a bonus and a further reason for producing the *Gaelic American*, which was first published in October. Engaged in a political and commercial war with such competitors as the far more successful *Irish World*, it specialised in venomous and exaggerated attacks on its enemies. Clarke the youthful schoolteacher had long since given way to Clarke the ruthless propagandist.

In his new job, Clarke dealt with advertisers, commissioned articles, designed layout, wrote headlines, reproduced material from Irish papers and books of Irish interest and edited the paper in Devoy's frequent absences. Prosperous Clan members bought shares in it and it sold enough copies to keep going. Its message was straightforward: England, cruel and ruthless, was the cause of all Ireland's problems and was intent on taking over the world through force and cultural imperialism. As his biographer Michael Foy points out, while Clarke was well-informed about international relations, in his loathing of England he sometimes tied himself

in excruciating ideological contortions. After the Anglo-Japanese alliance of 1902, the *Gaelic-American* accurately predicted a Russo-Japanese war in which it sided with a

Czarist autocracy despised by every European liberal while simultaneously lambasting England for helping a coloured Asiatic people challenge white European – and American – interest in the Far East. One *Gaelic American* headline ran 'The Yellow Peril'.[85]

Devoy, unconcerned with liberal credentials in general, would have been happy to ally with Czarist Russia in 1878 had it not disappointed him by not going to war with the United Kingdom.

Clarke and Devoy pursued their Anglophobic agenda wherever they could, being particularly hostile to any political developments that might have the potential to help the British in time of war. One of their targets was the proposed Anglo-American defence alliance, which was opposed by the United Irish American Societies, the new umbrella organisation Devoy had helped bring into being and of which Clarke was correspondence secretary. Devoy campaigned against the alliance in towns and cities across America and Irish America helped defeat it. A similar proposal in 1905 was opposed just as vigorously, this time with the support of German-American societies.

As Devoy's most trusted aide, Clarke learned from him how to acquire, retain and use power to attain a well-defined objective. He would, however, show himself to have a priceless quality that Devoy lacked: like his mentor, Clarke wanted to be in control, but he wanted neither status nor recognition. He was happy to join organisations as a foot-soldier, an observer, an infiltrator, an enabler or whatever other role would help the cause. He joined the Irish-American Athletic Club and the Clan's military wing, the Irish Volunteers, at the rank of Regimental Adjutant, where he practised rifle-shooting. In the newspaper he ran dozens of articles on Irish Fenians and in his spare time he found further ways of honouring his heroes, seeking out Fenian graves, having them looked after and instigating an annual memorial day. He also introduced an annual pilgrimage to the grave of Wolfe Tone's widow.*

---

* Martha Witherington (1769–1849) was renamed Matilda by Wolfe Tone, with whom she had four children: one died in infancy and two of tuberculosis

Much as he loved what he did and remained focused on his mission, domestic problems made it impossible for Clarke to stay at the *Gaelic American*. Kathleen had frequent bouts of ill health, some so serious she had to recuperate in the country or in Ireland, and medical advice was that she should live permanently in the country. He was devoted to her, so in 1906, they bought a small market garden farm in Long Island and he gave up his job. However, although he made the best of it – both of them enjoyed the country and they worked very hard raising crops and chickens – this life was clearly not going to be a commercial success. Nor had it anything to do with what he saw as his life's work: making Ireland a republic.

Clarke had become an American citizen in 1905 and had passed the exam for a well-paid, permanent civil service job as a city inspector, but to Kathleen's chagrin he had refused to take it on the unconvincing grounds that a friend had told him that if the authorities discovered his past he might be deported. It is hard to avoid the inference that he resisted being sucked into a life that had nothing to do with Ireland.

He still kept up with foreign news, always probing for clues to potential British weaknesses. As Devoy had been furious about what he thought were Stephens's missed opportunities, so Clarke, furious that the British had won the Boer War, had chafed about the failure of the IRB to strike while they were under pressure. Now he talked to

---

in their teens. After Tone's death the family stayed in Paris with, after 1803, a government pension. In 1807 Martha took her surviving child, William Theobald Wolfe, to America, then returned to Paris where he became a cadet, and – after Matilda had accosted the Emperor Napoleon as he hunted and reminded him about her late husband – William was given privileged status and citizenship and had an honourable army career.

After Napoleon's defeat they returned to America, with Matilda now accompanied by her new husband, a Scottish businessman. She and William, who had inherited his father's literary flair, edited Tone's literary legacy, which was published in 1826 as *Life of Theobald Wolfe Tone . . . written by himself and continued by his son*. Tone's attractive personality, lively style and Pepysian frankness made the book a bestseller in Ireland. William died in 1828, but his mother kept the flame alive. Their joint grave is in New York.

Kathleen obsessively about growing Anglo-German commercial and
military rivalry and an inevitable war that would line up England,
France and Russia against Germany, Austria-Hungary and Italy. It
would be a tragedy, he told her over and over again, if Ireland missed
the opportunity to make a bid for freedom and so broke the tradition
of generations and became resigned to staying part of the British
Empire: 'The thought of such a thing happening was to him intolerable; to avert that fate from the country he loved he was ready to sacrifice everything, self, wife, child.'[86]

Clarke had stayed in close touch with Devoy, and, at his request, he
organised a 1907 lecture tour for the gifted, eloquent and precocious
twenty-four-year-old Bulmer Hobson. A grocer's son from a Belfast
Quaker family, Hobson had attended the Friends' School in Lisburn,
had fallen in love with Irish culture and, at fifteen, inspired by the
centenary of 1798, became a republican. In quick succession, he had
founded a boys' debating club, become secretary of the Belfast junior
branch of the Gaelic League and the Antrim board of the Gaelic
Athletic Association and had founded Fianna Éireann, a boys' hurling
league.

In 1904, at twenty-one, Hobson was sworn into the IRB by another
dynamo, Denis McCullough, whom he had met in the Gaelic League.
Just ten days his junior, McCullough was a publican's son from a Belfast
IRB Catholic family with a Christian Brothers' education who had
founded the first Belfast hurling club. A piano tuner who would run a
successful music business, he had been sworn into the IRB in 1900 at
the behest of his own father, who was one of the convivial, heavy-
drinking, unfocused old guard in Belfast whom he and Hobson
despised and now displaced. 'They were mostly effete and many of
them addicted to drink,' remembered McCullough. 'In a year or two,
after I had organised one or two new circles of young men to support
me, I got most of these older men retired out of the organisation,
which had been split up into about three factions by their personal
squabbles.'[87]

In 1901 both men had joined Cumann na nGaedheal (The Society
of the Irish), a nationalist umbrella group, but, though the organisation
became influential and set up new branches, to Hobson and
McCullough it was insufficiently serious of purpose.

In 1905 they founded a more radical organisation that they could control, the Dungannon* Clubs, a non-sectarian, separatist IRB front that opposed any participation in Westminster politics. 'The Ireland we seek to build is not an Ireland for the Catholic or the Protestant, but an Ireland for every Irishman irrespective of his creed or class,' said its first manifesto. The following year Hobson, a printer and journalist, founded its mouthpiece, the *Republic*.

The lecture tour for Hobson had been proposed by Pat McCartan, a farmer's son and another young northerner who became a nationalist under the influence of the 1798 centenary. After he left school, he worked as a barman in Philadelphia, where he became close to another native of County Tyrone, Joseph McGarrity, who initiated him into the Clan.

McGarrity, a successful businessman and generous financial backer of the revolutionary-minded, made it possible for McCartan to return to Ireland in 1905 to study medicine in Dublin. He transferred from the Clan to the IRB and became a member also of the Gaelic League, established Dungannon Clubs and joined Sinn Féin, an organisation dedicated to Irish independence and self-sufficiency. An Irish correspondent of the *Gaelic American*, he was a constant source of information to McGarrity and Devoy about people and politics.

Clarke organised a two-month tour for Hobson that included Boston, Chicago, Philadelphia and other cities with a strong Clan presence. It began in February with a packed New York meeting at which Hobson told the audience that the new generation would refuse to sit in a Westminster parliament and would live up to Wolfe Tone's promise about uniting Catholic and Protestant, north and south, as Irishmen.

Hobson deeply impressed Devoy, who appointed him an Irish correspondent of the *Gaelic American*. He also convinced Tom Clarke

---

* The title was inspired by the Dungannon Convention of 1782. During the American Revolution, with the regular army fighting thousands of miles away, in Ireland local militias of part-time soldiers were recruited to resist potential French or Spanish invaders. Known as the Volunteers or the Irish Volunteers, in 1782 they held a convention in Dungannon that successfully demanded greater legislative freedom for the Irish parliament. In 1798 a minority of Volunteers supported the United Irishmen's rebellion.

that if he returned to Ireland he would have young, energetic, talented and dedicated troops available. Kathleen would say later that his reasons for leaving America were wholly political, but there were family and economic reasons too: five-year-old Daly was turning into an American and, except for Clarke's sister Maria, all their relatives were in Ireland. Clarke's sister Hannah, who had a newspaper and tobacco shop (and who was the Dublin circulation manager of the *Gaelic American*), offered him help in setting up a similar business, which Madge Daly was prepared to back financially. Kathleen was fearful that in Ireland Clarke would get into trouble and be sent back to prison, but she was a good Fenian wife, so, against her better judgement, she agreed, Clarke sold the farm, booked the sailing tickets and went to break the news to Devoy. 'There was not a more surprised man in the USA than Devoy,' said Kathleen. 'He promised him all the help in his power, a promise he kept faithfully.'[88] The move certainly suited Devoy, who could see that now there would be an experienced man to steer the young Turks in the right direction.

The arrival in Cork in November 1907 of Thomas J. Clarke, 'ex-convict and dynamiter', was noted by the police.[89] The family set up their base with the Dalys in Limerick and Clarke embarked on a quick tour of Dublin, Londonderry and Dungannon to meet old IRB friends and new contacts. The Clan were the paymasters of the IRB, so Devoy's letters introducing him as a trusted ally were taken very seriously. He wrote delightedly to Devoy's assistant that 'the young fellows . . . who take the lead in the Sinn Féin movement impressed me very much by their earnestness and ability. I am delighted to find them away above what I had expected.'[90]

While Kathleen, who was pregnant, stayed in Limerick, Clarke lived with his mother and sister and spent several weeks finding and doing up premises for his tobacconist's shop at 55a Amiens Street, which opened in February 1908. Despite his lack of Irish, the name over the door was T.S. Ó'Cléirigh, in Irish lettering, and reflecting his American years was the large gold '55' he put on the front window against Hannah's advice but on the sound premise that it would get people talking. He applied himself with his customary flair and industry to promoting the shop with advertising in the *Gaelic American* and *Sinn Féin* newspapers and he had cards distributed far and wide by IRB contacts, but in the spirit of commerce and Fenian non-sectarianism he also stocked titles of interest to Protestants and unionists.[91] He worked in the shop from 6:30 a.m. to 11:30 p.m.; exhausted, after going to Limerick to the funeral of Kathleen's sister Annie he came down with the typhoid that had killed her and was absent for months in hospital or convalescing in Limerick. Kathleen stayed in Dublin with Daly and baby Tom, to run the shop with the help of her brother Ned.

Clarke's life was back on an even keel in 1908 as the shop became not just the means to keep his family in reasonable comfort but the centre of the conspiracy that would lead to rebellion. Yet though he had the financial backing of the Clan, Clarke was hamstrung. His sentence had been for life, so at any time the authorities could pick him up and return him to jail, and he knew well that the police kept a close eye on him.

From among the young bloods who gathered around him and became his allies and trusted friends, this cautious man needed one who was single-minded and whom he could trust implicitly. He found him in a clever, handsome, charming young man who had failed as a teacher, a gardener and a tramcar conductor, and who was now a Sinn Féin organiser. He became Tom Clarke's eyes, ears and mouth, the travelling spy, persuader and recruiter who understood and carried out obsessively a strategy that he knew must end in both their deaths.

Chapter Two

SEÁN MAC DIARMADA[1]

> He was a wonderful organiser, full of charm and magnetism,
> and very handsome. He never spared himself, he was here
> and there, in Dublin, out of it, all over the country. He was
> a very lovable character, and became Tom's loyal and loved
> comrade. He did all his organising under Tom's guidance;
> Tom being older and more experienced, he trusted him
> completely. Indeed, they trusted each other completely.
>
> *Kathleen Clarke, c.1939*

It took John Joseph McDermott (who as an adult Gaelicised his name to Seán Mac Diarmada*) longer than Tom Clarke to become a revolutionary, but he was born in different times, began on a different and more conventional path, and had to wait to find a direction, a cause and a guru.

Born in January 1883,[2] the same month and year as Bulmer Hobson and Denis McCullough, he was twenty-six years younger than Clarke. The eighth child of ten of Donald and Mary McDermott, he was brought up in a three-roomed thatched farmhouse on a smallholding in boggy Corranmore, near the village of Kiltyclogher, a beautiful part of County Leitrim near Fermanagh, close to what is now the border with Northern

---

* He was John McDermott until 1907, when he began calling himself Seán MacDiarmada or Mac Diarmada. His biographers call him MacDiarmada, he signed the Proclamation Mac Diarmada, the Dublin street named after him is Seán McDermott Street, the Sligo railway station is Mac Diarmada, and so is his entry in *The Dictionary of Irish Biography*, which works on the principle that Mac names in Irish should have a space between the Mac and the follow on. I think that the signature a person puts on his death warrant is the one he is serious about, so I'm calling him Mac Diarmada, and, to avoid confusion, I will give · him that name from the beginning.

Ireland. The area was miserably poor and wet; memories of the Famine were strong, and shortly before Mac Diarmada's birth the family's land-lord, Colonel Arthur Loftus Tottenham, a Conservative MP, had evicted thirty-nine tenants, including – according to McDermott family recol-lection – the McMorrows, the family of Mary McDermott.[3]

It was not an easy childhood, as Seán's mother was 'in decline' for a long time before she died in 1892 at forty-five: he was nine and his father was sixty-five.

Clarke's sister-in-law and benefactress Madge Daly, who like her Uncle John became a friend of Mac Diarmada's, would later recall that 'he often told us that when a boy he was blamed for all of the mischief in the parish.'[4] Kathleen Clarke said that he told her once that he had never known a mother's love and had always longed for it.

Still, Donald McDermott was a carpenter, so his family was better off than many of their neighbours, and young Seán aspired to being a teacher. Like Tom Clarke, he became a school monitor, but, unlike Clarke, he appeared determined to pursue his ambition, even though for him it was a hopeless one. Though he did well at his local school, he consistently failed his mathematics exams.

His biographer Brian Feeney eloquently describes how tough was the route to becoming qualified. Before having a chance at getting to a teacher training college, the pupil-teacher had to endure a five-year apprenticeship, often with inadequate teaching and poor resources, and the compulsory, competitive King's Scholarship examination that drew on rote learning in a wide range of subjects had an absolute requirement to pass drawing, English, mathematics, music and penmanship. The one-roomed Corracloona National School could not give him the help he needed, so Mac Diarmada had extra tuition. 'I hate Euclid and I'm afraid that the old rascal will have revenge on me if he catches me at the examination,' Mac Diarmada told a friend, and, although he had taken two years longer than the norm and a corre-spondence course, Euclid duly did. At twenty-one, escaping the igno-miny of the status of failed teacher, Mac Diarmada went for a short while to Edinburgh to work with a cousin as a gardening labourer; then, after a few months at home, he went to neighbouring County Cavan to take a six-month night-school course in Irish, book-keeping and shorthand. It was another false start as far as practical skills were concerned, so in the spring of 1905, in search of a job, Mac Diarmada followed one of his elder brothers to Belfast.

He was already a long way down the nationalist path. For a start, there had been the influence of his father, who according to a 1913 obituary in a newspaper then managed by his son had been a participant in the Land League, a member of the IRB and a friend of John Daly.[5] Then, although Gladstonian land reforms, much to Colonel Tottenham's disgust, gave tenants the oft-demanded 'fair rent, free sale and fixity of tenure', there was more trouble after he became insolvent. Under new ownership from 1883, during a period of widespread agitation (which included the boycotting of agents and landlords and attacks on livestock and property) in pursuit of compulsory purchase, tenants demanding the right to buy refused to pay rent. There were in consequence over a hundred evictions locally and a famous run-in with the police led to prosecutions in Kiltyclogher and the imprisonment of the local MP.

Calm descended in 1903 with the Wyndham Land Purchase Act that generously subsidised land sales to tenants, but by then Mac Diarmada's nationalism and Anglophobia were well entrenched. Even the dog he took rabbit-hunting was politicised: he named it Kruger.

Like so many of his contemporaries, Mac Diarmada was moved by the widespread and enthusiastic commemorations in Leitrim and much of Ireland of the 1798 rebellion, the United Irishmen and especially Wolfe Tone, which intensified his reading of history, the subject that had most interested him as a teenager. His books included Abbé James MacGeoghegan's *Histoire d'Irlande*. Published in France in the mid-eighteenth century, its sympathies were with the deposed Stuarts and its theme the oppression and heroism of Irish Catholicism. Translated into English in the nineteenth century, its narrative was continued to 1868 by John Mitchel, that purveyor of epic hate, and later revised again by an American-based Young Irelander; it became a best-selling work of popular nationalist Anglophobia in Ireland and Irish America.

The Irish peasantry in pre-Famine Ireland 'were proverbially known throughout the earth as "the worst housed peasantry in Europe"', the book explained. More significantly for Mac Diarmada, it banged the drum about the loss of Irish identity: 'the "national schools" were teaching Irish children that there is no such thing as nationality, and that it is a blessed privilege to be born "a happy English child".'[6] 'In every way the colonies are of use to this nation [Britain]', Mac Diarmada wrote in an essay about the English and Ireland, 'but for poor Ireland nothing is of any use 'till the yoke of English tyranny is shaken off'.[7] Patrick McGauran, the teacher to whose night-school he went in 1904, later remembered Mac Diarmada as 'anything but a bookworm' except when it came to Ireland, 'her language, her heroes, or her history', along with patriotic poetry and that of Robbie Burns. 'Many a time at dances and gatherings he recited Emmet's Speech from the Dock and Father Mullin's poem "The Celtic Tongue".'[8]

Seventy lines long, Father Michael Mullin's 'The Celtic Tongue'[9] was a test of memory as well as a mawkish plea for the Irish language, which Mac Diarmada was trying to master. A sample:

> The Celtic tongue is fading and we coldly standing by –
> Without a pang within the heart, a tear within the eye –
> Without one pulse for freedom stirred, one effort made to
> save
> The language of our fathers, lisp the language of the slave!
> Sons of Erin! Vain your efforts – vain your prayers for
> freedom's crown
> Whilst you crave it in the language of the foe that clove it
> down.

Emmet's speech from the dock was another labour of love but one of much greater significance for Mac Diarmada. If Tone, the United Irishmen and the Fenians were Tom Clarke's prime inspiration, Robert Emmet* was Mac Diarmada's, and his was a much more personal devotion than Clarke's for Tone.

---

* Born in 1778 in Dublin to liberal Protestants, Emmet was the fourth surviving child of seventeen of the state physician, who encouraged him to venerate the principles of liberty and freedom as expressed in the American War of Independence and made him ambitious to be an Irish George Washington. Academically brilliant, in Trinity College Emmet excelled as an orator, having a remarkable natural capacity to speak fluently and extempore; he also, in 1796, joined the United Irishmen, which was proscribed, and with his elder brother Thomas Addis attended meetings of the executive. In 1798 Trinity expelled him over his 'wicked' political activity.

Unlike Tone, who came to republican separatism gradually, Emmet had been brainwashed as a child. A close family friend would mimic Dr Robert Emmet, father of Temple, Thomas Addis and Robert, 'giving his children their "morning draught"' of patriotism: 'Well, Temple, what would you do for your country? Addis! Would you kill your brother for your country? Would you kill your sister for your country? Would you kill me?'[10]

Temple died at twenty-seven, Addis would be imprisoned and exiled for his role in the United Irishmen, and Robert, fourteen years his junior, would be hanged in 1803. Their sister Mary Anne died in 1804 worn out from grief and worry; her lawyer husband, who was sympathetic to the political sympathies of his brothers-in-law, had been imprisoned for a year after Emmet's rebellion.

Irish nationalist legend did not bother itself much with collateral damage, so the Emmet whom Mac Diarmada came to love was simply a hero who had sacrificed himself. He had the advantage of being more uncomplicatedly romantic than Wolfe Tone and appearing to have no unacceptable baggage. Like Clarke, Mac Diarmada was a lifelong teeto-taller, but, unlike Clarke, as a young man he was a pious Catholic. This would have been a barrier to venerating Tone, whose candid diaries showed him to have been a highly convivial drinker and womaniser.

And there was the suicide of which many disapproved and was condemned by A.M. Sullivan, who liked his heroes perfect, as 'yield-ing to a weakness which every Christian heart should be able to conquer'.[11] So severe was the Catholic Church about the wickedness of suicide that it is only comparatively recently that particularly devout keepers of the republican flame stopped alleging that Tone had been murdered in his cell for mysterious, sinister British reasons.* He had

---

During the rebellion he was a United Irishmen agent and messenger; after-wards he wrote the report on why it had failed, with particular emphasis on the indiscretions of members. Passionately opposed to the Act of Union, he was part of a United Irish delegation that went to France in 1801, where he met Matilda Tone and developed a deep dislike of French politics and society.

* An alternative explanation is that – knowing friends were searching for a means to have his life spared – he had been trying to injure himself just enough to secure a stay of execution, hence his remark not long before he died: 'I am sorry I have been so bad an anatomist.' That, however, would also have been thought inglorious.

also insulted the conventions of Irish nationalist mythology, which required its Irish heroes to laugh in the face of the hangman.

And that, certainly according to the legend, was what Robert Emmet did on the scaffold in 1803, giving him – at a time when disillusionment about the French Revolution was spurring romanticism to ever greater intensity – the most important ingredient for an Irish hero. He was only twenty-five. He was a fine orator, handsome, gifted, careless of his life, and remembered as cutting a fine figure in his elaborate green regimentals, his white waistcoat and cashmere pantaloons, Hessian boots and black velvet stock. There was also a doomed romance with Sarah Curran, whose death in 1808 from consumption after a happy marriage to a British army captain was decreed by legend to have instead have been caused by a broken heart that had pined for Emmet. For good measure, there was a second tragic heroine, Anne Devlin, Emmet's sixteen-year-old housekeeper, who had carried messages from Emmet to Curran and refused to give information on him despite being tortured and imprisoned.

Emmet's incompetent rebellion had been an utter failure; indeed he had called it off when he witnessed the brutality of some of those who had joined in. Having no control over them, he was unable to save the life of the liberal Lord Chief Justice of Ireland, Lord Kilwarden,* who was dragged from his carriage along with his clergyman nephew and hacked to death with pikes. As the military restored peace, among the dead were about twenty soldiers and fifty rebels, fifteen of whom were hanged.

But, as with the victims of the United Irish rebellion, all that mattered subsequently in nationalist legend were the good intentions and the rhetoric of the young leader. Dr Richard Madden, an opponent of physical force nationalism who in 1846 published the first biography of Emmet, mixed fact and fiction in his elaborate construct of a sinless hero. In language later echoed in the petitions about Tom Clarke, Madden insisted that Emmet was morally in the clear: 'No

---

* Coincidentally, Kilwarden had given Tone a chance of survival when he granted him a stay of execution on a technicality, but by then Tone had already cut his throat.

motive of Robert Emmet could be impure, selfish, venal, or ambitious.'
Rather, 'he was the victim of deception . . . he was deluded, misled,
and sacrificed by designing men, whose machinations, his youth, his
inexperience, his confiding nature, were unfit to cope with'.[12]

As Emmet had spoken without a prepared text, there were myriad
versions circulated of his speech from the dock, and there were different notes made in court. However, the version published by Sullivan
would almost certainly have been the one available to Mac Diarmada,
though at almost 3,000 words it seems unlikely that any party would
want the full piece.

Emmet's was magnificent declamatory prose. In the Sullivan text,
the last part begins with Emmet's indignant rejoinder when the judge
interrupted him to say that 'his sentiments and language disgraced
his family and his education, but more particularly his father, Dr.
Emmet, who was a man, if alive, that would not countenance such
opinions'.

'If the spirits of the illustrious dead participate in the concerns and
cares of those who were dear to them in this transitory life,' retorted
Emmet,

> oh! ever dear and venerated shade of my departed father,
> look down with scrutiny upon the conduct of your suffer-
> ing son, and see if I have, even for a moment, deviated from
> those principles of morality and patriotism which it was
> your care to instil into my youthful mind, and for which I
> am now about to offer up my life.

It was the peroration that became part of the Irish nationalist popular
narrative:

> I am going to my cold and silent grave – my lamp of life is
> nearly extinguished – my race is run – the grave opens to
> receive me, and I sink into its bosom. I have but one request
> to ask at my departure from this world, it is – THE
> CHARITY OF ITS SILENCE. Let no man write my
> epitaph; for as no man who knows my motives dare now
> vindicate them, let not prejudice or ignorance asperse

them. Let them and me rest in obscurity and peace; and my tomb remain uninscribed, and my memory in oblivion, until other times and other men can do justice to my character. When my country takes her place among the nations of the earth, *then* and *not till then*, let my epitaph be written. I have done.

Less industrious than Mac Diarmada, most of Emmet's admirers have confined themselves to learning just the second-last sentence, which has been used by a succession of revolutionaries to justify violent nationalism in the name, first, of Irish freedom, and, later, of a united Ireland.

After the legend of Robert Emmet took hold of the Irish nationalist imagination, there were many who lamented that the authorities had not had the sense to exile him to Australia. But then there would later be many who lamented that rather than executing Fenians like Devoy – and of course Clarke – they had been kept alive to wreak havoc.

Of all the songs that were written about Emmet, the finest were written by his friend Thomas Moore, the master of the sentimental ballad and the darling of the London drawing rooms. 'Music is the first faculty of the Irish,' he had said once. 'We will endeavour to teach the people to sing the songs of their country that they may keep alive in their minds the love of the fatherland.'

Reflecting Emmet's prohibition of any mark for his grave, Moore wrote in his *Irish Melodies* a poem that began:

> Oh, breathe not his name,
> Let it sleep in the shade,
> Where cold and unhonoured,
> His relics are laid;
> Sad, silent and dark
> Be the tears that we shed,
> As night dew that weeps
> On the grave o'er his head.

It was that melancholic lament that 'set the tone for the legend', wrote Marianne Elliott. 'Emmet himself, brooding and rather humourless, was Ireland's perfect romantic hero.'[13] Lord Byron begged that if he died a tragic death Moore 'would at least celebrate him with another "Oh breathe not his name"'; 'The Broken Heart' was a eulogy Washington Irving wrote about Emmet and Sarah Curran in his *Sketch Book* of 1819–20; Hector Berlioz dedicated to Emmet *Elégie* – the last of his *Neuf Mélodies irlandaises*.[14]

A hundred years after Emmet's death, centenary celebrations had whipped nationalist Ireland into a frenzy of admiration for their dead hero and Anglophobic anger at his perceived persecutors. His virtues were stressed even from the pulpit and in the singsongs in societies and pubs the favourite would have been 'Bold Robert Emmet'.

> The struggle is over, the boys are defeated,
> Old Ireland's surrounded with sadness and gloom,
> We were defeated and shamefully treated,
> And I, Robert Emmet, awaiting my doom.

There would even now be many who could sing along to the refrain:

> Bold Robert Emmet, the darling of Ireland,
> Bold Robert Emmet will die with a smile;
> Farewell! companions both loyal and daring,
> I'll lay down my life for the Emerald Isle.

In heavily industrialised Belfast, in November 1905, Mac Diarmada found a job as a tram conductor and occupied his spare time with the Gaelic League and the AOH, which was being turned into an instrument of Redmond's Irish Parliamentary Party (IPP) by a brilliant organiser, the charismatic MP 'Wee Joe' Devlin. A mirror image of the Protestant Orange Order, its members paraded on Catholic holy days wearing green collarettes and carrying banners showing popes, saints and Celtic imagery. Its membership expanded from 10,000 in 1905 to 60,000 four years later, at a period when the IRB had around 1,000.

Pat McCartan in Ireland and his mentor Joe McGarrity in Philadelphia both loathed the AOH: McGarrity thought it 'only keeps religious strife alive in Ireland': McCartan described its members as 'no good, ignorant, bigoted creatures'.[15] Both of them reflected the underlying anti-clericalism of many members of the IRB. The Catholic bishops were blocking reform, McCartan told McGarrity in April 1906: 'if the Church continues to oppose the advance of Nationalism the history of France will undoubtedly be repeated in Ireland. Of course it will take time and perhaps a Voltaire.'[16]

At the end of 1905, Hobson had persuaded McCartan to found two Dungannon clubs in Carrickmore, the Tyrone village from which he and McGarrity came. McCartan extolled Hobson as 'a Protestant and a thorough nationalist' who worked hard 'to blend orange and green'[17] and was full of optimism, but, as he reported shortly afterwards, at Mass the local parish priest had warned his flock against the clubs. 'Wouldn't an act like that make you curse the day you left a free country? One can hardly keep from thinking that Ireland is unworthy of freedom. God knows it is hard to blame the Orangemen for their fear of Home Rule.'[18] He was coming to the conclusion that Irish Protestants were 'not actuated by love of England but hatred of the priest in politics'.

McGarrity was equally enthused: 'I think Hobson may yet make Protestant Ulster Irish and National. Give him all the help and encouragement you can. Convey to him my sincerest good wishes. If he achieves the conversion of Ulster to Nationalism his name will be cherished by generations of Irishmen to come.'

The then devoutly Catholic Seán Mac Diarmada was lodging in Ardoyne, a small Catholic enclave in north Belfast, and it was almost certainly his landlord (another of that rare Protestant republican breed), a member of the Dungannon Club and the IRB, who drew him into political circles. The Dungannon Club promoted temperance, and one of its members, who had been purged by Bulmer Hobson and Denis McCullough from the IRB for drunkenness, was said to have asked McCullough: 'Well, if you won't have me, would you have a promising young fellow from the country who doesn't drink?' Mac Diarmada (remembered McCullough), was 'a raw country boy with no deep national understanding'.[19]

Initially, his piety was a real problem, for he was reluctant to join a secret organisation of which his church disapproved, but Hobson was a very persuasive man and in the spring of 1906 Mac Diarmada joined both the Dungannon Club and the IRB. Spotting that he was someone with a desperate need to dedicate himself to a cause, his two mentors set about ridding him of his religious baggage and giving him a sense of political direction. 'One of our earliest converts', said Hobson, he 'came over to us from the AOH and soon became one of our most active workers. He was a very handsome youth with an ingratiating manner and, after a little practice, became a fairly good speaker. His sincerity and energy made him a valuable recruit.'

Mac Diarmada's rapid education away from sectarian nationalism was helped by the weekly club meetings, which centred around partisan political lectures and debates. According to McCullough, they often ended in a nationalist singsong, the quality of which was not improved by the involvement of Hobson and Mac Diarmada, who he claimed were so tone deaf that 'you could not tell whether they were singing "God Save Ireland" or "God Save the King"'.

By early summer an enthusiastic member of an evangelical trio, Mac Diarmada was to be found with his two new friends pulling around promising areas a borrowed cart containing a borrowed magic lantern, used to show slides with statistics about such subjects as emigration, industry and venereal disease among British soldiers. Their message was that Ireland should become politically independent and economically self-sufficient. Belfast audiences were lively: as McCullough reported, 'the lantern was often battered with stones thrown by hostile crowds, but was never put out of action'.[20] This was an excellent training for Mac Diarmada's future career, for, as Hobson said, 'When one has learned how to handle a hostile mob in Belfast, other audiences seem pretty easy.' Not that Belfast was the only rough district. In Newry, critics hurled mud and vegetables, and the pair were chased out of another location in a hail of stones.[21]

Mac Diarmada's first public speech and first appearance in police records was in June 1906, in Clonard Street in West Belfast. The police estimated the crowd was about 1,500 and reported that 'Bulmer Hobson, Denis McCullough and John McDermott spoke and advocated doing away with all things British. Those present were advised to refuse jury service as a means of making the British Government powerless. Recruiting for the army was also condemned.'[22] Hobson recalled that there were present 'a great number of factory girls' who 'started jeering McDermott and being very friendly with the police. McDermott lost his temper and let loose on them. Forever afterwards he was much in demand by the platform patrons, who always sought out 'the young fella with the fiery tongue'.

The Dungannon Clubs were expanding quickly, with a second branch in Belfast and others in Londonderry, Tyrone, Newcastle, London and Glasgow, but progress was not fast enough for Hobson and McCullough. More interesting to the police than the press, they had realised early on that they needed some kind of journal. In May 1906 McCartan sent McGarrity Hobson's prospectus for the *Republic*. There were four directors, he told him, two Protestant (Hobson, the editor, and his friend Jack Morrow, a Belfast artist who used to show his cartoons through the Dungannon Club's magic lantern) and two Catholics (McCartan and McCullough), and there would be 'no half measures'.

The journal was the product of impatient young men, and McGarrity's reaction was to fear that the directors might end up in jail, but McCartan was insouciant. That would not happen, he explained, for the new Liberal government was in the business of 'giving nothing but sympathy' to Ireland, and to get young people interested the tone needed to be 'a bit hot' and the aim shown to be 'something noble'.[23]

The *Republic* was launched by the Dungannon Club in December 1906, with financial help from Roger Casement, with whom Hobson had been friendly for a couple of years. 'We stand for an Irish republic', explained Hobson's editorial, 'because we can see that no compromise with England, no repeal of the Union, no concession of Home Rule or devolution will satisfy the national aspirations of the Irish people nor allow the unrestricted mental, moral and material development of our country. National independence is our right; we ask no more; and we accept no less.' Its masthead declared: 'Not to repeal the Union, but the Conquest; not the Constitution Wolfe Tone died to abolish but the Constitution Tone died to obtain.'* Hobson gave the paper's anti-sectarian message uncompromisingly:

---

* A quote from James Fintan Lalor.

The old hate and the old bigotry that have kept Catholic
and Protestant divided – the old grovelling spirit of toady-
ism, must be killed and forgotten by the people. The ineffective and out-worn political movements, Unionist and
Nationalist, must be superseded and silenced and in their
place a national movement, virile and militant, that recog-
nises no creed save that of Irishman, no party save the
national, must be established.[24]

Needing to spread that gospel further and more vigorously, a full-time
organiser was needed to found new clubs, look after those already in
existence and generally spread the message. The by now messianic
Mac Diarmada, a chain smoker who had been sacked in the summer
for puffing on a cigarette on the platform of his tram, was making what
was described as an 'erratic' livelihood and was the obvious candidate.
'They simply got thirty members of the Dungannon club to agree to
pay a shilling a week each . . . into the organising fund,' recalled one
member, 'and without more ado Seán went on the road.'[25] According
to another source, all he got was half of that. But he *was* given a
bicycle.

    Although he would also visit Antrim, Derry and south Armagh,
Mac Diarmada's instructions were to focus on Tyrone, whose inhabitants Hobson referred to disparagingly as 'the Hibs' or 'the Ribbonmen,'*
a county and a group so threatening he was mock-seriously presented
at the club with a lead pencil holder they told him was a 'revolver'. Mac
Diarmada met plenty of trouble, for his message that Irishmen should
not take seats in Westminster went down very badly. He was also
'having some very narrow escapes from the Ribbonmen in Tyrone', as
he reported to Joe McGarrity. 'Their leaders and National Chaplain are
very aggressive and often brutal in their opposition.'

* An early nineteenth-century reincarnation of the sectarian Defenders, who
had been suppressed after the 1798 rebellion, the Ribbonmen dwindled in
numbers from the 1850s onwards and were often hostile to Fenians. Unionists
delighted in undermining AOH respectability by calling them Ribbonmen or
Molly Maguires, another secret agrarian society from which the American
AOH had partially derived.

McCartan was assiduous in promoting the reputations of his colleagues. In the *Gaelic American* published just before Hobson arrived, in February 1907, to begin the lecture tour Tom Clarke had organised for him, he was described as being representative of the 'heroic tradition' of such Protestant nationalists as John Mitchel and Clarke's beloved Henry Monroe.[26] His brilliant platform performances there had enthused not just McGarrity but Devoy and the *Gaelic American* about the Ulster activities of nationalism's New Model Army. They in turn had impressed on Hobson the importance of uniting the separatist forces back home and he set about the task with a will. McCartan's reports from Ireland covered the amalgamation in April 1907 of the Dungannon Clubs with Cumann na nGaedhael under the title of the Sinn Féin League. This development did not please Arthur Griffith, who had not only founded Cumann na nGaedhael in 1900, but edited a newspaper called *Sinn Féin* ('We Ourselves') after the political policy he had been developing for several years.

As Michael Laffan described him, Griffith was – like many nationalists – 'a geographical determinist' who believed that 'irrespective of their background or religion, all the people living on the island were Irish and were equal members of the Irish nation – whether they liked it or not'.[27] Uneasy about violence, Griffith had left the IRB: his policy was that the Irish should develop parallel institutions such as courts, leave Westminster, and sit in an independent parliament in Dublin and practise passive resistance of the kind that had caused Austria to yield to Hungary's demands in 1867. To placate unionists, Griffith proposed that a separate Ireland should share a monarch with Britain (as had happened with Austria-Hungary), yet he believed in economic self-sufficiency and protectionism – unpopular ideas in Belfast, which as the only industrialised part of Ireland depended on free trade within the British Empire.

Feeling the young men were too extreme in their insistence on a republic, Griffith resisted Hobson's suggestions that the new League should also incorporate his grandly named National Council, a collection of local groups that in 1904 and 1905 had won a few council seats in Dublin. Hobson was disappointed, but otherwise he and his colleagues were now riding high. The amalgamation had solved the clubs' considerable financial problems, not least because the *Republic*, which had found it impossible to attract advertisers, was then subsumed into the Dublin-based Cumann na nGaedhael-linked *Peasant*. Hobson, who lost several jobs because of his politics, was appointed a sub-editor, and, with fifty pounds McGarrity had sent him, he was able to keep going with his writing and speaking. Seán Mac Diarmada was appointed Ulster organiser for the League and set about winning recruits to the Sinn Féin platform and founding more branches.

However, national political events then changed everything, and sent Mac Diarmada and his bicycle back home to Leitrim.

Since the demise of Gladstone's Second Home Rule Bill in 1893, most Liberals had wanted nothing to do with an Irish policy that had brought them only grief and division. What was more, the English electorate had taken umbrage at Irish support for the Boers, and the House of Lords would be certain again to reject any Home Rule bill. The Liberal Party had won a huge majority in the election in January 1906; they had no need of the votes of the Irish Parliamentary Party (IPP) and there was no commitment to Home Rule in their manifesto. From the Irish perspective, however, since most of Ireland outside Ulster had voted for Home Rule parties, this was a betrayal of decades of co-operation.

As a gesture of goodwill, in May the government introduced the Irish Council Bill, which offered a measure of administrative devolution and reform but left the Chief Secretary with the power to overrule any decisions he disliked. To persuade parliament that it was innocuous, Prime Minister Campbell-Bannerman described it as 'a little modest, shy, humble, effort to give administrative powers to the Irish people', thus succeeding in maddening a large swathe of Irish opinion. A besieged IPP withdrew its earlier tentative support for what was now being described as an 'insult', the bill was dropped in June, and the young MP for North Leitrim, Charles J. Dolan, said constitutionalism had been tested and found wanting and that he would fight a by-election on the policies of Arthur Griffith.

The *Gaelic American* reported Mac Diarmada's speech in Newry that month:

The heroic men of '98, '48 and '67 had their enemies and the policy could endure this also. The Sinn Féin party had been told that they sprang into existence when we were going to get something from beneficent England. Well, he (the speaker) thought that the argument should have exhausted itself by this time. The Sinn Féin party had as its ultimate aim the destruction of foreign domination over Ireland and in order to carry out that policy some sort of organisation was necessary.

He recommended passive resistance, for with the death of Parnell 'fell the last hope of ever being able to wrest anything from England by parliamentarianism'.

Long before Dolan had resigned his seat, Hobson and Mac Diarmada went straight to Leitrim, Hobson telling McGarrity that if they won that seat for Sinn Féin other MPs would resign and 'we will rouse the whole country . . . Four or five others are ready to come over to us and others can be forced presently. Things are moving very fast but not yet as fast as I would like. We are doing all we can to hurry them however.'[28]

There was not, though, much Hobson could do to hurry things along in Leitrim. On 8 July, McCartan wrote to McGarrity that 'Hobson had to leave today because he is a Protestant.' Hobson elaborated a few weeks later to McGarrity about how 'they demonised me from the Altar as a dangerous person and the local press described me as a Salvation Army preacher from Belfast and an Orangeman, etc. I thought my presence would do more harm than good.'[29]

Still, away from that 'backward ignorant county', he increased the pressure on Griffith. Even though its membership contained many who would have settled for a pre-union Irish parliament, the National Council agreed in Dublin in August to join the League and form the Sinn Féin party with Griffith as president, Hobson as vice-president. To reflect their different emphases, both organisations, for a while, kept their separate titles. On what was almost certainly his first visit to Dublin, Mac Diarmada was at that meeting and became a member of its Executive, and the following month he was there too outside the

Mansion House as part of an aggressive Sinn Féin group who – having failed to crash a meeting of the IPP – held an open-air meeting themselves. There was no point trying to reason with 'such a despicable gang as Independent Redmond, the Italian Nanneti or Toady "God Save the King" Devlin', he told them. The job was to destroy 'the last link that binds Ireland to Great Britain (cheers)', something that could not be achieved 'by men going over to England to take an oath of allegiance to England's king'. What Irishmen had to do was to 'paralyse British government in Ireland'.[30]

Mac Diarmada had fallen in love with Dublin and now had a base there, sharing a house with McCartan, who was still studying at the Royal College of Surgeons, but his main work was still in Leitrim. Griffith threw the weight of his *Sinn Féin* paper behind Dolan, Hobson wrote and Mac Diarmada published locally a weekly Sinn Féin paper, the *Leitrim Guardian*, and money and press support came from America, particularly McGarrity, John Devoy and the *Gaelic American*.

'John McDermott, our Dungannon Club organiser is down in Leitrim,' Hobson told McGarrity in the autumn. 'He has turned out splendidly and is doing great work.'[31] He was there off and on for a long time, for the by-election did not take place until February 1908. And though he was an indefatigable worker, he was up against a very well-resourced IPP that was gradually becoming more united than it had been in years. One of Dolan's local organisations had abandoned him for the IPP candidate, Francis Meehan, a county councillor and president of Manorhamilton AOH, who was publicly backed by the local bishop. Mac Diarmada's brother, Patrick McDermott, helped set up a Sinn Féin *cumann* (society) in their local village, but there were few other local activists.

More importantly, the Leitrim electorate had little or no interest in arcane discussions of Hungarian solutions when the only question they were interested in was that of the land. They relied on government to provide subsidised food when crops failed; as far as tenant farmers were concerned, Westminster was delivering the means of getting rid of the landlords through heavily subsidised land purchase, and even the landless labourers were on their way to having cottages with an acre attached.

Pat McCartan was one of the young enthusiasts to whom Leitrim gave some education in reality, telling McGarrity that it

> had a tendency to cool my ardour about Republicanism. The National Spirit is completely killed by poverty in some places and the idea of doing anything against the Government is out of the question. They would ask you what would the poor people do only for the government and so on.[32]

A recognition that a relatively benign government was the enemy of radicalism fanned the flames of the young men's loathing of the parliamentarians. In turn, the IPP – proud of all it had achieved for Ireland through patient work and tough negotiation at Westminster – despised what it saw as the forces of ingratitude and irresponsibility whose policies would lead only to division and violence. The deep antagonism between the two camps sometimes ended in fisticuffs, with IPP forces sometimes augmented by tough guys from Belfast sent by Wee Joe Devlin, the party's 'enforcer'.

Public appearances were sometimes lively even by Belfast or Tyrone standards. In January 1908, as Mac Diarmada and Diarmuid Lynch, a fellow IRB member, attempted to address parishioners in Drumshambo after Mass, they were first drowned out by booing and groaning, and when they relocated to the town centre Mac Diarmada was dragged from the makeshift platform by the local UIL organiser. A local newspaper reported:

> The two organisers doggedly fought their way to the hotel where they remained for some time outside the door and when Mr. Barry [another UIL member] approached MacDermott blows were exchanged freely with the result that Mr. Barry received a nasty blow on the side of the eye. The crowd grew very excited and rushed in on Mr. MacDermott who escaped a severe mauling by slapping the hall door in their faces.[33]

The final tally – 3,103 for Meehan and 1,157 for Dolan – was, in the circumstances, a very good result and in advanced nationalist circles

'made Mac Diarmada an *sar-fhear* [superman] of Leitrim'. With plenty
of admiring coverage in *Sinn Féin* and the *Gaelic American*, he was now
respected in Sinn Féin, IRB and Clan na Gael circles. He was confident, sociable, attractive and twenty-five years old, had had more than
enough of Leitrim and had no urge to return to Tyrone.

Within a few weeks of the election, Bulmer Hobson joined his two
friends in their Dublin house on the north side of the city centre and
introduced Mac Diarmada to the legend that was Tom Clarke.
McCartan has described what Clarke, now fifty-one, was like in his
new role as a Dublin shopkeeper:

> A lean or thin type of man who wore glasses and smoked
> many cigarettes. If he did not know a person he pretended
> to know nothing about Ireland or Irish organisations and
> seemed just a businessman. To those he knew well –
> mostly IRB men – he talked freely and liked a joke and
> could enjoy one heartily. He knew what was taking place
> in all Irish organisations as the IRB had members in all,
> but to the stranger he knew nothing outside the news in
> the press. He looked straight into a customer's eyes if one
> spoke to him and seemed to study them with those pierc-
> ing eyes of his.[34]

Was a life of constant uprooting evident in his accent? Born in Tipperary,
infancy in the Isle of Wight, seven years in South Africa, eleven in County
Tyrone, two in New York, where his circle were mostly a mixed bunch of
Irish immigrants and exiles, fifteen in an English jail under the silent rule,
a year in Dublin with his Dungannon family, punctuated by visits to his
adopted family in Limerick, New York for seven years in the Irish-
American bubble, most of the time with his Limerick wife, he finally
settled in Dublin, where he was surrounded by a small group of young
people the majority of whom were from Ulster.

Clarke was already close to McCartan, McCullough and Hobson,
whom Kathleen Clarke claimed he saw as another John Mitchel, but
Hobson was intellectually fully formed, naturally questioning and
lacked the vulnerable charm of Seán Mac Diarmada, the delightful but
slightly lost young man who seemed in search of a family as well as a

cause. He found in Clarke a hero to worship and a ready-made cause to believe in, while in him and Kathleen he also found a surrogate father and mother. He quickly accepted the authority of the first, the care of the second and the affection of both.

Apparently set on a path as an organiser and election agent for Sinn Féin, Mac Diarmada was keen to relate tales of his exploits in Leitrim. 'He was full of fun and laughter,' recalled Kathleen,

> relating all the tactics they had resorted to win the election. When he had finished, Tom turned to him and said, in a very severe tone, 'Seán, I would rather lose an election than resort to tricks to win it. Our cause is too sacred to be sullied with electioneering tricks. No matter who else may indulge in them, we should not, neither should we participate in an election to the British Parliament.'
>
> Opening his big beautiful eyes and looking startled, Seán said, 'Tom, I never looked at it that way before. I see now you are right.' He held out his hand to Tom, saying, 'There's my hand on it.' They shook hands. 'I promise you never to take part in such proceedings again.' He kept his word, and later resigned his position as organiser for Sinn Féin.[35]

Apart from her tendency to report conversations long in the past as if she had taped them, Kathleen's recollections also suffered from having been written decades after they happened, but she was an honest woman. Here, though, she slightly misremembered. Mac Diarmada stayed on for now as a paid Sinn Féin organiser, albeit one who was primarily working for the IRB.

The Clarke of Kathleen's anecdote was presenting his Robespierre side, incorruptible according to his own lights and utterly rigid. As another young friend remembered:

> Some say that he had the face of a fanatic. I'd prefer to say that it was clear from his countenance that he was a man who would hold vehemently, closely, faithfully, and earnestly to the basic opinions and principles which were dearest to him, that he should direct his life accordingly,

and that no one would be able to make him retreat, deviate, desist or abstain from that, irrespective of whatever obstacles might be put in his way.[36]

Yet what honest Tom Clarke was inspiring his young friends to do was to join as many nationalist organisations as they could and infiltrate and subvert them mercilessly in the interests of the revolution. Lying was legitimate: Fenianism permitted its members to lie and cheat even to friends for the sake of the cause. Mac Diarmada, the man whom Hobson and McCullough had found so easy to convert from piety and parliamentarianism, willingly accepted he should follow a more absolutist and deceitful path and put his gifts at Clarke's disposal. Kathleen exaggerated the extent of Clarke domination. He set the strategy as well as the objective, but Mac Diarmada had considerable tactical gifts, was often unable to consult with Clarke on everything and sometimes thought he knew better. But he had the highest regard for Clarke's courage, his convictions and his wisdom, as well as for his close relationship to Clan na Gael, who were, through Devoy, the paymasters.

Sinn Féin were on a roll following the Leitrim by-election and, with Mac Diarmada's assiduous help, was busy infiltrating cultural organisations. In February 1908, for instance, some of its leading members were elected to the leading posts in the Gaelic Athletic Association (GAA),* attracting from police Special Branch the gloomy comment that this 'would eventually place the GAA "entirely in the hands of the Sinn Féin ring in Dublin who were probably tempted by the large finances and other considerations".[37] From a security point of view, matters were much more serious, for the IRB was infiltrating the infiltrators and spreading its separatist message widely. The police were aware of this by November, when they concluded that the IRB was controlling many GAA activities. Their records noted a dance committee in County Offaly that had passed a resolution banning any soldiers or policemen from their functions, something Mac Diarmada regularly recommended, as 'only for whom, although being their own kin, Ireland would now be free'.[38]

* Founded in 1884, the GAA's objectives were to promote Irish identity by reviving and popularising Irish sports.

Mac Diarmada had joined the Keating branch of the Gaelic League, of which McCartan was already a member, the Laurence O'Toole Gaelic Football Club, its pipers' club, and, of course, was an active participant in the Teeling circle, his local IRB group. The Keating Branch, which existed to promote the Munster dialect of the Irish language,* would become an IRB fiefdom, but for now it was a centre for myriad cultural and sporting activities: Mac Diarmada acted in its drama society and played in Phoenix Park with his home-made hurley. He attended meetings of the Celtic Literary Society and spoke to Sinn Féin clubs all over Dublin. Covered occasionally by the *Peasant* and regularly in *Sinn Féin*, he gave talks on such subjects as 'Our Critics, A Reply to their Arguments' and 'The Young Ireland and Sinn Féin Movements. A Contrast'.[39]

In 1908 the counties he visited included nearby Kilkenny, Kildare and Wicklow, but he undertook a tour of Ulster clubs too, including an open-air meeting in County Down in August, which *Sinn Féin* alleged had an audience of 2,000. He was working hard to improve his Irish, though he must have annoyed some of his more bigoted Keating friends by going to the Connacht Gaeltacht for a week. In Scotland in the autumn, he spoke in Glasgow and Edinburgh, where a few weeks later his younger brother Daniel was elected president of the new Sinn Féin John Mitchel club.

His greatest success that year was the first Aonach na Nollag (Christmas Fair) in the Rotunda in Dublin, an event that Sinn Féin hoped would assist its self-sufficiency agenda by giving Irish manufacturers 'an assured Christmas market'. Mac Diarmada not only sold all the available space but booked the bands, choirs and pipers. 'The Christmas Aonach . . . was a great success,' wrote Clarke to a Clan friend,

---

* Named after Geoffrey Keating, a seventeenth-century Munster priest who wrote *Forus Feasa ar Éirinn*, a history of Ireland from the creation to the Norman invasion, and was popularly believed to have been murdered by Cromwellian soldiers. Dialect wars were a feature of the Gaelic League, with the speakers of Munster Irish the most venomous warriors. Followers of Connacht Irish, like Éamonn Ceannt and Patrick Pearse, were members of the Central Branch.

exceeding all our expectations, and can be taken as
evidence of the strength and spirit of the industrial revival.
But after all the one man that may be thanked for its being
such a success is young Seaghan* MacDermott (he was
Sinn Féin organiser in Leitrim in the late election contest
there). He it was who attended to the securing of exhibi-
tors and looked after the details generally. He surely bids
fair to make a name and a reputation for himself that any
Irishman might envy.[40]

Mac Diarmada revisited Scotland in 1909 and redoubled his efforts in
Ireland, making a particular effort to convert Munster: to the bicycle
and the trains had been added a 'ramshackle' motor car. Under the
influence of Clarke, he was learning to hate ever more fiercely and to
embrace violence, as he demonstrated publicly in March. Tom Kenny,
the IRB Centre for Galway, had been arrested and still was the main
suspect after the murder of an RIC man in a land-ownership dispute;
his blacksmith's business was being boycotted by the local IPP supporters. Mac Diarmada's attempt to mediate got nowhere because party
officials refused to speak to him. Defiantly, in a subsequent speech, he
accused the authorities of having 'kept in prison, knowing him to be
innocent, Thomas Kenny, one of the truest Irishmen of the present
day, and for what? For shooting a policeman of whom there were too
many moving about at the present time.'[41]

   Mac Diarmada was becoming his master's Fenian voice. In November
1909 a police report of his speech at the annual Manchester Martyrs'
rally in Macroom, County Cork, said he 'endeavoured to justify the use
of physical force in '67 and at the present time, if opportunity offered.
Any means were justifiable in trying to rend their hereditary enemy
from Ireland even to scatter the fires of hell in the face of that enemy.'[42]

   Yet though the infiltration was proceeding apace with the IRB's
active members, there was a severe shortage of recruits: the IPP and

---

* It seems to have taken quite a while for Mac Diarmada and his friends to
reach a definite consensus about how to spell his name. On his 1911 census
form, he called himself Seaghán MacDiarmada. Sometimes, in correspondence, Clarke referred to him as Shawn.

the Catholic Church were hostile, the authorities were ubiquitous and few people cared about such an abstract concept as Irish freedom. With only about 1,000 members, the IRB tended to be rather an old Fenians' club, passed on from father to son by those proud of coming from Fenian stock. All Mac Diarmada's cycling, driving, speechmaking, private persuasion and informal swearing in of likely talent in the four provinces of Ireland and beyond could not stop the decline of both Sinn Féin and the IRB, or the revival of the fortunes of the IPP. After four years in which the Conservative-dominated House of Lords had thwarted the will of the Liberal-dominated Commons, its unprecedented voting down of a (popular) budget forced a general election in January 1910 that delivered a Liberal majority of two. That of December – fought on the issue of Lords reform – was a dead heat. In exchange for support in removing the Lords' veto, the government promised the IPP Home Rule for Ireland. There was euphoria throughout most of nationalist Ireland, and a loss of interest in both republicanism and the doctrine of abstentionism.

In any case, Sinn Féin was already badly split, for the differences between Griffith (dual monarchy) and Hobson (complete separation) – exacerbated by the clashes between two strong personalities both of whom wanted their own way – had come to a head. Although Hobson had successfully blocked an attempt of Griffith's to do an electoral deal with dissident parliamentarians, he was fed up with pointless argument, and he and McCullough abandoned the Sinn Féin ship late in 1910 to concentrate on the IRB, which Tom Clarke was in the process of taking over.

Clarke's troops were the 'splendid set of young fellows – earnest, able and energetic, around Dublin, with whom it is a pleasure to work', he wrote to a Clan friend, 'fellows who believe in *doing* things, not in gabbing about them only. I'm in great heart with this young, thinking generation. They are men; they will give a good account of themselves.'[43] Their task was to take over the IRB Supreme Council. The writer, language enthusiast and revolutionary Piaras Béaslaí described how

> Tom Clarke's friends used to come to the shop in Parnell Street at night before closing time. There, they often used

to surprise Tom sitting on a chair in the same position as,
when a convict, he used to sit on a stool in his cell, trunk
erect, gazing into the distance, his eyelids hardly moving,
his hands resting on his knees.[44]

They joked, they talked politics and they plotted how they would take
control. Clarke already had one friend and two protégés on the
Council: Major John MacBride, the best man at Clarke's wedding,
represented Connacht, lived in Dublin, rarely went west and was a
heavy drinker of little organising ability; P.S. O'Hegarty, a live-wire
who worked as a post office clerk in London, had been elected
Southern England representative to the IRB in 1907 and was 'shocked
at having metaphorically stumbled into a cobweb-infested museum
whose aged curators' sole ambition was to prevent it being closed
down and boarded up'.[45] He had become devoted to Clarke: 'the lean
figure with worn frame but unconquerable soul that used to stand for
hours behind a shop counter, selling papers and tobacco to all and
sundry and exchanging jokes with his more intimate friends'. Rather
than being 'broken-spirited and inert', Clarke 'was as supple as steel
and as spontaneous in laughter as a boy'. 'Clear-headed, vital, and
neither warped nor embittered', he had 'an intense energy for national
work and a contempt for drones'.[46] Denis McCullough was co-opted in
1908 when it was impossible to ignore the young men running the
Ulster IRB: for Fred Allan, P.T. Daly and John O'Hanlon – the troika
who ran the Council – he was preferable to the dynamic, brilliant and
arrogant Hobson.

Although Tom Clarke was an obvious candidate for co-option, the
old guard were wary of him, but he patiently continued to cultivate
them and await his opportunity. It came when Daly reluctantly admitted in the spring of 1910 to having embezzled £300 of the annual £600
subsidy from the Clan just as the investigator sent from America by
John Devoy was due to meet the Council. Terrified that the Clan
would abandon them, they replaced P.T. Daly with Clarke, whose presence they knew was guaranteed to keep Devoy on board and whom
they thought a safe pair of hands.

To those except the few he allowed to know him well, Clarke used
his unassuming manner to conceal his ruthlessness. His first coup

was to persuade the duo to appoint Mac Diarmada national organ-iser; his second was to convince them to drop their opposition to the republican newspaper that his young friends passionately believed was vital for propaganda purposes, persuading the duo that it would be prudent to go ahead, since otherwise Hobson would probably fulfil his threat to launch a paper himself. He gave them a sense of false security by suggesting that Allan should be manager and Pat McCartan editor.

To provide cover for the paper and those running it, the IRB founded the Dublin Central Wolfe Tone Clubs Committee, nominally to direct the Wolfe Tone Clubs, which in turn had been founded

> to propagate the principles of the United Irishmen and the men of '98 who strove for the complete independence of Ireland; to encourage the union of Irishmen of all creeds and of all sections for the freedom of their country; to inculcate the spirit of self-sacrifice and self-reliance by which alone liberty can be obtained.

The editorial committee appointed was chaired by Clarke, Mac Diarmada was secretary and treasurer, and among the other members were Hobson, McCartan, Béaslaí and Seamus McGarry, a young IRB friend of Hobson's and McCullough's. Since the duo refused to have Hobson as editor, the committee affirmed that the editor of Irish Freedom would be McCartan and the business manager Mac Diarmada. Having by now sworn in or befriended the key IRB men in almost every Irish town, Mac Diarmada was in an excellent position to organise the distribution.

Since McCartan was now a busy surgeon, as it turned out and as Clarke well knew, it would be the duo's *bête noir* Hobson – with O'Hegarty's help – who in practice would do most of his job. *Irish Freedom* was launched in November 1910: Allan's editorial was run as an article and an article of Hobson's substituted instead.

'We stand', he wrote,

> not for an Irish Party, but for national tradition – the tradi-tion of Wolfe Tone and Robert Emmet, of John Mitchel

and John O'Leary.[*] Like them, we believe in and would work for the independence of Ireland – and we use the term with no reservation, stated or implied: we stand for the complete and total separation of Ireland from England and the establishment of an Irish Government, untrammelled and uncontrolled by any other government in the world. Like them, we stand for an Irish Republic.

All 'English legislation' was 'wrong and immoral' because it was English legislation and 'foreign interference in the affairs of this country'. Hence, the Irish should not vote in the following month's general election – a piece of advice the vast majority of the Irish people ignored.

The openly republican declarations worried the duo, but the backing of the Clan for Clarke and his young men stymied them. The balance of power in the Council began to tilt away from the old guard. MacBride resigned his Connaught seat, which was taken by Mac Diarmada, and the Treasurer resigned and was replaced by Clarke, which put him on the three-man executive along with Allan and O'Hanlon.

Then came a serious falling out over the visit to Ireland of King George V and Queen Mary scheduled for July 1911. Allan and O'Hanlon were concerned that the hot-headed young might make unwise public statements at the March Wolfe Tone Clubs' organised commemoration of Robert Emmet's birth. Clarke and McCartan had been organising opposition and *Irish Freedom* had announced that at the event there would be a debate on resolutions opposing the presentation of a loyal address by the Dublin Corporation. The executive then agreed that there would be no resolutions.

McCartan was an admirer of Patrick Pearse, the headmaster of St Enda's school, whom Clarke distrusted because he spoke well of the government and the IPP when they proposed or introduced measures he thought helpful to Irish culture or education. Yet Mac Diarmada had heard Pearse speak and he persuaded Clarke that he should be

* A leading Fenian who was convicted of treason-felony in 1865, spent five years in jail, and fifteen in exile in Paris and the USA.

asked to give the Emmet oration, saying that, if properly primed, he would say the right things.

So Pearse visited Clarke and was told what the right things were, and so eloquent was he that he fired up some of his IRB audience. McCartan was carried away by the line that Dublin 'will have to do some great act to atone for the shame of not producing a man to dash his head against a stone wall in an effort to rescue Robert Emmet'. Scribbling a resolution against the royal visit he showed it to Clarke, who said he could not comment, as he had been at the executive meeting where it had been decided to have no resolutions.

> The band was then leaving the platform and though I knew
> I was dashing my head against a stone wall of discipline I
> went over the footlights and proposed my resolution. To
> my surprise Tom jumped up beside me and seconded it
> and of course it was passed with enthusiasm.[47]

For once, Clarke had succumbed to impulse rather than calculation, and by failing to follow the agreed executive decision had shown his hand as well as committing the grave IRB sin of indiscipline, for which the normal penalty was expulsion. The duo avoided a showdown, deciding to wait for the next elections to get rid of undesirables. Fearful that he had put everything at risk, Clarke had to leave Dublin for a week's recuperation in June, writing to John Daly, 'For some time past I have had a bad tension in my nerves – all wound up like. I am eased very much after this rest – loafed and slept and eat all the time – that and nothing more.'[48]

Clarke's faction continued to play hardball, with *Irish Freedom* becoming ever more controversial and uncompromising, and Mac Diarmada working feverishly for an umbrella committee organising letters, rallies and support and making speeches 'to frustrate attempts to make Dublin Corporation grant an address to the King'.[49] He organised a day of protest on Coronation Day in June, with a banner erected across Grafton Street after midnight a few days before: strung between two poles draped in black and white, it bore streamers reading 'Do not miss the great Independence demonstration at Beresford Place, Thursday evening, 22 June' and

'Thou are not conquered yet, dear land', and was removed in the morning by the police.

The committee's efforts succeeded in killing off the corporation address and as well as their demonstration, they also achieved a modest black flag protest on the day of the royal visit in July, but for most purposes the city and much of the country was *en fête* on both occasions. On Supreme Council instructions, on the day of the visit, to avoid clashes, most of their members decamped for the day to visit Wolfe Tone's grave in Bodenstown, where both Hobson and MacBride made speeches. There was some drama at the Clarke's Parnell Street premises, though, where, in her husband's absence, that doughty Fenian Kathleen was looking after things. She recounted how large numbers of soldiers and sailors who had attended the reception for the King in Phoenix Park 'were met at the corner of O'Connell and Parnell Streets with a large poster outside our front door. On it, in large black type, was: "Damn your concessions, England, we want our country."' It was the *Irish Freedom* poster for that month, and it caused an angry crowd to collect and utter threats: a sailor

> took the poster off the hook it was hanging on and threw it into the shop. I walked out of the shop with the poster board and replaced it on its hook. Then I turned to the crowd and announced that I would have anyone who touched the board again arrested. The poster remained untouched after that, but the angry demonstration continued.[50]

McGarrity had been in Ireland for six weeks in the summer, tracked by special branch who spotted him visiting Clarke, John Daly, Hobson, MacBride and Mac Diarmada. Like other Clan visitors, he pointedly stayed away from the duo, who finally had their showdown with the Clarke faction at the turn of the year. It was an indiscretion of McCartan's that gave the duo their chance, as he had told his IRB circle that he was being censured when a man who had stolen IRB money had got away with it. Since the discreditable story of P.J. Daly was a secret known only to members of the Supreme Council, and since McCartan was close to Clarke, this gave the duo their chance.

At an emergency executive meeting, McCartan was sacked as editor, he and Hobson were suspended from the paper, and Clarke was given the choice of resigning from the Supreme Council or having an IRB trial. Allan – who had been on the Supreme Council since the year Hobson was born – threw the whippersnapper out of the paper's office, seized the edition of *Irish Freedom* that was going through the printers and published a safer version. McCartan then insisted on publishing the original version under the same title. Threatened with legal action by Allan and O'Hanlon, the new printer demanded surety of £100, which, nervously, Clarke agreed to lend McCartan from IRB funds.

With two competing *Irish Freedom*s, there could be no more post-poning a resolution of the split. In January 1912, at a Supreme Council meeting to which Hobson had been summoned by special invitation, Allan and O'Hanlon expected a quick win, but their opponents dragged proceedings out for more than six hours. Allan had the hammer-blow of learning that McGarrity had financed the McCartan *Irish Freedom*. There was, recalled O'Hegarty,

> some brilliant dialective [*sic*] by Hobson, some very clever leading questions by Clarke, and some very clever answers by MacDermott, the upshot of which was to confuse Allan and O'Hanlon, so that at the very end of the day they found themselves agreeing to whitewash everybody concerned, on the grounds that the whole business was a misunderstanding.[51]

The compromise was for Allan and McCartan to resign as manager and editor of the paper; they were replaced by Mac Diarmada and O'Hegarty. Outwitted and worn out by ruthless, clever men, the duo resigned a couple of months later from both the Council and the IRB, along with several other senior members. They were replaced by much younger men of whom Clarke approved. One of them was Diarmuid Lynch, another young admirer who had met Clarke in New York and picketed plays they thought anti-Irish and who had become one of Clarke's Praetorian Guard soon after he returned to Ireland. Mac Diarmada replaced MacBride as Connacht representative and Allan as secretary of the Supreme Council. With the old guard gone from the Supreme Council, the Clarke faction now had a majority of seats and the jobs that mattered: Hobson was co-opted in place of Allan and became Head Centre, leader of the Dublin IRB, and now Mac Diarmada became secretary; Clarke stayed as treasurer. It was typical of Clarke that he did not want to be president: the job was given to Seamus Deakin, chosen because he had no interest in it and did not attend executive meetings. Two officers made a quorum, so the IRB was ruled by Clarke and his right-hand man.

It was no wonder that they were, as O'Hegarty recalled, in an exult-ant mood. 'I shall never forget how happy and cheerful we were the day O'Hanlon and Allan resigned. Tom Clarke was like a boy. "By God" said he "now if we don't get something done, it'll be our own fault."'[52]

That Mac Diarmada was able to play his part in all these develop-ments was impressive, for in August he had been stricken with polio. At twenty-eight, he had virtually lost the use of his right leg, had a defective bladder and neuralgia. After four months in hospital and some weeks with Dublin friends, financed by a whip-around, he went to Limerick to convalesce. Madge Daly was shocked when she met him at the station: 'A few months before he was a joyous, buoyant lad, full of life and vigour. Then he looked a delicate, bearded, middle-aged man, only able to walk with a crutch and a stick.'[53] His friend Piaras Béaslaí saw him in the street some time later and failed to recognise him. But while his condition made travel more difficult for Mac Diarmada, it in no way diminished his appetite for plotting and intrigue.

Ill as he was, once he was on his feet, he was back to recruiting. One of the first things he did when released from hospital in December was to attend the Aonach that he had pioneered so successfully the previ-ous year. He had his eye on thirty-year-old Éamonn Ceannt, a pious and proper policeman's son, a local government clerk and an energetic campaigner for the Irish language and the principles of Sinn Féin. Ceannt had been on the committee opposing the loyal address and had helped Mac Diarmada with the banner protest.

Michael O'Rahilly, who had been co-secretary with Mac Diarmada of the umbrella group protesting against the royal visit, was also a colleague of Ceannt's in the Dublin Corporation and the Gaelic

League. He invited Ceannt outside 'to meet a Russian revolutionary', who turned out to be the now almost unrecognisable Mac Diarmada. Ceannt was discreet, but his wife subsequently guessed that this was the day he was sworn into the IRB, for he had written in his diary just a single entry: 'is iongantach an lá é seo, is iongantach an lá dom-sa frei-sin é [this is a wonderful day, it is a wonderful day for me too].'*54

* There is a difference of opinion between historians as to whether Ceannt was sworn in so early to the IRB: I'm with those who think the balance of probability is with this date.

Chapter Three

ÉAMONN CEANNT[1]

Because the paths to glory lead but to the grave.
The schoolboy Ned Kent as he reflected
on why he would not like to be a soldier

As I was writing this, I asked two well-informed Irish friends with a deep interest in history what they knew about Proclamation signatory Éamonn Ceannt. Both knew just two things about him: he was a Corkman after whom Cork's Kent railway station had been named.

'Wrong Kent,' I said. 'He was from Galway. And he had Galway station named after him. You're thinking of Thomas Kent."* There was a baffled shrugging of shoulders.

In life, as in death, Ceannt was the least memorable of the seven, for while reliable, competent Éamonn had passions so strong they set him and kept him on a path that led to revolution, he was an accountancy clerk who in his leisure pursuits took on the dull jobs. Tom Clarke was worshipped; Seán Mac Diarmada was loved; Ceannt was respected.

---

* Thomas Kent, born 1865, was a farmer from Castlelyons who was involved in land agitation, the Gaelic League and from January 1914 with some of his brothers in the Cork Brigade of Volunteers. During the Easter Rising of late April 1916 they hid for several days awaiting a general mobilisation and on returning home the night of 1 May were encircled by the police. In the ensuing gun battle, redolent of the American west – in which it was claimed their eighty-five-year-old mother enthusiastically participated – a policeman and Richard Kent were killed and David Kent seriously wounded. On 4 May, Thomas and William were tried under courts martial for 'wilful murder'; William was acquitted and Thomas was executed. At their mother's funeral in 1917 there was an enormous cortège. He was given a state funeral on 18 September 2015 as a part of the 1916 commemoration.

Two years older than Mac Diarmada, Ceannt was baptised Edward Thomas and known as Ned. The sixth of seven children, he was born in a police barracks in Ballymoe, a pleasant little village in County Galway, on 21 September 1881 to Constable James Kent and his wife Joanna Galwey, both Catholics from Cork.

During the 1880s, the RIC were reluctantly becoming politicised, for the Land League had exacerbated agrarian strife and police were being called in to deal with arson, the maiming of cattle and other kinds of violence and intimidation, and were required to enforce the law when tenants were evicted.

Ned was two when his father was promoted and transferred to County Louth. At five he was sent to the Christian Brothers' School in Drogheda, transferring to the De La Salle Brothers when the family moved to the Ardee countryside. Intensely shy and nervous when strangers were around, Ned loved the country, and with his brothers liked fishing and rambling over the bogs and the novelty of visiting circuses and the occasional slide show. He could mimic bird calls with great accuracy and was so keen on acquiring knowledge that his siblings nicknamed him 'Wiseacre'.[2]

The rural idyll ended when Ned was eleven and James Kent retired from the RIC and moved to Dublin, where he worked as a house agent. Ned went to another Christian Brothers' School near their home on the north side of the city. It was named after Daniel O'Connell, who had famously said that freedom was not worth a drop of blood. A conscientious, stoical and academically successful child, Ned won a steady stream of exhibitions awarded by the examining board as well as school prizes every year, with only a slight falling off when he was thirteen and his mother died suddenly of phlebitis. According to his brother Michael, Ned apparently took the news with 'silence and immobility'.

He was, as he would remain, a bit of a prig. 'The more we know, the more we wish to know,' he wrote in notes for a school project: 'we are never tired getting additional knowledge – after our school days are over'. He had initiative, though. Despite his shyness, he used to go with a friend down to the quays when a foreign boat came in in the hope of practising his French or German on foreign sailors.

The ethos of the school was nationalist: rugby, which he loved, was banned initially from the school grounds but then even outside the school, as extremists pushed the GAA towards banning 'foreign' games. Ned did not like being pushed around, so outside school for a time he continued to play rugby as well as hurling in the Phoenix Park.

Still, the effect of a nationalist school, which taught history as a continual heroic narrative of the struggle of a great Gaelic civilisation against English persecution and oppression, was already kicking in by the time he was fifteen. As his brother Bill was about to join the Royal Dublin Fusiliers, Ned wrote himself a list of reasons why he would not join the army, one of which was 'because I am Irish and no Irishman should serve in a foreign army'.

With predictably excellent results in his final examinations, he might have been expected to consider university: his father had his pension and a job and his elder brothers were working. It may have been that the family would not have wanted the expense, but it is more likely that Ned himself was determined to be self-supporting.

He left school and coached boys for civil service and university exams – two options he had ruled out for himself – while he decided on a career. By then, diligent and reliable Ned Kent was in a private emotional ferment, his nascent nationalism inflamed by the centenary commemoration of 1798 along with a burgeoning interest in Irish culture. He was not prepared to emulate his three elder brothers who had become a policeman, a soldier and a civil servant. In 1899, when his brother Bill was fighting for the British Empire in South Africa, Ned flew in the family garden a Boer flag he had persuaded his sister to make for him (until his father saw it and had it removed).

The civil service was ruled out because it was 'British'. He thought of becoming a journalist ('the pen is mightier than the sword' was another of his reasons not to join the army) and had an interview with the *Irish Independent*, but when told 'that he would be on duty by day and by night with little freedom, he changed his mind'. What he wanted was a steady job with regular hours that would leave him plenty of time to explore his expanding interests, so he took the competitive exam for the Dublin Corporation, which he considered legitimate because it was financed by Dubliners, and in 1900 became a clerk in the City Treasurer and Estates and Finance Office. His wife would recall that in his seventeen years of working there 'only once was he late, and that was a day on which he started from home on a bicycle and the storm blew him off it'. A corporation colleague said that 'a brain such as his, always crowded with ideas, novel and interesting, seemed to chafe at the humdrum of routine and sameness', but, in his methodical way, Ned Kent set out to lead a rewarding and culturally enriching private life. He had already shown curiosity about the Irish language: although he had chosen modern languages rather than 'Celtic' at school, at fifteen he had had a go at hibernising his name, writing 'Eamun Tomas Ceannt' in his school diary.

Then, in 1899, he had found *Simple Lessons in Irish* in a second-hand bookshop. This was written by Father Eugene O'Growney, who with Douglas Hyde, the son of a Protestant clergyman, and Eoin MacNeill, a historian from Antrim, had founded the Gaelic League six years earlier. Deliberately non-sectarian and non-political, its primary objective was to revive the declining fortunes of the Irish language, but it also encouraged music and dance, and it was growing fast.

In a paper to the National Literary Society in 1892 Hyde had sounded a call for cultural nationalism:

> I have no hesitation at all in saying that every Irish-feeling Irishman, who hates the reproach of West-Britonism should set himself to encourage the efforts which are being made to keep alive our once great national tongue. The losing of it is our greatest blow, and the sorest stroke that the rapid Anglicisation of Ireland has inflicted upon us.

To arrest the decay of the language would require the pressurising of politicians and the arousing of 'some spark of patriotic inspiration among the peasantry who still use the language, and put an end to the shameful state of feeling ... which makes young men and women blush and hang their heads when overheard speaking their own language'.

For bored and frustrated young people at the turn of a new century, the League offered both intellectual challenge and the extraordinary social freedom of an organisation where men and women could meet as equals and learn together. Yet, being full of civil servants, teachers, academics, intellectuals, priests and clerks, it was very proper. The acerbic Seán O'Casey would ridicule 'respectable, white-collared, trim-suited Gaelic Leaguers, snug in their selected branches, living rosily in Whitehall, Drumcondra, Rathgar, Donnybrook, and all the nicer habitations of the city', and indeed this was a very middle-class environment, full of keen, aspirational young people embracing a cultural revolution and, along the way, often falling in love with each other.

As Éamonn Ceannt, he joined its Central Dublin Branch in September 1899, where he met people like MacNeill and Patrick Pearse, with whom he would have a great deal to do at another time and in another arena. Although only two years Ceannt's senior, Pearse was so industrious and keen that he had already been co-opted onto the Coiste Gnótha (Executive Council).

Ceannt was in the same mould. After just over a year he was teaching Irish to newcomers; after two he had won the first prize at a feis (a traditional cultural festival) in an Irish essay competition for students of not more than three years' standing. He had discovered that his father was a native speaker of Irish, which, like so many people of his generation, he had hidden from his children because he wanted them to have the advantages of an education in English. Ceannt seems to have been successful in persuading his family to speak Irish at home: in the 1901 census all members of the family living there were recorded as speaking both languages.

He spent his holidays mostly in Irish-speaking parts of Connemara, swept romantically away, like so many middle-class young Leaguers, with the barefooted poor and expressing it in language reminiscent of rhapsodies about noble savages. In a paper he read some years later to a branch meeting, he described his first visit to Galway 'as a Gaelic Leaguer' and his delight in the village of Menlo in the 'chattering crowd of children – chiefly boys' who for a penny would 'tell a story or recite a poem with an accent and pronunciation that will fill you with delight as well as envy'. The women he met were 'fine, stout, rosy cheeked, weather beaten dames'. He described one young woman

> as she crossed a rock bearing in her hand a pail of water
> from the well. Her hair and eyes were black; a small dark
> shawl was thrown over her blue bodice. And a pair of bare
> feet projected from beneath the usual red petticoat, the

contrast being highlighted still more by a white apron partly tucked up round the waist ... It struck me at the time that many of our fine ladies could have learned a lesson in dress from that poor hard working, supple, active, graceful country woman.

Ceannt was also now on a branch sub-committee that arranged monthly musical and dramatic events that the League's newspaper said 'fought the music halls by showing that relaxation and sociability and enjoyment are possible in Dublin in a healthy natural atmosphere'. Like Ceannt, the League was very keen on temperance and clean living, of which he was a shining example. And unlike Clarke and Mac Diarmada, he also eschewed tobacco. He promoted dances and concerts, but tended to stay at home studying Irish rather than attend them.

Ceannt was a gift to committees, that rare member who likes administration and organisation, volunteers for work, deals with it efficiently, wears responsibility lightly and requires no thanks. He took on a lot, including being secretary and then president of a new branch near where he lived, and he also swam regularly and played hurling. But it was music that particularly attracted him, and his greatest enthusiasm was directed towards the Dublin Pipers' Club, founded in 1900 to promote both pipe music and Irish dancing. Coming from a musical family, Ceannt could already play the fiddle and the tin whistle, but his great passion was for the uilleann (or union) pipes. An old friend wrote emotionally decades after Ceannt's death about his memories of his playing: the pipes 'stir the blood with the strangest exhilarations, the subtlest intimations: I hear the voice of Ireland in the pipes; in the distance the thin, coiling cry of the pipes turns me cold with the sense of the far of sad romance of our country.'[3]

Ceannt practised assiduously, winning prizes at feiseanna (local festivals), and played devotedly throughout his adulthood, collected suitable ancient airs on his travels in Connemara and popularised the instrument with evangelical talks and articles (in Irish where possible). Helpful as ever, he produced a stylistically constipated pamphlet to address a problem: 'Gentlemen often expressing a desire to learn the Pipes have been prevented by not meeting with a proper Book of

Instructions, which has induced the author to write the following Treatise, which, it is presumed, with the favourite Collections of Tunes added thereto, will be acceptable to the Lovers of ancient and Pastoral Music.' He also bought a press on which to print a club journal.

Ceannt's shyness co-existed with considerable self-possession and an urge to show off in public: he was rather serious, commented one contemporary, but at times full of 'dash and fire'.[4] His brother Michael remembered that when they were out putting up concert posters 'Éamonn would lead the way playing Irish airs on his pipes.' When he became involved in 1902 in organising a 'Language Procession' on St Patrick's Day, it was his war pipes that signalled its start. Ceannt was one of the organisers who was shocked that Leaguers were working or drinking that day in pubs ('Do not drown the shamrock; wear it unstilled; wear it proudly' was the slogan), but the League's campaign to make it in future a dry day failed.[5] It became a huge annual event, though, hailed by Pearse: 'Dreamers of dreams, perhaps, were they who marched there, but stern purposeful men nevertheless – dreamers who have made their dreams into facts.'[6] Seán O'Casey was reliably more uncharitable: 'Here come the carriages holding the neatly-clad forms, trim beards, set faces, sober-hatted, silently-jubilant, respectomissima members of the Gaelic League's Central Executive.'

Thoroughly respectable (though privately a dreamer of dreams), in 1901, when he was only nineteen, big, handsome, reserved Éamonn Ceannt found a suitable girl on the Gaelic League's Central Branch annual outing to Galway. Twenty-year-old Frances O'Brennan, now known as Áine, whose father (who had died before she was born) had been a Fenian and whose mother claimed her grandfather was one of the United Irishmen, had joined the League after leaving school and going to work in an accountancy firm. She was attracted by this young man's 'wonderful whistling, sweet as a bird on a bush' and his sense of humour and he by her 'gentleness and sweetness'. It's hard to find evidence of Ceannt's humour, but occasional correspondence shows a playful streak with intimates, and his exhibitionist streak could startle people who knew the ordinary man, who seemed to be permanently arriving at meetings bearing with him a sheaf of neatly processed papers.

But at his first encounter with Áine, he showed his theatrical side: as the train crossed the Shannon, he called for 'three cheers' for the people of Connacht, and shouted greetings in Irish at people standing on station platforms.[7] Shortly after they returned to Dublin she joined the Pipers' Club, where she became treasurer.

Both lived at home and both were devout Catholics; their courtship was conducted slowly and with propriety. At the end of 1903 she accepted his proposal that she should be his 'little wife' and he her husband and protector: she would to him always be his 'little child,' his 'dearest pet'.[8] Áine would show herself in time to be formidable, but they were a conventional pair and at this period he certainly took a conventional view of the roles of men and women, having an argument with a female acquaintance about his disapproval of women in politics.[9] He set about making extra money, for convention required his capable fiancée to resign her job on marriage. Kathleen Clarke would not have been impressed.

Ceannt acquired a typewriter and offered an advertisement-writing service and also put a lot of time into a rather unsuccessful attempt to develop and market Kent's Blue, a whitener for laundry he hoped would both be lucrative and assist in Irish self-sufficiency. To the consternation of the Pipers' Club, he even gave up the secretaryship. Though Kent's Blue was ultimately a failure, no one could have faulted the extent of the research he did on manufacturing and marketing. As a home-owner he would similarly apply himself to finding the best methods of cultivating vegetables and raising hens.

Áine and Ceannt married in an Irish service in June 1905, a couple of months after one of his brothers died of the then prevalent tuberculosis. The ceremony was in Irish, and Ceannt used French francs rather than English currency to represent 'all his wealth'. The following month he complained because the registrar had added English versions of the Irish particulars. An old school friend wrote from London: 'Shy – bashful, retiring Ned, who used to blush when asked the boundaries of Europe – not merely engaged, mind you – but – married! Well, I'm blowed. I really am.' Áine almost died of septicaemia in childbirth the following year: Rónán would be their only child and, of course, Ceannt spoke to him almost exclusively in Irish.

He was unanimously selected in the autumn of 1906 by a committee that included Patrick Pearse for the evening job of registrar in the
new Leinster College of Irish, which trained teachers, but his implaca-
bility about what he considered matters of cultural principle held up
the opening. He was at the time engaged in a three-year battle with the
authorities over the registration in its Irish form of Rónán's name. Now
the Gas Company official with whom he was negotiating insisted on a
translation of his name, so, as the *Freeman's Journal* put it, 'Mr Ceannt
could not solve the problem by "translating" his proper name, and the
officials of the company informed him that the requisition would not
be accepted nor the gas supplied. Hence the present obscurity.' He
seems to have won the argument; the college was opened two weeks
late by Douglas Hyde and Archbishop William Walsh.

As registrar, Ceannt worked from seven to nine every weekday
evening, and twice a week taught for an hour afterwards, preparing
thoroughly and teaching well. He wrote notes reminding himself to
keep things lively, 'use gestures freely' and laugh with but never at his
pupils. He also found time to write a letter of complaint to Patrick
Pearse, who was editor of the League's Irish-language paper, *An
Claidheamh Soluis* (*The Sword of Light*).

At a time when there was magnificent poetry, prose and drama
emanating from Irish writers in English like George Moore, George
Russell (also known as AE) and W.B. Yeats, Pearse had offended
Ceannt by praising Yeats as 'the most powerful mind in the "present
literary movement"'. Pearse was desperately anxious to encourage
writers in Irish to break loose from their stultifying literary conventions and learn from contemporary writers in other languages, but that
annoyed the traditionalists who wanted to keep Irish culture unsullied
by foreign influences. Ceannt was predictably in that camp, having, he
explained, long believed that 'a straight line divided Gaelic literature,
past, present and future from all literary productions by Irishmen in
English'. The League was no place for talking up the literary efforts of
Irish people writing in English, however beautiful their English or
patriotic their aspirations and actions. Because their audience was so
restricted, Gaelic writers deserved special treatment. It was not that he
had no intellectual curiosity: it was that he had deliberately set rigid
boundaries.

Ceannt took umbrage also at criticism Pearse had made of amateur Irish actors ('it is only people who have an impediment in their delivery, or who are in a certain stage of intoxication, that speak in disjointed, staccato sentences, or rather segments of sentences, and even these do not, as a rule, bob up and down from their chairs as each segment is ejected'). He objected to Pearse taking 'the professional actors at the notorious "Abbey"' as his standard and recommending that Gaelic actors should learn from them. The League, said Ceannt, 'has not time to waste on Anglo Irish poets, dramatists, or literature. Their time has gone. Let the Gael have the field henceforth.'

Pearse took criticism well, though he responded toughly by saying that any Leaguer who confined himself to Irish '*does not* appreciate the full extent of the present day literary movement'. He had no effect on Ceannt, who was unshakable in his Gaelic tunnel vision, but relations remained civil.

A strange episode in Ceannt's life was his visit to Rome in September 1908 as the official piper of the Catholic Young Men's Society, which was part of a pilgrimage of its International Federation. Ceannt did not normally travel anywhere except in Connemara, for holidays were for improving his Irish. Still, he could not resist an opportunity to see the Pope. Since there was no English representation, the Irish were anxious to make a point of their presence and their individuality. Ceannt's first contribution was to decide to speak no English while he was abroad; he operated instead with a mélange of Irish, French and a little Italian. His second was to take with him a green and red costume made by his sister from what was thought to be an eleventh-century design.

As the ship to Liverpool pulled away from the quay, he played 'God Bless the Pope', and it is said that he played throughout the journey and was the 'life and soul' of the pilgrimage. When they reached Dieppe, Ceannt was delighted by the sight of a large cross on the quay, which he believed was a sign, 'showing to all and sundry that the country of France wasn't without religion'. This apparently provided some necessary reassurance to him that republicanism could co-exist with Roman Catholicism.

Although shocked by 'the fleshpots' of Paris, his Anglophobic evangelism never flagged. He reminded Irish speakers to leave their 'English' spectacles behind, to tell the world that Ireland had its own language, music and culture, and to emphasise to anyone they met that Ireland was not a part of England but a country in its own right.

On their arrival in Rome, in the rain, in his full regalia, Ceannt played the pipes at the front of the group all the way to the hotel, as he did a couple of days later as they marched to the Vatican to meet Pope Pius X. The Pope had been briefed that at this event he would be hearing an instrument 'that had not been heard in Rome for hundreds of years, some said not since the glory days of the earls of Ulster'.

The first part of the proceedings was for Seán T. O'Kelly, a Sinn Féin member of Dublin Corporation and a Gaelic Leaguer, and the rest of the Corporation delegation, to see the Pope for a private audience, where O'Kelly read out an official address in Irish to the Pope congratulating him on the fifth anniversary of his coronation.

Following that, the Pope walked towards his throne in the Grand Hall, greeting the two hundred and fifty or so people lined up on three sides and allowing them to kiss his hand. He then ascended his throne and read an address to the Irish people, after which the pilgrims sang him 'Song for the Pope', which had just finished when there was the skirl of 'O'Donnell Abú' on the pipes that Ceannt – in full costume – played into the hall. He

> marched into the 300-foot-long hall, walking its full length up to the steps of the throne and back down again. He did this three times until he came to a stop within a few paces of the throne. The Pope called him forward to examine the pipes and was startled when 'a most unearthly sound was emitted' by the bag and chanter. Having regained his composure, he asked Éamonn to play again, and Éamonn obliged with 'The Wearing of the Green'. The Pope then came down and patted him on the back before walking informally among the rest of the pilgrims.[10]

With photographs and many witnesses, the shy, retiring Éamonn Ceannt achieved considerable notoriety in Irish newspapers.

It had been inevitable that someone with Ceannt's views would gravitate to Sinn Féin. He had joined its Dublin Central Branch in

1907, been elected to the committee and by late 1907 he was on the National Council. This would involve him in two potential conflicts of interest. The first concerned the League, where Sinn Féin was intent on capitalising politically on the constant discord that was mainly fomented by bitter Munster factionalists in the Keating branch. As Tom Clarke's friend P.S. O'Hegarty wrote, the executive 'was composed of a number of strong-minded people divided into groups, who hated each other like poison, and would almost have assassinated each other if it would advantage the victory of the particular dialect of Irish in which they believed as the master dialect'.[11] Speakers of Connacht Irish were despised, and non-native speakers – those like Pearse and Ceannt who had learned the language for love of it – were beneath contempt.

The war extended beyond dialects to politics. Like Pearse, Ceannt did not believe that having different opinions should mean enmity: he could disagree with colleagues without venom and in his early years his clear priority was culture before politics. He took a stand on this when a young singer was booed from the stage at a League event because she was believed to have performed at a function at Dublin Castle. 'It was a brave, a very brave thing to face that hostility, and to risk his own reputation. He was as likely as not to be called "Castle hack" for his action.' He spoke from his seat with his arms folded, and the audience listened to him.

> His voice sounded aggressive and harsh, because he was trying to overcome his natural shyness, and it shook with intensity, as he told of the struggle of women like her, with a great gift cramped by poverty, to earn any kind of a living. And then, with a fine scorn, he pointed out that we all went to hear great artists of Irish blood and applauded them, without regard to their principles. Why not apply the same rule to all?

She was allowed to sing her song, 'and the audience went to the other extreme of applause, when the music was done'.

But politics would not go away. As Douglas Hyde wrote sadly many years later,

The Gaelic League, which was really a delightful body of
men and women so long as it was actuated by only one
desire, that of restoring the Irish language, began to lose its
charm when it became powerful. It was then worth captur-
ing and people, notoriously Griffith, set about to do so.[12]

Pearse put it bluntly in the *Claidheamh Soluis* in 1908 when he wrote of
growing enmities, ugly wounds and bad blood that had gradually
damaged the whole language movement like 'a foul disease'. The
'Wrecker Party', he wrote, 'seized every pretext to make virulent attacks
on the Coiste Gnótha', which had been accused of provincial bias,
corruption, misuse of funds, 'climbing backstairs to Government
patronage' and finally charged with 'trimming its sails in sympathy
with the wishes of a Castle Department'.

At this time, a bone of internal contention concerned the question
of paying fees to those teaching Irish during school hours. Pearse,
always more high-minded than everyone else, and wanting Irish integ-
ral to the system, opposed this, which caused predictable fury from
League teachers: it led his most vicious critics to call a special meeting
of the Árd-Fheis (League Congress) to attack the Coiste Gnótha in
general and Pearse in particular.

Responding to articles in Arthur Griffith's *Sinn Féin*, Pearse wrote
that it

is stated that there is an implied understanding, if not an
express agreement, that at the Árd-Fheis the Sinn Féiners
are to support the malcontents on the Fees Question . . .
that the whole party, embracing as it does many earnest
and able Gaelic Leaguers, is willing to wreck the language
movement at the bidding of a disaffected handful within
the movement itself, is, we hope and believe, untrue.

Ceannt went public on his affiliations at a League meeting in June. As
Pearse reported it, he 'avowed himself as a Sinn Féiner, both in the
broad sense in which the word was used by Gaelic Leaguers long
before the motto Sinn Féin was adopted by a political party, and also as
an official Sinn Féiner in the narrower [sense as] . . . a follower of the

political programme of the [Sinn Féin] National Council'. The news reached Ceannt's schoolfriend Peter Murray in London, who wrote to say he just about knew what a Sinn Féiner was and hoped 'that the shy bashful super-quiet Ned Kent of my schoolboy days . . . will never be called upon to wield a pike for what used to be called "The Ould Country"; and that he will wield any other more peaceful weapon for his native land gallantly and well'.

Perhaps significantly, having been nominated annually since 1902 by his branch as a candidate for the Coiste Gnótha – and having expressed himself in the *Claidheamh* as frustrated at the executive's failure to communicate properly with the membership – it was after Ceannt declared his Sinn Féin sympathies that in August he was finally elected. But he showed no clash of loyalties: for another while, the pen and the pipes were still Ceannt's weapons, and language and culture still his priorities.

The malcontents had failed at the special meeting, but increasingly the venom of the League's internecine warfare was driving away the talented and the idealistic, and the splits in the Catholic Church over language policy were an additional cause of distress to religious people like Ceannt and Pearse. There was another ferocious row in 1909 over the League's demand that Irish be a compulsory entrance subject for the new university colleges: many priests were in favour, while the bishops feared that such a requirement would favour Trinity College, which for sectarian reasons they wanted their flock to avoid. Under episcopal pressure, several priests resigned from the League, and the Maynooth Professor of Irish was fired for being too vociferously on the wrong side.

Although Ceannt's devotion to Catholicism would never diminish, this episode released in him an element of anti-clericalism that would be helpful to him later when he was sworn in to the IRB in direct disobedience to the Church's rules against oath-bound societies. In an article in 1912 he would extol Irish priests for their sacrifices for faith and fatherland, while savaging the bishops for standing shoulder to shoulder with the English. But although he would not allow them primacy in matters of politics, he reassured them that when it came to religion, the Irish would stay true to their teaching.[13]

The League eventually won this battle, but Ceannt was one of those who began to detach himself from the inveterate squabbling. Although he remained an active member of the League and wrote the occasional article for the *Claidheamh*, he did not stay long on the Coiste Gnótha, and by the end of 1909 had also stopped teaching at the Irish College.

The cultural subjects that kept him most interested were, inevitably, the pipes and now also children's education. Ceannt spoke publicly in support of the League view that the National Board of Education should insist on Irish being a compulsory subject for entrance to teacher training. He did not have an original mind: in a talk he gave at a League branch in County Kildare in December 1911, he regurgitated almost verbatim the conspiracy theories that Mac Diarmada had acquired in his schooldays from his updated version of the Abbé MacGeoghegan's *History of Ireland*. 'The schools were called National because they were anti National,' said Ceannt, 'and they were established with the one aim and object of wiping out every vestige of nationality in Ireland and substituting "happy English children" for happy Irish children.'

He drew on the educational thinking of Pearse in an article he wrote a few months later criticising the examination system, but there were heartfelt passages that suggested how frustrating he had found the system he had slogged through so successfully at school. In his school notebook when he was fifteen he had written that cramming for exams 'eleven hours a day, three days a week, and nine and a half hours the other three' should leave him in 'a pretty fair condition to spout our knowledge in seven weeks' time'. Now he wrote of the generation that had to work so hard before their youthful hearts 'if not utterly chilled as often they are, will again glow and expand under the cheerful rays of six weeks' summer sun'. He also betrayed his frustration with work, for the school system had been designed to 'make officials of the flower of Ireland's intellect' by providing 'our brainy young men with more or less well-paid soft jobs under the Government where their security of tenure enables them to shirk their responsibilities as citizens and renders them oblivious to the problems of the day'.

A man who never seemed to leave one committee without taking on two, on giving up his League responsibilities Ceannt's new emphases were on workers' rights and separatist politics. The first issue caused his second potential conflict of interest – the Dublin Municipal Officers' Association versus Sinn Féin politicians. The Association had been set up in 1901, the year after Ceannt joined the Dublin Corporation, for 'the purpose of recreation and mutual advancement';

he and his brother Michael, also a Corporation employee, joined. At the beginning of 1908 he had been elected vice-chairman, at a time of serious tension between employees and employers, the Lord Mayor and the members of the council. The issue was the decision by a majority of the councillors to postpone both annual salary increments and promotions: it was fought over for months. Sinn Féin members had additionally proposed changes to the promotion rules intended to encourage talent and had been accused of treating the lower ranks of officials like 'social parasites'.

Ceannt failed to persuade his colleagues to try to merge the association with two others, but they did agree to be more aggressive in negotiations. In 1910 he was unanimously elected chairman and, although he spent much of his year of office fruitlessly engaged in tedious and frustrating battles with the council, he had some successes in improving terms and conditions and made well-regarded speeches. One colleague recalled him as 'a staunch believer in the need for organisation in defence of one's rights' and with a 'genius for organisation'.

Released in 1911, he turned his attentions to opposing the impending royal visit, joining the United National Societies Committee that met at Sinn Féin headquarters and which was dominated by Seán Mac Diarmada, who though working covertly for the IRB was still the Sinn Féin organiser, and whom Ceannt knew slightly. The differences in their personalities and their family circumstances were rather strikingly exhibited on census night, Sunday 1 April 1911.

Éamonn (29 years) had meticulously filled out the form in Irish. He was living with Áine (30 years) and Rónán (4 years) at 4 Herberton Lane, New Kilmainham, Dublin. Áine's mother, Elizabeth O'Brennan (60 years), and her sister, Lily* (Eilís ní Bhraoináin, 32 years), lived with them.

* Lily was one of the few people Ceannt was playful with. On holiday with Áine in 1908, while she looked after their son, he wrote a postcard: 'To dearest Lily, of the long locks, defender of the orphan, waterer of the flowers, sender of Póga [kisses], seeker of a man, greetings!' He hoped Rónán was waking her up early and told her that she might like to know the 'fear an tighe [man of the house]' in which they were lodging was on the look-out for a girl with £200 a year.

All family members with the exception of Elizabeth O'Brennan, who was born in England, were recorded as speaking Irish and English.

That same night Mac Diarmada was filling in what became an untidy mess, partly due to Mac Diarmada's irregular entries but mainly due to the subsequent scrawlings of an official. Mac Diarmada called himself 'Seaghán Mac Diarmada', writing carefully in tight tiny old Irish script. He then seems to have decided to amuse himself with the census enumerator, giving his age in Roman numerals as 'XXVI' even though he was twenty-eight three months earlier in January 1911.

Beside this entry Mac Diarmada wrote

> '*Tá Móirín* co aois*' – meaning 'Maureen is the same age'. For religion he wrote '*Náisiúntacht na hÉireann*' – 'Irish nationalist'. He gave his occupation as clerk – *cléireach*. There then follow two bizarre entries. For his marital status he wrote, 'aonta acht ní fada a béidh' – 'single but not for long'. In the space for infirmities he wrote, '*croidhe craidhte eadh ón aontach*' – 'vexation of heart from the union'.

If he set out to baffle the census officials, he certainly succeeded. As with many census forms completed in Irish, civil servants pencilled in English versions. Against the religion of Mac Diarmada's fellow tenants who wrote '*Caitilioceach*', someone wrote at right angles 'All Catholics'. In Mac Diarmada's case, underneath his '*Náisiúntacht na nÉireann*', a confused official wrote 'Ch of Ireland'! Above his 'XXVI' the same person helpfully wrote '26' and drew arrows from '*Tá Móirín co aois*' to the 'XXVI'.[14]

The official gave up on the rest.

Although such frivolity was one of Mac Diarmada's attractive features, it played no part in the enterprises he took seriously: he was grateful for the competent if often mundane assistance Ceannt offered where he could. For instance, when it came to the banner Mac

---

* This was probably Josephine 'Min' Ryan, the woman with whom Mac Diarmada would be most closely linked, but at this stage she had been in London for a long time, he travelled around Ireland a great deal and he was very attractive.

Diarmada had strung across Grafton Street advertising a protest meeting on Coronation Day, there is reason to think Ceannt advised on how to get permission from the Corporation's paving committee to dig up the road to erect the poles. And with the Aonach he willingly took on such tedious jobs as organising newspaper advertising. Yet as he did his dull job and dutifully met all his family and other commitments, Éamonn Ceannt seemed more and more to be straining against his respectable bonds. Too extreme for the Gaelic League, in Sinn Féin, as he stood for the Executive Committee, he was in conflict with its president, Arthur Griffith, over workers' rights.

The dispute centred around James Larkin,* the founder of the Irish Transport and General Workers' Union (ITGWU), who had been invited to speak from the platform at the Gaelic League's September 1911 Language Procession. Having come to Dublin in 1907 with a mission to fight urban poverty, Larkin had begun to learn Irish and had sent his son James to St Enda's. A striking presence and a rousing speaker, not for nothing was he known as 'Big Jim Larkin', but he was anathema to many Leaguers. Douglas Hyde, the president, was annoyed to find himself speaking alongside two firebrands, Larkin and Pearse. He wrote about it years later, recalling Larkin as

> a tall blackhaired powerfully built man, with a great resounding voice and much fluency and energy, seeming to say a lot with great emphasis but really speaking

* Born in 1874 in Liverpool to Irish Catholics, Larkin worked part time from the age of seven, full time from eleven and from sixteen was a docker. A roamer, he reached America as a stowaway in 1893: deported and back working on the docks, and by now a socialist, he joined the Independent Labour Party and undertook charitable work in the slums. Initially suspicion of trade unions, he joined the National Union of Dock Labourers in 1901 under duress, in the 1905 strike made his reputation as a formidable leader and orator, lost his job as a foreman docker and became a union official. Sent in 1907 to Belfast, he became a militant and called a general strike that led to violence. Disgust with the settlement led to his move to Dublin, expulsion from the union over strikes and his foundation of the ITGWU, which in 1910 was admitted to the Irish Trade Union Congress (ITUC).

platitudes, the gist of his speech being that if Irishmen really wanted Irish taught to their children there was no power on earth that could stop them! Patrick Pearse, who spoke also, pronounced a great eulogy on Larkin, *he* at least he said was *doing something*, he was making history.[15]

Sinn Féin was no keener on Larkin than was the League establishment, Griffith seeing union militancy as a threat to native Irish industry. In August, in an article in *Sinn Féin*, with reference to foundry workers in Wexford being locked out for joining the ITGWU, he had referred to strikes and lockouts as 'weapons of destruction'. Ceannt wrote to disassociate himself from Griffiths' anti-Larkin tone and praise political agitation. Land reform, he said, had been achieved by agitators. As an aristocrat, Parnell would not have made the interests of the tenant-farmer class a priority without Michael Davitt's influence: 'Parnell's political sagacity was acquired in the hard school of practice, not in the easy chair of theory. Would it not be wise to take a leaf out of Parnell's book, if you will not take it out of Larkin's book, as gravely suggested by Padraig MacPiarais [Patrick Pearse] to the Gaelic Leaguers on Language Sunday.'

Sinn Féin should be helping to organise unskilled workers, 'the so-called lowest classes in the social scale'. What was more, it was no business of either the editor of *Sinn Féin* or employers to dictate to the men whether they should join 'a Social Union, a Political Union or a Trade Union', as 'the right of free speech, of public meeting, and of organising for a lawful purpose ought to be unquestioned and unquestionable'. The ITGWU was

an Irish union governed by Irishmen . . . Their methods may seem strange to those who are up in the clouds and give not half a thought to the cause of the labour volcanoes that are bursting forth all over the continent of Europe. But practical politics cannot afford to wait while these dreamers are awakened to their new, their startlingly new, surroundings. It is the business of Sinn Féin to use the grievances of the various classes in this country as a whip with which to lash the English tyrant out of Ireland.

On the following day he was elected to the party's Executive Committee.

With that kind of rhetoric, it was hardly surprising that Mac Diarmada should shortly afterwards, in December, have recruited Ceannt to the IRB. By March Ceannt was telling the Socialist Party that his own party was wrong to emulate other constitutional nationalists in abandoning Ireland's claim to nationhood and that, since no laws made by foreign powers were binding on conscience of the Irish people, agitation did not have to be confined to constitutional methods.

You knew were you were with Éamonn Ceannt, who had a straight-forward trajectory down the extremist path. Pearse, despite his incendiary success at the Emmet commemoration, was confusingly inclined to give even parliamentarians the benefit of the doubt and was therefore a figure of suspicion to separatists. Yet it was Pearse who gave Ceannt a new platform for his IRB views when in March 1912 he launched the short-lived *An Barr Buadh* [*The Trumpet of Victory*], a four-page weekly newspaper in Irish with the mission 'to preach the elementary political truth that the liberty of a people can only be guaranteed by its readiness and ability to vindicate it in arms'. Ceannt also became a part of Pearse's equally short-lived Cumann na Saoirse (The Society for Freedom), in which speakers could discuss politics and initiate political action in Irish.

Since contributors had to be both advanced nationalists and capable of writing in Irish, they were few, and Ceannt was in the forefront. For those in the know, this prominent Gaelic Leaguer and Sinn Féiner was pinning his new IRB colours to the political mast. His article in the first issue was a eulogy of the Fenians, whom he declared to have been a success, not a failure, for they had stirred the minds of Irish people and raised 'the old flag of Ireland, that was at that time hanging in the mud'. He specifically praised James Stephens and those who swore allegiance to the Brotherhood and often ended up in jail or exile and delivered a call to Irish youth to put their talents at the service of Ireland. Ceannt was nothing if not purist about whom he considered to be the Irish: in another article he spoke of the mission to awaken the 'true Irish' – by whom he meant Irish speakers – from their heavy sleep so they could show fellow Gaels that Ireland was worth fighting for.

The huge Home Rule rally in Sackville Street* on 31 March 1912 showed the gaps between some of those who would later be the closest of allies. Republicans boycotted it: like Clarke and Mac Diarmada, who wanted to destroy constitutional nationalism at all costs, most were distraught that the Liberal government had committed itself to Home Rule and were hoping desperately that it would be defeated by militant Ulster unionists. Ceannt – who was, of course, now an IRB agent within Sinn Féin – had been able to boycott it too, as that was Sinn Féin policy, but a fortnight later at a special party conference he was one of the delegates accepting the principles of the Bill while rejecting its provisions as a final settlement of Home Rule. He extolled this as proof that 'the old spirit of Freedom' was 'alive and bright among those Gaels' while regretting that there weren't twenty words of Irish to be heard.[16] It was, however, twenty words more than would be likely to be heard at IRB meetings.

Pearse, however, like John Redmond, the AOH's Joe Devlin and Eoin MacNeill, was on a public platform at the rally. Since he spoke in Irish, few would have understood, and he would have pleased almost no one since he welcomed the bill but promised 'the edge of the sword' and 'red war throughout Ireland' if the Gall[†] did not play fair. Displaying a pragmatism unfashionable in Irish republican circles, he said it would be foolish for a prisoner to refuse to have one manacle removed just because an oppressor was refusing to remove his second.

The splits in nationalist opinion were bitter. Despite now being on a stick and evidently crippled, Mac Diarmada was beaten up in Dublin that year by members of the AOH, who regarded him as a traitor and a threat to the parliamentary cause. Pearse's appearance on the platform increased the suspicion felt about him by IRB men, but, as ever, he was emitting contradictory signals.

At the first meeting of his Cumann na Saoirse, Pearse was the main speaker. Peadar Kearney, writer of 'The Bold Fenian Men', recorded the occasion.

> The keynote of his address was that a rifle should be made
> as familiar to the hands of an Irishman as a hurley. The

* Later renamed O'Connell Street.
† Meaning 'foreigner', it was used as a pejorative word for the English.

audience appearing to agree, it resolved itself into a question of ways and means. But it was plain to be seen that those present were growing uneasy as the evening advanced when it dawned on them that Pearse was determined to carry out his policy. The mere academic discussion of revolutionary methods and their practical application were two different things.[17]

Kearney was in the IRB, which at the time Pearse distrusted. Other members present included Éamonn Ceannt and Con Colbert, a drill adviser at St Enda's and close associate of Bulmer Hobson. Whether it was Ceannt reporting to Mac Diarmada or Colbert to Hobson, word of what Pearse was saying got back to Tom Clarke.

Chapter Four

PATRICK H. PEARSE[1]*

Pearse in his dashing moods struck you as quite insane, but as
one who knew he was and one with whom it was pleasanter to
go mad than with all the solid, sensible folk in the world.[2]

Desmond Ryan, 1934

I went to a Kilburn club in the 1980s to hear a performance by the
Wolfe Tones of what were mostly rebel songs like 'The Boys of the Old
IRA'. There were a couple of thousand there, seemingly mainly young
Londoners of Irish heritage, who were clapping and cheering and singing along with familiar words. Yet IRA bombs were a feature of London
life: only two years previously an explosion in Knightsbridge had killed
six and injured ninety-one. There were a few uniformed police outside
the hall turning blind eyes to the man selling IRA badges out of a
brown-paper bag.

Among the songs was the truly dreadful but admittedly catchy 'A
Tribute to Patrick Pearse', written in 1979 in honour of his centenary,
two years after an almighty public row in Ireland over my biography.
The chorus is:

> The poet and the Irish rebel
> A Gaelic scholar and a Visionary
> We gave to him no fitting tribute
> When Ireland's at peace only that can be
> When Ireland's a nation united and free.

* Pearse is often known as Pádraic Mac Piarais, but, despite his deep commitment to the Irish language, he chose to sign the Proclamation in the form by
which he was known to officialdom.

I had a drink afterwards with the Wolfe Tone who had composed the song and asked if he had read my book before he wrote it. He said he had read some of it and thought there had been no call for me to put in the negative bits.

It was unsurprising, though slightly dispiriting, to find a republican songster still so incurious about the real man behind the face and voice of the Easter Rising. But then, as Pearse pointed out himself, he was hard to understand, which is why after his death most republicans settled for some variation on Pearse the martyr and saint while a tiny number of doubters whispered behind their hands about his being bloodthirsty and possibly paedophile.

Was Pearse, as one of the schoolbooks said, probably the noblest man in Irish history? Or was he mad? Was he bad?

He was certainly dangerous to know.

He worried about it himself. 'Pearse, you are too dark in yourself,' he wrote in Irish in an obscure magazine in 1912.

> You don't make friends with Gaels. You avoid their company. When you come among them you bring a dark cloud with you which lies heavily on them . . . Is it your English blood that is the cause of that, I wonder? . . . I suppose there are two Pearses, the sombre and taciturn Pearse and the gay and sunny Pearse . . . I don't like that gloomy Pearse. He gives me the shivers. And the most curious part of the story is that no one knows which is the true Pearse.[3]

This tormented man, who had exceptional gifts and deep flaws, could provide enough material to keep a symposium of psychiatrists arguing for a week. Certainly, in recent decades, in books and essays, fascinated historians have been struggling to disentangle myth from reality in putting together the story of Patrick Pearse as he was, rather than how in his writings and speeches he so brilliantly simplified, romanticised and packaged himself for posterity. We have made enough progress for Pat Cook, an ex-curator of the Pearse Museum, to say hopefully, 'it is possible at least partially to deconstruct this mythic stereotype and discover a personality that was trying, by declaiming a patriotism simple in its certainties, to fly the nets of a troubled identity'.[4]

Born in Dublin in 1879, Patrick Henry Pearse* was, as he put it himself in 1912, the product of two 'very widely remote traditions – English and Puritan and mechanic on the one hand, Gaelic and Catholic and peasant on the other; freedom loving both, and neither without its strain of poetry and its experience of spiritual and other adventure'.[5] This was part of an autobiographical fragment written as politics were becoming a preoccupation and he was under attack from republicans for favouring compromise with parliamentarians. Seeking to reconcile two aspects of his identity, perhaps it was because the depth of his Irishness was again in question that – as Brian Crowley points out – 'he associates his Englishness with the negative aspects of his personality, his melancholia and emotional distance from others'.[6]

The unfinished autobiography was self-censored, written as it was in the full knowledge that, since his father was dead, for the sake of his mother, his siblings and posterity, it was his maternal influences he had to favour. It is therefore no surprise that he did not dwell on the intellectual disparity between his parents. James Pearse was a rational man of exceptionally wide interests and deep intellectual curiosity, who thought for himself: Margaret Brady, the attractive but uneducated twenty-year-old shop assistant who became his second wife, was a practical but highly emotional romantic who was an unquestioning transmitter first of her family's and later of her sons' Catholic and nationalist values.

James Pearse could be brusque, and culturally he would have stood out among loquacious Dubliners: negative adjectives applied to him in the 1940s by contemporaries of his sons included 'rough, dour, aggressive, choleric, dogged and impulsive', but, post-Rising, Anglophobic religiously conservative Ireland wanted their Pearse with unsullied Gaelic and Catholic credentials, so denigrating or airbrushing out his

* The birth of Patrick Pierce on 10 November was registered by his absent-minded maternal great aunt, who was also put in charge of organising his Catholic christening. Her mistakes were discovered when his school needed his birth certificate: his father had to swear a special declaration in 1891 to have him re-registered as Patrick Henry Pearse.

English heritage came naturally. Published extracts from Pearse's auto-biography in a book edited by his younger sister left out most of what he had written about his father.[7] In 1937, a few years after their mother Margaret Pearse's enormous state funeral, Patrick was given a meta-phorical virgin birth with the help of a hagiographical pamphlet called 'Pearse the Patriot was his Mother's Son'.

Yet 'It is much for a boy to start life with the conscious knowledge, "I am the son of a good father,"' Pearse wrote in 1909 in reflections about the pupils in his school, and there is no doubt that he was includ-ing himself. His own recollections are mostly very positive about this loving, generous family man who by Victorian standards was an atten-tive husband and father. When Margaret's father and sister died in the 1890s, her husband wrote poems for her.

Yes, he seemed often abstracted, but then the issues that preoccu-pied him would not have been ideal for conversation with Margaret or with children, and though he was rather taciturn at family meals, Patrick recalled, he would interrupt 'some reverie to say something kind to my mother or something funny to one of us'. Very occasionally he seemed 'a little sorrowful' but 'in order to please my mother he would rouse himself to exercise the wonderful social gift that he had, and then my mother's face would flush with pleasure, and we would laugh in pure happiness or join shyly in the conversation.' He kissed his children every night, had close friendships and cried when he heard of his father's death. Given to fisticuffs, sometimes to test the mettle of his own workmen, he abhorred violence towards children and once threatened to sack the father of one of Patrick's classmates because he had failed to fight a teacher who had hit his own son. On another occa-sion, when Patrick was struck by a Christian brother in punishment for something he had not done, he refused to hold out his hand for further punishment and ran down the street to his father. The Pearse boys were fortunate: few parents in either island would have objected to corporal punishment in schools at that time.

Born in 1839 into a poor London family that moved a few years later to Birmingham, James Pearse was sent to work very young first in a chain factory and then as a printer's devil, read voraciously in his spare time and took evening classes in drawing. A frame-maker's son who hoped to make an artistic career, he apprenticed himself to a sculptor, but economic reality intervened and he settled for being a stonemason whose craftsmanship would be widely admired. With the rise of the Catholic middle classes, church building was booming in Dublin, where, like many other Birmingham tradesmen, James settled in the 1860s. In 1867, the year of the abortive Fenian rebellion, he was dispatched by his Dublin employers to help carve twenty-six princesses for the Queen's robing room in the House of Lords.

All his life, James Pearse remained close to the Birmingham artistic circle in Dublin, and Birmingham friends and relatives visited from England. The substantial library of often expensive books he acquired included art, architecture, history, literature and religion, his interests so wide they included Islam, Judaism, the Franco-Prussian war, the ill-treatment of Native Americans in the US and Gibbon's *Decline and Fall of the Roman Empire*. Like many of his Birmingham family and friends, he espoused radicalism, and was an enthusiastic follower of the atheist free-thinker MP Charles Bradlaugh (whom he knew), an anti-imperialist whose causes included women's rights, universal suffrage, birth control and the rights of subject peoples, once saying that only his own father 'ever took the same hold upon my affections as Mr Bradlaugh'.[8]

James's father was free-thinking and his mother Unitarian; James had found Sunday school intellectually unsatisfying and had embraced atheism. But in Ireland in 1870, married to his first wife, a Protestant, having two children to support and making most of his living from commissions from Catholic churches for altars and statuary – mostly in the elaborate style of the Gothic revival – he went through the motions of conversion and had a letter from the relevant priest to flourish when rivals tried to have him boycotted for religious as well as racial reasons. *Labor omnia vincit* (Work conquers all) was his firm's motto: he would end up the proprietor of the most successful stonemason's business in Ireland.

In 1900, with his second wife and their twenty-year-old son Patrick, James visited Birmingham and collapsed from a brain haemorrhage in the house of his elder brother William. When a priest was requested, William asked the dying man, 'Are you a Catholic, Jim?' 'If it makes them happy, let them do it their way,' he replied. His Irish death notice would emphasise that he had died 'fortified by the rites of the Roman Catholic Faith'. Yet in 1884 he had discreetly loaned £50 to Bradlaugh's anti-religious Freethought Publishing Company, for whom he almost certainly wrote, as 'Humanitas', a series of pamphlets with titles like *The Follies of the Lord's Prayer* and *Is God the First Cause? Being also a reply to Father Burke's Theory of Science and Received Religion.* Instinctively anti-ideological, he also wrote *Socialism, A Curse.*

In his pamphlets, he reveals such extreme free-thinking views, says Brian Crowley, that he was 'living an almost Wildean double-life. In Ireland he was a pious purveyor of ecclesiastical statuary while, at the same time, in England, he was a free-thinking firebrand, scornful of all forms of religious belief.'[9] To add to this confusion was the high regard he won among politically-minded Catholic nationalists for publishing at his own expense in 1886 a lengthy denunciation of the Trinity moral philosopher Professor Thomas Maguire, who had infuriated him with an attack on Home Rulers as degraded oafs. Expressing his admiration for Charles Stewart Parnell and Michael Davitt, Pearse urged that the British government should respond to the democratically expressed will of the Irish people by introducing Home Rule, so that 'bitterness and strife may depart from the land in spite of all the professors and owls who hoot and screech from the walls of old Trinity'.

James Pearse does not seem to have embraced Bradlaugh's republicanism, for formal dinners at home ended with the singing of 'God Save the Queen'. His bookish son Patrick read children's classics like *The Swiss Family Robinson* and *Uncle Tom's Cabin* as well as British favourites such as *Alice in Wonderland* and *Treasure Island*. In his autobiography, Patrick wrote of the identification with martyrs that began when he was given a gigantic scrapbook, and would contribute to his terrible childhood nightmares:

> I began straight away to people our house with the crea-
> tures of that book, and to see myself going into the perils
> that were pictured there. This was my way with every book
> that was read to me, with every picture that I saw, with
> every story or song that I heard. I saw myself daring or
> suffering all the things that were dared or suffered in the
> book or story or song or picture: toiling across deserts in
> search of lost cities, cast into dungeons by wicked kings,
> starved and flogged by merciless masters, racked with Guy

Fawkes, roasted on a gridiron with St Laurence, deprived
of my sight with the good Kent.*

None of these martyrs was Irish, for in addition to the books at home the
children's books and magazines his father bought him were inevitably
mostly English. As he grew older, he borrowed English authors like Charles
Dickens from his father's shelves, and his lifelong favourites would include
Shakespeare, whom he read incessantly, Milton and Wordsworth.

An intensely imaginative child, Patrick starred in many epic adventures on Dobbin, the wooden rocking-horse his father had carved for
him. There were few companions, mainly his three siblings: dull,
conscientious Margaret (1878), devoted William James (1881) and
sickly Mary Brigid (1884). After an initial battle for supremacy with
his big sister, Patrick established dominance over all three and a couple
of younger cousins, and had them acting in the plays he wrote – with
occasional bits of Shakespeare thrown in – directed and starred in.

Not given to understatement, when fundraising for his Irish-
Ireland school in America in 1914 he represented this period of his life
by telling how the system of education 'that I was subjected to grap-
pled me insensibly and by degrees. The books that were put into my
hands ignored Ireland. They did not attack Ireland; they simply ignored
Ireland . . . I began to write composition about OUR empire, and
OUR fleet, and OUR army and OUR colonies.'

That was probably true of his early education, for until he was eleven
he was at a small private school, and his father was too discriminating
a reader to have given shelf-room to the kind of nationalist propaganda
posing as history that had so influenced Clarke, Mac Diarmada and
Ceannt when they were in their teens. In his attack on Maguire, James
Pearse cited *The Popular History of Ireland* by Thomas D'Arcy Magee,
but though as a young man Magee had been a Young Irelander and a
rebel, he became a Canadian politician who opposed the Fenians,
supported Canadian Confederation and was ultimately assassinated.

Yet at home there was some counter influence passed on orally from
the maternal side. Margaret's father Patrick Brady was a farmer turned

---

* It was Gloucester who was blinded in *King Lear*; Kent was Lear's faithful and
heroic protector.

coal factor; family folklore claimed he had supported the Young Irelanders in 1848 and the Fenians in 1867 and that *his* father had fought in 1798, as had a great uncle who had been hanged by the yeomanry. Pearse's mother Margaret sang her children some old ballads as lullabies, but it was Great Aunt Margaret who passed on nationalist lore by singing her favourite nephew bits of songs and telling snatches of stories: 'She loved all who had striven for Ireland from the shadowy heroes of old to those of her own blood and ours who had died in '98 or been imprisoned in '67.' Tone, Emmet, O'Donovan Rossa and Napoleon* were among the heroes Patrick remembered her mentioning.

At his court martial, Pearse would claim that 'as a child of ten I went down on my bare knees by my bedside one night and promised God that I should devote my life to an effort to free my country'. His brother Willie had a variation on it: 'as an infant he had knelt down at his bedside at Pat's command and they had both taken an oath to live for Ireland and die for Ireland when they grew up'. It is possible that this might have happened in one of his dramatic moments, but it did not fit the general persona of the young Patrick, the studious boy following the reading interests of his radical English father.

His family provided a willing audience when Patrick recited Shakespeare (Mark Antony's oration was a favourite) or gave lectures with the help of his father and the magic lantern he had bought him, but there were no friends there: his mother's social aspirations ensured that throughout their childhood the children were cut off from ordinary Irish influences. Although they lived over the shop in a working-class neighbourhood, they were not allowed to play with local children. So when in 1891 Patrick and Willie were sent to the nearby Christian Brothers' School, which had many poor children, they were set apart not just because they were socially awkward but because they were wearing tight velvet jackets and Eton collars and had accents that owed as much to Birmingham as Dublin. One contemporary thought Patrick 'an odd English rather than Irishman'.[10] A classmate judged him 'not the type to cut down Union Jacks. There were boys in the school

---

* Notices issued by perpetrators of agrarian outrages were often signed 'Napoleon'.

who had strong views on politics no doubt reproduced from what they had heard at home, but he was not one of them.'[11] To another, 'in early youth the two Pearses were very pro British.'[12] One contemporary remembered one of the Christian Brothers telling him 'to write of an Irish hero and this set him off. The subject was "Was Napoleon or Wellington the greater general?" P. spoke for Wellington and praised him qua Irishman.'[13]

Pearse would never learn anything much from his peers because he would never get close to them: he and they made each other uncomfortable. He had a stutter, 'a cold, clammy handshake & let one's hand drop', and was cripplingly shy, not least because of the cast in his left eye, which seemed like a squint and about which he was so self-conscious all his life. He looked at people sideways and always insisted on being photographed from the right.[14] 'No one knew Pearse. I sat beside him for 4 years in Westland Row but knew nothing of him. He was aloof.'[15]

Pearse's avoidance of athletics or games or any kind of horseplay further distanced him from his peers, as did his impeccable behaviour, his earnestness and his obvious lack of interest in his fellow students. According to a schoolfellow, he

> was gentle and quiet and always went home by the rere way from Westland Row thru the lane. The boys would go under the railway arch noisily but he seemed to like to be alone. He wore a big round collar, type now no longer seen. This riled the boys. I remember a rough boy once holding him up – they all mocked his collar – and began to bully him. I intervened. 'Let the chap alone,' said I. The tough lad turned on me and in the end I got a black eye. Pearse walking away quietly whilst I was being beaten.[16]

He would have slipped away from embarrassment, not cowardice. He stood up to bullies, quick to rush to Willie's aid if he was being mistreated by pupils or teachers, which, of course, made his brother ever more prone to idolise him. 'As a boy', wrote Pearse of Willie in his autobiography, 'he was my only playmate; as a man he has been my only intimate friend. We have done and suffered much together, and we have shared together a few deep joys.' Willie would follow his big brother's lead through life into death: 'He agreed to his every decision and seldom put forward an argument of his own,' recollected a theatrical friend.

> This submission could be rather irritating to the onlooker unfamiliar with the brothers. But Willie's deference was not born of lack of character. To those who knew them the most remarkable thing about these two was the similarity of their views on all subjects. This, with the admiration they lavished upon each other, made them almost unique. What P. H. thought, Willie believed; whom Willie liked P. H. admired.[17]

All this would often rattle outsiders, especially when in public they reverted to a baby dialect that even the loyal Desmond Ryan found 'weird in the extreme'.

Willie was academically undistinguished but artistically inclined and left school at fifteen to work with his father and attend the School of Art. Although he was hardworking and steady rather than brilliant, Patrick was a star pupil: like Éamonn Ceannt, two years younger and in a Christian Brothers' school on the other side of Dublin, he won exhibitions every year. He excelled particularly in Irish, at which he worked so hard that after only three years of study he won second place in Ireland. He also came under the influence of two nationalist Christian Brothers, one of whom he claimed reacted to a line in one composition about how 'our empire would weather the storm as she had weathered many storms before' by writing on it 'No marks' and telling Pearse to try to be Irish, something which had a profound effect on a sensitive boy who did not fit in.

He finished his exams in 1896 at sixteen, rejected the idea of a civil service job as 'soul destroying', but though awarded a scholarship to university was two years too young to matriculate. However, the Brothers hired him to teach Irish while he waited. He filled his time helping his father with administration and, inspired by a book about Irish literature he had won as a prize,[18] founded with Edward O'Neill, the boy to whom he was closest at school, the New Ireland Literary

Society ('high-class yet popular'), which for almost two years met weekly to discuss Irish literature and gave this shy but ambitious boy the chance to practise public speaking. He also joined and threw himself into activities of the Gaelic League and swiftly imbibed the argument that Ireland must be de-anglicised before it was too late, a position which for many, including the young Pearse, went hand-in-hand with opposing modernisation.

Dismissive of all contemporary literature as immoral and worthless, his obsession was to save the nation – and indeed perhaps the world – by preserving the Irish language and its literature. He read and published three precocious but derivative lectures on literature, folk-songs and the intellectual future of the Gael when he was eighteen, which blindly followed his maternal tradition. One intensely emotional paragraph would reverberate throughout his life:

> Closely connected with, and indeed, directly dependent on this love of the Gael for nature, is his capacity for worshipping his heroes. Hero-worship, no doubt, is often carried to extremes; we are prone too frequently to mistake the hero for the cause, to place the man before the principle. But there can be no doubt that hero-worship, in its highest form, is a soul-lifting and ennobling thing. What would the world be without its heroes?

By the time Pearse was twenty-one, he was running a business, had two degrees and was a hardworking rising star in the Gaelic League. His father had died in September 1900 and since Willie was still at art school he and Patrick ran James Pearse & Sons together for the financial benefit of the immediate family, a half-sister and her son and a cousin. He was, said a friend, surrounded by 'a monstrous regiment'.

In 1901 he had taken a second-class BA in English, Irish and French from the Royal University (with a special prize for excellence in Irish) and had been called to the bar as a barrister. He had avoided as far as possible entering into student life. The Royal University was merely an examining body and he chose its option for the first two years of private study rather than lectures in an institution like University College Dublin (UCD), which he had to attend in his third year. There he managed to become friends with Tom Kettle, later a nationalist MP, but he hastened away after the Trinity lectures he had to attend for his law studies, and keeping terms at the Kings Inns and eating dinners there were clearly torture for him. One contemporary remembered 'a big, shy boy who neither drank nor smoked, nor joined in our adventures or took part in our debates. If one of the wits, who never failed in that company, let fall a jest too risqué over the coffee and the wine, Pearse would hurry away blushing.'[19] He already hated the law and lawyers, and would take only two cases, both unsuccessful. He also hated alcohol: his father's enjoyment of an occasional binge with friends had been disapproved of at home.

In the Gaelic League, he was on the committee of the Central branch, where 'quiet, reticent and anxious to avoid the limelight,'[20] Éamonn Ceannt was a member. Pearse was the most assiduous attender at the Coiste Gnótha, sat on sub-committees for education and finance, and as unpaid secretary to the Publications Committee from 1900 over three years of prodigious work he turned the League into a successful publishing company that printed classic Irish texts and commissioned new work. This intensely ambitious young man was now corresponding with the most senior people in the movement, including Archbishop William Walsh. He was also making a name for himself as a speaker, acting at feiseanna as the League's adjudicator for Recitation, Dialogue and Oratory, lecturing or debating at any branch or acceptable organisation (like the temperance movement) that invited him or suggesting himself as a speaker in areas where he went on the firm's business. He even addressed after-Mass crowds in Irish-speaking areas.

He had no natural talent as a speaker ('The lecturer is quite a young man with a peculiar, jerky, pistol-shot-like delivery that becomes trying to listen to after a time' said one sufferer), and his voice was not strong, but like a craftsman he learned through hard work, practice and studying the techniques of his oratorical betters. He would never master impromptu speeches and everything was prepared, written and – if necessary – memorised in advance, and emphases, cadences and pauses were planned. But this labour paid off and, along with his fervour and his strength of personality, created within a decade a performer that even the sceptical Tom Clarke would regard as an asset worth taking a risk to acquire.

He had to work hard too to become an effective teacher. When he first taught adults – in 1899 in UCD – his awkwardness was very evident; James Joyce dismissed him as a bore and dropped out of his class because he was so irritated by Pearse's denigration of English the better to eulogise Irish. His idealisation of native Irish speakers reached quasi-religious heights:

> What wonderful faces one sees in Irish-speaking crowds! Truly the lives of those whose faces are so reverend and reposeful must be beautiful and spiritual beyond your and my ken . . . I often fancy that if some of the old Masters had known rural Ireland, we should not have so many gross and merely earthly conceptions of the Madonna as we have.

Pearse was, though, learning the hard way that there were among educated Irish speakers many quarrelsome, bigoted and downright unpleasant people. Like Ceannt, he had acquired fluent Irish by long hours of study and frequent visits to the west of Ireland, yet he was derided by native speakers, especially those from Munster. Father Dineen, his chief tormentor, brought malice to an art form: he satirised Pearse's tendency to flourish his graduate credentials in signing himself as P.H. Pearse B.A., B.L. by nicknaming him 'Babble' and sniggered publicly about unwitting double entendres in his writing. Pearse's natural reserve and desperate shyness – especially with women – brought accusations of pride. Brought up to be respectably turned out and always careful with his appearance, because in early days at League formal functions he thought a frock coat, top hat and bow tie appropriately respectful, he was derided for snobbery and vanity. Throughout his adult life he would dress in black, his hair 'always sleeked down, never out of place . . . his tie always at the right angle'.[21]

Before he was twenty, he was the target of vicious criticism in a bitter argument about the Pan-Celts. More outward-looking Leaguers like Douglas Hyde and Eoin MacNeill approved of joint festivals of Irish, Scots, Welsh, Manx, Cornish and Bretons, but met with bitter opposition from those who associated Pan-Celts – who included many Protestants and were headed by Lord Castletown – with the aristocracy and the Dublin Castle circle. Pearse was dispatched to the Welsh

Eisteddfod and the Scots Highland Mod to give addresses on behalf of the League but acquired enemies at home when it emerged that he had drunk a toast to the Queen and hobnobbed with Castletown. The political passions erupting in Ireland over the 1798 centenary, the Boar War and Queen Victoria's 1900 visit had largely passed him by: he saw the Pan-Celtic events as opportunities to gain more experience to help him pursue his language evangelism ever more successfully.

He was upset by the venom, but he was toughened up by it and learned to view the unreasonable Munster critics as 'moral thugs'.[22] He extricated himself from the battleground and concentrated on adding to his reputation for talent and industry by bombarding *An Claidheamh Soluis* with reports and articles and, when it became clear that the editor was to be sacked, canvassing for his (paid) job far and wide and with a detailed prospectus.

Even though he was only twenty-three when he became editor, Pearse already had a deserved reputation for being egotistically convinced of his own rightness, listening politely to his opponents but sticking to his opinion, ploughing ahead and getting what he wanted – which, considering his naivety about people and politics and his social inadequacy, would cause him many problems then and in the future. When things went wrong it was always rather a shock to him and came of people having failed to live up to his expectations. Obsessive in his commitments to his series of causes, he never understood that few were as single-minded as he was. A friend recorded him almost weeping with frustration at the news that Eoin MacNeill was getting married and might therefore have less time for the League.

As editor, what happened was predictable. He ignored those urging caution, made extravagant improvements to the newspaper, worked on it devotedly for six years and had to be saved from financial catastrophe by wiser heads. He had honed his natural facility for writing through years of practice and the subjects on which he contributed innumerable articles included history, literature, theatre, education, politics and religion. Nothing, he told his audience over and over again, mattered as much as the preservation and spread of the Irish language, which would 'carry all kindred movements with it. Irish music, Irish art, Irish dancing, Irish games and customs, Irish industries, Irish politics – all these are worthy objects. Not one of them, however, can be said to be fundamental.'

Pearse had no difficulty in following the non-political line of the League. Stirred by the publication in 1904 of Griffith's *The Resurrection of Hungary*, which he thought of great importance, he explained that it described how the Hungarian language revival of 1825 had laid the foundation of the Hungarian nation of 1904. 'And so it shall fall out in Ireland.' Even though there was no bar on Leaguers joining whatever they liked, he had no inclination to join any political organisations.

He had a courteous exchange in 1905 in the *Claidheamh* with his UCD friend Tom Kettle, a supporter of parliamentary Home Rulers, who had written a well-argued letter to say that the political movement was indispensable since 'the Ireland of the future must be free as well as Irish'. He was sure, answered Pearse, that Kettle would come to realise that 'the language movement' was 'on a different and altogether higher plane' from the political movement: political autonomy was not in itself 'an essential of nationality'.

That viewpoint landed Pearse in many arguments, quite a few with the Catholic clerical establishment, with which he tangled several times when he was finding the bishops and individual priests wanting on support for the language. Although his commitment to Catholicism never wavered, he was without sectarianism, and was his father's son when it came to taking an independent view of the conduct of the clergy.

He had attracted a great deal of criticism and abuse because he was prepared to give praise to Chief Secretary Bryce, a Liberal who had supported the Irish language; on being attacked for this by Griffith's *Sinn Féin*, he reiterated that 'Gaels will retain kindly memories of the official who, in spite of all the forces against him . . . has done these things'. He had also proved himself even more open-minded than Irish parliamentarians when he supported the Irish Council Bill of 1907 because it gave educational home rule. Among his most choleric critics was Tom Clarke's friend Piaras Béaslaí, of the Keating branch, who raged to Eoin MacNeill in 1908 about Pearse's readiness to defend what he thought were enlightened government reforms and his habit of taking up positions in the *Claidheamh* without consulting the Coiste Gnótha.

Pearse might have been an obsessive, but he had, as Kettle put it, 'a largeness of view' that was a combination of a generous spirit, a curious mind and wide reading. The youthful ignorance and bigotry that had had him sneering at Yeats in 1899 as 'a mere English poet of the third or fourth rank' and talking of the need to 'crush' the '"Irish" Literary Theatre' had given way to profound admiration for the talent and commitment of Yeats and his circle: indeed, Yeats became a poet he read and re-read. His *Claidheamh* argument with Ceannt showed Pearse had wider horizons than those imposed by Ceannt's intellectual tramlines. By now he was committed to the idea that Irish literature – including drama – must take account of international developments and modernise. He had called unsuccessfully on the Gaels to get writing and had turned his hand with mixed success to writing fiction and poetry.

What he still had no time for was politics. In 1908, a year after Ceannt had joined Sinn Féin's National Council and Mac Diarmada was busy subverting the League, the GAA, Sinn Féin and any other organisation he and his IRB recruits could infiltrate, Pearse was fuming about the failure of Seán T. O'Kelly to do his job for the *Claidheamh*. 'What the Manager is doing I don't know,' he wrote furiously to Eoin MacNeill.

> He is hardly ever at the office . . . What occupies him or where he is all day I can't say. He may be at Corporation meetings. He may be doing Sinn Féin work. He may be doing Coiste Ceanntair [Dublin Gaelic League] work. He may be doing St Vincent de Paul work. But I am perfectly sure he is not doing the work he is paid for – managing 'An Claidheamh Soluis' . . . The present situation is intolerable and is getting on my nerves.

He left out the IRB, of which O'Kelly had been a member since 1901, but then he believed it moribund and Tom Clarke had only just returned to Dublin.

In any case, by then Pearse's and therefore the *Claidheamh*'s emphasis had shifted to education. Like many of those who had gone through it, he reviled the Intermediate system for its intellectual limitations, its relentless emphasis on rote learning and its brutality. He had studied Continental educational thinking, he had seen bilingualism in operation in Wales and had visited Belgium for a month to study it in depth, he corresponded with radical educational reformers abroad, and by now he was an experienced teacher at both Intermediate and university level and was impatient to put his ideas into practice.

Education, he wrote in 1904, 'is not the imparting of knowledge but the training of the child to be a perfect man or woman . . . The real education consists in the forming of the child's character, the drawing out of his faculties.' Like all good propagandists, Pearse believed in repeating the message: he wrote about fifty articles based on his Belgian visit. 'In season and out of season', wrote P.S. O'Hegarty, 'he urged bilingualism, and in season and out of season he brooded on the question of Irish education, seeing in that, as so many have done, the spear-point of English influence in Ireland.'

Disillusioned at the League's splits and limitations, Pearse had become convinced that it was only through education that de-anglicisation could be achieved through 'the creation in the schools of an Irish atmosphere, the Irishising of the hearts and minds of the children, setting before them of a great and glowing ideal of *Duty*'. Having despairingly concluded that the teachers of Ireland would not rise to the challenge, he had to take on the mission himself.

Reforms of 1907 had removed all restrictions on bilingual teaching and allowed him free rein in developing ideas for his ideal school, informed by his Dublin teaching experiences and even more by children in the west of Ireland with whom he spent as much time as he possibly could. He idealised them, of course, but had become more realistic, worrying that they had 'a certain lack of veneration for the truth' and had a primitive cruelty about the weak and about animals. Still, the Irish-speaking child 'is the fairest thing that springs up from the soil of Ireland . . . purer than any monk or nun, wiser than any seer' and needed a teacher who would be a wise and tolerant friend rather than a 'man of terror', a person of 'fine character and high ideals' and 'warmly Irish in sympathy'. 'The teacher whose every act does not show that to him untruth and injustice, unkindness and meanness are things unholy and abhorrent', he told *Claidheamh* readers in 1908, 'will preach and teach in vain.'

Children needed to be 'constantly reminded of and made to realise the fact that they are a separate race from England, that it is a disgrace and a badge of slavery for a race to use the language of any other in preference to its own'. They should hear stories of the stirring deeds of heroes and learn to recite ballads and heroic poetry and legends about them. The more Pearse dwelt on that theme, the more emotional he became, and although he still had no truck with violent separatism the Irish-speaking version of the prospectus for his school included an aspiration to inculcate in pupils 'the desire to spend their lives working hard and zealously for their fatherland and, if it should ever be necessary, to die for it'. (Such sentiments were common in the English magazine *Little Folks* read by him and his siblings in the 1890s.)

In bringing his school into being, he had the help of the teacher and poet Thomas MacDonagh, thirty to Pearse's twenty-eight when it opened, whose extroversion had conquered Pearse's reserve when they met on visits to the Aran Islands. Together they had chosen Aran's patron saint* as the name for the school: Sgoil Éanna, St Enda's, the 'educational adventure' for the nationalist boys he hoped would labour as selflessly for Ireland as he had always done, opened in September 1908 in Cullenswood House. It was 'one of the noble old Georgian mansions of Dublin', wrote Pearse, with 'memories of its own' that included a wood that had often sheltered Irish rebels and was also redolent of the contribution to Irish scholarship of the famous historian William Edward Hartpole Lecky, whose family owned the house in the nineteenth century.[†23]

Among the obstacles Pearse had successfully overcome were his lack of money and the entrenched opposition of the Catholic hierarchy to lay schools. The school was financed by a combination of the Pearse family's now slender resources (for despite Willie's best efforts,

* A fifth-century mid-Ulster king, converted to monasticism by his nun sister, who died as an abbot in Aran.
† Such was the fame of Lecky (1838–1903) as an historian of Europe and England as well as Ireland that he was made a Privy Councillor and awarded the Order of Merit. Pearse would have appreciated his sympathetic writing about the sufferings of Irish Catholics and seemed ready to overlook the opposition to Home Rule, which caused him in 1895 to become a unionist MP for Trinity College Dublin.

there was a depression in the building trade and Pearse & Sons was failing), government pupil subsidy, school fees and the contributions of rich well-wishers.

Fresh, stimulating and full of cultural references, the striking decorations in St Enda's included patriotic friezes by Willie and by Bulmer Hobson's friends the Morrow brothers, who contributed a fresco showing Irish mythological hero Cúchulainn taking arms, framed by his famous declaration 'I care not though I were to live but one day and one night provided my fame and my deeds live after me.' Pearse was far too reckless to worry about unforeseen consequences, but one of the artists did: 'I had painted an allegorical picture of a seated, hooded figure of Cathleen ni Houlihan,' wrote Beatrice Elvery later,

> with a child on her knee, presumably Young Ireland, stretching out his arm to the future, and behind her a ghostly crowd of martyrs, patriots, saints and scholars. Maud Gonne bought this picture and presented it to St Enda's College . . . Some time later I met one of the boys from the school and he told me that this picture had inspired him 'to die for Ireland!' I was shocked at the thought that my rather banal and sentimental picture might, like Helen's face, launch ships and burn towers.

In the early years of St Enda's, it was Cúchulainn who dominated Pearse's pantheon of heroes. Mythologised in the Ulster cycle of early and medieval Irish heroic literature, Cúchulainn is the champion of the Red Branch warriors and the central character of the 'Táin Bó Cuailnge' ['Cattle Raid of Cooley']. He occupies a strange place these days in Irish tribal politics, an all-purpose mythological hero garishly painted on gable ends in Belfast in both republican and loyalist strongholds: Pearse's favourite warrior-hero, a semi-divine image of fearless self-sacrifice, doubles as the 'Hound of Ulster' who at seventeen single-handedly and to the death repelled those from the south trying to force their way into Ulster to steal a bull. But even in Pearse's time Cúchulainn sent out conflicting messages.

As a youth Pearse had been fascinated by the Irish sagas, which around the time of his birth had been popularised and sanitised in the two volumes of *The History of Ireland* by the politically mercurial pantheist Standish James O'Grady.* The books had such a powerful effect that Yeats called O'Grady the 'father of the Irish literary revival': they spawned many versions of the sagas for adults and children, in poetry, prose and dramatic form. Cúchulainn appeared in some of Yeats' poems and plays from 1892 onwards and his picture was on a wall in the Abbey Theatre that Yeats co-founded in 1904. In 1898, the year in which many impressionable young people were being politically radicalised by tales of the United Irishmen, the eighteen-year-old Pearse was telling the New Ireland Literary Society 'that the noble personality of a Cúchulainn forms a true type of Gaelic nationality, full as it is of youthful life and vigour and hope'.

A decade on, Pearse had his school and wanted his pupils to be a mixture of Cúchulainn and the young Jesus, a 'conflation of pagan and Christian Celticism' that produced an image of a Christian warrior. The name he gave them was *macaomh*, which in bardic literature meant a young warrior scholar and was given to Cúchulainn, but Pearse had applied it also in 1906 to Íosagán [little Jesus] in a story (derived from Wilde's 'The Selfish Giant') about an old man who had lost his faith but whose soul was saved through friendship with a Christ-like child who would get a priest to his deathbed. The boys would be taught how to be masculine in an Irish way, fighting for truth, purity, Christianity and an Irish Ireland.

Among the seventy children in the preparatory and secondary schools were many relatives of various prominent Leaguers including three sons and a nephew of Eoin MacNeill, a son of the Protestant Redmondite MP and language enthusiast Stephen Gwynn, and

---

* Like all sagas, the Ulster cycle had plenty of sex and violence. Unexpurgated, Cúchulainn's exploits included exhibiting a battle-frenzy that turned him into a hideous, unshapen monster in which he failed to distinguish between friend and foe, killing his foster brother and best friend after three days of combat by sticking a magic barbed spear up his anus, and unwittingly killing his own eight-year-old son, who had been born when Cúchulainn was ten.

Desmond Ryan, whose anti-clerical father W.P.* was the editor of *The Peasant*, the weekly newspaper where Hobson was sub-editor. Ryan recalled his first day at school, being addressed by that 'grave, tenacious idealist in his black gown' who addressed them

> in English and Irish, swaying slightly from side to side . . .
> He strikes us as a very good and enthusiastic man, not quite a Sunday school teacher, as some irreverent wight whispers. In Irish lettering the names of Ireland's heroes, saints and sages, run around the wainscoting of the walls. Some hear Irish for the first time. We shall all hear it in future until it has grown as familiar to us as English.
> He urges us to work hard.
> He persuades us we shall work hard. He begins to tell us the Cúchulainn saga which he subsequently continues every day after religious instruction, until the 'dark, sad boy, comeliest of the boys of Eire' has become an important if invisible member of the staff.

Pearse's deputy, the poet Thomas MacDonagh, took over then, assuring

> the diffident audience of mingled sizes and ages that knowledge was a wondrous power. He assumed with great confidence we should master the tongue of Keating and O'Growney in three months. During a few hours he had strayed into innumerable bye-paths of knowledge where

* Tipperary-born London literary journalist W.P. Ryan returned to Ireland in 1905 to edit the *Irish Peasant*. The controversies he caused included his condemnation of clerical opposition to mixed Gaelic League classes and Irish party MPs' support for Catholic education in England; he also encouraged lay participation in running Irish national schools. When ecclesiastical pressure closed the paper in 1906, Ryan merged with Hobson's *Republic*; in 1909 it was renamed the *Irish Nation and the Peasant*, edited by Ryan with major contributions from Hobson. By 1910, Ryan had abandoned Catholicism and embraced pro-labour nationalism: his son Desmond would become Pearse's secretary and a republican socialist who died a Catholic.

Cúchulainn elbowed Dante and Catullus walked down
arm-in-arm with Canon O'Leary* and Edmund Waller. . .[†24]

Money was short. Faithful follower Willie Pearse taught Art and
English and, after the family business was sold in 1910, acted as his
brother's full-time assistant; various other Pearse relatives helped out
where they could. Members of the interesting and accomplished staff
sometimes left when they were unpaid, but there were famous visiting
lecturers like Douglas Hyde and Yeats and, overall, Pearse's clarity of
vision and sense of purpose prevailed to make happen what seemed
impossible. The school buzzed with excitement, enthusiasm, hope and
achievement.

Pearse had become a creditable Irish scholar of Gaelic literature, but
he was fascinated too by Germanic culture and particularly by Wagner's
use of Celtic and Norse mythology to link 'masculinity, national identity and cultural regeneration'. As Wagner used opera, so Pearse would
use pageants and plays in St Enda's.[25]

Only six months after the school opened, MacDonagh and Willie
Pearse successfully staged two plays – a Christian morality tale by
Douglas Hyde set in a monastic community in which children meet a
young saint, and Standish O'Grady's *The Coming of Fionn*[‡] with Gwynn
and Yeats in the audience to hear O'Grady's post-performance speech

---

* Father Peadar Ó Laoghaire, a pioneer in the 1890s of a modern literature in
Irish and hence a hero of the Gaelic revival.

† A seventeen-century author famous for 'Go, lovely Rose': the poet sends a
rose to a young lady instructing it to tell her that she's 'just as sweet and fair as it
is' and recommending her urgently to go into the world so she can be desired,
since life is short and she'll soon be in the grave.

‡ In Irish tradition and politics, Fionn Mac Cumhaill always played second
fiddle to Cúchulainn, not least because he did not die young. But as with
Cúchulainn, his admirers had quite some bowdlerising to do over such happen-
ings as his pursuit of Diarmuid and Gráinne. The daughter of the High King,
Grainne was promised by her father to the aging Fionn, but ran off with
Diarmuid, one of the Fianna, with Fionn in hot pursuit. After a very long time
peace was made; years later, on a boar hunt suggested by Fionn, he failed to save
a badly gored Diarmuid, and by the time his grandson Oscar had forced him to
do the decent thing and provide the necessary magic water, Diarmuid was dead.

urging Ireland to take to the hills and the simple life as enjoyed by
Fionn and his companions. Eoin MacNeill would blame O'Grady for
infecting Pearse 'with an unhistorical and pagan imagery of self-regard-
ing Celtic heroism'.[26] Yeats – who was frequently the butt of vicious
criticism from belligerent nationalists and was in very low spirits
because Synge was dying – referred to St Enda's as 'one of the few
places where we have friends' and wrote to Lady Gregory apropos the
Fionn play that 'the waiting old men of the defeated clan seemed so
like ourselves'.[27]

In theatre-mad Dublin, O'Grady's play received an excellent reaction from the audience and the press, exceeded only by the accolades
accorded the June pageant, *Mac-Ghníomharta Chúchulain* [*The
Boy-Deeds of Cúchulainn*]. Written by Pearse, who had now thrown
himself into theatre, its purpose was to send the boys home for the
summer 'with the knightly image of Cúchulainn in their heart and his
knightly words ringing in their ears'. There were plaudits too for the
first issue of *An Macaomh*, the school magazine, in which Pearse
explained his motivation in setting up the school.

> I am conscious of one motive only, namely, a great love of
> boys, of their ways, of their society; with a desire, born of
> that love, to help as many boys as possible to become good
> men. To me a boy is the most interesting of all living things,
> and I have for years found myself coveting the privilege of
> being in a position to mould, or help to mould, the lives of
> boys to noble ends . . . my school should be an Irish school
> in a sense not known or dreamt of in Ireland since the
> Flight of the Earls.

The actress Máire Nic Shiubhlaigh, who met Pearse often but never felt
she knew him well, described him as being transformed when he was
with the boys. 'He knew all their separate traits', she said, and when in
their company 'he had a sort of boyish enthusiasm which set him on a
level with all of them. He really loved his boys.'

In an era of rigid and harsh educational practices, Pearse was probably the best-informed educational theorist in Ireland, a radical many
decades ahead of his time, his approach child-centred long before that

became fashionable. 'I knew one boy who passed through several schools a dunce and a laughing-stock', he wrote in one of his educational articles;

> the National Board and the Intermediate Board had sat in judgement upon him and had damned him as a failure before men and angels. Yet a friend and fellow-worker of mine discovered that he was gifted with a wondrous sympathy for nature, that he loved and understood the ways of plants, that, in short, he was the sort of boy likely to become an accomplished botanist. I knew another boy of whom his father said to me: 'He is no good at books, he is no good at work; he is good at nothing but playing a tin whistle. What am I do to with him?' I shocked the worthy man by replying (though really it was the obvious thing to reply): 'Buy a tin whistle for him.'

Pearse would not be the first or last brilliant schoolmaster whose ability to understand, inspire and relate to his pupils was rooted in both arrested emotional development and homoeroticism. It is a sign of the broadening of the Irish mind that unlike in 1977, when my biography caused much outrage by drawing attention to how Pearse's prose sang when he wrote of the physical beauty of boys, the issue of his sexuality is now freely discussed publicly.

It is difficult to challenge Séan Farrell Moran's 1994 assessment that 'at the age when the sexual drive anarchically manifests itself' Pearse's developing preoccupation with 'moral abstinence and purity' suggested

> a substantial maladjustment in his personal development. The obsession with boys obviously had its roots in his lack of maturity, a kind of stunted sexuality. It also means, however, that he was able to control his sexual desires by sublimating them into his truly creative and innovative work as an educator.

As Moran also says, even though this was a period when 'Peter Panism' was at its height (the play was produced in 1904), Pearse's writings

were 'far more openly homoerotic than other works'.[28] But then he was
writing for a Dublin audience, which was much less sophisticated than
its London counterparts.

In 2004 Elaine Sisson, in her examination of the St Enda's cult of
boyhood, discussed the public debate about Pearse's sexuality and
helpfully unpacked the layers of confusion caused by ignorance.

> The homoerotic is a love and desire for the same sex that is
> primarily filtered through a visual or literary sensibility and is
> not usually understood to involve sexual acts. Homosexuality
> is a socio-sexual identity that may or may not be defined in
> terms of sexual activity with the same sex. Paedophilia is a
> much more closely defined activity expressed as a sexual
> interest in, and engagement with, children.

And pederasty is a usually erotic homosexual relationship between an
adult male and a pubescent or adolescent male.

In this, as in so much else, Pearse was complicated and it is certainly
wholly anachronistic to try to claim him as gay in the sense in which
that is now understood. There is no doubt about his homoerotic
tendencies, but, like Moran, I believe they were sublimated, and that
– as Sisson puts it – it was this sublimation of his sexuality 'that
produced such a remarkable interweaving of discourses on aesthetics,
martyrdom, masculinity and nationhood, which found literary, visual
and dramatic expression in the highly eroticized figure of the *macaomh*'.

Pearse had woven into his thinking the athleticism, heroism and
eroticism of Greek and Roman culture as seen through the code of
honour of the Victorian public school about which he had read so
much as a child. Not long before he set up St Enda's, he gave a lecture
claiming that ancient Irish literature was superior in humanity and
spirituality to that of Greece, that both valued youthful masculinity
and the beauty of the male naked body and that the 'horror of comely
nakedness' was a British and imperial invention. In the merry boyish
Red Branch games of tearing off each other's clothes, Cúchulainn was
inevitably by far the most accomplished, being able, in Pearse's admiring words, 'to tear off not only the cloaks and tunics, but the kilts of any
three'.[29]

Those were innocent times, and Pearse was an innocent man, and in the rather bohemian world of his father as a child he had modelled nude. Yet as Joost Augusteijn, his most recent biographer, discovered, there were disturbing aspects to some of his relationships that were discussed in private correspondence in the 1940s.[30] 'Pearse used to kiss the young boys,' wrote one ex-pupil. 'He tried to kiss me but I would not have it.'

In Edwardian times a teacher kissing a boy was not an arrestable offence, but it was unusual enough to have been regarded as odd and for him to have been given by a few boys the nickname 'Kiss me Hardy'. Seamus O'Sullivan, the poet and editor of the *Dublin Magazine*, a direct contemporary of Pearse's, claimed in a letter in the 1940s that Pearse 'was under a cloud because it was known that he used to kiss boys in his school'.

Pupils noticed that his favourites were good looking, particularly Frank Dowling, who was chosen to play in the pageant because 'in face and figure and manner' he resembled

> my own high ideal of the child, Cúchulainn; that, 'small, dark, sad boy, comeliest of the boys of Eire', shy and modest in a boy's winning way, with a boy's aloofness and a boy's mystery, with a boy's grave earnestness broken ever and anon by a boy's irresponsible gaiety; a boy merely to all who looked upon him, and unsuspected for a hero save in his strange moments of exaltation, when the seven-fold splendours blazed in his eyes and the hero-light shone above his head.[31]

Studio shots of Dowling in that role became St Enda's postcards, 'images which suggest that Frank Dowling (as a representative St Enda's boy) and Cúchulainn, the legendary *macaomh*, are one and the same'.

Posthumously, anxious hagiographers would create a heterosexual romance with a young woman whom Pearse knew in the League and who had drowned in a tragic accident in Kerry, but there was no evidence for it whatsoever.[32] Delight in the faces and bodies of male children and adolescents along with suppressed desire ran and would continue to run throughout Pearse's literary writings, though it would be a few years before anyone drew attention to it.

By any criteria, although Pearse had his father's positive views on women's suffrage and their rights in general, he was deeply uncomfortable in their company, and the women in his fiction were maternal or allegorical, mostly engaged in nurturing a dying child or calling for young men to free her from evil oppressors. Sydney Gifford – whose sisters Muriel and Grace would marry MacDonagh and Joseph Plunkett – wrote of a visit to St Enda's with Muriel in its early days:

> We were all standing in the library talking, when MacDonagh suddenly got me by the arm and said: 'Come outside, I want to talk to you about something.' So I went out, leaving my sister in the room with Pearse. [MacDonagh said:] 'Wait till you see Pearse! Wait till you see Pearse! He won't stay in the room for a minute with her!' And the next thing the door opened and Pearse shot down the passage with his head down like as if he was pursued by devils . . . it was so funny.[33]

Pearse lived within the emotional protection of his family bubble, which since James Pearse's death had offered no intellectual challenge. Although he had never rejected his father and always admired much about him, the identity crisis with which he had struggled was eased when he could adopt and adapt as he chose the uncritical nationalism of his mother's family and harness his closest relatives in the service of his causes. They were an odd family: none of the children married or ever seem to have formed any normal relationships, seeming to exist to serve their Pat in their various ways, even if his sisters were often at loggerheads. The cantankerous nationalist-turned-unionist Ulster dramatist St John Ervine would say privately in the 1940s that 'I thought Pearse a degenerate, a witless man with an over-emotionalised nature who really ought to have been certified in his youth. The whole family was mawkish and maudlin.'[34]

Oddest of all was the Pat–Willie relationship. Apart from speaking to each other in their baby dialect, as adults they still played familiar tricks on each other – even tickled each other – with Willie delighted that having reprised their childish dressing-up game and presented himself at the door of St Enda's in the guise of a beggar-woman, he was ordered away by Pat.

Willie was quite attractive in an arty sort of way ('[a] slight, long-faced man with a lisp and melancholy eyes and dark hair sweeping back in a curve above his forehead'[35]) and easier to talk to than his big brother, but his only recorded interest in a female was his obsession with Mabel Gorman, who modelled nude and clothed for him from the time she was eight and to whom he wrote and sent presents until she got bored with him when she was about fourteen. Not that he had much opportunity. The Pearse family mutual protectiveness extended to the younger daughter, Mary Brigid, insisting in all joint theatrical ventures with Willie that she must play the female lead lest someone 'make love to' her brother.

To Pearse, though, with their intense loyalty and acceptance of his vagaries, his family were perfect. None of them put up a fight when towards the end of St Enda's second highly successful year he put both the school and the family finances at grave risk because – in tune with his belief that prudence was a vice – he followed what to him was the incontrovertible logic that since St Enda's 'had the highest aim in education of any school in Ireland: it must have the worthiest home'. He found it in the Hermitage, a large, beautiful eighteenth-century mansion outside Dublin set in equally large and beautiful grounds, where Robert Emmet, who had walked there with Sarah Curran, began to displace Cúchulainn in his heroic affections. 'Whereas at Cullenswood House I spoke oftenest to our boys of Cúchulainn and his compeers of the Gaelic prime,' he wrote in *An Macaomh*, 'I have been speaking to them oftenest here of Robert Emmet and the heroes of the last stand.'

Desmond Ryan would write many years later that

> if a locality can preserve the past and haunt a receptive mind with past good and evil, assuredly the Hermitage haunted the mind and personality of Pearse ... Robert Emmet's memory haunted Pearse, and this haunting is clamant throughout Pearse's later speeches: he seems to see Emmet tapping his cane along the Rathfarnham roads,

rambling through the Hermitage grounds and plucking grapes from the vines or lying hidden among the heather on Kilmashogue Mountain, which Pearse could see from his study windows, or standing on a scaffold before a silent Dublin crowd.

It was this identification with Emmet that gave Pearse the passion that inspired Denis McCullough and Tom Clarke after his oration in March 1911 to defy IRB rules and provoke a debate about the July visit of King George and Queen Mary. Áine Ceannt would later recall that he came to one meeting of the committee set up to prevent an address being made to the king by the Dublin Corporation. He was with MacDonagh, 'and that was the first time that Pearse, to my knowledge, took any interest in Irish affairs outside the Gaelic League'. And Sydney Gifford said that during a protest outside City Hall 'Pearse arrived and was attempting to force his way past the police when Tomás MacDonagh intervened and nearly dragged him away, telling him that if he was arrested it would mean the end of his school. He yielded to Tomás's persuasion although he seemed very excited.'[36] Still, Pearse was drifting inexorably towards politics, though he still was still unclear about which path he was on – cultural, parliamentary or revolutionary.

One he had ruled out was that of Sinn Féin, for which he had 'little affection': hating mean-spiritedness, he blamed Arthur Griffith for almost killing his political child because of personality deficiencies that included hardness, obstinacy, narrow-mindedness, paranoia and undue respect for his own opinion,[37] and thus succeeded in 'repelling the more vital and Irish-Ireland elements of the Irish Party by nagging personalities and carping criticism'.

Pearse's open-mindedness did not just antagonise Griffith – it made him an object of deep suspicion within the IRB. At the great Home Rule demonstration in March 1912 that Clarke, Ceannt and Mac Diarmada were boycotting, Desmond Ryan was a witness to Pearse's lonely involvement.

Three green flags towered over three platforms in the main street, where thousands of citizens cheered wildly and waved miniature replicas of the floating emerald and harp as a carriage drove slowly by with Mr. Joseph Devlin, M.P., smiling, bowing and turning on a spit, as it were, to the roasting applause of the roaring multitude.

Devlin went to his platform near the General Post Office

> bounded forward with his tiny green flag and yelled above all the frantic plaudits: "This is Ireland's answer to the taunt that she does not want Home Rule!" Another shattering roar from the citizens and Wee Joe dived into a whirlpool of popular oratory – "a good speaker", as Pearse described him, who knew "how to please the people".

Ryan watched Pearse standing up, 'shy, austere, alone', speaking in Irish 'in the future shade of his last stand', and Devlin listening to his speech respectfully. 'We do not seek to destroy the British Empire, we seek Irish freedom,' he said.

> We are all agreed in this: it is our duty, willy-nilly, to achieve freedom for our race. Some of us would be content to remain under the lordship of the English king, others (and I am with them) have never bent their knees or bowed their head to the King of England, and never shall. But I feel I should betray my people if I had not answered this call to-day, since it is clear to me that this Home Rule Bill here recommended to us will make for the advantage of the Irish and strengthen them in their struggle. He who is of that mind would be a coward if he withheld his aid.[38]

Afterwards, Devlin wrote to Pearse to thank him, regretting that he could not understand Irish but hoping for his support in future. Had he understood Pearse's peroration with its threats of violence if Ireland was betrayed, he might have been less sanguine.

What Pearse could not bear was having his courage or his patriotism questioned, especially by people he thought were all talk and no action, like the IRB. Desmond Ryan accompanied him to a public meeting where he spoke from the floor.

> Pearse's plea for a charitable attitude towards the Irish Parliamentary party drew taunts that he was a moderate, very boorishly and ignorantly expressed with all the crudity of exasperated doctrinaires. Pearse made a remarkable reply which ended: "Yes, give me a hundred men and I will free Ireland!" ... As we left the meeting Pearse's eyes burned and he talked all the way to the Rathfarnham tram at the Pillar, saying intensely: "Let them talk! I am the most dangerous revolutionary of the whole lot of them!"

His desperate need to express unchallenged his rather complicated opinions had led him the same month in which he defended Home Rule to found Cumann na Saoirse and the weekly *An Barr Buadh*, in which Éamonn Ceannt played so prominent a part. Inviting the small number of eligible people to a meeting, he explained a Home Rule parliament would need Irish speakers, but if Home Rule was not introduced, 'a sustained agitation will be needed, in which we must ensure that the battle cry is not sounded in the foreign tongue. Only those who are prepared to defend the rights of Irishmen against all and sundry and who are Irish-speakers will be admitted to the association.'[39] The membership was tiny, but at least four (Ceannt, Colbert, Cathal Brugha and Seán T. O'Kelly) were members of the IRB.

From his new pulpit, Pearse wrote letters in Irish to public figures, most of whom would not have understood them. He called on warring members of the Gaelic League to unify in the cause of the Irish language, on the Irish Parliamentary Party to unify for the sake of a good Home Rule bill, and criticised suffragettes and the Labour movement – with both of which he was sympathetic – for putting their own causes above Irish freedom. Yet an increasingly emotional state that gloried in death was becoming ever more evident as he idiosyncratically harnessed famous names in Irish history to justify physical force in lyrical form. Two poems in *An Barr Buadh* were testimony to this. First was the marrying of religion and nationalism in 'Mionn' ('Oath') in his idiosyncratic and almost blasphemous pantheon of

Irish heroes: 'In the name of God, / By Christ His only Son, / By Mary His gentle Mother, / By Patrick the Apostle of the Irish,' it began, and taking a gallop through various tragic deaths of patriots, it ended with:

> By the bloody wounds of Tone,
> By the noble blood of Emmet,
> By the Famine corpses,
> By the tears of Irish exiles,
> We swear the oaths our ancestors swore,
> That we will free our race from bondage,
> Or that we will fall fighting hand to hand
> Amen.[40]

And in true nineteenth-century nationalist style, 'Mise Éire' ('I am Ireland') personified Ireland as a broken-hearted old woman, the mother of Cúchulainn the brave, who had been shamed by being sold by her own children* to an enemy who continually tormented her, was sorrowing because she had lost all those she trusted and was now lonelier even than the mythological old hag of Beare.†

In May a crisis in St Enda's, mainly caused by the financially calamitous move to the Hermitage, put an end to the paper and the society. Realising that his new focus on politics had almost allowed St Enda's to drown in debt, Pearse instructed himself in *An Barr Buadh* to disregard politics, and embarked on the job of saving the school, which had haemorrhaged students because it was too far away for most day boys, and teachers because he could not pay them, and had creditors literally banging on the door. 'I was mad!' he said to Desmond Ryan, 'to start such a paper when the school

* In 1167, the High King of Ireland deprived Dermot McMurrough, the King of Leinster, of his kingdom. The Vikings, who in 911 had been granted the duchy of Normandy, had won the crown of England by force in 1066 and were well entrenched in Wales. McMurrough invited King Henry II to involve himself in Irish affairs; in 1169 a small army of Welsh Normans invaded Ireland and began a long and uneasy conquest.
† The 'Lament of the Old Woman of Beare' was a tenth-century poem about a woman who had seven periods of youth and lost to death by old age every man who lived with her.

was trembling in the balance. Why didn't you stop me?' The question was rhetorical, for no one could stop Pearse when his blood was up.

Bulmer Hobson, to whom he went for help, recollected asking Pearse with what money he had begun *An Barr Buadh*:

> he said 'none'. I could hardly credit this, and asked him to explain. He said that one evening when walking around St Enda's he had got the idea of such a journal, had gone into Dublin, and given the contract to a small printer, Curtis. No payment was ever made. It was a heavy loss for Curtis, but this did not bother Pearse.

It was not that Pearse was personally extravagant: apart from the little cottage built for him in Rosmuc, in Connemara, and books, which he could not resist, he was frugal, and he and his family drew out of the business only what they needed to live on. But the debts were large and increasing and yet more fundraising from the Gaels produced very little. Yeats was one of those to whom Pearse appealed successfully: he put on at the Abbey Rabindranath Tagore's play *The Post Office* along with Pearse's *The King* – about a king who loses all battles because of his 'polluted hands', but whose troops are led to victory by Giolla, a Christ-like boy, who offers to do 'this little thing' – and gave him two-thirds of the profits. A good friend persuaded the now more than a hundred and twenty creditors to accept two shillings in the pound for now and St Enda's was safe for another year. St Ita's, the girls' school he set up in Cullenswood House after St Enda's moved but had little to do with, collapsed in a heap of unpaid bills. Pearse put all his faith in an American fundraising tour, but at this stage Irish America was uninterested.

Yet his interest in politics was merely in abeyance and was to become intense following the sectarian political chasm being opened over the prospect of Home Rule. Once the outcome of the 1910 election had indicated that a Home Rule bill was inevitable, unionists – who were mostly Protestant – had sought to find effective means of making clear their opposition to any kind of legislative autonomy. In 1910, Dublin-born Sir Edward Carson, the famous London barrister, parliament-arian and fine orator, had been offered and accepted the leadership of the Ulster Unionists. There were unionists, mostly Protestant, in many parts of Ireland, but they were concentrated in the north-east of the island, in the home counties of Tom Clarke, Bulmer Hobson, Pat McCartan, Denis McCullough and Seán Mac Diarmada of the IRB. Southern unionists mostly kept their heads down.

Above all, Carson wanted to defeat Home Rule throughout Ireland, but he also wanted to minimise the sectarian violence that accompanied times of political tension by providing a safe channel for Protestant working-class rage. In September 1911 he had recommended to a mass unionist rally in Belfast that there should be immediate resistance when Home Rule was enacted, but to show the leadership meant business he decided to stage a piece of political theatre of the kind so beloved by both Irish unionists and nationalists.

To that end, Saturday 28 September 1912 was appointed 'Ulster Day', when there would be widespread Protestant religious services, after which a 'solemn covenant' signed a few days previously by Ulster Unionist Council delegates would be 'proclaimed throughout the Province' and made available to congregations so they could pledge themselves to it. A terse document of only 206 words, it declared that Home Rule 'would be disastrous to the material well-being of Ulster as well as the whole of Ireland' as well as 'subversive of our civil and religious freedom, destructive of our citizenship and perilous to the unity of the Empire'.

Although they worried that Home Rule might presage a break with the United Kingdom and that somehow it might threaten their prosperity as the only industrialised part of Ireland, what most troubled Protestants was their perception that in a Catholic-dominated island Home Rule would mean Rome Rule, which Protestants mostly associated with European authoritarianism and monarchical absolutism.

As the Gaelic League's struggle with bishops demonstrated, the tentacles of the Catholic Church were visibly reaching ever further into Irish public life. And Pius X – the pope honoured in 1908 in prose and music by Seán T. O'Kelly and Éamonn Ceannt respectively, and an uncompromising opponent of modernism – had helped embed that perception by issuing the previous year the *Ne Temere* decree by which marriages not performed by a Roman Catholic priest were now sacramentally invalid. Priests had discretion to refuse to perform them,

or insist on such conditions as that children be raised Roman Catholic*
and agreement by the non-Catholics to attend religious instruction
designed to convert them.

This was particularly divisive in Ireland: as recently as January 1912,
the Ulster Women's Unionist Council had collected 100,000 signa-
tures for a protest against *Ne Temere*. With the Ulster Covenant, the
signatories numbered almost 500,000 out of an Ulster Protestant
population of 891,000. 'The signing itself was surrounded by great
pageantry,' wrote Liam Kennedy.

> Sir Edward Carson, using a silver pen, was the first to sign
> at Belfast City Hall, which was one of the many centres
> where signatures were registered. That a Dubliner with no
> obvious Ulster connections was the first to sign was an
> irony that went largely unnoticed. The ritual and the spec-
> tacle were integral parts of what was in effect a massive
> exercise in ethnic mobilisation.[41]

The third and fourth signatories were the Moderator of the General
Assembly of the Prebyterian Church in Ireland and the Church of
Ireland Bishop of Connor, in whose diocese Belfast lay. The Protestants
of Ireland were finally united.

It was the establishment of the Ulster Volunteer Force a few months
later, in January 1913, that would create the circumstances that would
propel into uniform those two unworldly poets and teachers, Patrick
Pearse and his best friend Thomas MacDonagh.

---

* While in many mixed marriages the boys followed the father's and the girls
the mother's religion, this had not applied in the families of Tom Clarke or
Pearse, nor would James Connolly apply it in the case of his own children.

Chapter Five

THOMAS MACDONAGH[1]

What was fundamental in him . . . was an eager search for something
that would have his whole devotion. His dream was always of
action – of a man dominating a crowd for a great end. The historical
figures that appealed straight to him were the Gracchi* and Owen
Roe O'Neill†. In the lives of these three there was the drama that
appealed to him . . . the thoughtful man become revolutionist; the
preparation of the crowd; the fierce conflict and the catastrophe.[2]

Padraic Colum, 1916

There was nothing in Thomas Stanislaus MacDonagh's immediate
family background that encouraged violent revolution. Born in
Cloughjordan, Tipperary, on 1 February 1878 to apolitical, cultivated
national school teachers, his convivial, kindly father Joseph, who loved
classics and literature, had rejected the Fenianism of his own father,

---

* The Gracchi brothers both served as reforming tribunes in the late second
century BC. Tiberius tried to redistribute land from the rich to the poor and
with 300 followers was clubbed to death at the behest of angry senators. The
Roman poor turned against Gaius when he tried to extend rights to non-Roman
Italians; he committed suicide before the mob could assassinate him, but 3,000
of his followers were subsequently killed.

† After forty years as a Spanish mercenary, during which he failed to persuade
the Spanish monarchy to invade Ireland, O'Neill returned home after the Irish
rebellion of 1641, and won some notable victories for the Irish Catholic
Confederacy during a turbulent decade of complicated war and diplomacy. He
agreed an alliance with royalists shortly before the Cromwellian invasion and
died a few months afterwards, probably of an old wound. Romantics like
Thomas Davis thought otherwise: 'Did they dare, did they dare, to slay Owen
Roe O'Neill?' / 'Yes, they slew with poison him they feared to meet with steel.'

who was a member of the IRB – he dismissed nationalist activists as 'great cry and little wool, like the goats of Connacht'.[3] Thomas's mother Mary, who shared her husband's political views, was the daughter of a Unitarian Englishman who worked as a compositor in Greek for the Trinity College Dublin Press; she was an accomplished pianist who wrote short stories, essays and poems.

They met in County Offaly as schoolteachers and Mary became an enthusiastic convert to Catholicism, regular prayer, a nightly rosary and charitable works. After marriage, they moved to Cloughjordan to run a new Catholic school. Thomas was the third child of six, and their eldest son.

In their musical and literary home Thomas played the piano and sang, had a mischievous sense of humour, loved the countryside, read avidly, revelled in ghost stories and, like his siblings, acquired from his mother her 'grave high sense of moral purpose'.[4] One brother would become an actor and playwright, another a musician, and a sister became a nun.

He was sent as a boarder to Rockwell College in Cashel, a school in Tipperary run by the Holy Ghost Fathers, who were teachers, missionaries and workers among the poor. Academically strong, it was uninterested in nationalist culture of any kind. MacDonagh excelled in English and Latin and the humanities and was keen on cricket and rugby, where he played in the forwards. 'Tom was small,' remembered a contemporary, 'but a handy little fellow.'[5]

He was happy there: 'I found thee when my childhood's home I left, / And grew to love thee fondly through the years' he would write in 'The Parting,' the night before he left Rockwell forever. In 1894, at sixteen, shortly after his father's death, MacDonagh wrote to the Superior General asking for acceptance into Rockwell's Junior Scholasticate, explaining that he had always wanted to be a priest: 'having tried by every means in my power to find out to what life I have been called' he had realised he had 'a decided taste for the missionary and the religious state'. The interim stage before going on to the priesthood was to become a prefect, which involved dormitory and games supervising and some teaching in addition to private prayer, daily mass and the intensive study of Catholic doctrine.

He was accepted and moved out of the college to the Scholasticate's Lake House and having matriculated in 1896 became a junior master, thoroughly enjoying teaching English, French and Latin. His life suited someone alternately gregarious and reclusive, but he was temperamentally a free spirit who did not easily fit the rigid mould of Catholic dogma. He once told Yeats what life was like there. "'O,' he said, "everybody is very simple and happy enough. There is a little jealousy sometimes. If one brother goes into town with a Superior, another brother is jealous."'6 A simple life was not enough for MacDonagh. Suffering a profound crisis of religious doubt – probably precipitated by the death of a fellow-student – which mainly focused on death and an afterlife, in 1901, when he was twenty-three, he wrote 'with sorrow' to ask to be released from his obligations. 'The house in the wood beside the lake,' he would write, 'That I once knew well I must know no more. / My slow feet other paths must take.'

He spent six reclusive weeks in Paris before taking up a job in September 1901 teaching English and French in St Kieran's Secondary School in Kilkenny, where he was carried away in class with the poetry of Keats and Wordsworth. A contemporary there recalled that he became a great friend of Francis Skeffington, a pacifist and doughty fighter for women's rights, who was becoming an atheist, had just left the staff but was still in the neighbourhood: 'MacDonagh small, stocky, neat, almost dapper, interested in rugby; the other bearded and untidy with a passion for long walks and legendary among his students.'

At the end of 1901 he sent Yeats a collection of poems he intended to publish at his own expense. Yeats replied that 'you have a thoughtful and imaginative mind – but you have not yet got a precise musical & personal language'. He advised him to postpone publication, 'to read the great old masters of English, Spenser, Ben Jonson . . . perhaps Chaucer – until you have got our feebler modern English out of your head' and translate a great deal from Irish 'literally, preserving as much of the idiom as possible'.7

MacDonagh published them anyway in 1902 and dedicated them to Yeats. *Through the Ivory Gate** contained poems he had written in

---

* In Homer's *Odyssey* and Virgil's *Aenead*, false dreams come to mortals through the ivory gate, the true through the gate of horn.

Rockwell during his tormented period. They showed, he explained, 'a struggle of soul from the innocence of Childhood through disillusion, disappointment and ill doubt; and thence through prayer and hope and the pathos of old memories to lasting Trust and Faith'. Its few reviewers struggled to label this account of a religious crisis, though one correctly spotted Yeats' influence in its interplay between dream and reality.[8]

Was it Yeats' recommendation that sent MacDonagh to a meeting of the Kilkenny branch of the Gaelic League? He would claim he went to scoff, but 'instead was moved to a conversion of Pauline peremptoriness, his self-described "baptism in nationalism"'.[9] Always busy and efficient, by April 1902 he was forging ahead with language lessons, was an energetic collector for League funds, was elected to the executive and even acquired a kilt and a Tara brooch as a public demonstration of his new commitment to cultural nationalism. He hurled himself into promoting his new cause with all his eloquence and intensity: 'the League was doing the work of a messiah', saving the nation's soul so it could be self-sufficient, culturally restored and free of British influence. That year he made the first of his many visits to the Aran Islands, at the mouth of Galway Bay, which – being beautiful, wild in their scenery and weather, almost exclusively Irish-speaking and virtually untouched by modern life or British influences – were a mecca for lovers of Connaught Irish. His first visit was around the time of one of Éamonn Ceannt's more exhibitionist and skittish moments, which illustrates the gaps between the sceptical natives, the dilettantes and the dedicated.

A group of earnest young Leaguers who had gone to the islands to 'perfect themselves' in Irish in a fortnight travelled back through Galway afterwards rather dejected by their limited progress. Ceannt heard of their arrival and turned up with a skirl of the pipes, solemnly preceding them all the way to the railway station.

> Heads were popping, children running alongside and everyone gasping at the sight. The young Irish students 'would have been glad if the ground opened up to swallow [them], or if they could have wrung Éamonn's neck'. At the station, he marched up and down until a cheer was raised as the train moved off.[10]

MacDonagh was no more a dilettante than Ceannt or Pearse. He worked hard at the language and bonded with the locals, who – as his son wrote in the 1940s – enjoyed him for 'his eager friendship, his exhilarating talk, his archaeological interest, and as the man who introduced the strange song "Malbrouc se va t'en guerre"* into the islands'.

He was still writing poetry and, though his first collection had been a financial failure and a critical non-event, he published *April and May* – again at his own expense – in April 1903. While several of the poems had been written at Rockwell in his less despairing moods and dealt with resurrection, there were new themes from his new life that owed much to the established nineteenth-century nationalist graveyard tradition: the formula was 'premature death, the lonely grave, eternal life through memory, inspiration signalling national renewal, disputation between Soul, Death, Sin, etc'.[11] His first poem, 'To Ireland', was subtitled '(In memory of the things that came to pass in April and May, 1798)' and began 'Let Erin remember the heroes brave, / And gild their names in her story, / Who nobly died their land to save / When knaves forgot her glory.' His adulatory 'To William Rooney'† ended 'But thy music in souls shall thrill, / The loud harps dumb, / And the life-throb have echoes still / When the Dawn has come.' He had also

---

* This rollicking eighteenth-century folksong ('Marlborough has left for the war') – which has the same tune as 'For he's a jolly good fellow' – was almost as popular in England as in France and was among favourite pro-French ballads sung in Ireland. It was based on a false rumour that the apparently invincible general and scourge of the French John Churchill, 1st Duke of Marlborough, had died in 1709 after the Battle of Malplaquet, his last victory in the War of the Spanish Succession.

† An admirer of the Young Irelanders, in 1893, at twenty, Rooney founded the Celtic Literary Society. A leading member of the 1798 centenary committee, in 1899 he co-founded with Arthur Griffith the *United Irishman* (most of which he wrote) and with him fostered pro-Boer sentiment, began to develop what would be the Sinn Féin policy and in 1900 co-founded Cumann na nGaedheal. He died at twenty-seven of tuberculosis. Griffith called him 'the Thomas Davis of the new movement', Yeats dedicated the first edition of *Cathleen ní Houlihan* to his memory and James Joyce savaged his poetry as the product of 'a weary and foolish spirit, speaking of redemption and revenge'.

faithfully taken Yeats' advice and translated the Irish poem
'Druimfhionn donn dílis', the first of the translations that are among
his finest poetry.

The book was another commercial and critical failure, even if one
reviewer celebrated his decision to abandon 'morbid irritability' in
favour of an 'irresistible desire to make sweet and pleasant and musical verses': sales of the two little books were a hundred and
eighty-four.

From 1903, he was among those trying to open League branches
throughout the county, but only one lasted for any length of time.
Then St Kieran's refused his plea to add Irish to its curriculum and individuals in the local League fell out acrimoniously over whether the
organisation should be purely cultural or aim for national renewal by
supporting Leaguers who stood for political office. MacDonagh, who
resembled Pearse in his profound moral courage, started a huge row at
the annual general meeting by denouncing two friends on the committee who had disobeyed instructions from the executive by voting
against a League activist in a municipal election. He would not be
doing his duty if he remained silent, said MacDonagh, and refused to
stand for re-election.

He was touched and amused by the encomium that followed, which
he described to a friend as 'a rather high-flown resolution of confidence': 'Devoted heart and soul to the loftiest ideals of the Gaelic
League, unselfish in his motives, kind, tactful, and gentlemanly in his
actions towards all, and absolutely fearless in the discharge of the
duties which his position, as Secretary or Committee-man, imposed
upon him.'

With Irish culture his new religion, MacDonagh could no longer
stand either the anti-nationalism of St Kieran's or the bad feeling in the
Kilkenny League. In June 1903 he took a job at St Colman's College in
Fermoy, County Cork: it was 'Gaelic to the spine', the teachers were
'scholars and gentlemen' and there was a lively Gaelic League branch
about ten miles away. He worked hard at his Irish, became in turn
secretary, treasurer and vice-president, helped organise festivals and at

---

* The dear brown white-backed cow – one of the allegorical names for Ireland.

the annual convention of the Gaelic League argued for the establishment of an Irish-language university. He also collaborated with an
Italian composer on a cantata about the escape of the Israelites from
Egypt that won first prize at the most important Irish music festival
and was published in London.

He had also been working hard on his third book of poems, *The
Golden Joy*, which was published in Dublin in 1906 and was better
received than its predecessors. In two parts – 'The Praises of Beauty'
and 'Quest' – and with a long preamble, there was much rumination
on beauty and truth and trust and love and youth as well as on the role
of the poet as the bridge between the physical world and the
spiritual.

By now he was becoming so fed up with the Gaelic League and its
internal arguments that he was set on leaving Fermoy, which had
become 'a horror' to him. His disillusion would gradually plunge to the
depths by 1909 when he told Yeats that he was

> losing faith in the League. Its writers are infecting Irish not
> only with the English idiom but with the habits of thought
> of current Irish journalism, a most un-Celtic thing. 'The
> League', he said, 'is killing Celtic civilization.' I told him
> that Synge about ten years ago foretold this . . . He thought
> the National Movement practically dead, that the language
> would be revived but without all he loved it for.[12]

MacDonagh had toyed with moving to London in search of literary
recognition, but his conversations with Pearse in Aran about St Enda's
had borne fruit, and in the summer of 1908, a few months after Tom
Clarke had opened his shop, MacDonagh moved to Dublin and threw
himself into a new world and new preoccupations. He had not hesitated to join forces with Pearse, whom he liked and admired, believing
he had the potential to be 'the greatest of Irish writers in imagination
and power, if not in language'. As his son would write, 'this was an
adventure which led directly to Kilmainham in 1916'.[13]

Both idealists, they wanted St Enda's to become some kind of Boy
Republic. Both were sincere, but Pearse's strength was to motivate
them through oratory ('MacDonagh used to say jestingly that Pearse

had started a school to be able to make as many speeches as he liked'[14]),
while MacDonagh charmed and laughed them into intellectual curiosity and disputation. It was he who decided that teachers and boys
would sit together during meals and have adult conversations.

Desmond Ryan, who was one of his pupils, recollected his idiosyncratic approach with great affection. MacDonagh's

> talk was not idle talk and his instalments of his life-story
> were in much demand: how he had tried to join the French
> Army and found too late there were three vacancies per
> annum for Irishmen in the Austrian Army ever since some
> great battle in the days of the Wild Geese; how he had
> nearly been a priest; how he had been the greatest West
> Britisher in Ireland and suppressed the Irish language and
> played Rugby football in a South of Ireland College; how
> he was very properly held up to popular odium for this in a
> Dublin paper and saw the light, learning Irish in some
> quick flashes of time, all as a matter of course.[15]

Unlike Pearse, who lacked spontaneity, MacDonagh was easily
distracted, and the boys quickly realised he could be sidetracked with
interesting questions that sent him rummaging in 'the rich storehouse
of his imagination'. But, as one of his contemporaries saw it,

> MacDonagh's learning sat lightly on him, and whether his
> audience was a public meeting, a classroom, or a small
> gathering of intimate friends, they would often, after leav-
> ing his company, realise on reflection how much know-
> ledge he had imparted to them during what seemed to be a
> light-hearted and informal talk.

In a testimonial for a job in the newly established National University
of Ireland that MacDonagh failed to get in 1909, Yeats wrote: 'He
would create a taste for reading & for reading the best literature & that
is the one thing that matters.'[16]

He was loved too at St Enda's because of his ability to find the fun in
everything. He teased even Pearse at every opportunity. Fortunately,

although Pearse took himself seriously, MacDonagh was never pomp-
ous and could laugh at aspects of himself. Reminiscing in 1913 about
the early days of St Enda's, Pearse wrote that MacDonagh

> has told me how, when we were preparing the first number
> of *An Macaomh*, I came to him one evening with a face of
> portentous gravity and begged him to be humorous.
>
> I explained that *An Macaomh* was too austere, too
> esoteric: it needed some touch of delicate Ariel-like fancy,
> some genial burst of Falstaffian laughter. Mr. MacDonagh
> is one of the most fanciful and humorous men, but even he
> could not become Ariel-like or Falstaffian to order. He and
> I sat in our respective rooms for a whole evening lugubri-
> ously trying to be humorous; but our thoughts were of
> graves and worms and epitaphs, of unpaid bills, of
> approaching examinations, of certain Anglo-Irish
> comedies: the memory of it is still dreary.[17]

When in June 1910 the Pearse brothers and MacDonagh took their
actors to perform the Cúchulainn pageant at a feis in County Louth,
they arrived back to Dublin to some commotion as they marched from
the station.

> Some of us carried battleaxes borrowed from the school
> museum, others held tall gilded spears which glinted like
> polished bronze in the lamp-lit streets. A crowd gathered
> round, wondering at our strange weapons and our dusty
> faces. They followed us, and soon they were singing 'Who
> Fears to Speak of '98' as they tramped and surged around
> us. MacDonagh was delighted at the commotion we had
> raised. 'Egad!' he said, as the crowd swelled to the dimen-
> sions of a riot, 'They expect us to lead them against the
> Castle.'[18]

Like the Pearses, MacDonagh was devoted to the theatre, but unlike
them he was effortlessly at home socially in the middle of that world.
Ryan wrote of his appearances at the Abbey that

Thomas MacDonagh watches the stage pensively, his head on one side, and then wakes up to talk the other poets around him under the floor, and the wits say that MacDonagh has all the ideas and the other poets listen and then express them, though Thomas writes a hundred lines on the most meagre day wherever he is. His staccato laugh and 'begad!' cross the stalls and enter the ante-room with his gaily waved hand, and Thomas is soon at home with the critics and *literati*.[19]

From 1904 MacDonagh had worked on *When the Dawn has Come*, a play that took its title from his poem about William Rooney and reflected some of the obsessions of *The Golden Joy*, which dealt with leaders and patriots and rebels and sacrifice and martyrdom. One of its poems, 'A Fragment (Written of a Patriot who suffered unmerited disgrace and death)', echoed the theme of his oddly prophetic first play, which, as outlined in his diary, was about a council of seven planning an Irish insurrection.

The Abbey rejected the first draft in 1907 and with the help of Padraic Colum, who was already successful, MacDonagh revised it. It was turned down again, both J.M. Synge and Yeats thinking it too sentimental and in need of rewriting. The final version was staged in October 1908, the month after he began teaching at St Enda's. Set fifty years in the future, its hero, the poet and revolutionary Turlough McKiernan – whom MacDonagh thought of as 'a great mind reasoning with little ones' – had decided to 'cheat the English by posing as a spy'. In this version he no longer died in exile in disgrace, but succumbed to his wounds after a victory in battle.

Not only did the play have a confusing plot, but it was poor on characterisation and long on tedious speeches, which do little justice to the conflict between McKiernan and his less intelligent and more fanatical colleagues; it was also disastrously badly staged, acted and produced. The St Enda's teachers and boys attended, while Yeats and Maud Gonne saw it on the same night as Douglas Hyde, who called for the author at the end, Yeats told Lady Gregory, 'but only to see what he looked like'.[20] MacDonagh's distress over its failure was as nothing compared to that he felt over his mother's illness and her death that November, which left him 'crushed'.

MacDonagh's appetite for life and experience did not confine him to teaching and writing: he wanted to participate in public life, but for a time he looked in vain. Although he was an Irish-Irelander and contemptuous of the Irish Parliamentary Party, he thought Sinn Féin had not much of a natural constituency, as had indeed been shown by their failure in the 1907 North Leitrim by-election where Seán Mac Diarmada had acted as election agent: 'the present state of politics is pitiable', he wrote to a friend in 1909.

He became involved at the fringes of the labour movement, becoming in July 1909 a founder member of the Association of Secondary Teachers of Ireland, whose pay and conditions were miserable compared to those of national teachers, who had been unionised since 1868. It was suffragism, however, that engaged him, as he had shown in his play, where two women counsellors were in the inner revolutionary circle, and though not on the seven-man council, were on equal terms with them.

MacDonagh's first Kilkenny friend, who since his marriage to Hannah Sheehy had become Francis Sheehy-Skeffington, was, alongside his wife, a leading light in the Irish Women's Franchise League. MacDonagh made innumerable friends in the League and made speeches and wrote articles on its behalf, although he publicly deplored its invitations to British suffragettes to address meetings. 'If it coquets with West Britain and puts forward speakers who will give us talk of "our army", and "our parliament" . . . it cannot grip Irish sentiment or support, as it must do if it is to win here.'

St Enda's was not enough for MacDonagh, for although he loved much about it there were disappointments. Telling Yeats in 1909 that he was very sad about Ireland, he said

> he finds a barrier between himself and the Irish-speaking peasantry, who are 'cold, dark and reticent' and 'too polite'. He watches the Irish-speaking boys at his school, and when nobody is looking, or when they are alone with the Irish-speaking gardener, they are merry, clever and talkative. When they meet an English speaker or one who has

learned Gaelic, they are stupid. They are in a different world.[21]

It was unsurprising that MacDonagh began that year a part-time university course, graduating the following year with a BA in English, French and Irish. He took a more critical look at his own poetry and decided to abandon most of it by destroying *Through the Ivory Gate, April and May* and *The Golden Joy*. In the grounds of St Enda's, Desmond Ryan watched him

> unload some hundreds of these booklets with a smile into a ritual bonfire beneath a tree in the playing field. In the spirit of his quip that no poet burns a poem unless he has a second copy, he saved some of these for his definitive edition. He told me, too, that his *Songs of Myself* was nearly ready for the press, a book he would never burn.

This, the second year of St Enda's, was traumatic, for MacDonagh fell desperately in love with Mary Maguire, for whom he had found a job at St Ita's. She was a graduate in modern languages with a deep interest in Irish literature, a suffragette, a lively member of Dublin artistic and literary circles, a wholly undomesticated free spirit and a friend of both MacDonagh and Padraic Colum. Her firm refusal to accept his proposal coupled with Pearse's impulsive decision to move St Enda's to Rathfarnham left him miserable. Saying he needed what he called 'a desert where I could begin again without shackles', he resigned his job, telling a colleague he would miss Patrick Pearse most of all.

Paris offered MacDonagh his preferred mixture of solitude or company according to his inclination. He would write of being 'Silent and free as a hawk in the sky, / Unnoticed and alone'[22] and he read and wrote a great deal, but he also improved his French by chatting companionably in cafés near the Sorbonne and attending the theatre. His poetry was benefiting from the generous and good advice Yeats had continued to give him. Though Yeats was cautious about MacDonagh because he thought his politics too radical, he liked him. 'I often ask myself when I have written a poem,' he had written to

MacDonagh in the spring of 1910, 'could I have said this or that more simply in prose, and if I could I alter the poem.'[23]

Songs of Myself, which MacDonagh published at the end of the year when he returned to Dublin from the self-imposed exile that lasted only six weeks, was full of intensely subjective poems about lost love, death and even suicide. As William Irwin Thompson neatly summed him up, his poems over and over again 'rehearse a personal agony, a love that died, a youth that fled, a disappointment with Fate, and over and over again he proclaims against this suffering that he is a mystic caught up in the ineffable joy-sorrow beyond human ken.'[24] The collection includes one of his best poems: MacDonagh had 'an intimate knowledge of the humours of popular life in the country and the country town', observed Padraic Colum, 'a knowledge which he seldom put into his writing, but which has become vivid in that unique poem "John-John".'[25] The inspiration almost certainly had come from reading his mother's papers after her death, which included her poem 'Children of the Wandering Poor' about society's rejection of an itinerant mother and her child.

A vivid demonstration of MacDonagh's humanity, empathy and lack of sentimentality about rural Ireland, 'John-John' is about a settled woman who goes to the fair to search for her husband, one of the thimble men who cheated innocents by rigging a challenge to identify the pea under the thimbles. They had married five years earlier ('The neighbours' shame of me began / When first I brought you in; / To wed and keep a tinker man / They thought a kind of sin') and he had stayed for only two years. She's glad to see him, but she knows he was never cut out to 'go to Mass and keep the fast / and till the little patch', so she shares what she has with him that afternoon and sends him away ('But here now, it is six o'clock / And time for you to step. / God bless and keep you far, John-John! And that's my prayer.')

The collection was a success, especially 'John-John'. The last poem was 'Envoi,' which declared its intention 'to lay the ghost of my youth', to let his unrequited love go, to take to the road with John-John 'And leave this life behind; / We'll be free on the road that we journey on / Whatever fate we find.'

MacDonagh did not take to the road, not least because he was already in love again, and this time it would be requited. He went back into the bosom of St Enda's, teaching part-time and living down the road from the Hermitage in a gate lodge rented from David Houston, a prosperous and cultivated Scots bacteriologist who was a professor at the Royal College of Science. This was to be the place where alone he would find his path: 'Make your mansion, pray and sin,' he wrote in 'Grange House Lodge': 'Pray for grace yourself to be, / To be free in all you do / For a straight sincerity, / Grace to see a point of view . . .'

The intention was clear, but MacDonagh's reclusion, as usual, did not last as long in practice as he had planned. Ryan recalled:

> Thomas MacDonagh returns to his lodge half a mile away on the Dundrum road with his little dog frisking round him . . . The poet and his dog are well known on the Rathfarnham roads as Thomas goes with his long neck-tie floating in the wind talking to anyone for hours on anything. He lives in his little lodge rather than in the Hermitage for solitude and freedom. He respects Pearse too much to be quite at ease with him, for Thomas must argue or die. Thomas knows Pearse could not endure religious controversy, but Thomas must thrash out all such questions with those so inclined and he has a more robust humour than Pearse and wider interests. He is more a European, he says himself, and cannot get to the heart of Gaeldom so profoundly as Pearse. There are moments when the native speakers and the Gaeltacht bore him stiff and he returns to Elizabethan poetry and France and Greece and Rome, and rounds it all off with a night with the poets in his little lodge.[26]

Among the regular visitors were some of the most distinguished names in literary Dublin, including Seamus O'Sullivan, Padraic Colum, Francis Ledwidge (the gifted poet who was a protégé of Lord Dunsany, conservative unionist Meath landowner and writer of fantasy fiction) and James Stephens, a poet and admirer of Arthur Griffith, who as 'The Old Philosopher' wrote a humorous topical column in *Sinn Féin*. Stephens would achieve success in 1912 with his delightful comic novel *The Crock of Gold*, which affectionately parodied the beliefs of his mentor, George Russell, otherwise known as AE* and another occasional sipper of whiskey at MacDonagh's primitive home.

It was a period of happy bohemianism for MacDonagh: 'one Hallow Eve they melted all his window-weights and cast magic spells'.[27] 'I am within striking distance of the life I want', he wrote to a friend in March 1911, the same month that, with financial backing from David Houston, MacDonagh launched with Padraic Colum, Mary Maguire and James Stephens *The Irish Review*, a new monthly magazine.

MacDonagh was the contributing sub-editor, believing the journal would 'speak for itself and say something for me too'. Among those writing on culture and politics were the four founders and a wide range of distinguished Dublin figures that included Arthur Griffith, Standish O'Grady, Pearse and Yeats. Every issue had an art plate from such artists as Beatrice Elvery, Casimir Markievicz, Jack Morrow, Jack B. Yeats and MacDonagh's future sister-in-law Grace Gifford. MacDonagh would publish there his second play, *Metempsychosis*, a satire on theosophy, reincarnation and other esoteric beliefs. Its intention was to make fun of some of the stranger preoccupations of Yeats and his circle, but when staged by a small amateur group in 1912 the audience failed to get the joke and thought it boring and incomprehensible. It reflected MacDonagh's irritation with Yeats, partly because of the fate of *When the Dawn has Come*, but also because he thought him a 'snob' – albeit loveable – who through his relationship with Lady Gregory was tainted 'with that rottenest of taints in Ireland's ground, the ascendancy taint'.[28] Class-consciousness was becoming a feature of MacDonagh's thinking.

The St Enda's connection still offered more than occasional teaching. In the spring of 1911 MacDonagh helped with what was probably Pearse's finest dramatic production, *An Páis*, a passion play in Irish

---

* George William Russell (1867–1935) was a close friend of Yeats, a poet, painter and mystic who after reading Standish O'Grady focused some of his occult beliefs on Cúchulainn. A nationalist, in 1903 with Maud Gonne and Douglas Hyde he became joint vice-president of the Irish National Theatre Society.

staged in the Abbey that was imbued with his personal devotion to, and identification with, the suffering and crucified Christ. Pearse and MacDonagh played the crucified thieves; Willie, who was usually a diligent but unconvincing actor, was praised for his Pontius Pilate. The audience was rapt. In the *Irish Review* Colum praised it as a breakthrough in Gaelic drama.

Even more useful for MacDonagh's career ambitions was an MA thesis on metrics and rhyme in Elizabethan poetry with particular reference to the poet and composer Thomas Campion, which was so original that it won him a first-class honours degree from UCD toward the end of 1911 and a full-time assistant lecturership. He was overjoyed that he would now have the money to marry his new love, Muriel Gifford, who had red-gold hair like Mary Maguire, but was otherwise much more retiring.

Although Muriel's solicitor father was Catholic, her domineering mother insisted that all twelve of their children be brought up in the Church of Ireland. The six boys emigrated, without any rebellion against their parent's unionism, but all the girls became involved in feminist and nationalist politics, with Muriel being the least evangelical. In 1908 MacDonagh had been introduced to three of the Gifford girls, Grace (a cartoonist), Sydney (a journalist) and Muriel, who had given up nursing because of a breakdown. She was emotionally fragile, quiet, sweet-natured and warm-hearted. They fell in love in 1911 and kept their relationship secret for several months for fear of a violent reaction from her anti-Catholic mother. Yet as MacDonagh put it to a friend, 'Muriel and I are of the same religion, which is neither Catholic nor Protestant nor any other form of dogmatic creed, neither of us ever go to Church or Chapel, but for the sake of several things and people we are willing to conform for a marriage ceremony.' Chief among those people were Muriel's mother (who would learn to put up with it) and MacDonagh's nun sister, who would become very fond of her sister-in-law.

MacDonagh was happier than he had ever been. 'Now no bitter songs I sing', he wrote in 'A Song for Muriel': 'Summer follows for me now; / For the Spirit of the Spring / Breathes upon the living bough: / All poor leaves of why and how? Fall before this wonder, dead: / Joy is given to me now / In the love of her I wed.'

At their small, informal wedding in January 1912, Patrick Pearse, who had agreed to be best man, exceeded his reputation for unpunctuality by failing to turn up at all, causing MacDonagh to tease him for having stayed away because he was too fat to get into the kilt he had been instructed to wear. Ten months later, the MacDonaghs were having their son Donagh christened in a Catholic church when coincidentally Pearse dropped by to pray. 'Well,' said MacDonagh, 'you got here in time for the christening anyway!'

'Wishes for My Son' was written at this time:

> Now, my son, is life for you,
> And I wish you joy of it,
> Joy of power in all you do,
> Deeper passion, better wit
> Than I had who had enough,
> Quicker life and length thereof,
> More of every gift but love.

'Love I have beyond all men, / Love that now you share with me', the poem continued, neatly describing what was most remarkable about MacDonagh himself: of all his many gifts, his greatest was for love. Among the long list of people who regarded him as their best or one of their best friends were Pearse, Francis Ledwidge, who would be killed at Ypres in 1917, and James Stephens, who would write *The Insurrection in Dublin* from the point of view of a horrified observer. 'I have seldom known a man in whom the instinct for friendship was so true,' wrote Stephens after MacDonagh's death, 'nor one who was so prepared to use himself in the service of a friend. He was intensely egotistic in his speech; so, it seems to me, were all the young Irishmen of that date [1910]; but in his actions he was utterly unselfish.'[29]

'Wishes for My Son' also, though, showed the side of MacDonagh that was to lead him into a more perilous world, for he wished for Donagh to know 'more than I / Ever knew of glorious deed', including 'Wild and perilous holy things / Flaming with a martyr's blood, / And the joy that laughs and sings / Where a foe must be withstood, / Joy of headlong happy chance / Leading on the battle dance.'

*   *   *

Happy in his university job, his various literary ventures, his little family and his friendships, life was sweet for MacDonagh, but the inner doubts and the questing romantic spirit were not contained for long. What would take him beyond cultural nationalism and beckon him towards more dangerous paths was the experience of watching people being batoned on the streets of Dublin.

Domesticity might have tamed some of MacDonagh's bohemian-ism, but bourgeois convention held no attractions for him. Contemporary debate was full of social as well as political fervour and even Patrick Pearse was kicking against the gentility and social constraints of his claustrophobic family circle. In May 1913, in what would be the last issue of *An Macaomh*, Pearse deplored the way in which teachers brought their pupils down to their level by substituting for their 'vision of ultimate beauty and truth . . . the mean philosophy of the world, the mean code of morals of the counting houses. Our Christianity becomes respectability.' He listed the six commandments of Respectable Society:

> Thou shalt not be extreme in anything – in wrong-doing lest thou be put in gaol, in right-doing lest thou be deemed a saint; Thou shalt not give away thy substance lest thou become a pauper; Thou shalt not engage in trade or manufacture lest thy hands become grimy; Thou shalt not carry a brown paper parcel lest thou shock Rathgar; Thou shalt not have an enthusiasm lest solicitors and their clerks call thee a fool; Thou shalt not endanger thy job.[30]

Although Pearse admired James Larkin and had admitted his children to St Enda's when they were unwelcome in every other school, MacDonagh was far ahead of him in developing a preoccupation with social justice, for he was now living and working in central Dublin, mixing in new and more radical circles, and becoming aware of the terrible conditions in the slums where a third of Dubliners lived. The city was agog with controversy about the upheavals in labour relations resulting from the industrial unrest that had been spreading from Britain.

Like so many of his contemporaries, MacDonagh was inspired by
the mesmeric, theatrical, rebellious, larger-than-life Larkin, who by
now was a major Dublin figure: a spell in jail in 1910 over what was
perceived as a vindictive and unjust prosecution by his old union had
added to his popularity. By 1913 his ITGWU had 20,000 members
and he was president of the ITUC, which now had a political wing – in
1912, with his right-hand-man James Connolly, he had founded the
Irish Labour Party. He was also editor of a successful weekly newspaper, the *Irish Worker*, which eloquently and venomously reflected his
and Connolly's advocacy of class warfare and their syndicalist gospel
that preached that through industrial action one big union could overthrow capitalism.

Larkin's major target and most formidable enemy was William
Martin Murphy, the President of the Dublin Chamber of Commerce, a
devout Catholic and home ruler who believed that Ireland should stay
within the British Empire, who had worked well with the Dublin
Trades Council but welcomed only well-behaved craft unions that
worked in harmony with employers for the good of industrial development. Murphy's many business interests included the Dublin United
Tram Company and the *Irish Independent*, a paper as belligerent as the
Irish Worker. He believed Dublin needed more capitalists, saw Larkin
as 'an irresponsible demagogue waging war on church and state to grat-
ify his vanity' and the ITGWU as 'no more a legitimate trade union
than "a pirate ship"'.[31]

Larkin had won several victories over the wages of the unskilled
by persuading other workers to refuse to pass pickets; Murphy had
won other disputes by adopting similar tactics with the bosses, his
task made easier by their bad experiences in trying to make peace
with Larkin. In July, the Chamber of Commerce and the Trades
Council had agreed to establish a conciliation board to mediate
future disputes, but on learning that Larkin was recruiting in his
Tram Company Murphy decided on making a similar pre-emptive
strike. As Larkin acquired members among Murphy's employees,
Murphy began dismissing them; in August 1913 Larkin called a
general strike and Murphy and over 400 employers demanded their
workers sign a pledge not to join the ITGWU or engage in sympathetic strikes. Twenty thousand workers were locked out, blackleg

labour was employed and so began a terrible period for the Dublin poor, which was unnecessary and probably happened primarily because of 'the peculiarly perverse personalities'[32] of Larkin and Murphy.

Helen (Nellie) Gifford, who travelled around Ireland as a domestic economy instructor, was the most formidable of MacDonagh's formidable sisters-in-law. A supporter of radical land agitation and women's suffrage, she was a friend of Constance Markievicz*, with whom Larkin stayed on the night of Saturday 30 August, the day before he was due to address a banned rally on Sackville Street. In severe riots the night before, angry strikers flinging sticks and bottles had been backed up in nearby Monto – where the brothels flourished – by prostitutes whose missiles included jam pots and clinkers. Two men would die from injuries from police batons and around three hundred casualties among civilians and police alike had to be treated in the nearest hospital. Passions were high, but Larkin was determined to defy the ban.

In a false beard and frock-coat, he pretended to be the deaf uncle (so he would not have to reveal his strong Liverpool accent) for whom Nellie had booked a room at William Martin Murphy's Imperial Hotel, just opposite the General Post Office. Unable to step on to the balcony in his room because it was blocked by an enormous window box, Larkin rushed into the dining room and stepped out on its balcony. His triumphant 'I am here today in accordance with my promise' was drowned out with shouts of 'It's Larkin! It's Larkin!' after which he ran toward the hotel's rear exit. He was arrested inside without any trouble,

---

* Constance Gore-Booth, of planter stock, was born in 1868 and brought up in Lissadell, County Sligo. One of five children, beautiful, gregarious, brave, adventurous and a daring rider, she and her favourite sister Eva would be immortalised as 'two girls in silk kimonos' in Yeats' 1927 poem 'In memory of Eva Gore-Booth and Con Markiewicz'. Their education in the liberal arts extended to a European grand tour with their governess. As a debutante in 1887, Constance was presented to Queen Victoria. She studied in London at the Slade School of Art and in Paris and in 1900 married fellow art student Casimir Dunin-Markievicz, a Pole. Their only child, Maeve, was mostly left in Lissadell with her grandparents. From 1903 the Markieviczes were at the centre of Dublin artistic, thespian and social circles; they separated around 1909.

but the crowds outside the hotel kept growing, Markievicz, who had arrived with Sydney Gifford, called for three cheers for Larkin, a large window in William Martin Murphy's Clery's department store was smashed and the police feared a mob was forming to rescue Larkin or damage other property. As they tried to push back the crowds, the police began to lay about them with their batons.

Thomas MacDonagh, who had cycled into the centre of town out of curiosity to see how Nellie was getting on that lunchtime, had a perfect view. He would later tell the Disturbances Commission that nothing happened until Larkin had been taken out of sight, but that when he was about to get on his bicycle a man advised him to get out of the way because there was about to be a baton charge. Around 300 police in Sackville Street, nervously fearing more trouble, mistook a surge in the crowd for an attack on them and charged wildly. MacDonagh, who had abandoned his bicycle and taken refuge in the offices of the *Freeman's Journal*,

> saw the police batoning the people and striking them on the head ... I saw sometimes three policemen attack a single individual. I saw them attack an old woman with a shawl over her head, and baton her brutally. I saw them baton a small man who had lost his hat, and he was bleeding ... I heard the continual rapping of batons on people's heads.[33]

This brutality would change the course of MacDonagh's life, and that of his now closest friend, twenty-five-year-old Joseph Plunkett, who was less than two miles away visiting his parents' house for the excellent weekly family Sunday lunch. It had not even occurred to Joe that anyone would disagree with his belief that it was inevitable and right that workers should unionise. As his sister Gerry remembered events, his mother denounced him

> in passionate and dramatic tones as having taken the side of the devil himself in the person of Larkin. Ma attacked him with fury, screamed and roared, flouncing about the place, in and out of the dining room, wanting to know how

her own family could actually tell her that the men were right . . . 'I never heard of such a thing! They demand work! Well the world is coming to an end!' she said.[34]

Joe and Gerry finished their meal in silence, left the house under a cloud of disapproval and did not return for two months.

Chapter Six

JOSEPH PLUNKETT[1]

As different as Pearse, MacDonagh, and Plunkett were from
one another, they shared a common desire to live a myth. A
certain amount of self-dramatization is natural to man, but
few individuals attempt more than a temporary imitation . . .
The exaggerated passions of Pearse, MacDonagh, and Plunkett
show the self-mythicization that a romantic age finds . . .
congenial . . . The poet-rebels chose to image themselves as
sacrificial heroes taken from the old mythologies of torn gods.[2]

William Irwin Thompson, 1967

Seán Mac Diarmada and Éamonn Ceannt lost their mothers when
they were nine and thirteen; Pearse was over-mothered until his death
at thirty-seven; Joseph Mary Plunkett was tormented throughout his
short life by a maternal monster.

Plunkett is remembered mainly for one poem, 'I See His Blood
Upon the Rose', written when he was a tubercular twenty-three-year-
old. It is so religious, so full of mystical imagery and yet so simple that
most Catholic children in an independent Ireland would be required
to learn it by heart.

> I see his blood upon the rose
> And in the stars the glory of his eyes,
> His body gleams amid eternal snows
> His tears fall from the skies
> I see his face in every flower;
> The thunder and the singing of the birds
> Are but his voice – and carven by his power

Rocks are his written words.
All pathways by his feet are worn,
His strong heart stirs the ever-beating sea,
His crown of thorns is twined with every thorn,
His cross is every tree.

Joseph Plunkett was born on 21 November 1887, the second child and eldest son of George Noble Plunkett and his wife Josephine Mary. Five of the seven children, who were born over eleven years, had Mary as a first or second name, and four had Joseph or Josephine, but there was only one George and no Noble.

George's and Josephine's fathers, the upwardly mobile Patrick Plunkett and Patrick Cranny, had married first cousins whose dowries had enabled their husbands to move from the shoe trade to become builders of comfortable houses suitable for letting to the middle classes in south Dublin. The marriage settlement of George and Josephine included sixteen houses and three farms.

Clever, bookish George had been sent to France and Italy as a young boy to escape the tuberculosis that would kill his sister and so spoke fluent French and Italian. Back in Dublin he acquired a sound Jesuit education in classics, philosophy, maths and science. A natural poly-math – as his eldest son would also become – he subsequently studied art, wrote poems and articles, and later went to Trinity, where he read law lackadaisically and had an eclectic collection of friends, including Oscar Wilde.

Apart from art and literature, his passions included Irish history and politics and Catholicism: at thirty-two, in recognition of his extreme generosity to a group of English nursing nuns who were setting up a branch in Rome, he was made a papal count. A few months later he married the twenty-six-year-old Josephine, who was very beautiful but largely uneducated. She had been looked after materially but neglected emotionally by her largely absent father and her rigid and tyrannical mother; she would always, said her daughter Geraldine Mary Germaine, otherwise known as Gerry, stay 'the wild Irish girl' he had fallen in love with when she was fourteen.

After a two-year honeymoon in North and South America, the Plunketts settled into the tall, thin Georgian house they had been given in Upper Fitzwilliam Street, 'an address suitable for a gentleman' full of fine paintings and sculptures collected by George. There was a basement for servants and on the ground floor a dining room and conservatory as well as a large study, lined with books and with papers all over the floor, where George Plunkett – an obsessive reader – spent most of his time.

The first floor had two elegant drawing rooms, the second their two big bedrooms, and on the top floor, originally set up for a baby and two nurses, there were eventually the seven children and two or three 'girls or women who were supposed to be nurses but very often were completely unqualified or ignorant or violent or all three'. One used to heat a poker until it was glowing red and threaten to shove it down Joe's throat when he cried. 'Ma hired them from the Irish Times Agency and, as she could not look her staff in the face, a habit acquired in her upbringing, she had no idea about their competence or value.' She visited the nursery every day for half an hour; otherwise, apart from a daily walk and occasional visits downstairs, the children stayed in their quarters. Periodically, though, their mother sent one or more of them to stay with relatives, and occasionally there was a long family holiday: when Joseph was seven, for instance, the family spent three months in Brittany.

Josephine was a happy traveller and loved and admired her husband, but she was totally unsuited to being a mother or running a house, not least because she was a social climber who was appalling to servants. Believing that 'the lower classes' were 'made of different clay' and less sensitive than their betters, she over-worked and fired them frequently, usually on a whim. They also went hungry, since she believed overfeeding them caused immorality.

George claimed rather unconvincingly that he used his title only because the Vatican requested he should do so; his wife certainly insisted on being called Countess. Being ashamed of the family background in trade and her husband's journalism, she bullied him into practising as a lawyer, 'a profession for a gentleman', and though he was too frightened to speak in court he worked in chambers. Josephine could not prevent him from socialising, mainly with literary or political friends: a devoted follower and friend of Parnell, he stood unsuccessfully for the IPP several times. He was friendly too with old

Fenians, having known Jeremiah O'Donovan Rossa in Ireland and New York, where he had also got to know John Devoy. In 1898, the year he came closest to getting into parliament, he used to sing 'Who fears to speak of '98' around the house.

Although he was a devout Catholic and on good terms with the ecclesiastical establishment, in politics the gentle Plunkett displayed the courage he never showed at home, stood by Parnell throughout the adultery scandal and remained a Parnellite after his death. When the Irish Party reunited in 1900, it needed to field respectable candidates, and romantic Parnellite rebels were no longer required.

At home, Joe Plunkett contracted a virulent form of bovine tuberculosis when he was two, which for the rest of his life would flare up frequently and confine him to bed. His and his siblings' circumstances improved greatly when he was four and Gerry's arrival brought another nurse, Biddy Jenkins, who was kind, sensible, intelligent and looked after the children properly for nine years until sacked by Countess Plunkett for impertinence. She was also a Parnellite who taught them their religion and Irish songs.

George Plunkett lived in his own world and Josephine was uninterested in education, so in their early years the children's only teachers were Biddy Jenkins or a series of governesses as varied in competence and temper as the nurses. The only real intellectual stimulation available to these clever, enquiring minds came from their father, who talked to them freely of art and books and history and took them to galleries and theatres, yet left all decisions about their school to their ignorant mother. She sent her children to schools and took them away again as the whim took her and sometimes sent them away from home, especially if another baby was due. Her unconventional attitude to child-rearing was evident when in 1897 she rented a house on the outskirts of Dublin and dispatched there for a year six children, two servants and a wild, angry governess from Alsace who – in addition to teaching the children French poetry – taught them anti-French songs and curses. The Countess visited occasionally to check that they were speaking French at dinner, but frequently forgot to send them food. Neglect had the positive side of allowing the children unusual freedom, and with a friendly pony and a trap they explored the countryside.

They were back in Dublin the following December, when eleven-year-old Joe was sent to CUS (Catholic University School) in Leeson Street, where after four months he came down with pneumonia and pleurisy and was expected to die. On this occasion, his mother came up trumps, for, with plenty of help, she was an excellent nurse who carried him to recovery after months of illness. Her fits of responsibility rarely lasted long, though. Deciding that he should recuperate in Rome, she stopped by Paris and instead put him in a boarding school in the suburbs while she led an active social life. Unfortunately, the French climate was unsuitable, and he developed the first of many enlarged glands in his neck.

By the time they went home at the end of the year to convalesce, his father had had a windfall from a successful book on Botticelli, and – wanting to give the children country air – had taken a seven-year lease on Kilternan Abbey, a house in the foothills of the Dublin mountains where they roamed freely and happily and had horses, dogs and cats. On the plus side, the Countess read to them well and was often good fun, but after she sacked Biddy Jenkins and proved incompetent in organising such basic care as clothing them properly, she became frustrated and began to beat the children irrationally with her fists, a cane and a horsewhip. From then on, Gerry would shake when her mother came into the room.

Joe knew his mother better than did his siblings, was grateful to her for saving his life and was better than most at manipulating her, but she still took a horsewhip to him. He fainted, though, and he was henceforward spared. The hatred for her mother felt by Gerry – Joe's closest sibling – continued to intensify in line with the harsh and arbitrary decisions, including the Countess's instruction to the coachman to drown all the cats because she became annoyed with them. Count Plunkett was rarely around: he was either working in Dublin, travelling around Europe giving lectures, or living in a bungalow in the grounds writing; in 1902–3 he mainly lived in Cork, where he was Secretary to the Cork International Exhibition, and on the occasion of the visit of King Edward VII and Queen Alexandra presented to the Queen a little bell with an amethyst clapper. Looking after the family he saw as his wife's job, and anyway, being too scared of her to intervene, he pretended to notice nothing wrong.

From October 1901, when he was well enough, Joe went to Dublin daily to the Jesuit Belvedere College, which required a round trip of sixteen miles by bicycle, train and bicycle. On the homeward journey, the hill was too steep for cycling, so his siblings tried to meet him with the pony and trap to spare him walking. Badly dressed and unaccustomed to school, he seemed 'cold, haughty and independent towards strangers', wrote a contemporary. 'He was inevitably misunderstood. He was not a boy like the rest. His companions classed him with those whom they called "queer fellows." He puzzled them. They joked at his expense and treated him sometimes with school-boy harshness.'

Joe spent his lunch money in the little shops on the quays on pet mice, curios and books, among them the chemistry books that inspired him to set up a laboratory in the basement of Kilternan and persuade his mother to buy him some basic equipment. He and Gerry spent hours conducting experiments, but his mother's insistent questions about what he had discovered ultimately sapped his confidence: instead he began building radio sets, which he would continue to update regularly all his life.

After two years, Joe's health deteriorated so much he had to leave school. Lancing the swollen glands in his neck required a long convalescence. His mother went abroad for months, and, since the elder girls were at school, she left the twelve-year-old Gerry in charge of the household: a resourceful girl, she even taught herself how to make clothes for the family. An operation on Joe's neck was so badly botched he would never again be able to wear an ordinary collar.

The three boys were sent to a Catholic school in England in the autumn of 1904 but removed in the spring; Joe was ill again and had to be taught at home by a tutor who came in twice a week, but who succeeded in teaching Joe and Gerry so well that four years later, on the basis of his lessons, she was able to get into university to read medicine. He also taught the younger Plunketts to read and write. 'We were all so deprived of learning', remembered Gerry, 'that we jumped at the chance of learning anything at all.'

Yet there were many positive influences that compensated for the erratic parents, the chaotic homes, and the interrupted and mostly inadequate education. Although the siblings were often separated, they were affectionate and clever: their creativity had even extended to producing from 1903 a few issues of a joint magazine called *The Morning Jumper*, which encouraged Joe to write stories. ('"Father are you very busy, I have something to tell you," said a tall dark and very pretty girl of nineteen coming into the laboratory of Mr Lexonbridge the celebrated chemist when he was engaged in research on radium' is a fragment of a story begun when he was sixteen.) Their mother became so enthusiastic that she joined in with everything and meddled so thoroughly that she killed off the children's interest in the whole enterprise.

While the children never had access to their father's books, their parents did leave in Kilternan novels, detective stories and magazines they bought to read on trains from Dublin. There were also several adults and children who befriended them. The O'Morchoes, whose father was the local rector, provided a friendly house and close play-mates for several years. Evelyn Gleeson, a friend of William Morris, who lived nearby and who had set up the Dun Emer studio and press craft centre with Lily and Lolly Yeats, sisters to the poet Willie and the artist Jack, was at the centre of a creative ferment. Named for Cúchulainn's wife, to whom folklore attributed great beauty and artis-tic ability, the centre was a counterpart to the literary revival in produc-ing beautiful Celtic-inspired rugs, vestments, tapestries, banners and books, and won international acclaim. Joe and Gerry attended art classes given by the Yeats sisters and revelled in meeting the artistic and literary people who visited.

Then there was Count Plunkett's friend William Rafferty, the local coroner, who became guide and mentor to the neglected and undisci-plined Plunkett children. Apart from teaching them manners, he treated them as adults and taught them how to examine evidence and make informed opinions, even encouraging them to read RIC reports on violent deaths and give reasoned arguments for holding or not holding an inquest. His profound effect on the children continued after they returned to Dublin in 1907. As Gerry put it:

> I loved the Raffertys and Springfield dearly and went there
> as often as I could, often to stay overnight. Like the others,
> I made the decision to have a new method of living based
> on what I found there, but the decision and the method

had to be secret because if they were suspected by Ma, they
would have been smashed to pieces. It was the most beautiful place in the world to us and when I think of it now, it is
in those memories of sitting on the porch steps on wet
days, watching the rain drift through the Scalp mountain
pass.

At eighteen, in October 1906, Joe was well enough to be dispatched
along with his twelve-year-old brother George to yet another school.
The Jesuit college Stonyhurst, in Lancashire, England, had a two-year
'Gentleman Philosophers' course, which was claimed to offer school-
leavers an education comparable with Oxford and Cambridge*, and
was in many ways superior. It was perfect for such an eclectic and
cosmopolitan mind as Joe Plunkett's. He revelled in being the only
Irish student: the other ten Gentlemen included an American, a
Belgian, an Italian and a Maltese, Alfred Asphar, who shared his interests, became his closest friend and would entertain him in Malta in the
summer of 1907.

   He had an early clash over humour with Father Gibb, the English
priest in charge of his class, when set an essay on 'People I would like
to have seen'. He began with the Mad Hatter, who

> has always appealed to me why I cannot say unless it be
> that he forever seems 'let us move one place on and start
> again'. That is so hopeful it shows such a determination to
> get where there is to be got in this eccentric world. 'We're
> all mad here, you're mad, I'm mad, the Cheshire cat's mad.'
> All the more reason to move one place and start again.

---

* Religious tests kept non-Anglicans out of Oxford and Cambridge until 1854
and 1856 respectively. Until 1895 the Roman Catholic hierarchy barred its
members from attending what it considered endangered their faith: in Ireland,
an episcopal ban on attending Trinity College Dublin was maintained by the
Archbishop of Dublin until 1970. The Jesuit classes in philosophy were also
intended for potential recruits to the priesthood, but Plunkett's ill health would
have ruled him out. So, like MacDonagh, he was a man who might have been a
priest, which unconsciously drew him further along the path to sacrifice.

Shakespeare and the music hall artist Dan Leno were chosen because
he thought they would have been fine collaborators, and the fourth
choice was Lady Baltimore, the subject of a 1906 book by the American
novelist Owen Wister, author of *The Virginian*. Wister's 'description of
her is so felicitous that is not to be wondered at that many readers of his
book have desired to make her further acquaintance'. (Lady Baltimore
was in fact a cake: 'Oh, my goodness!' says the hero. 'Did you ever taste
it? It's all soft, and it's in layers, and it has nuts – but I can't write any
more about it; my mouth waters too much.') Father Gibb was unamused.

The days were structured to include lectures, study, religion and
sport, which Plunkett was excused on health grounds, giving him even
more time to satisfy his rapacious intellectual curiosity in the fine
library and afterward in debates and in informal discussion with
students and staff. Being interested in military matters, he regretted
not being fit enough to join the Officer Training Corps and encouraged George's participation. While scholastic philosophy (based on
the teachings of Aristotle and the Church Fathers) and Catholic mysticism were his principal focus, as his sister put it, 'he was fiercely interested in everything intellectual – philosophy, mysticism, physics,
poetry – and in chemistry, wireless and aeronautics'.

He was influenced in his historical thinking by a lecture on Cromwell
from the witty, pugnacious polemicist Hilaire Belloc, devoted defender
of the Roman Catholic Church, but it was Belloc's friend and close
associate, the benign G.K. Chesterton, an Anglican who was a Roman
Catholic fellow-traveller, who was his hero. Plunkett loved his humanity, his intellectual profundity, his whimsicality, his ability to see the
fun in even the most serious subjects and his paradoxically down-to-
earth appreciation of mysticism. This was well displayed in Chesterton's
fine appreciation of Francis Thompson, whose mystical poetry
Plunkett would always deeply revere and whose use of cosmic imagery
transfixed him, in, for instance, 'The Hound of Heaven', where the
flight of the soul from God reaches to 'the gold gateways of the stars'.

'Great poets', said Chesterton, in his column in the *Illustrated
London News* mourning Thompson's death in 1907,

> use the telescope and also the microscope. Great poets are
> obscure for two opposite reasons; now, because they are

talking about something too large for any one to understand, and now again because they are talking about something too small for any one to see. Francis Thompson
possessed both these infinities.[3]

Chesterton cited an example where Thompson 'was describing the
evening earth with its mist and fume and fragrance, and represented
the whole as rolling upwards like a smoke; then suddenly he called the
whole ball of the earth a thurible, and said that some gigantic spirit
swung it slowly before God'. That was 'the image too large for compre-
hension', while the one that was too small was where

> he says that abyss between the known and the unknown is
> bridged by 'Pontifical death'. There are about ten historical
> and theological puns in that one word. That a priest means
> a pontiff, that a pontiff means a bridge-maker, that death is
> certainly a bridge, that death may turn out after all to be a
> reconciling priest, that at least priests and bridges both
> attest to the fact that one thing can get separated from
> another thing – these ideas, and twenty more, are all actu-
> ally concentrated in the word 'pontifical'.

Thompson was the poet Plunkett aspired to be, but he would not live
long enough to reach his potential. The poem he wrote as a tribute to
him was heartfelt, but would suffer so badly from youthful literary
pretension that it was one of those he would later suppress: 'Weep,
Daughters of Mnemosyne! / Chant not th' Epithalamium / For maiden-
widowed Poesy' it began. 'The fluttering wings of ecstasy / Have ceased,
for now his voice is dumb – / Weep, Daughters of Mnemosyne!'*[4]
   Everything new attracted Joe Plunkett: as his sister put it, 'he took a
violent interest in everything intellectual'.[5] During his 1907 summer
holiday he helped set up the Irish Esperanto Association, and, when he
heard of the Lumière brothers' colour photography process, he wrote

---

* Mnemosyne was the personification of memory in Greek mythology; an
Epithalamium was a poem in honour of a bride on her way to the nuptial chamber; poesy is the art of composing poetry.

to them for instructions and addressed himself very seriously at home and at school to a procedure that involved film being processed via eight different baths. Given a room to himself at home because of his ill health, his decorations included his painted copy of a poster by the actor-manager Henry Irving, and on the door some Egyptian figures: he liked to claim the similarity between the shapes of their skulls proved he was the reincarnation of the pharaoh Rameses the Great.

The subject of his final essay at college was 'The Truth, alleged as the basis of Pantheism and Deism, find their only fully and complete expression in Theism', and the reading list in his notebook shows how seriously he took it:

> Revelations; Mother Julian of Norwich; St Teresa; St John of the Cross; The Psychology of the Saints, Joly Sweden-burg; R.H. Benson, Mysticism; The West Molest Lectures; The Mirror of Shalot; Tauler, Mystical Workes; William Blake, Mystical Poetry and Prose; Francis Thompson etc., Delacroix, Les Grands Mystiques; Vaughan, Silex Scintillans, Evenings with the Mystics.

The £5 he won for first prize was spent exclusively on poetry when he got home to Dublin.

Stonyhurst had a profound effect on Plunkett. He would continue to study scholastic philosophy and 'was very much influenced by mystical contemplation "or loving inclination towards God".'[6] Henceforward, the books he read most frequently were by the Spanish mystics St John of the Cross and St Teresa of Avila, founders of the Discalced (or Barefoot) Carmelites, who dedicated their lives to prayer, the German Dominican mystic Johannes Tauler and the Italian mendicant preacher St Francis, The prospect of imminent death was often a part of Plunkett's vibrant life of body and mind, so it was no wonder that he drew comfort from such reflections as, for instance, this verse from Francis's 'Canticle of the Sun':

> Praised be You, my Lord, through our Sister Bodily Death,
> from whom no living man can escape.
> Woe to those who die in mortal sin.

Blessed are those whom death will find in Your most holy
    will,
for the second death shall do them no harm.
Praise and bless my Lord and give Him thanks
and serve Him with great humility.

By now the family were as settled as they ever had been, being back in
Fitzwilliam Street, with Count Plunkett now Director of the Dublin
Museum of Science and Art.* Accustomed in Stonyhurst to rational
discussion and the peaceful pursuit of knowledge, and missing his
friends, Joe found home hard to bear. It had not been improved by the
addition of a cousin from Minnesota, Sarah Ferrall ('dried-up, middle-
aged, haggard and high-voiced, uneducated and opinionated', whom
the Count found 'an intolerable bore' and whose opinions Joe 'found
appalling'), who had been invited by the Countess to help with the
children but instead drove them crazy.

'Joe was far too logical for ordinary life,' said his sister, 'and at first did
not understand the family atmosphere, the continual awful rows, upset
tempers and natural reactions, always defensive. The house was full of
hair-splitting arguments which got worse when he got home.' The Count
was usually out at work or in his study and 'the Countess ran a continuous
battle with any or all of her children, now aged from thirteen to twenty-
two. It was sometimes violent, sometimes silent, often ending in a refusal
to give them whatever money they needed.' Countess Plunkett was as
erratic and inefficient with money as she was with child-management,
spending wildly on luxuries and travel yet being unable to pay basic bills.
She also used it as a means of keeping her children under her control.
When her brother died in 1904, leaving two houses to his goddaughter
Mary Josephine Patricia, known as Moya, and five between the other six
Plunkett children, their parents, who were his executors, held on to them
even after the children became adults. Indeed, when Moya became a nun
in 1914, she was persuaded to sign over her property to her mother.

Plunkett was twenty-one that November and mulling over what to
do with his life other than try to become a gloomy romantic poet. 'The

* Now the National Museum of Ireland.

Gull', the first poem he ever published, appeared in *The Weekly Freeman* in January 1909 under the perplexing pseudonym of Joseph Ó Cahan. It compared the 'wheeling and shrieking' gull to the lost soul 'Calling and crying / For rest thro' all time, / Never finding, but flying / From the curse of its crime.' He was bent on taking the Matriculation entrance examination for University College Dublin, and, although Irish would not be a compulsory subject until 1913, he decided to take it anyway.

According to Gerry, Ma had put an advertisement for a private tutor in a newspaper that was answered by Thomas MacDonagh*: Padraic Colum said MacDonagh had told him that the Countess had called at St Enda's to ask him to help her son with his Irish studies, which sounds much more likely. She and her husband moved in the theatrical circles that were supportive of St Enda's and its teacher-poets. Either way, MacDonagh was delighted with his new pupil, reporting to a friend that he 'is great at genealogy and the like; he knows Egyptian and out of the way things and has studied philosophy at Stonyhurst under Father Maher†'.[7] This suggests strongly that Plunkett had spent some of his time at home reading his father's extensive research into the family tree, which he had traced back to the eleventh century. What the Count was proudest of was the connection with Archbishop Oliver Plunkett of Armagh, who was unjustly found guilty of high treason in June 1681 and hanged, drawn and quartered at Tyburn, probably the last Roman Catholic martyr to be executed in England. But there were other Plunketts who over the centuries had made some historical mark fighting or campaigning for their country or their religion.

MacDonagh and Plunkett developed an instant friendship. 'They were both poets,' wrote Gerry,

> loved theatre, read history, argued fiercely about politics and
> were full of humour and wit. There were nine years between

---

* The Plunketts always called him Tomás.
† In 1890 Stonyhurst College published *Psychology: Empirical and Rational* by Father Michael Maher, its Professor of Mental Philosophy. Well written and intellectually sophisticated, for fifty years in various editions it was a standard textbook in Catholic colleges and universities on both sides of the Atlantic.

them but from the beginning it was a deep, personal and important relationship for both. They haunted each other – if [Tomás] didn't come to see Joe, Joe went out to see him.

Their common interests were legion, underpinned by their philosophical and religious studies as well as their light-heartedness – they shared a love of comic songs and nonsense verse, and Plunkett would play music-hall songs on his fiddle. But what was to bring about their deaths was their eager search for a heroic meaning to their lives.

Plunkett, wrote Padraic Colum, 'had a conqueror's will. His and MacDonagh's friendship was one of the finest things I know of. MacDonagh's influence brought him from the study into affairs, continually adding to his qualities of decision and command.'[8] And as Pearse had led MacDonagh, so MacDonagh led Plunkett on the path to execution.

It was presumably Plunkett's new enthusiasm for Irish that informed his mother's decision to send five of her children, along with Cousin Sarah, to Achill, an island off the Mayo coast, for three months in the summer of 1909 to a lodging house someone had recommended to her. When they reported that it had a dreadful atmosphere and asked to be allowed to move, she refused. They all went to classes run by the Gaelic League (Plunkett briefly hibernicised himself to Seosamh Ó Pluingcéad) and, while his siblings swam in a little harbour, Joe braved the big waves, for despite his frequent bouts of ill-health he loved strenuous physical activity, including skating and dancing. 'This island is fascinating', he wrote in a letter describing what happened when the highest mountain

puts on a mantle of mist and like wilful majesty becomes incognito . . . He sings of little people on the mountain at night and the soft low whispering of the wind across the crannies in the rocks . . . I have been for some distance round the coast discovering beaches of shining yellow sand and rocky strands with caverns fit for smugglers, places where drowned men's clothes are washed up at high tide and left in a melancholy line with seaweed and strange shells.

The terrible poverty of Achill had shocked the family and provoked Plunkett to more gloomy poetry.

The Irish teacher took the family to the mainland at the end of July for the annual pilgrimage to Croagh Patrick, but the two-and-a-half-hour climb caused Joe to collapse, and he was once again bedridden. When they returned to Dublin he was still unwell and desperately tried to build up his strength with the help of devices like spring-grip dumb-bells and rubber strands for stretching, popularised by the famous performing strongman Eugen Sandow. He exercised, said Gerry, 'until muscles stuck out in lumps all over him. It didn't do him any good and may even have done him some harm, but he found the lack of exercise when he had to stay in bed very tedious.'

Plunkett was rescued by the Raffertys, who took him to Kilternan where almost a year of mountain air and kindness nursed him back to health. He and William Rafferty 'became great friends', and

> although they did not agree on politics, Joe valued highly all their detailed discussion on moral issues. I think that the kindness and consideration he received there, both intellectually and physically, gave his confidence a great boost and allowed him to follow his strongest belief, that no intellectual decision should be made lightly.

Joe continued to read voraciously, and to work at his Irish, visiting Dublin from time to time and becoming every closer to MacDonagh, who encouraged his poetic experiments, both serious and frivolous. In March 1910, for instance, in the midst of writing all manner of serious poetry on serious themes, having failed in his attempt to write a prose appreciation of Chesterton (whose books he bought and read as soon as they came out), he wrote lyrics to the tune of 'The Night before Larry was Stretched', an upbeat song about an execution.

'Now Gilbert you know you're our man', it began, 'The only one equal to seven / Tho' you stand on the earth yet you span / With your hands the four quarters of Heaven.' That he addressed him as 'Champion of all that's sublime, Our madly magnificent mountain' (Chesterton was enormous) was in itself a demonstration of why

Plunkett so loved Chesterton, who could write and speak about the most fundamental mysteries of life with contagious gaiety.

He sat the Matriculation and was very dejected when he failed, probably because his education was too unorthodox for a conventional exam. He was well enough in the summer of 1910 to go for a few months to an Irish summer school in Gortahork, in Donegal, where he was taught Ulster Irish, which did not sit easily with the Connaught Irish he had learned in Achill and with MacDonagh. He fell madly in love with Columba O'Carroll, a medical student six years his junior, whom he had known since childhood, and embarked on five years of unrequited passion, which inspired much poetry. 'Joe's love for her was quite unreal and got no response from her,' wrote Gerry, 'though she was fond of him and kind to him. I don't think she liked sick people and he had no money so he couldn't bring her around.' In the spring he visited his Maltese Stonyhurst friend and met Ma in Italy and travelled with her in Italy sightseeing, smoking and, increasingly, coughing. An omnivorous reader of novels of all kind, including detective stories, Plunkett was a particular fan of Chesterton's *The Man Who was Thursday: A Nightmare*, a metaphysical thriller he bought in Florence although he had already read it three times since its publication in 1908. About a seven-man anarchist central council that consists of seven men, six of whom turn out to be secret policemen, it would help make him as obsessed with secrecy as Clarke and Mac Diarmada.

Back in Dublin, in May, Plunkett was bedbound again for a couple of weeks, but improved after being prescribed what was thought to be a new miracle cure by a Hungarian doctor, involving injecting radioactive mentholated iodine for thirty days. He was buoyed up when MacDonagh visited and told him his poem 'The White Dove' had been accepted by the *Irish Review*. Shortly after his death, a hagiographical literary critic was perhaps exaggerating when he described it as 'A thing of purest beauty, of fresh and dew-dropt delicacy', but he was right about its 'fragrant' lyricism.[9] ('White Dove of the wild dark eyes / Faint silver flutes are calling, / From the night where the star-mists rise / And fire-flies falling / Tremble in starry wise, Is it you they are calling?' ran the first of the three verses.)

Plunkett managed to take and pass the Matriculation examination for the Royal College of Surgeons, but, after a sociable and poetically productive summer, he was physically unfit to take up a place. 'Went to Dr Meenan,' he wrote in his diary at the beginning of September. 'He says I must go away for the winter early in October. I don't want to.' A few days later MacDonagh 'came to supper and stayed well into the night working at my poems to get them in order which we did at last thank goodness'. Just before Plunkett left Ireland he wrote in a few hours late one night 'I See His Blood Upon the Rose'.

Plunkett went travelling initially with his father, who was going on a tour of continental museums, and visited galleries, theatres, cinemas, churches, bookshops and restaurants in London and Paris before going to Algiers, the destination that his mother had chosen for him. Egypt, about which he was both well-informed and curious, would have been ideal for his health and his happiness, but she decreed other-wise on grounds of cost and kept him and his sister Moya, who had gone there to look after him, short of money. Their mother loved her son – she enjoyed his company enormously, and when travelling or socialising they got on well – but her extraordinary perverseness and intermittent parsimony often put his health at risk.

Still, he made the best of it, learned Arabic, threw himself into Algerian culture, wrote innumerable letters and several poems and danced, skated, socialised and drank when he was strong enough. He and Moya had to leave abruptly when the weather turned bad in March, but, rather than send them to Egypt, Ma summoned them home, took offence over the complications of settling their bills, and refused to speak to them or help them when they returned in time for a 'raw cold Easter'. A request from Plunkett for a decent overcoat was ignored: within a couple of months, his doctor found him walking home in the rain because he lacked the money for the tram, drenched, and with a temperature of 103. He had a major lung haemorrhage, and spent the rest of the year in hospital, a convalescent home, or, when he was well enough, at home in Fitzwilliam Street, where he had another haemorrhage.

Fitzwilliam Street was no more a suitable place for an invalid than it had ever been. Gerry records a monumental row precipitated by Moya's request that Josephine Mary (known as Fiona), the youngest girl, be given a winter coat. As her mother began screaming hysteri-cally and hitting Moya with her walking stick, Count Plunkett

– rushing from the study and mistaking Moya as the attacker – began hitting her with his, causing Joe to arrive and break his father's stick over his knee and his mother to redouble her screaming.

> Joe comforted Moya while Pa, realising his mistake, stood helplessly patting her on the head to show he was sorry. By the time I [Gerry] came in, Pa had retreated to the study, Ma to the dining-room, and Joe was still trying to soothe poor Moya. Joe, as always happened after an affair like this, was boycotted by Ma, but she did give Fiona the coat.

On a later occasion, while the twenty-one-year-old Gerry was sitting by the twenty-four-year-old Plunkett's bed telling him of a recent violent attack on her after a similar maternal outburst that she had fended off, their mother came in and said

> 'I suppose you've told him all about it.' Joe told Ma she shouldn't do such things and Ma said, 'Do you mean to say that I should apologise to my own children?' Joe said it would be the right thing to do. 'Well, all I can say is . . . I'm sorry.' For a considerable time, she avoided me, but that was the last physical violence on any of us.

A joyful consequence was that the Countess decided to lend Plunkett and whichever sister agreed to look after him a two-storey house in Marlborough Road in Donnybrook; he moved in with Gerry before Christmas 1913. Naturally, Ma was mean with furniture, but they had a 'rather mad' housekeeper and enough money for decent food for the invalid. Gerry could not keep up with university work because of looking after her brother, who was never really well and often confined to bed, but she earned some money as a demonstrator and private tutor so they could manage when Ma held money back. They were very happy, for this was 'a new era of independence for both of us. This independence was spiritual, political, philosophical, in some ways financial, and even more wonderful was the absence of criticism of every step we took.'
They shared their interests and confidences and held open house for their friends, who included Tommy Dillon (Gerry's chemistry

lecturer and fiancé), science students and a mixture of literary types. At the circle's hub was Thomas MacDonagh, who had selected Plunkett as godfather to his son Donagh. The cosmopolitan Plunkett was an exotic addition to the Dublin literary and thespian worlds to which MacDonagh introduced him. 'Frail as he was', wrote a contemporary,

> it was not that impression the man himself left with you. There was nothing small in his personality . . . curiously made up of strength and sweetness. His conversation had wondrous charm, a rare combination of vivacity and reposefulness, of alertness and poise. With Plunkett it was not so much his courtesy that struck one as his courtliness, not so much his politeness, as his kindness and grace.[10]

Gerry described her brother at the time as being

> about five foot nine but looked rather less as a rule as he stooped in repose and was very thin and muscular. He was dark-haired but his beard did not grow strongly. His skin was white and he had a good deal of colour in his lips and cheeks. His eyes were very large, his nose thin, high-bridged and delicately cut and his mouth was finely drawn and mobile.

He was viewed as an eccentric, his unusual appearance enhanced by his striking choice of clothes, which had arisen because of differences of opinion with his mother.

At one stage, after he had had wearisome arguments with Ma about a coat, a sibling suggested he should ask for a cloak. This notion appealed to Ma so much that she made him a circular, unlined cloak in royal blue with a velvet collar. He shared with MacDonagh a liking for flamboyance, 'which Joe', said Gerry, 'carried a bit further. He also liked colour, materials and fine work of all kind, especially rings, not for their value as jewels but for their beauty.'

He cared too about the appearance of books: on the strength of having bought a small printing hand press from MacDonagh on his return from Algiers, he had founded the Columba Press, which mainly published his own poems. The twelve-page *Sonnets to Columba*, for instance, published in 1913 and dedicated to the still-desired and still-unattainable Columba O'Carroll, was printed on handmade paper with a print run of twenty-five.

Since their first meeting in 1909, MacDonagh had encouraged and helped Plunkett at every turn, taking his volume of poetry *The Circle and the Sword* through to publication and printing some of his poems in the *Irish Review*. The pair argued vigorously as equals about everything they wrote. MacDonagh's review of *The Circle and the Sword* in January 1912 was, of course, very favourable, but not uncritical, and written from the perspective of an established literary critic assessing a young poet. He quibbled slightly about Plunkett's occasional archaisms and obscurity, but predicted he would 'come to a more concentrated power'.

Their approach to writing poetry was very different. Plunkett, said Gerry, would compose in his head with difficulty and, once his verse was written, rarely altered it. 'In this he differed in an extraordinary degree from Thomas MacDonagh, who suffered in equal measure from a too great facility in verse writing, and would alter a completed poem repeatedly till he was satisfied that it approximated to the poem of his imagination.' Their 'critical standards and judgments were alike', as was their spoken criticism: 'both of them as quick to destroy, to praise as to blame, not sparing in either, though Thomas MacDonagh was the more severe of the two'.[11] Poets, explained MacDonagh,

> Like all the men and matters of the universe . . . may be divided into two classes, those who begin by being accomplished and come to power along the road which leads to straight simplicity, and those who begin by stammering, those who have slowly to master the craft. Mr. Plunkett is of the former class. He is amazingly accomplished. Yet it is safe to prophesy that he will never produce work of what may be called Art for Craft's sake. He will come rather to see that craft and technique and all the creature of prosody are only the hand maidens of poetry.

It was, he ended approvingly, 'better that the reach should exceed the grasp . . . This poetry aspires. It is sincere mysticism.'[12]

For his part, when, two years later, Plunkett reviewed MacDonagh's *Lyrical Poems* along with AE's *Collected Poems* in an essay on obscurity and poetry, he divided obscurity into two kinds: 'the obscurity of Art and the obscurity of Nature. They may be called the obscurity of mist and the obscurity of mystery.' An artist, he explained, 'is one who has the power of unveiling Nature, only to substitute the veils of Art'; his vision 'penetrates these veils and thus can view the realities underlying them'. AE was often obscure, but probably deliberately, and when he wished to express anger or disgust 'all his immutable immensities go by the board . . . and his meaning stands clearly forth'.

He did not think MacDonagh immune to the obscurity charge, but Plunkett pointed out that Francis Thompson had said 'There is not one great poet who has escaped the charge of obscurity, fantasticalness, or affectation of utterance.' In MacDonagh's book, he thought, the 'quiet depth of meaning' and 'calm splendour of expression throughout the great poems in this book' raised them 'to the region of essential poetry. Tried by any of the touchstones of criticism, clarity, lyrical beauty, perfection of imagery, effortless rapture, sympathy of human feeling, profundity of Vision – everywhere we catch the glint of perfect gold.' If some of his work was very difficult to interpret, there was always the 'clarity of Vision' Plunkett regarded as essential. Soaring to rapturous enthusiasm, he compared MacDonagh to Blake – one of his own great influences – in 'stating his Vision of all Being in eight short lines':

> The phases of the might
> Of God in mortal sight
> I saw, in God's forethought
> Fashioned and wrought,
> Now wrought in spirit and clay,
> In care and common day,
> And shown in symbol and sign
> Of power divine.

MacDonagh's universe, his friend judged to be the

true dominion of the mystic. In his symbolism Mr. MacDonagh shows the same power: 'The flowers of heaven and earth, / The moons of death and birth, / The seasons of the soul,' are three clear images which illustrate and illuminate the obscurity of his form and the precision and plenitude of his meaning. And indeed the first of these serves to remind us of the essential teaching of all the great mystical poets from Solomon to Francis Thompson – the doctrine that binds AE and Thomas MacDonagh in the same service of beauty, the creed subscribed to by all who have experienced the divine vision; for the flowers of heaven and earth are the same flowers.[13]

Plunkett had no such reverence for the poetry of Patrick Pearse; his friend's friend was still to him an admirable but rather distant figure whose simple style was very plain fare for such an intellectual gourmet. Discussing in the *Irish Review* in January 1913 a lecture Pearse had given on education under Home Rule, Plunkett described him as 'an educationalist who is incidentally a poet and a playwright'. He mentioned approvingly Pearse's passion play as 'an innovation in Gaelic drama, because it set forth a grand theme and because it took up with the origins of European drama', but otherwise concentrated exclusively on his educational innovations.

Plunkett would soon get to know Pearse much better, for in mid-1913 he took over the debt-ridden *Irish Review*. Professor David Houston had had disagreements with the editors Padraic Colum and his now wife Mary Maguire, who consistently produced a journal with high standards and low circulation and who insisted that given time they could find a financial backer. They were 'impossible in matters touching real affairs', Houston told MacDonagh, who introduced him to Plunkett, who was delighted at the idea and managed to extract the necessary £200 from Ma and become the proprietor in June. The Colums were upset at what they saw as MacDonagh undermining them and staging a coup with Plunkett, 'a delicate young man' who might have 'to put the whole thing aside on a doctor's order'.[14] There was a temporary estrangement.

For Plunkett, who made himself editor, this was bliss. The Marlborough Road drawing room became the *Review*'s office, and when he was bedridden MacDonagh would bring the necessary people to visit. 'Joe and I both read all the books sent for review', said Gerry; 'we would have read very few of them otherwise. Joe had been very broadminded about literature until he read these books but now he developed a hatred of sloppy thinking and writing and became very critical of his own work.' MacDonagh had to persuade him to keep trying to write good prose. They were 'usually in complete agreement, expressed after heated argument and at great length, on literature and politics'.

The literary relationship with Pearse was more complicated.

When it came to poetry, Plunkett and Pearse did not drink from the same inspirational well; the far more technically proficient MacDonagh drew from both, though not as deeply as either. The poet and critic Brendan Kennelly said that Plunkett should be remembered as having 'a unique visionary intensity', 'that some of his best poetry is born out of deep inner conflict; that he was concerned with the problems of good and evil in a way that Pearse and MacDonagh were not; and that occasionally, despite all his uncertainties, he speaks with a mystic's certainty, insight and authority', and that frequently 'his mystical experiences overwhelm his power of articulation . . . His own dream-battle which was to become a grim reality, is symbolic of the struggle between good and evil in the heart of man.'[15] William Irwin Thompson said less kindly that though the poems show talent 'it is anybody's guess if their baroque and chryselephantine lusciousness could ever be brought under control, and once under control, directed towards greatness', although he added that, had Yeats been executed at Plunkett's age, he would have been a minor poet remembered by few.[16]

But while MacDonagh and Plunkett had poetry at their centre and from adolescence had written, experimented and ultimately rejected and suppressed much of their own output, Pearse had been so busy in both languages with his speeches, his prolific journalism and his essays, short stories and plays, that he published the small amount of poetry he produced quickly and without undue agonising about merit. He saw the need for the development of a modern Irish literature, he contributed to the best of his ability, and then moved on to the next challenge, for his purpose was ever to educate and encourage his audience to embrace, share and take forward his preoccupations of the moment. While all three were writing religious poetry, for such an

intellectual as Plunkett there was little to attract in the simplicity of
Pearse's ideas and language, and the sentimentality of much of his
fiction and poetry would have repelled him.

Yet Pearse was a frequent contributor to *the Irish Review*: from its
inception in March 1911 he had been steadily publishing instalments
of what were to be two anthologies of Gaelic poems with translations
that were literal, except where he 'tried to preserve something of the
march of the originals'. Those in *Specimens from an Irish Anthology* –
which was intended as a collection of 'all that has been most nobly said
in verse by Irish-speaking men and women from the beginning to our
own time' – had mostly been collected during his Gaelic League days.
Their gloom was unrelieved, for as well as keens (lamentations) for the
dead or exiled there were love songs that were no more cheerful. As
Pearse explained it, 'The love of an Irish peasant, if his love songs give
it true expression, is not a thing of gladness but a thing of sadness, with
a terrible passion at its core.'"

Pearse was also producing a few poems of his own in Irish, and the
Review, which under Plunkett had begun publishing some books of
poetry, would issue in January 1914 a very slim volume called
Suantraidhe agus Goltraidhe, which translated as *Songs of Sleep and of
Sorrow, Lullabies and Keens*. MacDonagh reviewed it in an essay called
'Criticism and Irish Poetry'[17] in which he lamented that while 'original
literature in Ireland is still but stammering, criticism already speaks
with a full voice, almost too fluidly, too loudly'. An Irish poet wrote in
'one of the fresh languages of the country' – modern Irish or in 'Anglo-
Irish, English as we speak it in Ireland, a language yet unspoiled by the
overgrowths of literature.' After a lengthy elaboration on his criticism
of criticism, he declared he was not providing an apology for Pearse's
book, 'which is one of the first books of the new literature', and, being
written in Irish, would be ignored by one lot of critics and blamed by
others for having 'something of the note of recent Anglo-Irish literature', yet he thought the poems 'good' and 'true'. In his loyalty to his

---

* Plunkett at least would have been aware of Chesterton's 1911 'The Ballad of
the White Horse' in which he wrote 'For the great Gaels of Ireland / Are the
men whom God made mad, / For all their wars are merry / And all their songs
are sad.'

dear friend he went to the trouble of translating some of the poems for the benefit of non-Irish-speaking readers. He also dealt with the problem that had caused him and Plunkett much heart-searching. 'A mhic bhig na gleas' had first been published in *An Macaomh* at the end of 1909 and reprinted in *An Claidheamh Soluis* apparently without raising any eyebrows, but they knew that 'Little Lad of the Tricks' would be a different matter.

Little lad of the tricks,
Full well I know
That you have been in mischief:
Confess your fault truly.

I forgive you, child
Of the soft red mouth:
I will not condemn anyone
For a sin not understood.

Raise your comely head
Till I kiss your mouth:
If either of us is the better of that
I am the better of it

There is a fragrance in your kiss
That I have not found yet
In the kisses of women
Or in the honey of their bodies.

Lad of the grey eyes,
That flush in thy cheek
Would be white with dread of me
Could you read my secrets

He who has my secrets
Is not fit to touch you:
Is that not a pitiful thing,
Little lad of the tricks?'

In 1975, when I was researching my biography of Pearse, I visited Plunkett's sister Gerry, who suddenly blurted out that 'Joe and Tomás' had to tell Pearse what people would read into 'Little Lad of the Tricks'. He had apparently been as shocked as they were embarrassed. In her excellent analysis of this 'highly sexualized love poem to a young boy', which she describes as 'the most striking example of the fusion between the paternal and the erotic gaze', Elaine Sisson remarks that MacDonagh 'was certainly more worldly-wise than Plunkett'.[18] Well, what with his wide reading, his experience of boarding school, his visits to Paris and his sophisticated friends, MacDonagh was, no doubt, well informed about homosexuality, but in this, as in so much else, Plunkett had always been precocious.

Joe Plunkett was eight years old when Oscar Wilde, his father's close friend since university, was sent to jail for gross indecency with other men. 'Long after Wilde's scandal was already old', reported Gerry, there had been a discussion about the fifty or so letters in the house from Wilde (with whom Count Plunkett would stay friends until the end), 'and Ma took one of her fits. "Oscar Wilde – that disgraceful man!" she said, and threw all the letters in the fire. She had only the vaguest notion of what the so-called scandal was about.'

Ma had a horror of Irish boarding schools because she had heard of a boy being expelled from one for something 'unmentionable', but she had heard good things from a relative about their English equivalents. The school where she deposited her three sons (Joe, sixteen, George, nine, and Jack, six) in 1904 was St George's Catholic School in Weybridge, but a few months later, while quarantined in Ireland because of an outbreak of scarlet fever at school, Joe managed to persuade her that the school 'was very unsuitable because of what went on there. She was horrified: "Surely the English couldn't allow such things in their schools" and said she would write to the government about it.' Plunkett's sophistication would have been enhanced by his wide reading, intense curiosity about everything, the artistic world in which his parents moved and his extensive travelling.

Apart from a trip to Paris as a member of a Pan-Celtic delegation in 1900 and to Belgium in 1905 to investigate bilingual education, with his big sister Margaret in tow, Pearse did not travel outside the United

Kingdom until 1914, and his world was one where the norm was sexual repression. Having been told by his friends how his poem would be interpreted must have added greatly to the emotional strain on this already troubled man. MacDonagh and Plunkett solved the problem by publishing the poems in Irish and having MacDonagh provide translations for all but a few in his review article, where he explained that there were in Pearse's book 'a series of personal or dramatic lyrics' some of which 'do not well bear translation. Judged by present English standards, which are hostile to sentiment, the mere words would give a false idea of the originals.'

'Little Lad of the Tricks' contains 'a self-directed revulsion at the irruption of impure thoughts'.[19] What *were* the secrets that would cause dread in a child he was unfit to touch? How could a man of obsessive purity cope with the knowledge that he was betraying himself as a pederast? Did he look at some of his recent writings and wonder about their sexual implications? 'Why are ye torturing me, O desires of my heart?' was the first verse of 'Why do ye torture me?' in *Songs of Sleep and Sorrow*. 'Torturing and paining me by day and by night? / Hunting me as a poor deer would be hunted on a hill, / A poor long-wearied deer with the hound-pack after him?' And even Pearse's prose writings were full of the same implications, focusing, as they increasingly did, on the sacrifice of the beautiful boy. 'I dreamt I saw a pupil of mine, one of our boys at St Enda's,' he had written in *An Macaomh* in May 1913, 'standing along upon a platform above a mighty sea of people; and I understood he was about to die there for some august cause, Ireland's or another.'

> He looked extraordinarily proud and joyous, lifting his head with a smile almost of amusement; I remember noticing his bare white throat and the hair on his forehead stirred by the wind, just as I had often noticed them on the hurling field. I felt an inexplicable exhilaration as I looked on him, and this exhilaration was heightened rather than diminished by my consciousness that the great silent crowd regarded the boy with pity and wonder rather than with approval – as a fool who was throwing away his life rather than a martyr that was doing his duty. It would have

been so easy to die before a hostile crowd: but to die before
that silent, unsympathetic crowd.[20]

In the introduction to a collection of poems by Pearse, MacDonagh
and Plunkett that he edited in the 1960s, Desmond Ryan recalled: 'If
we do nothing else', said Pearse, much amused by his jest, as he sat
revising his writings in the early spring of 1916, 'we will rid Ireland of
three *bad* poets!' They were not bad, but compared to their contemporaries they were not especially talented and would probably have been
forgotten had it not been for the dramatic end to their lives that added
such significance and poignancy to some of their work. MacDonagh
would observe that 'Propaganda has rarely produced a great poem. A
great hymn, whether of religion or patriotism, is rarely other than the
cry of a poet calling to his God or his country as if he alone experienced the emotion that he sings.'[21] Yet in truth, in their poetry as well
as their lives, the three of them were becoming propagandists for their
own myth.

Pearse was by now possessed by what Yeats would describe as 'the
vertigo of self-sacrifice'.[22] His Irish poem that he translated as
'Renunciation' would be seen in Ireland, said William Irwin Thompson,
'as an expression of an unflinching devotion to an ideal, a self-sacrifice
of the noblest order . . . But for those of us not involved in Irish patriotism, the fear of failure expressed in the first quatrain is like the religious
fanatic's fear of sin . . . humanity and sanctity are opposed, violently
opposed.'[23]

> Naked I saw thee,
> O beauty of beauty,
> And I blinded my eyes
> For fear I should fail.

In other verses he renounces the vision's music and the sweetness of its
mouth. 'I have turned my face / To this road before me', it ends, 'To the
deed that I see / And the death I shall die.'

If Pearse was bent on finding a way to exit heroically from a life that
was crushing him with desires and disappointments, Plunkett was well
on the way to finding a better death than the painful, debilitating

respiratory failure that often seemed imminent. 'The Spark', written in June 1915, showed that after many years of fighting to live, he had decided to fight to die.

> Because I used to shun
> Death and the mouth of hell
> And count my battle won
> If I should see the sun
> The blood and smoke dispel

He used to pray to live, to be freed and given strength, but now, recognising the shame of denying 'my soul's divinest flame', he would 'seek to die' at the hands of others, and to achieve that 'No more shall I spare blood.'

Unlike his tormented friend Pearse and his terminally ill friend Plunkett, MacDonagh had a happy life, yet it was undermined by his craving for an all-consuming passion. "How many of our own patriots . . . might never have taken to guns had the muse been kinder?"[24] asked Terence de Vere White once, in a question particularly relevant to MacDonagh. Yeats had written of him in 1909 that he was

> a man with some literary faculty which will probably come to nothing through lack of culture and encouragement . . . In England this man would have become remarkable in some way, here he is being crushed by the mechanical logic and commonplace eloquence which give power to the most empty mind, because, being 'something other than human life,' they have no use for distinguished feeling or individual thought . . . within his own mind this mechanical thought is crushing as with an iron roller all that is organic.[25]

A revised version of his tribute to Willie Rooney – now called 'Of a Poet Patriot' – would serve as a fitting farewell to the world for a man who believed himself to be a good poet but not good enough to achieve immortality. MacDonagh was an artist manqué who, unlike his friends, had no desire to die, but, being unable quite to make art out of life, he made his life into art.

> His songs were a little phrase
> Of eternal song,
> Drowned in the harping of lays
> More loud and long
> His deed was a single word,
> Called out alone
> In a night when no echo stirred
> To laughter or moan.
> But his songs new souls shall thrill,
> The loud harps dumb,
> And his deed the echoes fill
> When the dawn is come.

The three poets did not abandon literature, but increasingly they made it a servant of their ever more extreme politics. Plunkett took over the *Irish Review* in June 1913: the lockout began at the end of August and fell on fertile ground in 17 Marlborough Road. For the previous year, Gerry had been buying Labour weekly papers regularly in Tom Clarke's shop in Parnell Street, along with *Irish Freedom*. She and Joe were sympathetic to the Dublin poor and horrified by the events of 31 August that MacDonagh had witnessed and that had led to two deaths. On top of this there had been the collapse a couple of days later of two tenements in the slums of Church Street, with seven dead, including two small children, and another eight tenants badly injured. Eleven families were left homeless. This tragedy brought home to those ready to hear that more than 25,000 families lived in dreadful conditions in Dublin, mostly in a single room. Unlike in English cities, little had been done to regulate or clear slums.

The following day, Keir Hardie, the leader of the British Labour Party, was at the funeral of James Nolan, an ITGWU member and one of the two fatal victims of police brutality on 31 August. The procession of more than 10,000 stretched for over a mile. Larkin was absent, being in a police court on a variety of charges, but he was released the following week and resumed his energetic leadership. Plunkett went to him with a contribution for the striking workers and had it rejected. The following day, in a speech, Larkin referred to this, adding, 'His people have rotten tenements.' Plunkett was very upset about this, for he thought his family property solely suburban houses. He would never know that one reason his mother was so hysterically anti-Larkin was that she had secretly bought a four-storey house with an adjacent block of flats in Upper Abbey Street, which were let in single rooms.

'The sole objects of government', Plunkett wrote that month,

> should be the peace and prosperity in the fullest sense of all the individuals composing the nation – that all other objects, such as the furtherance of law and order, the cultivation of relations with other powers and peoples, the extension of boundaries, the building up of trade, the development of resources, the subjection of enemies, the pursuit of the arts, sciences and philosophies, the promulgation of ideals, should entirely and completely subserve those first named.

But

> the destinies, the habits of life and labour, the ideals and religion of the individuals composing the nation should as far as possible be their own free choice. This alone is liberty . . . The collectivist theory of government makes the state (as embodied in the government) more important than the governed – which is precisely the fallacy of oligarchy and aristocracy.

So Plunkett was not to be tempted by Marxism, but nonetheless, in October 1913, he gave pride of place in the *Irish Review* to an article he had requested from James Connolly, whose punchy, lucid writing he admired. Called 'Labour in Dublin', this was a skilful appeal to an intellectual audience that drew on international history for justifications of sympathetic strikes and appealed to the higher instincts of his audience: the ITGWU was painfully evolving, among its members, a higher conception of mutual life, a realisation of their duties to each other and to society at large, and are thus building for the future in a way that ought to gladden the hearts of all lovers of the race. In contrast to the narrow, restricted outlook of the capitalistic class, and even of certain old-fashioned trade-unionism, with their perpetual insistence upon 'rights', this union insists, almost fiercely, that there are no rights without duties, and the first duty is to help one another. This is indeed revolutionary and disturbing, but not half as much as would be a practical following out of the moral precepts of Christianity.[26]

Plunkett was focused on trying to help bring about industrial peace. In October, Tom Kettle, Pearse's university friend, Irish Party MP for East Tyrone until in 1910 he resigned his seat to take up the chair of Economics in UCD, wrote articles in the *Freeman's Journal* criticising both sides in the dispute and set up an Industrial Peace Committee. Kettle, a brilliant, decent man who, though prone to melancholia and drunkenness, was seen by many admirers as a likely post-Home Rule prime minister of Ireland, was far more even-handed than most. Faced with disorder on the streets, reports of strike waves in Britain, Europe and the United States, and the syndicalism they associated with industrial anarchy being preached by the charismatic Larkin, the middle classes were closer to Ma's point of view than that of her children.

Kettle became Chairman and his friend Thomas Dillon, Gerry's fiancé, and Plunkett were co-secretaries, for which Plunkett had the priceless qualification of having a motorbike with a sidecar – an invaluable asset during a transport strike. When the Committee went public, only two businessmen were on the platform, which also included two Catholic priests, a Protestant clergyman, Padraic Colum, Thomas MacDonagh and Joe Plunkett. 'If there was anything wrong with Kettle's platform,' said Padraig Yeates, 'it was that it was too literary in composition, theatrical even.'[27] Other members included Rabbi Hertzog, MacDonagh's old friend Francis Sheehy-Skeffington and W.B. Yeats.

There were several meetings and the committee laboured hard to bring people together, but they were meeting the usual fate of peacemakers in having all sides turn on them. In an emotional, hand-wringing, plague-on-both-their-houses, well-informed and fair-minded article in the *Review* in November called 'The Agony of Dublin', Tom Kettle spoke of how for eight weeks Dublin's citizens had been forced to watch 'a very apocalypse of waste, impoverishment and social disorganisation' with the prospect of 'a tempest of violence'. The workers 'have talked wildly, and acted calmly; the employers have talked calmly, and acted wildly'.

In England, he concluded, public opinion was the ultimate tribunal that decided the outcome of industrial wars. Since in Ireland, as a result of political calamities, public opinion hardly exists, let us create it.' Unfortunately for the peace committee, public opinion was being stirred up by the AOH and other Catholic activists enraged by an offer from supporters in London to take in and look after strikers' starving 'kiddies'. In Dublin, as the English Marxist suffragist Dora Montefiore and her helpers attempted to shepherd children to the boat, they found themselves besieged by hysterical crowds. Ma, who was convinced there was a sinister plot to convert the children to Protestanism, visited Liberty Hall, the ITGWU headquarters, to protest against the kiddies scheme and was thrown out. She marched off to the nearby Westland Row presbytery and extracted from priests details of some of the children 'rescued' from Montefiore and lodged a formal complaint of kidnapping, which had one of the women arrested. Larkin denounced the protesters, saving

> some of his most scathing comment for Countess Plunkett
> and her friend Mrs Bridget Dudley Edwardes* [*sic*]. She
> had earlier announced that she was organising accommo-
> dation in Dublin to take 150 children, rather than see them
> sent to England. 'Women of the type of Lady Plunkett and
> Mrs Edwardes and their class never knew until now that
> there were slums and poverty in Dublin. They have their
> cat shows and hang about on the skirts of the so-called
> nobility, and they look at the workers with scorn.'[28]

* My grandmother.

True to form,

> Ma became involved in all this and got up a committee to
> save the workers' children from being proselytised. She
> bought Sandymount Castle, an empty boys' school, and
> put in a matron of some kind. Her committee was supposed
> to get the workers' children and house them there but as
> far as I could make out, not a single striking worker's child
> ever arrived there.

Her son's work was little more productive, for, despite Kettle's best
efforts, intransigence ruled and no one wanted to listen to a peace
committee: hunger would break the strike by January 1914. But by
then, with the foundation of the Irish Volunteers in November 1913,
six of the Seven had for the first time found common cause. The poets
were on the march, and the IRB, which Clarke and Mac Diarmada now
rigidly controlled and of which Ceannt was a faithful servant, at last
had an army to infiltrate. Observing from the sidelines was James
Connolly, the proponent of socialist internationalism, whom events
were driving into the arms of advanced nationalism.

Chapter Seven

JAMES CONNOLLY[1]

The men and women of your class, tell them their wrongs and yours,
Plant in their hearts that hatred deep that suffers and endures,
And treasure up each deed of wrong, each scornful word and look
Inscribe it in the memory, as others in a book,
And wait and watch through galling years the ripening of time
Yet deem to strike before that hour were worse than folly – crime.

From 'The Legacy' by James Connolly, 1914

At birth – as throughout his life – James Connolly would be by far the poorest of the Seven. Clarke's father had the financial security of a British soldier, Mac Diarmada's was a carpenter as well as a small farmer, Ceannt's was a policeman, Pearse's a successful stone-mason, MacDonagh's a teacher and Plunkett's parents were rentiers. Born on 5 June 1868, the youngest of three sons, Connolly was brought up in the Cowgate, a grim Edinburgh slum in 'little Ireland'. Like most of their neighbours, his parents, John Connolly, whose job was shovelling up and carting away dung from the streets, and Mary McGinn, who had been a domestic servant, were desperately poor Irish Catholic immigrants. With 13,000 families crammed into squalid single rooms, conditions resembled those Connolly would later see in Dublin.

The harshness of the life of the Connolly family was exacerbated by the chronic bronchitis that would plague Mary Connolly from after the birth of her first son to her death thirty years later. James left St Patrick's Catholic Primary School aged eleven in 1879, the year Charles Stewart Parnell was elected president of Michael Davitt's new Irish National Land League. The following year Parnell would be elected Chairman of the Home Rule Party. This development linked militant obstructionist parliamentary tactics with often violent agrarian popular activism. But in November 1880 the popular ostracism of the landlord and land-agent Captain Charles Boycott gave a dangerous non-violent weapon to the cause of radical land reform.

Connolly joined the *Edinburgh Evening News*, where his elder brother John was an apprentice compositor, running errands and cleaning the ink from the mighty print rollers. John joined the British Army and went to India; James got the sack because a factory inspector declared him too young for the job he was doing. He worked for two years as a baker's apprentice from early morning to late at night: 'Often I would pray fervently that I would find the place burnt down when I got there,' he would tell his daughter Nora. His health was not up to such a punishing routine, and it gave him nightmares, so he moved to a mosaic tiling factory. A voracious reader, he strained his eyes reading by the embers, using charred sticks as pencils; he would grow up with poor eyesight as well as – like Pearse – an eye defect. His literate and intelligent father did not discourage him.

At fourteen, he lied about his age and enlisted under a false name, probably – like his brother – in the King's Liverpool Regiment, which had a dark green uniform, a harp surmounting the crown on the badge and played Irish airs during marches. He might have been born in Scotland, but, like many inhabitants of the Cowgate, he thought of himself as Irish. 'If you knew what the newspapers call the [lights and shadow] of Scottish character as well as I do,' he wrote to his Irish-born future wife in 1889, 'you would like them less. Such affectedly pious God-fearing hypocritical skunks as the majority of them are not to be found on this side of the globe. Thank God. But when you do find a good old Scotsman or woman they are pure gold.'[2]

His battalion was sent to Cork at the end of July 1882 after a tumultuous period in Ireland. Parnell and three colleagues had not long since been released after being imprisoned under the 1881 Irish Coercion Act they had resisted. Davitt too was in jail, having had his ticket-of-leave under his 1870 fourteen-year sentence voided. Just a few days after Parnell and Gladstone had agreed what was known as the Kilmainham treaty, which traded reform for an end to land agitation, had come the Phoenix Park murders of 6 May 1882.

Connolly's battalion would remain in Ireland until 1889 to help keep the peace during a time of frequent unrest, rising crime rates, the imposition of tougher coercion laws, concerted action by tenants against rent levels and the calming effect of a series of land acts. At Westminster, this was a period of high political excitement during which the Liberals split over Home Rule and the *Times* made the allegations about Parnell, the investigation of which would briefly involve Tom Clarke. The battalion left Cork in 1884 for the Curragh and was then based in Dublin from October 1885 until the autumn of 1888, when – with only a few months to serve – Connolly deserted. The likely reason is that his unit was due to go to India in September and he was in love.

We know nothing of his military career except that camaraderie seems to have had little part in it: he came to hate the British Army, a 'veritable moral cesspool corrupting all within its bounds' that exuded a 'miasma of pestilence'. The moral atmosphere of a typical barrack room was of the 'most revolting character' and the language of the soldier 'the most bestial conceivable'. Short (five feet six) and with bow legs, probably because of poor nutrition, it is all too likely Connolly was the butt of jokes for his appearance, the stammer it would take him years to conquer, his love of reading and his left-wing views. A regiment containing a high proportion of Liverpudlians, famous for being gregarious drinkers and merciless jokers, was not a friendly environment for a high-minded teetotaller who responded badly to mockery. As an adult, Connolly was thin-skinned, irascible and quick to take offence, as was clear even in his few surviving letters to his future wife, Lillie, in the first flush of their relationship.[3]

Lillie Reynolds, who came from a Protestant Wicklow family, found a job in domestic service in Dublin through the Church of Ireland's Girls' Friendly Society. Gentle and well-spoken, she was better educated than Connolly, whom she would help with his grammar and punctuation in his early writing days. Hired as a maid by the prosperous Wilsons of Merrion Square, she was highly regarded and promoted to assistant governess. Her prospects were good until she fell in love with the young soldier she met while waiting for a tram and agreed to marry. After he had deserted from the army and borrowed enough money from her to go back to Scotland, she abandoned her job to join him in Perth. 'When I left for Scotland to be married I was the happiest girl of my acquaintance,' she would say later, but that mood was dashed when it turned out that James had gone to Dundee and had no intention of coming to see her. The letter he had received from her, he said, instead of being as 'effusive and affectionate' as usual, was

> like unto a summons for rent. I was rather amused to see that you treated my proposal to visit me in all seriousness. Do you think me 'daft' or what. I am getting vexed you see. I mean to say, I wish to tell you that I cannot bring myself to ask to meet you Tuesday, or any other day for some time yet.

Dundee was only twenty miles from Perth, and there was a train service, but what was preventing him from visiting Lillie was what he referred to in another letter as the 'necessary habiliments'. A brilliant autodidact who believed he had found in socialism the answer to all the problems of the world, Connolly was humiliated enough by being in and out of awful jobs, including that of manure carter, but, always smarting from imagined as well as real slights, he put his pride ahead of Lillie's need to see the person for whom she had sacrificed her security. He was 'afraid of shaming' her, though he loved 'the girl who could lower herself to be seen speaking to one who has descended so low in the social scale'.

Connolly could be affectionate: sometimes he signed himself 'Your loving Jim', and he appreciated Lillie's 'sweet face and loveable ways', but he was frequently carping and cross. When he was back in Edinburgh and Lillie working in London, her failure in April 1890 to adhere strictly to his instructions about when to return to Perth to establish residency for their forthcoming wedding made him furious: 'Lil This is a letter full of reproach, abuse, and scolding. This is not a love letter. This is a letter written by me, James Connolly to my intended wife, Lillie Reynolds, on the style and after the manner of an old husband of nine or ten years standing.'

She would need all her 'good nature' before she had finished reading it, he warned her. He was 'very angry indeed, because of your seeming or real carelessness of the interests of yourself and your humble serv- ant, and because of your sublime ignorance of the most common and well known facts and thirdly for so easily forgetting what you have been told was necessary to remember'. Having set her right about what she had done wrong and should now do right, he had 'another distasteful job'. He had applied for a dispensation to marry a Protestant:

> I am informed it can only be granted on condition you promise never to interfere with my observance of my religion (funny idea, isn't it) and that any children born of the union should have to be baptised in the Catholic Church. Now, I know you won't like that especially as the priest will call on you to ask you. But, Lillie, if your brother attended chapel for nearly a year for the sake of his sweetheart, surely you will not grudge speaking for a quarter of an hour to a priest especially as the fulfilment of these promises rest with ourselves in the future. Though I'd like you to keep them.[4]

The letter was signed just 'Yours Jim'.

Although Lillie was anxious to please and was the giver in a relationship with a driven self-centred taker, she was not a doormat, and her 'very indignant' answer elicited what he called 'a love letter', even if it was double-edged:

> This is a letter written by me Jim to the nicest girl between here and anywhere, to tell her that all her mistakes, her wilfulness, her troublesomeness, only make me love her the more, and make me more than ever determined to have the possession of a delightful bundle of contradictions all to myself.

In the last letter before the marriage there was a portent of how their future would be.

> By the way if we get married next week I shall be unable to go to Dundee as I promised as my fellow-workmen in the job are preparing for a strike on the end of this month, for a reduction in the hours of labour. As my brother and I are

ringleaders in the matter it is necessary we should be on the ground. If we were not we should be looked upon as blacklegs, which the Lord forbid.

Both twenty-two, they were married in Perth on 30 April 1890, and went to live near the Cowgate.

Connolly had attended socialist meetings during his year in Dundee, where he had met the gifted speaker and writer John Leslie, a friend of his brother's, who appreciated his seriousness and courage. 'I noticed the silent young man as a very interested and constant attendant at the open-air meetings,' said Leslie after Connolly's death,

accompanied by his uncle whom I knew to be one of the Old Guard of the Fenian movement, and once when a sustained and virulent personal attack was being made on myself and when I was almost succumbing to it, Connolly sprang upon the stool, and to say the least of it, retrieved the situation. I never forgot it. The following week he joined our organisation, and it is needless to say what an acquisition he was. We shortly had five or six more or less capable propagandists and certainly cut a figure in Edinburgh, but with voice and pen Connolly was ever in the forefront.[5]

Leslie was the first secretary of the recently founded Scottish Socialist Federation (SSF) and Connolly's brother John the secretary of the Edinburgh branch. The British Social Democratic Federation, founded by Henry Hyndman, had split in 1884 when socialist purists like William Morris and Marx's son-in-law Edward Aveling – who disapproved of the organisation's policy of working with political parties to secure reform – set up the breakaway Socialist League. The SSF's purpose was to accommodate Scottish socialists who held dual membership and sought unity.

A generous-spirited man of wide reading and considerable gifts as a writer and speaker, Leslie was an ideal mentor. Through contact with him and his associates, Connolly had the opportunity to apply his logical, quick and powerful mind to the disciplined study of Marxist theory and its application to what were his twin preoccupations of Irish nationalism and social inequality. At study groups, where he acquired a thorough grounding in such socialist literature as Marx's *Communist Manifesto* and *Capital* and the writings of Frederick Engels, Connolly, unlike most of his contemporaries, did not avoid the difficult challenges; he had a natural gift for languages and learned French and German to read otherwise inaccessible works.

Wedded to the pursuit of a classless society without poverty, where free and equal citizens co-operated for the greater good, Connolly became a bitter ideological enemy of imperialism and capitalism. He was pragmatic about involvement in politics: when in 1893 the socialist MP Keir Hardie set up the Independent Labour Party (ILP), of which Leslie became Edinburgh secretary, Connolly became active in that too. The two organisations benefited each other – the SSF's propaganda brought recruits to the ILP, and the ILP's increasing popular support brought the trade union movement closer to socialism.

In addition to expanding his knowledge through reading and SSF meetings, Connolly was making his name as an efficient organiser and administrator and in 1892 succeeded his brother as secretary of the SSF. He did not fall into the trap of so many of the self-educated and use esoteric language to show off his own erudition: his writing style was trenchant, blunt, vigorous, and spiced up with furious abuse and brutal humour. In 1893, in *Justice* – the journal of the Social Democratic Federation – he reported that the SSF was gaining public support in Edinburgh, a city 'largely composed of snobs, flunkeys, mashers, lawyers, students, middle-class pensioners and dividend-hunters'. Even the working-class seemed to have imbibed 'the snobbish would-be respectable spirit of their "betters"'. Yet socialism was becoming so respectable that the SSF intended to set up a branch in Leith, which being an industrial centre had 'its due proportion of sweaters, slave-drivers, rack-renting, slum landlords, shipping-federation agents, and parasites of every description'.

Connolly had not, though, developed an intellectually coherent view on Ireland until Leslie, who was half-Irish, delivered a superb series of lectures from 1892–3 that would later be published as a pamphlet called *The Present Position of the Irish Question*. His primary purpose was to undermine the Irish National League, the Land

League's successor and an adjunct of the IPP, which had supported the Liberals against the ILP in the Edinburgh municipal elections.

Leslie skilfully harnessed the writings of the Young Irelander land reformer James Fintan Lalor to make a socialist analysis: Ireland's problem was not that it was represented in Westminster but that 'the means by which the Irish people must live are in possession of a class, which class will not allow the people to use these means unless by so doing a profit will accrue to this class'. In his view, the great lost opportunity was the alternative to the Gladstone–Parnell Kilmainham deal. A short, sharp and decisive struggle at that stage would have 'uprooted the poison-tree of landlordism thoroughly and for ever': instead, there had been years of pointless parliamentary struggle over land bills and Home Rule.

Leslie honoured Parnell, 'a Titan strangled by pygmies', whose death 'brought about a conflict between clerical authority in Ireland and all that is large-hearted and generous in the country'. Now that Parnell was dead, there was no reason for the Irish masses to support his party, all of whose factions were run by 'gintlemen'. Irish working people should not accept rule by capitalists, 'the meanest, the most sordid, the most cowardly, and most despicable class that ever dominated society'. Instead, they should

> declare, as Fintan Lalor did, that the emancipation of their class from economic bondage means the emancipation from all bondage; that the interests of their class are paramount and before the interests of all other classes in society; if they refuse to be any longer the mere pawns in the great chess-game of the lay and clerical State-gamblers for power and place, then they will clasp hands with the workingmen's parties of all other countries, they will come into the great International movement for relative economic freedom that is pulsating through the world today.

He emphasised that to ally themselves with the Socialist party would merely be to 'join hands with the English party that hates the English exploiting classes as deeply as do the Irish themselves hate them'. It was wrong that 'the Alpha and Omega of the Irish Question consisted in the hoisting of the green and gold banner above the old Parliament House in Dublin': the problem was private property.

It was Leslie's arguments that would decisively move Connolly away not just from Catholicism but from the nationalism he had imbibed in 'little Ireland' and from the patriotic publications churned out by A.M. and T.D. Sullivan. In July 1894, it was clear in a letter he wrote to Keir Hardie in his capacity as secretary of the Central Edinburgh branch of the ILP that Connolly had fully accepted Leslie's arguments. 'As an Irishman who has always taken a keen interest in the advanced movements in Ireland', he said, he knew that being middle-class, both factions in the Irish Party were unfriendly to the Labour movement.

> Their advanced attitude upon the land question is simply an accident arising out of the exigencies of the political situation, and would be dropped to-morrow if they did not realise the necessity of linking the Home Rule agitation to some cause more clearly allied to their daily wants than a mere embodiment of national sentiment of the people.

He suggested Hardie should address a meeting in Dublin in 'rebellious, anti-monarchial' terms and attack 'the fleecings of both landlord and capitalist, and the hypocrisy of both political parties'. He could then get a resolution passed 'expressing the sympathy of the Irish people with the Labour movement in Britain, and, as Dublin is the very heart of Parnellism, you would force the hand of Redmond and his clique'.

Old enmities were still intact in October, though, when Connolly was chosen to contest a ward in the city council elections. He had been steadily improving as a public speaker, having in Leslie's words conquered his stammer 'by an effort of will'. The open-air meetings, at which he denounced Conservatives and Liberals (and their Irish National League supporters) as people of property, were well-attended, and he won 14 per cent of the vote. He wrote of his opponents' tactics in the *Labour Chronicle*, an SSF-supporting journal in which, under the pseudonym 'R. Ascal', he wrote a monthly column called 'Plain Talk': Irish Catholics had been told 'that Mr Connolly was a Freethinker, who wanted to overthrow the Church'; 'old Scotch women of both sexes' had been told that he was 'an Irish Papist who wanted to introduce the Scarlet Woman'; and Home Rulers had been wooed by calling in support every leader 'who could be induced to sell his name, and voice, and birthrights for the ill-smelling pottage of Liberal promises'.

Standing in the same ward in April 1895 in the Poor Law elections, he won the same percentage of the vote and was roundly defeated by a local priest. But by then he was looking for a route out of Edinburgh. Always intolerant of those he considered knaves or fools, he was impatient about squabbling within the SSF about its relationship with the ILP, angry about complaints about Hardie communicating with him directly and he was hardly able to feed his wife and daughters Mona and Nora.

In the harsh winter of 1894–5, the city council had stopped using private contractors for refuse collection, and Connolly had lost his job. He opened a cobblers' shop, advertising it in the SSF journal with the ringing 'Socialists Support One Another'. Unfortunately, he proved to be both hopeless at business and unable to mend shoes. His political work, which included organising public lectures by socialist luminaries, gave him only a pittance and an attempt to secure paid engagements as a lecturer failed.

Lillie was pregnant again and Connolly was desperate enough to apply to the government of Chile for assistance with emigration, but Leslie persuaded him to await the result of a special appeal in December's *Justice*. 'Here is a man among men,' wrote Leslie.

> I may say that very few men have I met deserving of greater love and respect than James Connolly.
>
> I know the movement in Edinburgh to its centre, and I say that no man has done more for the movement than Connolly, if they have done as much. Certainly nobody has dared one half what he has dared in the assertion of his principles. Of his ability I need only say he is the most able propagandist in every sense of the word that Scotland has turned out. And because of it, and for his intrepidity, he is today on the verge of destitution and out of work. And we

all know what this means for the unskilled workman, as Connolly is.

Was there 'a comrade in Glasgow, Dundee, or anywhere else who could secure a situation for one of the best and most self-sacrificing men in the movement . . . an unskilled labourer, a life-long total abstainer, sound in wind and limb. Married, with a young family, and as his necessities are therefore very great, so he may be had cheap.'

The only response came from the Dublin Socialist Club, which offered him a job as its paid organiser at a weekly wage of £1. A third daughter was born in March and in May 1896, with the help of a subscription raised by Edinburgh friends, the Connolly family and his books and press cuttings moved to Dublin. At this time, Tom Clarke was about to enter his thirteenth year in jail, Pearse was founding the National Literary Society, MacDonagh was beginning his priestly training, Ceannt was studying hard for his school exams, Mac Diarmada was struggling to become an apprentice teacher and Plunkett was making the best of yet another governess. At the time, none of them had any more interest in the urban proletariat than Connolly had in the cultural revolution that was sweeping through the Irish middle classes. When in Ireland, he had been isolated in barracks. He did not know the country.

Lillie would later say that her time in Edinburgh was the best of her life. They moved several times, but, although always very poor, they had for much of the time had enough space and money for Connolly to have his few friends in to sit around the kitchen table, drink the tea provided by Lillie and argue about socialism. Now they were in one room in a stinking tenement that was worse than anything they had endured in Scotland. It was a world whose denizens Desmond Ryan described as

> cap-crowned, livid, hopeless, half-fed workers with lined faces and rotting teeth and casts in their eyes, their swarming children and betimes drunken wives, no book worth reading in their sorry homes and little romance save a picture of Parnell or Emmet or a red light before a statue of th e Virgin or Christ.[6]

Where the Connolly family lived, the floor was bare boards with strips of lino between the beds, water had to be carried in a bucket from the yard and cooking was done on a single gas ring. Lillie retained her self-respect and kept the room, the children and herself looking as good as possible. According to Nora,

> she looked so much nicer than the other mothers in the big house where they lived. She was so small and young [she and Mona] had decided to call her 'little mother'. She was always so clean and her brown hair looked so nice piled on top her head, with the little curls dancing at her neck. Then she had such a nice face – it was not red and dirty like some of the other mothers – it was white, and soft, and clean.[7]

What helped was that her husband was full of energy, purpose and optimism. As he had once told a visitor to Edinburgh, he believed that once socialism had taken root in Ireland it would grow more rapidly there than anywhere else,[8] and he threw himself into making this happen, despite unpromising omens. In 1894, as Connolly had urged, Keir Hardie had spoken in Dublin and launched the ILP with initial success, but soon there had been a split, enthusiasm had evaporated and the Dublin branch had dissolved and been reborn as the tiny Dublin Socialist Club. At their first meeting, in a pub where five of the eight present drank lemonade, the group yielded to the insistence of their strong-minded new organiser that it be renamed the Irish Socialist Republican Party (ISRP). In a whirlwind of activity, Connolly set in motion socialist education classes, lectures and public meetings, one of which was broken up when his accent so infuriated a Dubliner that Connolly was interrupted by a barrage of cabbage-stalks and cries of 'You're not an Irishman!'

The elaborate manifesto that Connolly wrote and the IRSP would publish in September was mainly inspired by the Social Democratic Federation. It was headed with an aphorism from the French revolutionary Camille Desmoulins – 'The great appear great because we are on our knees: let us rise' – which Connolly had borrowed from the masthead of the *Labour Chronicle*. Aims included 'public ownership by the Irish people of the land and instruments of production distribution and exchange'. Immediate political objectives included the nationalisation of railways and canals; the establishment of state banks issuing loans at cost; a graduated income tax; state pensions for the aged, infirm, widows and orphans; free maintenance for children; a forty-eight-hour working week; a minimum wage; extension of public ownership; free education; and universal suffrage. In deference to the nationalism of those he was trying to convert, it also denounced the 'subjection of one nation to another, as of Ireland to the authority of the British Crown', and called for an 'Irish Socialist Republic'. This was a novel idea that Connolly developed in three articles in the ILP's weekly, *Labour Leader*, designed to persuade British Marxists to abandon their belief that Home Rule for Ireland was a necessary stage before the proletariat took over throughout the British Empire. 'The interests of labour all the world over are identical, it is true,' he said, 'but it is also true that each country had better work out its own salvation on the lines most congenial to its own people.'

Connolly had spent a lot of time in the National Library preparing his arguments as well as a pamphlet of extracts from Fintan Lalor's writings. He based his pleas for flexibility in applying Marxist historical determinism to Ireland on a reading of history that claimed that until the English government had smashed the system there had been a pattern of common ownership of land that was a form of primitive communism. Political nationalists were predominantly bourgeoisie who were prepared to extend ownership to tenants; this would do nothing for labourers, so the only answer was land nationalisation (which was advocated by Michael Davitt) and modernisation. It was an argument based on a view of clan ownership as romantic as Pearse at his most misty-eyed and showed little understanding of the land hunger and yearning for peasant ownership in rural Ireland. Still, even if partly based on false premises, it was a powerful start to his project of hibernicising Marxism.

He also contributed to the *Shan Van Vocht*, which was open to anyone its co-founder Alice Milligan thought would help to unite Irish patriots as Tone wished by substituting 'the common name of Irishman in place of the denominations Protestant, Catholic and Dissenter'. In January 1897, in an article called 'Nationalism and Socialism', Connolly

wrote the famous passage for which he owed so much to the inspiration of John Leslie:

> If you remove the English army tomorrow and hoist the
> green flag over Dublin Castle, unless you set about the
> organisation of the socialist republic, your efforts would be
> in vain. England would still rule you. She would rule you
> through her capitalists, through her landlords, through her
> financiers, through the whole array of commercial and
> industrial institutions she has planted in this country and
> watered with the tears of our mothers and the blood of our
> martyrs. England would still rule you to your ruin, even
> while your lips offered hypocritical homage at the shrine of
> that Freedom whose cause you betrayed.

Alice Milligan sent her young brother Ernest to meet Connolly, which
resulted in the setting up of a short-lived Belfast branch of the ISRP.
The ISRP would publish his *Labour Leader* and *Shan Van Vocht* articles
as a booklet called *Erin's Hope: The End and the Means*, which helped
boost his reputation.

But poverty kept getting in the way. After a strike in the building
trade, at a time when Lillie was pregnant again, Connolly's wages dried
up, Lillie pawned her last treasure – a tiny gold watch – and, although
Connolly was only twenty-eight, malnourishment left him too weak to
do heavy labouring, the only work he could find. It was Lillie who
provided their meagre rations. She took Ina, who was born in
November, to show her old employers, who – according to custom –
put money in the baby's hand. Lillie was happy, but Connolly was
irate: 'To use my child for charity is more than I can bear.'[9]
Henceforward, she volunteered no information about how she kept
them eating, which during the bad times was mostly with the help of
local women as poor as herself.

Connolly would leave Ireland for America in September 1903
disappointed and bitter with the meagre fruits of seven years of unstint-
ing work and sacrifice. Yes, there were some impressive achievements.
He had made an impact on Dublin life and had made some influential
friends, not least the egregious Maud Gonne, who was acquainted

with Alice Milligan's circle, and had written in January 1897 to the ISRP asking to meet Connolly. She had agreed to speak at a meeting of protest on the eve of the celebrations for Queen Victoria's Diamond Jubilee. Gonne, who was as violent in her right-wing opinions as she was in her radical nationalism, changed her mind when she discovered the politics of the ISRP. Yeats wrote in his journal:

> I find Maud Gonne at her hotel talking to a young working-man who looks very melancholy. She had offered to speak at one of the regular meetings of his Socialist society about Queen Victoria, and he has summoned what will be a great meeting in the open air.
>
> She has refused to speak, and he says that her refusal means his ruin, as nobody will ever believe that he had any promise at all. When he has left without complaint or anger, she gives me very cogent reasons against the open-air meeting, but I can think of nothing but the young man and his look of melancholy. He has left his address, and presently, at my persuasion, she drives to his tenement, where she finds him and his wife and children crowded into a very small space – perhaps there was only one room, and moved by the sight, promises to speak.[10]

In their reckless physical courage and love of the flamboyant gesture, Gonne and Connolly were natural allies: together they planned what would be the ISRP's most dramatic contribution to Irish life. She provided black flags (the symbol of the unemployed) embroidered in white with statistics of famine deaths and emigration during Victoria's reign given her by Connolly and hired a window on the chosen route from which to throw onto a large screen lantern slides of eviction scenes and Irish patriots who had been executed or died in prison.

On Jubilee Day, a workers' band playing a funeral march led a procession, at the front of which was a handcart draped like a hearse bearing a large black coffin made by an ISRP member on which was inscribed 'British Empire'. Gonne and Yeats were at a convention of the '98 Commemoration Committee in City Hall, and when the music was heard she suggested all delegates join the procession, as she and

Yeats, dispensing flags, did along with several others. When the police used batons to disperse the crowd and block the procession from crossing O'Connell Bridge, Connolly ordered that the coffin be thrown into the River Liffey, shouting 'Here goes the coffin of the British Empire.'

Connolly was arrested and the lantern show interrupted by another baton charge: angry crowds rampaged down Sackville Street smashing the windows that had Jubilee decorations. 'Further clashes between police and crowds left Gonne exultant and laughing,' reported Yeats:

> I read in the morning papers that many have been wounded; some two hundred heads have been dressed at the hospitals; an old woman killed by baton blows, or perhaps trampled under the feet of the crowd; and that two thousand pounds' worth of decorated plate-glass windows have been broken.[11]

Gonne visited Lillie to tell her about Connolly, sent him breakfast in the Bridewell police station, engaged a lawyer to defend him (which annoyed him because it meant he could not speak in court) and paid his fine. 'Bravo! All my congratulations to you,' she wrote to him. 'You may have the satisfaction of knowing that you saved Dublin from the humiliation of an English jubilee without a public meeting of protestation.'

Such excitements were few. There would be another outing with Gonne in late 1899 in support of the Boers, which involved Connolly driving a wagon with protestors through a police cordon. Seán O'Casey watched as 'A stout, short, stocky man, whose face was hidden by a wide-awake hat, was driving them . . . and with them was a young woman with long lovely yellow hair, smiling happily, like a child out on her first excursion.' And in 1900, along with Arthur Griffith, he was injured by police batons in a protest against Queen Victoria's visit to Ireland.

Connolly was elected by the United Labourers Union to the Dublin Trades Council, but lost heavily when he stood in 1902 and 1903 as a Labour candidate for Dublin city council. Most of those years were spent on the ceaseless labour of speaking and writing and organising protests. In 1898 there was a rare rural visit: he reported on a famine in Kerry for a Scottish socialist newspaper, and then, with the help of £50 donated by Keir Hardie, there was the foundation of the ISRP's paper, the *Workers' Republic*. It was printed by P.T. Daly, the ISRP sympathiser whom Clarke would replace on the IRB Supreme Council in 1910. Advocating 'an Irish Republic, the abolition of landlordism, wage-slavery, the co-operative organisation of industry under Irish representative governing bodies', it was launched on 14 August 1898 to coincide with the laying of the foundation stone of the '98 memorial. Connolly assailed the Home Rulers for claiming that the United Irishmen had been a 'union of class and creed', for Tone's principles could be realised only in a socialist republic. Tone 'was crucified in life, now he is idolised in death, and the men who push forward most arrogantly to burn incense at the altar of his fame are drawn from the very class who, were he alive today, would hasten to repudiate him as a dangerous malcontent'.

The *Workers' Republic* collapsed in October; revived the following year, it was printed by Connolly on a small hand-press that was broken in a police raid after the pro-Boer protest. Back in business again in May 1900, there were several more crises, as there were in Connolly's domestic life. Moira was born in January 1899 and Roderick in 1901, and although the family now had a tiny cottage the comrades rarely came up with Connolly's wages and he was incapable of holding down manual jobs. Still, he made some money writing articles and giving lectures around Scotland, England and, after September 1902, America. Between 1900 and 1916, Connolly would be separated from his family for a total of more than four years.

His impecuniousness had much to do with his uncompromising ideology and his difficult personality. At this period he seldom had more than a tiny number of followers: few Irish nationalists would tolerate socialism, and few socialists outside Ireland had any affinity for nationalism. Keir Hardie and the ILP lost sympathy after hearing that he was leading mobs 'brandishing the Boer Flag and shouting for an Irish Republic and for the defeat of Britain in the Transvaal.'[12] As Fergus D'Arcy summarised: 'His approach differed from the state socialist Marxism of the Second International, the Leninist orthodoxies of the Third International, and the Marxism of the Social Democratic

Federation.' He became even more absolutist when he came under the influence of the extraordinary Daniel De Leon, a brilliant, egotistical, intolerant intellectual from South America who had studied in Europe and in the 1870s settled in the United States, where in the early 1890s he became the de facto leader of the Socialist Labor Party (SLP).

A proponent of the syndicalist or 'one big union' movement, De Leon believed this should be achieved through 'dual unionism', which would involve creating socialist industrial unions subordinate to an ideologically pure party as rivals of the existing craft unions. In his revision in 1902 of his *Erin's Hope* for publication in the United States, Connolly showed he had switched from social democratic reformism to the hard-line sectarianism of De Leon: 'No revolutionist can safely invite the co-operation of men or classes whose ideals are not theirs and whom, therefore, they may be compelled to fight at some future critical stage.'

In addition to his increasing ideological unorthodoxy and absolutism there was his oversensitivity and aggression. Many people admired Connolly, only to fall out with him because he gave no ground, was vicious when criticised, yet brutally castigated comrades who stepped out of line or failed to work hard enough. He would admit that 'I have such an unfortunate knack, as you know, of saying things that turn my best friends into enemies.'[13] 'He cares for nothing but the cause,' Lillie told Maud Gonne. But while she was devoted and said she 'would not have him otherwise' and would always support him unstintingly,[14] she was exceptional.

De Leon admired Connolly's work and had published some *Workers' Republic* articles in *The People**, the SLP paper he edited. He followed this up with an invitation to come on a lecture tour, offering travelling expenses and a wage. His twin objectives were for Connolly to persuade Irish emigrants to forget about Home Rule and vote socialist and to return home ideologically purified. Connolly arrived in New York in mid-September 1902 and was described by *The New York*

---

* After a split in the SLP in 1899 and a tussle over the paper, the De Leon faction's paper became known as *The Weekly People* and then *The Daily People* and later became *Weekly* again. Although the original title went out of existence in 1901, it seems simpler here to call it *The People*.

Times as 'an Irish Socialist agitator': he was welcomed by a large audience on his first booking and a resolution was passed welcoming him cordially on his mission 'to destroy the influence of the Irish Home Rulers and the bourgeoisie in Ireland, and their allies who trade on the Irish vote in this country to the economic detriment of the Irish working men in this country'. His gruelling cross-country tour lasted three-and-a-half months and did not improve his temper, especially when he found that even though he was sending money back to the ISRP there were publication delays with the *Workers' Republic*.

'Here am I', he wrote,

> knocking life out of myself, travelling from 200 to 600 miles every day at least, and talking every night, canvassing hard for subscriptions and in order to get them, telling everybody that the paper will appear more regularly in the future than in the past, and you people at home have not the common manliness to try and stand by my word by getting out the paper as promised. You may think it all a joke, but I think that you all ought to be damned well ashamed of yourselves. It is so hard a job for you to get together enough matter to fill a paper once a month – such a terrible strain on your nerves! I am ashamed, heartily ashamed of the whole gang of you.[15]

It was not all sunshine with De Leon either. Connolly fell out with a couple of SLP members, made a complaint about one of them to the party National Executive and wrote in the *People* that the party 'has its full share of the American national disease, swelled head'. Asked at his last meeting what he thought of the United States, he said some positive things about the country and the SLP, but condemned American individualism and described the country as backward in its understanding of class struggle. De Leon responded testily that it was the Old World socialists who needed to get it into their heads that America would be the strategic battleground when it came to the showdown between capitalism and socialism.

In the municipal election shortly after his return home in January 1903, Connolly's vote was halved from the year before. He blamed the idleness of his comrades: others attributed it to his running on a purely socialist platform. He then discovered that much of the subscription money he had painfully collected in America had been deflected to cover losses on the licensed bar that had been set up on the party premises during one of his absences in Britain. When the committee refused to pay a bill to avoid foreclosure on the printing press, he tendered his resignation, and to his dismay it was accepted.

The truth was that some ISRP members were fed up not just with what they saw as Connolly's puritanism, but with his intellectual tyranny. Having accepted with difficulty his brand of social democracy, they were being force-fed the rigid doctrines of De Leon, and none of them was capable of standing up to such a brilliant, articulate and forceful opponent. He rejoined, but the party was tearing itself apart, and Connolly hastened its collapse by failing to see anyone else's point of view and being uncomprehending that they lacked his single-minded commitment to the cause. Moreover, as one biographer put it, he 'could not tolerate the Irish (perhaps human) fondness for blurring issues, for postponing unpleasant decisions, for engaging in humorous chit-chat and when serious political problems had to be settled'.[16]

Connolly thought he had 'squelched the reptiles, but they dissimulated so well that, as you saw, my kindly intention to drag their scalps around as a trophy in the public gaze was frustrated and I have no doubt they will be allowed to crawl back'. He had therefore decided 'that the party here has no longer that exclusive demand on my life which led me in the past to sacrifice my children's welfare for years in order to build it up'. He would earn money on the British circuit and then emigrate to America.

As he put it bitterly in August to William O'Brien, one of the few erstwhile comrades for whom he maintained some respect, it was his 'quondam colleagues' who deserved the 'glory and pride' for that, for their 'willingness to believe ill of me, and to wreck my work, seems to have grown in proportion to the extent I was successful in serving them'. He listed some of his grievances, declared his own conscience clear and said those responsible should be assured that 'no amount of belated praise' would 'sweeten the bitterness of my exile. My career has been unique in many things. In this last it is so also. Men have been driven out of Ireland by the British Government, and by the landlords, but I am the first driven forth by the "Socialists".

He embarked for America from Dublin in September 1903, having been energetically involved in a doctrinal split in the Social Democratic Federation, which resulted in him being appointed for three months as a paid organiser of the new Scottish SLP. He gave this his very best efforts, but the new party never really got off the ground. A cousin in Troy, New York State, sent him his fare, but for now his family had to stay in Dublin. When he left, not a single socialist came to see him off.

Connolly's seven years in America would be marked by familiar domestic and organisational crises. He had acquired some training in Scotland as a linotype operator and had hoped to get work in New York City with the SLP's printers, but without a union card he was unemployable in that capacity anywhere and no one seemed prepared to help him obtain one. Staying with his cousins in Troy, he found a job as an insurance agent, and made enough money to pay for his family to join him and install them in a roomy house in August 1904. Their arrival was blighted because Mona, who was thirteen and the eldest, had died from burns after an accident the day before embarkation. The family could not postpone their journey to go to the funeral and she was buried in a pauper's grave. This was a terrible blow for an exceptionally devoted mother and a loving father, who was mostly absent and who read or wrote when at home, but who when paying attention encouraged the older children to read and think and talk and was tolerant of the small ones at play. Shortly afterwards, Connolly lost his job; from November he stayed in New York with an old ISRP colleague to whom he had become reconciled and took whatever occasional work he could. Lillie and the older girls also earned small sums from sewing and starching. In October 1905, with the help of a socialist foreman, Connolly became a lathe operator for the Singer Sewing Machine Company in Newark ('a pretty bum job'), where he installed his family, and then in New Jersey, to which he commuted.

Intellectually, though, Connolly was still firing on all cylinders. It was principled but reckless in March 1904 to challenge De Leon on his own territory with a letter to the *People* criticising on Marxist grounds the party's views on wages, marriage and religion. He disagreed that wage rises were useless because they would be immediately offset by price rises and that monogamous marriage was outmoded and would disappear in a true socialist society. Though he never admitted it publicly for fear of alienating potential recruits, Connolly had long since ceased to be a believer. 'For myself tho' I have usually posed as a Catholic,' he wrote in 1908 to his good friend John Carstairs Matheson in Glasgow; 'I have not gone to my duty for 15 years, and have not the slightest tincture of faith left.'[17] He nonetheless complained of the paper's increasing antipathy to religion: religion was about the soul and the hereafter; socialism was about the welfare of human in the present. De Leon denounced him in the paper on all fronts, a fiercely divided correspondence followed and the local branch threatened to expel him. Since the *People* would not print his defence, Connolly exacerbated the row by sending to the Scottish SLP's paper a defence that demonstrated what a friend called his 'fine, manly, titanic brutality'. In his absence, De Leon savaged his views at the party convention. The controversy died down and the enmity was contained for the time being.

Even when he was spending fourteen hours a day working and commuting, Connolly made time to write and speak on behalf of the party. He and De Leon still agreed that industrial unionism should be developed under party direction, that industrial unionism mattered as much as political action in overthrowing capitalism and that once the revolution had been achieved the 'one big union' would direct the party. Hence their support for the Industrial Workers of the World (IWW) – or 'Wobblies', as they came to be known – founded in 1905 to promote worker solidarity in the revolutionary struggle to overthrow the employing class through mass action and sympathetic strikes. 'All the actions of our class at the ballot box are in the nature of mere preliminary skirmishes,' wrote Connolly, 'and . . . the conquest of political power by the Working Class waits upon the conquest of economic power and must function through the economic organisation.'

The enmity between Connolly and De Leon took off again almost immediately after the IWW came into being at an SLP meeting in New York with Connolly in the chair and De Leon as the main speaker. 'Though little over fifty years of age,' wrote the Connolly biographer Desmond Greaves (a devoted communist implacably opposed to anarcho-syndicalism in general and De Leon in particular), 'De Leon affected a stoop and slow gait suitable to a man twenty years older. He entered the back of the hall and moved slowly up the side aisle towards the platform.'

When he had traversed two thirds of the distance an admirer noticed him. 'De Leon!' he shouted, and for the remainder of the great man's transit to his place in the sun the hall rocked with cheers and applause. Connolly's voice was drowned, and, experienced speaker though he was, he felt nonplussed and angry. He believed that De Leon had deliberately staged the scene as a personal affront. The ill feeling between the two men began to reawaken.[18]

However, the work went on relentlessly. Connolly not only became a prominent propagandist for the IWW, but in 1906 was organising protests against the arrest of radicals. Elizabeth Gurley Flynn, a remarkable young IWW activist, admirer and friend (who in 1964 as Chairwoman of the American Communist Party would be given a state funeral by the Soviet Union), described him then:

> short, rather stout, a plain-looking man with large black
> moustaches, a very high forehead, and dark sad eyes – a
> man who rarely smiled. A scholar and an excellent writer,
> his speech was marred for American audiences by his thick,
> North of Ireland* accent, with a Scotch burr from his long
> residence in Glasgow.[19]

Fired from his job in 1907 as a troublemaking union agitator, Connolly became even more involved in activism, and moved to a fire-trap New York tenement with his family – which had been augmented by a sixth daughter, Fiona – to earn what would be an uncertain living as an organiser for the IWW's Building and Construction Section. Having a successful track record in wooing Irish members for the SLP and the IWW, and having learned their language, he applied himself to recruiting Italians, which initiated more quarrels with De Leon.

---

* Connolly had two reasons to lie about his place of birth, which in the 1901 census he stated was County Monaghan. One was his desertion from the British Army; the other the xenophobia of the Irish.

Ideologically, Connolly disapproved of what he saw as De Leon's readiness to approve compromises between socialist and capitalist parties in Europe. For his part, on internationalist grounds, De Leon abhorred ethnic socialist groupings and Connolly's heretical view that Marxist teaching must be adapted to the varying cultures and traditions within a nation of immigrants. Both dictatorial, but seeing that characteristic only in each other (Connolly claimed putting too much faith in its leaders was an American trait), their mutual antipathy was becoming almost pathological. Tedious and varied disagreements within the party spilled over into the IWW, their paranoia about each other extended to De Leon believing Connolly to be a Jesuit agent and police spy and Connolly concluding De Leon had been 'purposely doing the work of the capitalist class'. The whole long-drawn-out, dreary and discreditable business would end with Connolly resigning from the SLP and joining the competing reformist Socialist Party of America and De Leon storming out of the IWW to found a doomed rival.

Connolly's sense of Irishness had been intensifying and many of the old wrongs were forgotten: 'as revolutionists', he wrote to a friend, 'the Irish comrades are immeasurably superior to anything I have met in America'. Deciding that to recruit Irish in America to socialism it was important to strengthen the movement in Ireland, he had established in New York for people 'of Irish race and extraction' the Irish Socialist Federation, which he affiliated to the ISRP's successor, the Socialist Party of Ireland (SPI). Its purpose was to explain the history of the class struggle in Ireland, steer members towards revolutionary class-consciousness and secure their help for the socialist movement of Ireland. In 1907 he published *Songs of Freedom by Irish Authors*, in which he explained that 'Until the movement is marked by the joyous, defiant singing of revolutionary songs, it lacks one of the most distinctive marks of a popular revolutionary movement, it is the dogma of a few and not the faith of the multitude.'* From December 1907 he

---

* It included the Richard Brinsley Sheridan translation of 'The Marseillaise', the Labour Party anthem 'The Red Flag', three songs by his old friend John Leslie and nine of his own, for Connolly loved writing doggerel, which included his translation of 'Auf Socialisten', sung at the Seventh Congress of the International in Stuttgart in 1907. 'For Labour's Right' began:

edited and largely wrote *The Harp*, which appeared monthly when he had the money. 'It was a pathetic sight', wrote Elizabeth Flynn, who was an active member of the Irish Socialist Federation, 'to see him standing, poorly clad, at the door of Cooper Union or some other East Side hall, selling his little paper. None of the prosperous professional Irish, who shouted their admiration for him after his death, lent him a helping hand at that time.'[20]

In its incessant calls for unity, *The Harp* demonstrated how the doctrinally pure socialist was becoming much more pragmatic. Connolly did not confine himself to discussing syndicalism, but sought to be constructive in his criticisms of developments in Ireland. When Griffith set up Sinn Féin in 1907, for instance, Connolly wrote approvingly of the doctrine of self-reliance as 'the dependency upon forces outside themselves is emasculating in its tendency, and has been, and will ever be disastrous in its results'. Unlike most socialists, he added, he was in favour of learning Irish (which he made some effort to do). Like Plunkett, he was an enthusiast for Esperanto, but while 'I do believe in the necessity, and indeed the inevitability, of a universal language . . . I do not believe it will be brought about, or even hastened, by smaller races or nations consenting to the extinction of their language.'

As he championed the right of socialists to feel Irish, Connolly denied also that there was any problem in being both a Marxist and a Catholic, making *Socialism Made Easy*, a collection of his *Workers' Republic* and *Harp* articles, a valuable contribution to IWW propaganda that enhanced his own reputation and helped him financially, since it sold in North America, the United Kingdom and Australia. The Socialist Party of America showed its approval by appointing him in June 1908 the party's middle-west organiser with a salary that was adequate and regularly paid. He was away from home for about eleven months lecturing, debating, and generally helping branches to flourish. This was hard on his family, who saw little of him. When he made

Up, brothers, up the drums are beating,
And see on high the banners wave,
Close up our ranks, let no retreating
Be ours whilst earth contains a slave . . .

a rare visit he took his older children to public meetings to hear him speak or sometimes took the family to Socialist Party of America outings where in addition to speeches there would be singing and dancing. Lillie did not enjoy lugging children around in hot weather. 'I can understand her remark', wrote her daughter Ina, 'when we returned from one such picnic: "I'd rather do two days' washing than ever again face such a day's pleasure".'

The Harp continued publication in Connolly's physical absence, now serialising *Labour in Irish History*, which he had been working on for a decade. 'Each country', it explained, 'requires a local or native literature and spoken propaganda translating and explaining its past history and present political developments in the light of the knowledge derived from a study of Socialist classic.' Looking in detail at Irish history from the late seventeenth century, the book showed evidence of wide reading, a perspective that was a welcome challenge to Irish parochialism, an ingenious mind, and the twin imprints of economic determinism and Connolly's own bitter hatred of the middle-class nationalist tradition. Where he wrote of traditional heroes, he gave them an internationalist or Marxist twist as circumstances required. Emmet, for instance, 'the most idolised, the most universally praised of all Irish martyrs', had decreed in his proclamation of a provisional government 'the wholesale confiscation and nationalising of church property' and had banned 'the transfer of all landed property, bonds, debentures, and public securities, until the national government is established and the national will upon them is declared'. Emmet had thus shown his belief that the 'national will' was superior to property rights, and could abolish them at will. (Or, perhaps, as with most revolutionaries, Emmet had shown his belief that his will was the national will.)

'The result of the long drawn out struggle of Ireland', said Connolly,

> has been, so far, that the old chieftainry has disappeared, or through its degenerate descendants has made terms with iniquity, and become part and parcel of the supporters of the established order ... Only the Irish working class remain as the incorruptible inheritors of the fight for freedom in Ireland.

He ignored what did not fit in with his theory, notably nineteenth-century Ulster, its unionist Protestant masses and human nature. The causes of the famine were manifold, not simply the Irish land system. As with nationalist historians, Connolly's villains were wicked, his heroes perfect and his idealisation of the communal paradise that he claimed was early Gaelic civilisation would have done credit to Patrick Pearse. What made *Labour in Irish History* so original, though, was that through his reading and travel it was permeated with ideas that had come from far beyond insular little Ireland. Ending on a syndicalist note, Connolly predicted that 'Irish toilers from henceforward will base their fight for freedom not upon the winning or losing the right to talk in an Irish parliament, but upon their progress toward the mastery of those factories, workshops and farms upon which a people's bread and liberties depend.'

Connolly justified to Matheson how his bad experiences in the SLP had made him realise that

> while our position is absolutely sound in theory, and might be sound in practice if adopted by men of large outlook, yet its practical immediate effects have been the generation of a number of sectarians, narrow-minded doctrinaires, who have erected Socialism into a cult with rigid formulas which one must observe or be damned.

This meant that 'the position we started from needs the corrective of association with Socialists of a less advanced type'. Socialists should henceforward be 'friendly critics and *helpers*' in the Labour move-ment rather than be in 'a separate organisation as hostile critics and enemies'.

Yet although his Socialist Party of America job was, he said, the best he had ever had, he had never liked America, 'this cursed country', and he had convinced himself that there was 'work to be done in Ireland I can do better than most any one'. He had not expected ever to be able to go back to Ireland, he had written in 1905: 'And at any rate I regard Ireland, or at least the Socialist part of Ireland which is all I care for, as having thrown me out, and I do not wish to return like a dog to his vomit.'

Yet from 1908 he was sending a stream of letters to a few old comrades, particularly William O'Brien, in whom he confided that his emigration to America was the biggest mistake of his life and that he was 'dying to go to Ireland'. The publications he sent to Dublin were having an effect, even if it was difficult for some of the less intellectually nimble to adapt to yet another change of direction. The teenage Desmond Ryan had been reading Connolly and had visited the SPI in 1908 to ask what the difference was between their revolutionary socialism and the gradual reformism of the British Fabian Society. He sat with half a dozen of them in a little room with an 'omniscient and aloof' Karl Marx over the mantelpiece. He was given pamphlets and told by Thomas Lyng, an ISRP founder, that revolutionary socialism had nothing in common with 'milk-and-water organisations', but also that 'there may be no violent revolution at all since history records that ruling classes sometimes abdicate through wisdom or weakness . . .'

> One name and one presence pervades the little room: Connolly away in the States. He is the master spirit who has called and held these men together, but somehow they lack his reality and fire. There is something sterile about the group that their long phrases culled from their God over the mantel and their aloofness both from the bright-garbed Gaels in kilt and classroom and the wild-eyed workingman who dogs and curses all their meetings. Only Lyng and William O'Brien seem conscious that they live in Dublin; the rest are a sect conning pamphlets and that long row of Marxist works in the bookcase yonder. The Irish language makes them smile, and again they smile at the ideal of a free Ireland.[21]

From thousands of miles away, Connolly was more engaged than his Dublin comrades in the public Irish debate. He was in W.P. Ryan's *Irish Nation* in 1909 discussing the Irish socialist reaction to the growth of Sinn Féin and recommending a conference of all socialists to find areas of common ground with Griffith. William O'Brien succeeded in reaching agreement with a reformed ILP on a commitment to independent labour representation on electoral bodies and support for the Irish language with the ultimate aim of achieving socialism in Ireland through democratic means. Although Griffith spurned an advance, O'Brien was sufficiently encouraged to tell Connolly he believed that the membership of the broadened SPI could be doubled 'if there was a man with the necessary tact and ability in the country, and I know of no one who would more likely succeed than yourself'.

O'Brien's suggestions for how a return might be financed were tentative, but Connolly rode roughshod over all his prudent caveats. Having first insisted he would not travel without his family and would return only if a decent wage were guaranteed, he was now determined to leave America as quickly as possible, and arranged for *The Harp* to be printed in Ireland by the *Irish Nation* despite O'Brien's warnings of lack of money and suitable help. 'The Connolly pattern was again evident,' said Samuel Leveson.

> In the same precipitate way that Connolly deserted the British Army during the last few months of his enlistment, abandoned jobs, and left Ireland for the US, he was now seeking to return to Ireland. In each instance he displayed a remarkable degree of independence, and a disregard for the advice of others that almost always led to disaster.

Further features of the pattern were that the big upheavals tended to come every seven years after a major falling out with comrades.

After a farewell dinner, 'a feast of mirth', and Irish songs and stories given by the Irish Socialist Federation, Connolly made it back to Dublin in late July 1910, having left his family in America, assuring Lillie that this was only a lecture tour and he would be back. He was now forty-two, and while more temperate and pragmatic than when he left, his was still not an easy personality. The city had changed in the seven years he had been away, not least because it now contained James Larkin, another overpowering man of a dictatorial bent. Via different routes (Larkin was uninterested in Marxist ideology), the two men had arrived at a roughly similar pragmatic position: they were socialists, internationalists and syndicalists who thought such beliefs compatible with nationalism and religion. But their styles were very different: Larkin was handsome, theatrical and had the common touch; Connolly was plain, cerebral and reserved.

Larkin would make a dramatic appearance on a balcony and instantly entrance his audience. His 'power lay in his ability to establish an emotional bond with his audience', wrote Padraig Yeates, 'rather than to persuade them by force of argument. He played on his listeners' grievances, which were many, and contrasted their abject state with the moral grandeur of their future if they had the courage to seize it. He quickly became "The idol of the Dublin working classes".'[22]

Connolly, said Darrell Figgis, 'would sit, a lifeless heap, the picture of gloom, till it came to his time to speak, when with three strides he would throw off his gloom like a cloak, and pour out eloquence like molten metal that scorched and burned all before it'.[23]

The journalist Cathal O'Shannon, a loyal follower of Connolly's and no Larkinite, made a barbed comparison: if Connolly's oratory

> did not arouse the wild and whirling enthusiasm evoked by the outburst of a demagogue, it created enthusiasm of a different kind. It compelled assent as well as respect, it carried conviction and it aroused enthusiasm of the more lasting kind, a quiet, enduring enthusiasm which forced the hearer to act on Connolly's side rather than cheer his words.[24]

But there was another reason why Larkin would be followed by thousands and Connolly, at best, by hundreds. 'The main defect in Connolly was his shyness,' recollected one of his closest colleagues. 'He could not tolerate company. He could not mix with the masses. After lectures or meetings he would rush away because he lacked that human warmth so characteristic of Jim [Larkin] and so essential in . . . labour organisers.'[25] Yet, as so often with style versus substance, 'Larkin knew how to draw a crowd but Connolly knew how to hold one.'[26] You might leave a Larkin speech ready to defy your employers, but if you took a pamphlet home from an encounter with Connolly you might read and discuss it.

The two men might have been on the same ideological side, but they never liked each other, and Connolly would quickly grow to resent, even hate, Larkin. He had good reason to be annoyed with him

before they even met. Unasked, Larkin had taken over the management of *The Harp*, and had instantly altered it from 'a tight and effec-
tively written propaganda sheet for thinking Socialists of the Irish and
Irish American variety' to a highly entertaining populist scandal sheet.
Of John Redmond, who led a 'ragged army', he wrote 'for the last thirteen years [he] had continually been presuming and venturing to say,
and desirous of pointing out, that in the not far distant day we shall
have our own again. Oh what a burlesque!' Unionists were 'the syco-
phants, privilege mongers, place hunters, nation levellers, blood suck-
ers, and carrion crows'; the 'ideal of the *Sinn Féin* Party or at least a
section who control the party, is to make cheap goods under sweating
conditions by cheap Irish Labour . . . for imported foreign capitalists,
such goods to be sold to any and every nation except England'.[27] In his
recklessness, Larkin had also rapidly killed the paper by incurring four
libel actions.

Yet because Larkin was now in jail because of a politically motivated
allegation of misuse of funds, Connolly's first duty in Ireland was to
visit him and begin what would be a successful agitation for his release.
As efficient as Larkin was inefficient, he began simultaneously organising a lecture tour, and dealt with the publication of *Labour in Irish
History* and *Labour, Nationality and Religion*, a pamphlet he had written
in his last months in America in response to a series of anti-socialist
Lenten sermons by a Dublin Jesuit called Father Robert Kane, who,
like most of the Catholic ecclesiastical establishment, was alarmed by
the industrial upheavals being caused by Larkinism.

Connolly had the advantage of being able to pose as a believing
Catholic and use Catholic history and the early Christian fathers as
ammunition. Mischievously, he reminded Kane that it was an important part of Catholic doctrine that 'the clergy are but the officers serving the laity' and should they 'profess or teach doctrines not in
conformity with the true teachings of Catholicity it is . . . the absolute
duty of the laity to refuse such doctrines and to disobey such teachings'. He noted regretfully that clergymen who were supposed to
model themselves on Christ 'should in their relation to the laity insist
upon service and humility being rendered to them instead of by them'.

The church, he argued, had adopted capitalistic values completely
divorced from the principles upon which it had been founded; he drew

on supportive saints like Chrysostom ('The rich man is a thief') and
Ambrose ('It is only unjust usurpation that has created the right of
private property'). He stressed the spiritual values of socialism and the
material aspects of Christianity, attacked Pope Leo XIII's encyclical
against socialism as unworthy of a schoolboy and denounced some of
Kane's arguments as claptrap and blasphemy. Kane's sermons might
not have been intellectually deserving of such attention, but they gave
Connolly a useful opportunity to deal head on with some of the thinking Catholic's reservations about socialism, they swelled his audiences
and made money through the sale of the pamphlet. At times they
would cause controversy: Connolly had to be escorted to Cobh train
station by police when some of his religiously-minded critics stormed
the platform.

Along with Francis Sheehy-Skeffington, Connolly drafted a new
manifesto directing the SPI to focus on winning elections 'through
independent working-class candidates pledged to a progressive policy
of social reform', which the party adopted in September 1910. Yet
there was still no offer of a living wage and he was threatening to go
back to America imminently.

Larkin got out of jail the following month and intervened impetu-
ously and so decisively in the tortuous negotiations about Connolly's
wages that the hitherto cautious SPI offered him enough to live on.
This was not good news for Lillie, who wanted to stay in America,
where she hoped her children could get reasonable jobs.[28] But told in
what Connolly described as 'the fateful letter' that she had two weeks
to dismantle their home and take the boat, she sighed and obeyed. As
she commented to one of her daughters, about every five years, when
she had really settled down, she always had to move.

Unsurprisingly, though Connolly was having some success in
setting up new branches, the party paid him erratically and sometimes
not at all and Connolly abruptly moved his family from Dublin to
Belfast, perhaps in the hope that Larkin would give him a job there.
Instead, though he did not slack in his work for the SPI, for months
there was another hand-to-mouth period, with his eldest daughter
Nora, a young socialist activist herself and increasingly her father's
right-hand woman, hurting his pride by supplementing his erratic
income through working for a pittance in a linen mill. He had already

turned against Larkin ('The man is utterly unreliable – and dangerous because unreliable') by the summer of 1911, not least because he had killed *The Harp*, but had also rubbed salt in the wound by launching the *Irish Worker*, which was hugely successful in promoting such syndicalist ideas as sympathetic strikes and Irish-Ireland organisations. Connolly went to Dublin occasionally; in the summer of 1911 he spoke in support of the protest against the forthcoming royal visit that Ceannt and Mac Diarmada were so caught up in. 'Stand by the dignity of your class,' he told his audience. 'All these parading royalties, all this insolent aristocracy, all these grovelling, dirt-eating capitalist traitors, all these are but the signs of disease in any social state.'

However, in July 1911, Larkin appointed him secretary and Ulster district organiser of the union; within a few days he had brought out 300 Belfast dockers in sympathy with cross-channel seamen. A deal was done with employers, and he had some success too in helping female mill workers sabotage humiliating petty rules, creating the Irish Textile Workers' Union. There was no doubt about Connolly's commitment to improving the lot of women workers. He was a doughty defender of female suffrage and women's rights in general, treated female activists as equals, and genuinely liked and got on with them. Admittedly, relations with women were often easier than with men, since the former were more inclined to be admiring than challenging, and he always put socialism ahead of the well-being of his wife and daughters, but, for his time, Connolly had very enlightened attitudes. Still, as an organiser, he failed to attract many members in Belfast, not least because miserably poor people grudged the modest dues, but Larkin brought him south for a while to settle a strike in Wexford and continue the building up of the union there.

In Belfast, as in Dublin, Home Rule was the issue dominating 1912. That Easter, Connolly organised a conference in Dublin to discuss socialist political unity. By avoiding contentious issues like republicanism and by catering for both syndicalists and social democrats, delegates from the SPI and the ILP agreed on a programme for an Independent Labour Party of Ireland. This was followed up at an ITUC meeting in May, when Connolly convinced Home Rulers that with a parliament on its way, the necessary machinery should be

introduced to ensure Labour representation. By leaving socialism out
of the resolution, and with Larkin's support, he secured a majority of
almost three to one for what would in time lead to the creation of the
Irish Labour Party. He developed his ideas on an Irish labour movement and how it would improve the people's lot in open-air meetings
during 1912, which were published in the *Irish Worker* and in 1915
issued as a pamphlet called *The Reconquest of Ireland*.

Trying to address sectarianism, he spoke of the sufferings of
Protestant workers under capitalism, and of Nonconformists under
religious persecution, for in Belfast he was trying vainly to make the
union equally attractive to green and orange – an incredible aim for a
man who trumpeted his republicanism and lived in an exclusively
Catholic part of the Falls Road. Connolly knew few Irish Protestants
and his difficulty in understanding Ulster unionists was evident in his
clash with the prominent Belfast trade unionist and Labour candidate
William Walker, whose belief that the future of Irish socialism lay in
the maintenance of the union was denounced by Connolly as false
internationalism. In fact, he dealt with rising unionist antipathy to
Home Rule as he dealt with any position that might undermine his
socialist analysis: he dismissed it. Impervious to the mood that had
led to the signing of the Solemn League and Covenant, he told a heck-
ler who waved a copy at him that 'your children will laugh at it'. When
in 1913, several months after the signing of the Covenant, he stood
unsuccessfully for the Belfast city council in a mixed area, his reformist election manifesto included the line 'As a lifelong advocate of
national independence for Ireland, I am in favour of Home Rule, and
believe that Ireland should be ruled, governed, and owned by the
people of Ireland'. Inevitably, the voting followed the usual sectarian
lines. In August, in Belfast, after the joint outing of the ITGWU and
the textile union, police protection was needed to escape countless
Orangemen who threw sticks and stones as the trippers left the
station.

Larkin was doing well with recruitment, but had failed to follow
through energetically on creating the Irish Labour Party, and, indeed,
fell out with the union's parliamentary committee; the issue slid down
the union's agenda. There were innumerable irritations that maddened
Connolly, who wrote to O'Brien in July 1913:

I don't think I can stand Larkin as a boss much longer. He is simply unbearable. He is forever snarling at me and drawing comparisons between what he accomplished in Belfast in 1907, and what I have done, conveniently ignoring the fact that he was then the secretary of an English organisation, and that as soon as he started an Irish one his union fell to pieces, and he had to leave the members to their fate. He is consumed with jealousy and hatred of anyone who will not cringe to him and beslaver him all over.

Larkin, claimed Connolly, had tried to bully him over money.

I told him that if he was Larkin twenty times over he could not bully me . . . I would formerly have trusted to his generosity in financial matters, now I would not trust him at all. Larkin seems to think he can use Socialists as he pleases and then, when his end is served, throw them out if they will not bow down to his majesty. He will never get me to bow to him.

At the end of the following month, Connolly received from Larkin a telegram summoning him to Dublin to assist in the lockout. Leaving his wife and family in Belfast, he hastened to the place where he would spend the rest of his life.

Chapter Eight

NO TURNING BACK[1]

If it was Tom Clarke who brought down the lamp of tradition, and held it firmly, without any thought for himself, until others were ready to take it from him; if it was Seán MacDermott who served the organisation of revolt with a fire that burned in him with a consuming flame, it was Patrick Pearse who gave insurrection a philosophy that was also a religion. And with him came others of a smaller mould, Thomas MacDonagh and Joseph Plunkett, who were in some sort disciples of his, who had received from him his doctrine that from the ashes of sacrifice would arise the new spirit of a nation.

At the other end stood two men of a different quality. One of these was Éamonn Ceannt, a dark, proud, aloof man, of so extreme a sensitiveness that he had schooled himself to wear for mask a cold and rigid manner. Patrick Pearse's doctrine found small echo in him. He went into insurrection looking for victory because the thought of defeat chafed his intractable spirit . . .

The other was James Connolly. In many ways he was the master-intellect of them all . . . but the splendid, massive machinery of his mind often produced results that were bewilderingly disproportionate to the intricate process by which they had been created.

Darrell Figgis[*], *1921*[2]

* Of Irish Protestant parentage, Darrell Figgis (1882–1925) was a gifted and perceptive London-based critic, a prolific poet and a friend of G.K. Chesterton who moved to Ireland in 1913, discovered Irish nationalism, became a propagandist, joined the Irish Volunteers and was an instigator of the gun-running in 1914. Arrested in his Achill home after the Easter Rising and interned in England, he would be the primary drafter of the 1922 Irish Free State constitution. Briefly a member of the Dáil, like most other Protestant rebels, he disappeared from the Irish consciousness, perhaps because his wife killed herself in 1924, his lover died after an abortion in 1925 and he committed suicide.

Sitting in his shop, Tom Clarke was observing every twist and turn to see how great events in Ireland and far beyond could be turned to the advantage of the IRB, which through his young lieutenants he now controlled almost completely. Indeed, the Supreme Council began to meet in the Clarke living quarters above his Amiens Street premises.

Seán O'Casey recollected that at this time

> Every aspect of this man showed weariness and age . . . Almost all his loyalties to the colours and enjoyments of life had been burned away, leaving but a slender, intense flame of hatred to what he knew to be England. Free himself, now, he plucked impatiently at those who wanted to let bad enough alone.
>
> Watch him locking up his tiny shop, slipping the key in his pocket, then giving a swift turn to where a Committee waited for him; a warm, rough, tweed overcoat belted firmly at his slender waist, a broad-brimmed hat set firm on his greying head, the frail figure went straight on, taking short, rapid steps with a tiny spice of jauntiness in them; straight on, looking neither right nor left, to where a drooping Committee sprang to interested alertness when he came among them, and bent low over the task of moulding the bullets that would tear rough and roguish gaps open in some of their own breasts.[3]

There was nothing democratic about Tom Clarke. He wanted a revolution whatever it took, and on his terms. When it came to the 1873 addition to the IRB oath, designed to prevent futile revolutions, he fully agreed with 'The I.R.B . . . shall, pending an emergency, lend its support to every movement calculated to advance the cause of Irish independence, consistently with the preservation of its own integrity.' But he utterly ignored the caveat that the organisation would 'await the decisions of the Irish Nation, as expressed by a majority of the Irish people, as to the fit hour of inaugurating a war against England'.

The intellectually confident and independent-minded Bulmer Hobson, who vied with Seán Mac Diarmada for the status of Clarke's favourite protégé, did not agree: in 1909 he wrote a pamphlet called *Defensive Warfare: A Handbook for Irish Nationalists*; they should fight to win, not to make a display of heroism. Because its message was unpopular with the IRB in Dublin,[4] he published it in Belfast, though at this stage his relationship with Clarke was strong enough to survive. Mac Diarmada, who was much more biddable and had now been well schooled, followed the Clarke line slavishly. Clarke's biographer Michael Foy believes that Mac Diarmada's charm 'concealed the icy calculation and nose for power of an intensely ambitious man, one set on being Tom's closest confidant but for the furtherance of his own aims'.[5] But Mac Diarmada's aims were Clarke's aims, they would differ very rarely and almost always on minor matters, and he seemed to have a deep emotional need to be close to his surrogate parents. Yet, as Brian Feeney points out, there was a 'sulphurous intensity' about him 'which sometimes manifested itself in his gaze. Under the surface of his *bonhomie* and easy-going friendliness there was the steeliness of a zealot.'[6] He did not tolerate political disagreement, interference or inefficiency, all the more obviously when the intolerance suddenly usurped the otherwise invariable charm.

Mac Diarmada was struggling with the physical and psychological effects of the polio he had caught in 1911. Even after his convalescence he still was weak, had a permanently bad leg, was often in pain and had frequent infections and good reason to believe he might not survive another operation. He was a young man now in an even greater hurry. Clarke sent him ('one of the finest young fellows of the young school') to America in the autumn of 1912 for business (as the IRB delegate to the Clan na Gael convention in New Jersey) and recuperation (visiting two sisters in New York). Mac Diarmada reported to the Clan's Foreign Relations Committee on the strength of the IRB in Ireland (1,660), in Britain (367) and the circulation of *Irish Freedom* (6,000). He estimated the membership of Fianna Éireann, the militaristic republican boy scout movement Hobson had founded in 1909, at 1,000. Under the heading 'Blocks in the Way', Joe McGarrity's notes of Mac Diarmada's briefing lists the following without further explanation: 'Hibernians, the Parliamentary Party, clergy, spy system, want of employment, want of money.' Clearly Mac Diarmada was impressive, for subsequently McGarrity had the budget for Ireland increased to $2,000 (about $48,000 in today's money), 'the first sum of any consequence that had been definitely set aside for some years for Ireland'.[7]

Henceforward, when Tommy O'Connor, a Clan courier working on the White Star shipping line, went from Liverpool to Dublin, he delivered the money to Mac Diarmada, who 'would make a note of the amount in his small, neat handwriting on a slip of paper, without any signature', and this would be given to John Devoy as a receipt on O'Connor's next trip to New York.[8] Clarke and Mac Diarmada had jointly the trust and financial backing of Irish America: there was no doubt about who called the shots in the IRB.

Ever the practical man, Éamonn Ceannt had ceaselessly been pointing out that if real shots were to be fired there had to be the means and the people to do it. In this he was echoing his friend Michael O'Rahilly*, who had written several times in *Irish Freedom* of the need for separatists to acquire arms and be trained to use them. In December 1912 Ceannt was elected to the National Council of the Sinn Féin Party as Joint Honorary Secretary and the following month, at a Council meeting, with O'Rahilly as seconder, he had successfully proposed the resolution that 'the Council of Sinn Féin is of the opinion that it is the duty of all Irishmen to possess a knowledge of arms'. Áine Ceannt later recalled that Arthur Griffith, who had not been present, angrily complained to O'Rahilly that 'he wanted no tinpike soldiers', being Anglophobe enough to see this as derivative of contemporary British fashion. But he was told that anything Ceannt took on he meant to do well and that he was already learning to shoot.[9]

Ceannt had offered to find a rifle range and by February he was practising on Sunday mornings with Cathal Brugha and a friend who provided the rifle the three of them shared on a site in Harold's Cross owned by an oil company. Seán Mac Diarmada joined them in their

---

* Michael O'Rahilly (1875–1916), independently wealthy and aimless, found his cause in Irish nationalism and gave himself the clan leadership honorific of 'The O'Rahilly'. Although he was an IRB fellow traveller, founder of a gun club and a contributor to *Irish Freedom* who told his readers to be prepared to use arms against the British, he disapproved of secret societies on religious and spiritual grounds.

second week. By June, Ceannt had his own gun; a few months later he was Secretary of the Banba Rifle Club at Larkfield (a house in Kimmage with eight acres that was Countess Plunkett's latest acquisition) for which he had bought five guns and two belts of ammunition. What Ceannt was working towards came closer when on 13 January 1913, with a recruitment limit of 100,000 signatories of the Covenant, the Ulster Volunteers were formally created by the Ulster Unionist Council. The British government wrung its hands and looked away at the illegal drilling it felt unable to control. Ceannt responded immediately, by successfully proposing at a Sinn Féin Special Congress the following month that 'the policy of Sinn Féin for the coming year be one of active hostility to the English Government in Ireland and that the attention of the Executive be directed especially to the fresh attempt at recruiting for the English army and navy now proceeding'. It was by his suggestion that an ass and cart with anti-enlistment slogans (sample: 'The British soldier's life is the life of a slave. His end's a pauper's grave') was sent around the streets.

Clarke was overjoyed at the increasing militarisation in the north east. Although he hated the whole idea of Home Rule, loathed the parliamentary party and was determined to destroy it, he saw great military possibilities as constitutional nationalist circles began to talk of the need to set up a counter-force to defend the bill. Seán T. O'Kelly remembered 'often seeing Tom Clarke rubbing his hands with glee when speaking about the reports of Ulster Volunteer activity. "Let them fire away, the more they organise the better," he would say. "Aren't they setting us a splendid example? Soon, very soon, we will be following in their footsteps."'[10]

As Mac Diarmada had grown closer to Clarke and to his family, he had begun to grow apart from Hobson. They still shared a house, but their differences in religious background and education, temperament (emotion versus reason), Mac Diarmada's secretiveness and Hobson's arrogance divided them. Mac Diarmada was Clarke's able and dedicated facilitator, Hobson a brilliant, free-thinking strategist who was often a solo flier: in his creation of the Fianna, along with Constance Markievicz, he had already developed a military organisation covertly run by the IRB. When he proposed to the IRB Dublin Centres Board in July 1913 the setting up of a militia, he could provide a nucleus of trained young men to begin the secret drilling. And when he suggested to the Supreme Council in October that the IRB should take the initiative in getting a Volunteer movement off the ground, he had yet more men to offer. It was Hobson's promise of this reliable core that encouraged O'Rahilly, now manager of *An Claideamh Soluis*, to accept his suggestion that Eoin Mac Neill* – Hobson's choice of frontman – be invited to mark the paper's revamp on 1 November 1913 with a leading article urging that nationalists emulate the UVF.

MacNeill's 'The North Began' (a title inspired by a Thomas Davis ballad about the 1782 Irish Volunteers – 'The North began, the North held on / The strife for native land; / Till Ireland rose, and cowed her foes') purported to explain the Ulster Question. MacNeill's almost wilful misreading of northern unionists as misguided, duped, fragmented people who were Home Rulers at heart was typical of nationalist thinking. Significantly, it assumed a comforting liberalism among the Ulster Protestant middle classes to avoid thinking of what its author really feared, the violence of the Protestant working class. But what mattered in 1913 was MacNeill's argument that the government's toleration of the Ulster Volunteers should extend to a mirror image down south. The UVF were drilling to resist the will of the government, so how could there be any objection if the rest of Ireland produced a militia in defence of it?

MacNeill would never be in the IRB and Pearse had not yet been invited to join, but via O'Rahilly Hobson was moving them into place. The week after MacNeill's article, in the *Claideamh* there appeared 'the ultimate paean to armed rebellion,'[11] an article by Patrick Pearse expressing his delight that

the Orangemen have armed, for it is a goodly thing to see

---

* Professor of Early and Medieval Irish History at UCD and a founder of the Gaelic League, Eoin MacNeill (1867–1945) came from the Glens of Antrim, a part of Ulster so peaceful that it inculcated in him the belief that Ulster unionism did not run deep but was artificially created by an elite. He was also convinced that Asquith wanted to renege on Home Rule and was encouraging unionist resistance to give him the excuse. He was a constitutional separatist but no Fenian.

arms in Irish hands. I should like to see the AOH armed. I should like to see the Transport Workers armed. I should like to see any and every body of Irish citizens armed. We must accustom ourselves to the thought of arms, to the sight of arms, to the use of arms. We may make mistakes in the beginning and shoot the wrong people; but bloodshed is a cleansing and a sanctifying thing, and the nation which regards it as the final horror has lost its manhood. There are many things more horrible than bloodshed; and slavery is one of them.

Variations on such sentiments were being paralleled all over Europe.

At Hobson's suggestion, O'Rahilly proposed to MacNeill that he chair a meeting to discuss setting up a volunteer force. Knowing he was seen as an extremist, Hobson did not attend: the ten others present included Ceannt, Pearse and Mac Diarmada, whom – significantly – Hobson had not invited but who had been asked along by Piaras Béaslaí. The committee swelled to thirty and agreed 'an overlong and stilted'[12] manifesto, largely written by MacNeill and Sir Roger Casement,* a romantic idealist like Pearse, MacDonagh and Plunkett. True to the nationalist instinct for self-delusion about what was driving the Ulster Volunteers, and despite Casement's earlier hopeless attempt to make nationalists of Ulster Protestants, the manifesto blamed the Tories for Ulster militarisation and declared the objective of setting up a corps of Irish Volunteers 'to secure and maintain the

---

* Roger Casement (1864–1916) was born in Dublin and moved to Antrim in 1873. Brought up and educated in the Church of Ireland, his Catholic mother, who died when he was nine, had had him secretly baptised. From adolescence he identified with the Irish rebel tradition. Having worked in various jobs in the Congo in 1895, he became part of the British consular service. Troubled by his homosexuality and probably bipolar, he was a mercurial and difficult employee, but at his best an outstandingly brave and independent-minded humanitarian. He became famous for his reports on atrocities in the Congo (1904) and in the Amazonian region of Putumayo in 1911, the year he was knighted. An Irish-Irelander and language enthusiast, by the time he retired in 1913 he was a committed Irish separatist convinced that independence could be achieved with German assistance.

Left: Ready to kill – Tom Clarke, the would-be dynamiter, in the early 1880s. (Nat. Library of Ireland)

Right: Seán Mac Diarmada in 1911, before polio struck.

Two Fenian ex-convicts, John Daly (left) and Tom Clarke, welcoming Seán Mac Diarmada (right), their spiritual heir, on his release from jail in 1915.

Left: Shy Éamonn Ceannt, who played his uillean pipes with 'dash and fire'. (Nat. Library of Ireland)

Right: The underestimated Áine Ceannt with their son Rónán after Éamonn's execution.

The redoubtable Kathleen Clarke, with (left to right) Thomas, John Daly and Emmet, after Tom's execution.

Left: 'You only have been my familiar friend,' wrote Patrick Pearse (left) in a poem to his brother Willie in 1916, 'Nor needed I another'. (Nat. Library of Ireland)

Right: The upwardly mobile Pearses circa 1890: (left to right) Patrick, James, Margaret, Mary Brigid, Willie and Margaret.

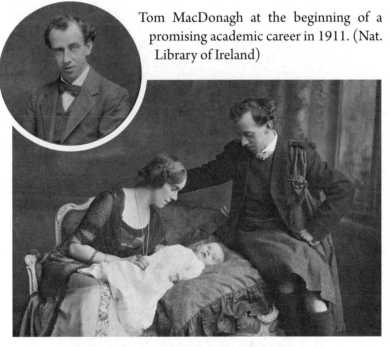

Tom MacDonagh at the beginning of a promising academic career in 1911. (Nat. Library of Ireland)

1912 – Tom MacDonagh and Muriel with Donagh, to whom he wishes 'Deeper passion, better wit / Than I had who had enough'. (Nat. Library of Ireland)

August 1908 – a rare moment of Plunkett domestic tranquillity. At the back (from left to right): George, Gerry, Joe, Moya, Mimi. At the front (from left to right): Fiona, Pa, Ma and Jack.

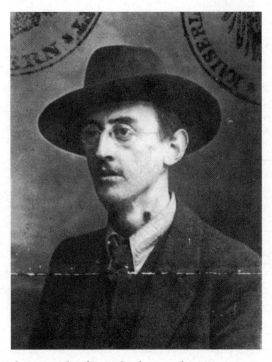

The 1915 photograph of Joe Plunkett on his German passport.

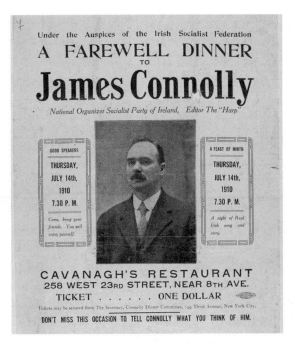

After seven years in America, James Connolly succumbs again to the lure of Ireland. (Nat. Library of Ireland)

THE LAST STAND 1916

'The Last Stand', General Post Office, 1916 (later known as 'The Birth of the Republic'), is a watercolour by Walter Paget drawn from photographic portraits that were in wide circulation after the executions. Connolly is on the stretcher with Mac Diarmada at his feet. Pearse, Clarke and Willie are together on the left; Plunkett is running to join the group.

Philadelphia, 1914 – Bulmer Hobson (right), the strategist for the IRB, visits Joe McGarrity, its dedicated Irish-American financial backer, to plot revolution.

The Proclamation of the Irish Republic, printed with great difficulty at Liberty Hall, and without access to fadas (acute accents).

Sir Roger Casement (left) and John Devoy in a Philadelphia procession, 2 August 1914.

Execution Yard, Kilmainham Gaol.

In 1966 a series of stamps were produced to commemorate the fiftieth anniversary of the Easter Rising. As well as the Seven, they depicted the burnt-out General Post Office.

During their lives, Yeats helped Connolly, MacDonagh and Pearse; after their deaths, he immortalised them in 'Easter 1916' along with the 'terrible beauty' to which they gave birth.

After a break of eighty years, James Connolly once more presided over (a rebuilt) Liberty Hall.

rights and liberties common to all the people of Ireland' by a permanent militia run by a national government. In the hope of winning the
support of Redmond – who was staying well away – it emphasised that
its ranks would be open to all men regardless of creed, class or
politics.

On his twenty-sixth birthday, 21 November 1913, Joe Plunkett saw
a newspaper announcement of a public meeting to be held in the evening four days hence 'for the purpose of establishing a corps of Irish
Volunteers . . . Eoin MacNeill, B.A., will preside'. Two days later, Jim
Larkin and James Connolly stole a march by setting up the Irish
Citizens' Army (ICA), an ITGWU militia; a fortnight earlier, at a rally
celebrating Larkin's early release from another prison sentence,
Connolly had said: 'Next time we are out for a march, I want to be
accompanied by four battalions of trained men with their corporals
and sergeants.' It was directed by a veteran of the South African War,
Captain J.R. White (whose father, Field-Marshal Sir George Stuart
White, had been the hero of besieged Ladysmith), who had become a
socialist.

Plunkett had been excited by MacNeill's article. Although he had
never met him, conscious that he was not in a fit state to be a useful
marching man, he called on MacNeill and was received kindly and
urged to attend. Including him, five of the Seven were at the meeting,
and one was there in spirit: Mac Diarmada and Pearse were among the
speakers, but Ceannt was now seen as so 'advanced' and therefore of
interest to Dublin Castle that he was among those asked not to speak,
and Clarke was in his usual place in the shadows. MacDonagh had
influenza and could not attend, but he told a friend he hoped the
movement could unite 'AOH men, Sinn Féiners, Irish freedom men,
Parliamentarians, GAA men and University men'.[13]

Apart from an attempt by some Dublin strikers to drown out the
reader of the manifesto because there was a labour dispute in his
father's business, the event was a great success. Of the 7,000 in the
Rotunda Skating Rink or in the overflow meetings, 3,000 signed up.
Clarke was well content: 'The Volunteer movement has caught on in
great style here in Dublin,' he reported to Joe McGarrity. 'Such an
outpouring of young fellows was never seen . . . the right spot has been
touched in them by the volunteering. Wait till they get their fist

clutching the steel barrel of a business rifle and then Irish instincts and Irish manhood can be relied upon.'[14] This would be especially true of Plunkett and MacDonagh, whose son Donagh, in an essay in 1967, would write of how

> two young poets, one of thirty-eight and the other of twenty-nine found themselves leaders in a desperate cause. They were neither of them orators, like Pearse; Marxists, like Connolly; felons, like Clarke; polemicists, like MacDermott; Irish Irelanders, like Ceannt, yet they too were willing to live that Ireland might live, or die that Ireland might live. They had said it in their poetry and nobody heeded it.[15]

The Volunteers would be Dublin-centred and, as the historian Charles Townshend put it, 'drawn principally (like the Fenians of the past) from the respectable working class'. One result of that was that the educated were afforded deference, which was part of the reason why MacDonagh, Pearse and Plunkett were on the first governing committee of the Volunteers. Also including Ceannt and Mac Diarmada, this committee had representatives from across the nationalist board, including Casement (a long-time friend of Hobson and MacNeill and the Volunteers' main financial backer) and Tom Kettle, the former IPP MP. Pearse, whom IRB members had blocked for years because of his moderation and his debts, was sworn into the IRB by Hobson that December, circumstances having overcome his natural wariness about secret societies. Hobson was arranging a lecture tour for him in America to raise money to save St Enda's, and for the Clan to co-operate enthusiastically IRB membership was a prerequisite.

The foundation of the Irish Volunteers and his induction into the IRB were heady days for Pearse, who worked even more frenetically than usual. He became Director of Organisation, opened up the grounds of St Enda's for the training of the Fianna and made recruiting speeches around the country to large audiences, extolling marching and drilling and rhapsodising about guns. In January 1914, for instance, he and Casement were the two Volunteer representatives at a big public meeting in Limerick. Casement, who was having the time of his life and 'relished what he described as intrigue and gross sedition',[16] had been billed as the chief speaker, but knowing Pearse to be a much superior orator he gave him the prime position. They stayed with John Daly and met local republicans, who helped to further focus Pearse's mind on Fenian history.

His stated position was, as usual, more complex and confused than that of most of his allies: to Pearse, the job of the Volunteers was to help Redmond obtain Home Rule, which he implied he would accept, yet Ireland should become wholly independent, which would be a job in the future for the Fianna. And while he was all fired up to fight the British, Pearse could see little likelihood that there would be any need to take arms against the Ulster Volunteers; on the contrary, he could see both sets of Volunteers fighting the British alongside each other.

MacDonagh's friend Francis Sheehy-Skeffington was one of the feminists who objected to the failure of the Volunteers to add 'without distinction of sex' to its manifesto, which said merely that 'there will also be work for women to do'. Asked what role women could play, Pearse recommended ambulance and Red Cross work. 'I would not like the idea of women drilling and marching in the ordinary way but there is no reason why they should not learn to shoot.' Nothing happened about this until in April 1914 there was an inaugural meeting of Cumann na mBan (League of Women). Unlike the ICA, which had a women's section that operated like its male equivalents, it was conventional, segregated and subordinate to the men, whom they were there obediently to support. Its members included Kathleen Clarke and Áine Ceannt, who set up the highly successful Central Branch, Ceannt's sister Lily O'Brennan and James Connolly's secretary, Winifred Carney, all of whom remained after the Volunteer split. Muriel MacDonagh was too timid to join and Joe Plunkett told Gerry to stay away as he needed her as his messenger.

Pearse embarked for America on 8 February and was away for three months. Lecturing almost exclusively under the auspices of the *Gaelic American*, he found little interest from audiences in culture or education: what they wanted to hear were accounts of the growth and militancy of the Volunteers and sanguinary speeches about Irish heroes. To 2,500 at an Emmet commemoration, he spoke of 'a sacrifice Christ-like in its perfection'. The new generation at home 'is reaffirming the

Fenian faith, the faith of Emmet . . . before this generation has passed
the Volunteers will draw the sword of Ireland'.

Pearse impressed Devoy and McGarrity even if he could not quite
convince them of the truth of his passionate assertions that there
would be a revolution. Indeed, senior Clan leaders were seriously sceptical about an open organisation like the Volunteers. For his part,
Pearse was invigorated by the hysterical nationalism on tap in the Clan
and the 'romantic lust for violence' of leaders and followers alike.[17] In
Philadelphia he had coincided with Hobson, who was in America to
deliver to Devoy a Casement memorandum on relations between
Germany and Ireland in the event of a European war. McGarrity had a
happy evening with them both when they all talked joyfully about the
prospect of successful negotiations for assistance between the Clan
and Germany:

> The hours seemed to fly so swiftly, the prospect of Ireland
> again standing in arms in defence of her ancient right, the
> prospect of help from a great power, the general awakening
> that was taking place in Ireland seemed to make us forget
> everything else for the time being and think only of the
> fight in prospect.[18]

With enough money to keep the creditors off his back long enough for
St Enda's to reopen in September, Pearse reached Ireland in mid-May
impatient to restart his Volunteer work, only to find the movement in
crisis. With the Home Rule Bill set to become law later in the year, and
with the Ulster Volunteers in full 'No-Surrender' mode, in March a
fearful British Liberal government and an inept high command had
helped create what was called the 'Curragh Mutiny' by appearing to
accept the refusal of some of its officers to impose Home Rule on
Ulster. The following month the Ulster Volunteers illegally imported
25,000 guns, and Irish nationalists' trust in the government to keep its
word on Home Rule was dangerously undermined. Irish Volunteer
numbers increased from around 27,000 in April to over 130,000 by
June and MacNeill and Casement began unofficially making overtures
to Redmond, who announced publicly in early June that the IPP now
supported the movement, but that it required 25 nominees added to

the 25-strong executive committee. Without that concession, he threatened to set up a rival organisation.

The Volunteer executive was in disarray. Hobson, one of the few who knew a secret arms shipment was due within a few weeks, believed a split at that time would be fatal and that compromise was the lesser evil. Clarke and Mac Diarmada wanted a fight with Redmond, but on 16 June, against the instructions of the IRB Supreme Council, Hobson not only voted in favour of the co-option of Redmondites but persuaded Casement and MacNeill, who knew of the shipment, to do so as well, and carried the day with a powerful speech. O'Rahilly and Plunkett voted with the majority: if MacDonagh had been present, he would probably have done so too, but then neither he nor Plunkett were yet in the IRB. Among the nine dissenters were Ceannt, Mac Diarmada and Pearse. Ceannt railed furiously against his friend O'Rahilly, the Volunteers' Treasurer, who was rendered so upset and disgusted with himself that he wrote a resignation letter that Pearse persuaded him not to send: according to Béaslaí many years later, on the night of the vote, Ceannt sent O'Rahilly a vicious anonymous letter.[19]

'I was with Tom [Clarke] when the news came,' wrote Seán McGarry,

> and to say he was astounded is understating it. I never saw him so moved. He regarded it from the beginning as cold-blooded and contemplated treachery likely to bring about the destruction of the only movement in a century which brought promise of the fulfilment of all his hopes. During his life he had had many, very many grievous disappoint-ments but this was the worst and the bitterness of it was increased by the fact that it was brought about by a trusted friend.[20]

At a showdown afterwards, which shocked Hobson with the level of its hostility, Clarke asked Hobson: 'What did the Castle pay you?'

Clarke never spoke to Hobson again and he and Mac Diarmada never forgave him. For the sake of IRB unity, Hobson resigned from the positions where he would have contact with them – the Supreme Council and the editorship of *Irish Freedom*. At Clarke's instigation,

Devoy sacked him as Irish correspondent for the *Gaelic American*, his main paid job, and Clarke believed that having 'showed the cloven hoof' Hobson was finished and would be an outcast. Pearse, as ever, was kinder, telling McGarrity that it would be 'an incalculable loss'[21] if Hobson left Dublin and asking that he be reinstated as a correspondent, but Hobson felt no gratitude for his support. He deplored Pearse's financial irresponsibility and distrusted the speed at which he had become wedded to physical force. Pearse had warned MacNeill at the inception of the Volunteers 'of the danger of allowing extreme nationalists like me gain control', Hobson wrote later, but six months after being sworn in to the IRB 'I wasn't nearly revolutionary enough for him.'[22]

Hobson was by no means finished, however: he stayed on in the highly influential job of Chairman of the Dublin Centres Board and his finest hour was still to come. He had been part of the group organising the transport in two ships of 1,500 rifles (old but serviceable Mausers) and 49,000 rounds of ammunition bought from Germany by O'Rahilly, who was Treasurer of the Volunteers and had Ceannt as his able book-keeper: they fiddled the books to bamboozle the Redmondites. The money had come from Casement and Mary Spring Rice, another Anglo-Irish Protestant, like Darrell Figgis and Erskine Childers, who collected the shipment from Germany. Paradoxically, Childers, British soldier and Irish nationalist, was famous for his best-selling *The Riddle of the Sands*, a sea-faring thriller about a German invasion published in 1903 (and still in print). Written from 'a patriot's natural sense of duty', it deplored British lack of preparation for a forthcoming war with Germany, and was highly influential in bringing about the creation of new naval bases.

It was Casement who in June appealed to Hobson to plan the landings, which Hobson agreed to do if no committee were involved. Deciding on the twin objectives of landing and distributing the arms successfully yet doing so with the maximum of publicity to encourage fundraising at home and in America, Hobson chose Howth, a harbour on the north of Dublin bay about seven miles from central Dublin, for the first landing. He and Childers decided on 26 July at noon. MacNeill was instructed to order the four Dublin Volunteer companies to hold joint route marches in the preceding weeks so that the authorities would get used to them; IRB carpenters were asked to make 200 oak batons for defensive purposes; some IRB members were instructed to be in Howth to help moor Childers' yacht, the *Asgard*; and others were told to take taxis and female escorts to Howth, order lunch in the hotel and then ditch the women and load the taxis with ammunition.[23]

The plan was a tremendous success, the six played varying parts in its implementation, and the police and army failed dismally. After a difficult and dangerous voyage, the heavily laden *Asgard* appeared on time with 900 rifles and 29,000 rounds of ammunition just as the first column of Volunteers arrived in Howth and began unloading, assisted by Fianna boys, who, having distributed the batons from their cart, filled it with ammunition. Hobson had instructed them to give no ammunition to Volunteers, for he thought them undisciplined and feared bloodshed that could have led to their suppression.

Ceannt was in charge of the fourth Dublin battalion, which arrived last and stationed men with batons at the start of the pier. Two policemen trying to gain access were turned away: Ceannt 'laughed at them saying: "In the name of the Republic you will not be admitted until this little operation is over."' His column was also in the rear when on the road back to Dublin the parade of armed Volunteers was stopped. The government had ignored the illegal Larne gun-running, but the Commissioner of the DMP was not prepared to overlook 'more than 1,000 men armed with rifles marching on Dublin, the seat of the Irish Government', regarding it as constituting 'an unlawful assembly of a peculiarly audacious character'. His deputy, Assistant Commissioner William Harrel, with military aid from the King's Own Scottish Borderers, met the Volunteers near Clontarf. In the ensuing stand-off, there was a brief melee mainly involving batons and bayonets, a few rifles were seized, Ceannt was said to have demanded ammunition and slightly injured a soldier by shooting him in the ankle, and a few Volunteers were bayoneted.

Hobson, who was trying to negotiate with Harrel, was joined by Darrell Figgis and Thomas MacDonagh. MacDonagh's arguments included pointing out that since it was not illegal to own a gun Harrel would have to prove the guns were imported. 'Either of them could have talked him blind', recalled Hobson:

that combined effort was overwhelming. I decided that
this colloquy would last for a considerable time, so I ran to
the back of the column and ordered the men to disperse . . .
to make their way home as quickly as possible and avoid
any conflicts or anything which would cause them to lose
their rifles. I saw company after company disappear
through the hedges and did not return until all but the last
company was left when I found Mr. Harrel, looking rather
dazed, still listening to Figgis and MacDonagh.[24]

Hobson had told very few in the IRB about his plans, but when Clarke
and Mac Diarmada heard they determined to be part of the proceedings. Both of them were unwell. Clarke told Devoy he was 'very much
run down, overwork and worriment is leaving its mark on me' and 'old
age appears to be creeping on me. Most of the time I feel "moidered"'.
He was now a prematurely old man in a hurry. The two were on the
sidelines, arriving in Howth by taxi and at one stage giving a lift to
MacNeill, whom by now they despised as a Hobson dupe. At Clontarf
they managed three times to fill their taxi with weapons and unload at
Clarke's house. The day after, Clarke cheered himself up by travelling
to Limerick to present a Mauser to Uncle John Daly, who was dying
slowly of syphilis and motor neuron disease.

Neither Pearse nor Plunkett were at Howth, but weapons were
delivered to and hidden in St Enda's, and the day after the gun-running,
MacDonagh and Plunkett collected rifles from all over the city that
would end up stored in Larkfield. A less public landing of the rest of
the shipment south of Dublin the following week was also successful.

In a triumphalist article about the gun-running in the *Irish Review*,
MacDonagh proclaimed that 'Ireland has now the strength to enforce
her choice of destiny.' For the Volunteers now, what was necessary was
discipline, vigilance and confidence. But the real public relations
victory had come courtesy of the 2nd King's Own Scottish Borderers,
some of them dripping with blood, who had responded to seemingly
incessant jeering and stone-throwing by losing control of themselves
and firing on the mob. Three members of the crowd were killed immediately and one died later in what was quickly termed 'The Bachelors
Walk Massacre'. Flags were flown at half-mast; there was an

international outcry, a huge public funeral where Volunteers fired shots, Redmond held an enormous demonstration in Dublin, and someone wrote a terrible ballad ending 'But we will yet avenge them and the time will surely come, / That we'll make the Scottish Borderers pay for the cowardly deeds they've done.' The extent to which the gentle Patrick Pearse had developed a dehumanised enthusiasm about bloodshed was to be seen in his exultant letter to McGarrity saying that the killings 'have given public sentiment just that turn that was desirable ... The whole movement, the whole country, has been rebaptised by blood shed for Ireland.'

A commission of inquiry would roundly blame Harrel for acting illegally in calling out the military for no good reason, but by then the damage had been done and the shootings were seen as further evidence of the government's instinctive pro-unionism. Yet as Townshend points out, what was really the case was that it was deeply apprehensive about provocative actions and had not the faintest idea what to do now that this small island was on its way to having two opposing trained armed forces that could be kept under control only by the use of the entire British Army. At the instigation of King George V, a three-day conference had been held in Buckingham Palace a few days before the Dublin gun-running to try to get agreement on what was to be done about Home Rule. Attended among others by Prime Minister Asquith, Edward Carson, John Redmond and other leading unionists and nationalists, it made each side more aware than before of the attitudes of the other, but that was about it. 'I have rarely felt more helpless in any particular affair,' wrote Asquith afterwards, 'an impasse with unspeakable consequences, upon a matter which to English eyes seems inconceivably small and to Irish eyes immeasurably big. Isn't it a real tragedy?'

A much bigger tragedy was unfolding as he wrote. On 28 July, Austria-Hungary declared war on Serbia, leading to Russian mobilisation and Germany's declaration of war on Russia on 1 August. This was followed by French mobilisation and Germany's declaration of war against France on 3 August and on Belgium the next day, which also saw Britain declare war on Germany over the issue of Belgium's right to neutrality. Insofar as the British government were now thinking about Ireland, they were hoping that one positive side effect of an expected international war would be at least temporarily to halt the feared descent into civil war.

Unionist and nationalist leaders agreed to support both the Government of Ireland Act that implemented Home Rule and an ancillary act suspending it for the duration of the war – which everyone thought would last only a few months – after which unionists were promised that special treatment of Ulster would be considered. Redmond offered Irish support for the war with a request but not as a condition that the Irish Volunteers be put in charge of the defence of Ireland and called for recruits for an 'Irish Brigade' to serve at the front: 'either madness or treachery', Pearse wrote to Devoy.[25] Convinced that Germany was a threat to the freedom of all Europe and that only whole-hearted support for the war could bring about the united self-governing Ireland he had fought for all his life, on 20 September, at Woodenbridge, County Wicklow, Redmond made a heartfelt speech about the interests of Ireland in a war 'undertaken in the defence of the highest principles of religion and morality and right'. It

> would be a disgrace for ever to our country and a reproach to her manhood and a denial of the lessons of her history if young Ireland confined their efforts to remaining at home to defend the shores of Ireland from an unlikely invasion, and to shrinking from the duty of proving on the field of battle that gallantry and courage which has distinguished our race all through its history.

Lord Kitchener, the Secretary of State for War, took his opposition to any concessions to promoting an Irish identity in the army to what Townshend calls a level of 'malign destructiveness'. There would be a 36th Ulster Division for the Ulster Volunteers with their own officers and emblems, but no equivalent for the Irish Volunteers. So while initially nationalist Ireland was fully behind Britain, France and Catholic Belgium, Kitchener badly damaged Redmond's attempt to bring Irish public opinion fully on board and was of steady assistance to Tom Clarke.

The moment of England's difficulty had arrived. According to Seán T. O'Kelly, IRB men welcomed the news of war 'with real joy'. 'If this thing passes without a fight I don't want to live,' Mac Diarmada told McCullough. 'And Tom feels the same.'[26] Their motion at the Supreme Council committed the IRB to an insurrection before the war ended, 'otherwise', said Clarke, they were 'damned for posterity'. That this violated the organisation's own constitution troubled neither them nor their supporters. Two dissenters were targeted. Clarke dispatched Seán T. O'Kelly to bully the Scottish representative, John Mulholland. He dealt himself with Seamus Deakin, the Council President – who was fearful that a rebellion would cause widespread death to civilians and destruction to Dublin – by cleverly playing on his fears about being spied on by the security services to frighten him out of the IRB, Sinn Féin and the Volunteers.

Clarke now decided to look for allies even among those of whom he had previously been suspicious, including James Connolly. While he and Mac Diarmada had sympathy for the plight of the Dublin poor and were pro-striker, and Clarke had written a letter of protest to the newspaper denouncing police brutality in the riots of August 1913, they were hostile towards socialism because of its internationalism and the closeness of the ITGWU to the British TUC. They also saw trade unionism as a distraction from the main job. Clarke was obsessed with vengeance on the British: Mac Diarmada, as Brian Feeney puts it, had 'a Manichean view of the British, or more precisely, the English. Quite simply, his attitude was: Irish good, English evil.'[27] He complained to McGarrity that 'the talk about the friendliness of the English working man and the Brotherhood of man, the English food ships etc. have a very bad unnational influence'. When a member of the IRB admitted he would put internationalism before Ireland, Mac Diarmada threw him out of the meeting. This worry had been mitigated by the breach that opened up when the British TUC, which was unsympathetic to syndicalism, refused to strike in sympathy with the ITGWU and in response to savage abuse from Larkin on union platforms cut off financial aid. But Clarke and Mac Diarmada looked with approval on some of Connolly's incendiary writing, beginning with his message to readers of the *Irish Worker* after the outbreak of war that if a German army landed in Ireland the next day 'we should be perfectly justified in joining it if by doing so we could rid this country once and for all from its connection with the Brigand Empire that drags us unwillingly into this war'.

Connolly had had a bruising year of riots and tensions and rows and arrests since his return to Dublin in August 1913. He had been there only a few days when he was imprisoned and went on a hunger-and-thirst strike that made him a hero among union members in Dublin and Belfast. After the Viceroy released him from jail, he recuperated at Surrey House in Rathmines, the home of Constance Markievicz. Like Maud Gonne, another society rebel, Markievicz found Connolly original and exciting. A restless, flamboyant, romantic attention-seeker, she sought out radical causes: from suffragism she had moved to nationalism after reading a bundle of back issues of *Sinn Féin* and the *Peasant*. Rebuffed by Arthur Griffith, who thought she must be a British spy, she was encouraged by Hobson, who facilitated her joining Sinn Féin and introduced her to Helena Molony, the feminist, separatist protégée of Gonne who brought her into the feminist Gaelicist Inghinidhe na hÉireann (Daughters of Ireland), In 1909, Markievicz had been closely involved with Hobson in setting up Fianna Éireann, the republican boy-scout movement much more militaristic than its Belfast equivalent. She soon became president. Her involvement was anathema to Clarke and Mac Diarmada, who were socially uncomfortable with her kind. As Hobson, who saw them as 'narrowly partisan', put it later, they were "very suspicious of my cooperation with men like MacNeill and Casement who belonged intellectually and socially to a different world',[28] and Markievicz came from a background they instinctively distrusted. In the Fianna, Markievicz was in her element, revelling in uniforms, drilling, shooting and all kinds of activism. In 1911 she was charged with assaulting a policeman while protesting against the royal visit and was let off with a caution.

In Sligo, she had been sympathetic to tenants, and it was inevitable that she would become interested in workers' rights, socialism and trade unionism. A hero-worshipper by temperament, when in 1910 she first met Larkin she thought him 'some great primeval force rather than a man',[29] and in 1911 she spoke at the launch in the autumn of 1911 of the Irish Women Workers' Union, a semi-autonomous branch of the ITGWU whose president was Larkin, whose secretary was his sister Delia and members of which at Jacob's Biscuit Factory helped to precipitate the lock-out through their loyalty to the union.

On Saturday 30 August 1913, with a warrant out for Larkin's arrest, he took refuge in her house, and after his appearance the following day at the Imperial Hotel, as he was being hustled out, Markievicz rushed up to shake his hand and was punched by a policeman. With Delia Larkin, Markievicz organised the feeding of strikers from the Liberty Hall kitchen, to which she was a generous donor, as she was to soup kitchens in the slums. Markievicz was genuine in her concern for the poor, but she did not take egalitarianism too far. Although she and her family had known before she married Casimir that his claim to be a count was bogus, she never disclaimed the title, and was always known as 'Countess', or, like Maud Gonne, as 'Madame'.[30]

Connolly was once more separated from his family. Lillie had hated leaving Dublin, where she was close to her twin brothers and had a decent house. She asked Connolly before they left if it would be the last time they would have to break up their home. Belfast was difficult for her, being a Protestant with Catholic children, but at least the financial problems were alleviated since Nora had a job and she and Ina did piecework on aprons at home. They did not tell their father what they were doing, 'as he thought making aprons was a form of slavery'. Ina later wrote: 'we were always on the alert for father's footsteps' and scrambled to hide evidence of their work before his arrival.[31] There seems to have been no suggestion of moving the family back to Dublin. Henceforward, Connolly would stay with Constance Markievicz, paying ten shillings a week. Although Connolly bristled at upper-class men, he had no problem with upper-class women like Gonne and Markievicz who admired and helped him. He travelled to Belfast to see his family when he could and he was assiduous with letters, but his energies were focused on Dublin.

Casimir had been livid in 1909 when Dublin was rife with rumours about Markievicz and Hobson and had successfully put an end to the financial disaster that was the agricultural commune they ran for a few months. Though Hobson disagreed, his son 'later interpreted some of his father's descriptions of eccentric behaviour by the countess as indicating sexual advances that Hobson was too idealistic and sexually naïve to recognise or reciprocate'.[32] After Connolly's execution Markievicz would write a poem to 'my Hero-love', so it seems likely they had a long affair. He lived with her for almost three years, she was clearly obsessed with him, she threw herself into all his activities, and as she became more socialist he became more nationalist. She was an honorary treasurer of the Irish Citizen Army where she was much involved in training and mobilisation. Not that she restricted herself to this world, for she still had the Fianna and was instrumental in merging Inghinidhe na hÉireann with Cumann na mBan. When Seán O'Casey – who could not stand her, partly because he thought she had a pernicious influence on Connolly – objected to this on the grounds that the Irish Volunteers was an army 'in its methods and aims, inimical to the first interest of Labour', the ICA backed Markievicz and he resigned.

When Connolly had recovered from jail, he led in October 1913 the campaign for the release of Larkin, who had been imprisoned for seditious libel. Speaking with George Bernard Shaw and George Russell at a gigantic protest in the Albert Hall in London, he called for all sympathisers to vote against the Liberals in three forthcoming by-elections. Asked why the government lost all three, Chancellor of the Exchequer Lloyd George suggested: 'There are explanations, the most prominent of which is, probably, Jim Larkin.' Larkin was released shortly afterwards.

The collapse of the strike was humiliating for the ITGWU leadership. 'And so we Irish workers must again go down into Hell, bow our backs to the lash of the slave driver,' wrote Connolly, 'let our hearts be seared by the iron of his hatred, and instead of the sacramental wafer of brotherhood and common sacrifice, eat the dust of defeat and betrayal.' Devastated, bitter and angry, Larkin and Connolly spoke more of nationalism and both were violently opposed to partition, which Connolly wrote should be 'resisted with armed force if necessary'. Back in Belfast, and squabbling again with Larkin about money, he could no longer delude himself that 'the Orange fanatic and the Capitalist-minded Home Ruler' would be consigned to history by working-class solidarity. He had only contempt for 'a people who have pawned their souls for a usurer's promise of prosperity'.

Connolly and Larkin seldom got on well, though they put on a united front in public. In June 1914, for instance, at the meeting chaired by Larkin that launched the ITUC and Labour Party, Connolly was the lead speaker in attacking partition. And later that month, after a still charismatic but exhausted, disillusioned and increasingly capricious Larkin had tried to resign his post, Connolly had led the appeal to his 'comrade' to stay, since he was 'the best man our class has turned out in Ireland'.

In August the tensions on the Provisional Committee of the Irish Volunteers had reaching boiling point. Pearse was one of those who had felt utterly sidelined by the Redmondites, complaining to McGarrity that he was 'scarcely allowed to speak' and that MacNeill capitulated at every turn and was 'weak, hopelessly weak'. There was violence at a poisonous meeting on 10 September when a row broke out after a defeated resolution from Ceannt and Pearse condemning British army recruitment and conscription. John D. Nugent, the toughest of the Redmondite nominees, who thought nothing of having opponents beaten up by his henchmen, accused both O'Rahilly and Ceannt of embezzling Volunteer funds and called Pearse 'a lying contemptible' cur, which caused the usually peaceable Pearse to punch him in the face. In the ensuing brawl, Pearse was rabbit-punched, and a priest challenged Ceannt to a gun duel. Ceannt smiled and told him to be quiet.

Redmond's Woodenbridge speech gave his enemies the excuse to implement the split they were already planning, with Ceannt, Mac Diarmada, MacDonagh, Pearse, Plunkett as well as Hobson and MacNeill among the twenty-one repudiating in a manifesto Redmond's policy as 'utterly at variance with the published and accepted aims and objectives' of the Volunteers, expelling his nominees and demanding the abolition of the Dublin Castle administration and its replacement by a 'National Government'. Redmond kept the leadership of 170,000 men who were renamed the National Volunteers, but since so many of its key people had joined the army it began to lose direction and haemorrhage members. Redmond's refusal to take a Cabinet seat (for fear of being accused at home of selling out) and Carson's acceptance helped unionism rather than nationalism and, with Home Rule on the statute book and so the IPP's *raison d'être* achieved, Redmond's main role became that of recruiting officer. Ireland was not pro-German, but after the initial enthusiasm recruitment began steadily to dwindle, partly because of Kitchener's stupidity and insensitivity, which as the novelist George A. Birmingham (otherwise known as Canon James Hannay) saw, resurrected 'a vague feeling that to fight for the British

Empire was a form of disloyalty to Ireland', and a visceral anti-English feeling, 'smouldering, lacking public expression, but strong'.[33]

MacNeill kept the name Irish Volunteers, the *Irish Volunteer* journal and the headquarters building and would have the loyalty and active involvement of around ten thousand men, themselves composed of three different groups: those against participating in the war and prepared to fight Britain if conscription were imposed; IRB members prepared to launch an insurrection – conscription or no conscription – but only if public opinion wanted it; and the tiny faction manipulated by Clarke, who was determined to destroy the man (for political, not personal reasons) and the party whose MPs had fought so hard decades previously to get him out of jail. For Clarke the split was the luckiest of lucky breaks. Though his protégées were few in number, they now had a real chance of subverting the Volunteers. To the intelligence services and increasingly the public, they would begin to be known inaccurately as Sinn Féin Volunteers.

The reaching out beyond the IRB had been assisted by an approach from Connolly, whose reaction to the crushing disappointment of seeing European socialist groups joining their own national war efforts was to seek potential allies to overthrow capitalism in Ireland. Independence, he had become convinced, was the necessary prerequisite if socialists were to achieve power in Ireland. Above all he was convinced that what gains Labour had made in the British Isles would be rolled back by a militaristic reactionary government enforcing brutal repression after victory in the war. Clarke was prospering now, having sold one shop, acquired a nice house for himself, his wife, three sons and his brother-in-law and surrogate son, Ned Daly, and even having the time to take it easy in the shop and have necessary recuperative holidays, but he was happy to help with a revolution to overthrow everything British, including or excluding capitalism.

Connolly had few friends who were not socialists, but his right-hand man, William O'Brien, told him 'that nothing could be done without the co-operation of such men as Tom Clarke and Seán MacDermott. He asked me if I could put him in touch with the right people, and I undertook to do so.'[34] O'Brien 'saw Eamon Ceannt with whom we were acquainted . . . He undertook to arrange a conference for Connolly and myself to attend.'[35] What he arranged was that on 19

September Clarke would chair a conference of advanced nationalists in Seán T. O'Kelly's office in the Gaelic League library. It was Clarke's first meeting with Connolly and the first formal meeting that included all the Seven; among the few other attendees were Arthur Griffith, John MacBride and William O'Brien.

Clarke called for a nationalist crusade against the war and a programme of action for achieving Irish independence. 'Everyone agreed to resist any British attempt to enforce conscription or disarm the Irish Volunteers and to co-operate with the Germans if they landed in Ireland – provided they only wanted to expel the British and recognised Irish independence.'[36] Failing any of that as the war was ending, an insurrection would be organised and a place claimed at the post-war peace conference. The agreement to establish two committees, one to contact Germany and the other to campaign against the British war effort, produced just a very short-lived Irish Neutrality League, co-founded by Connolly and Markievicz and soon suppressed by Dublin Castle. Clarke was already impressed by Connolly, yet he and Mac Diarmada were also wary of his impetuosity, which almost precipitated a catastrophe within a few days of the meeting. He tested the mettle of his putative allies by proposing that the Irish Volunteers and the ICA occupy the Mansion House a day before Redmond and Asquith were to address a huge recruiting meeting there. Connolly was hoping this would be followed by the takeover of the building, which would make any government actions to regain it to appear to be violent aggression. With luck, this might precipitate a revolution.

Clarke and Mac Diarmada wanted a protest, but a modest one, their plan being that sympathisers cut the lighting system just before the rally, something that proved to be impossible because of the level of security. Yet they were not prepared to be outdone by Connolly. The night before the event, eighty Volunteers and forty members of the ICA joined forces at Stephen's Green, but just before Connolly could set off at their head news arrived that the Mansion House was already occupied by soldiers with machine guns, so it was necessary to call the whole thing off. As Michael Foy put it, Clarke and Mac Diarmada had learned the important lesson 'that although Connolly was a dedicated revolutionary, his impatience and thirst for action whatever the odds made him almost as dangerous to his allies as to his enemies.'[37]

Henceforward, they were cautious with him, yet he was someone of increasing power whom they could not ignore, especially after Larkin disappeared to America the following month, never to return during the lifetime of the Seven.

Before he left for America, Larkin had told Connolly that he would be replaced by P.T. Daly, his long-time associate and secretary of the ITUC, while Connolly would take charge of the *Irish Worker* and the Insurance Section. Under pressure from a furious Connolly and also from the Executive Committee, Larkin capitulated, and on 24 October 1914 Connolly became general secretary, editor of the *Irish Worker* and commandant of the ICA. The union headquarters in Liberty Hall – now adorned with a banner saying 'We Serve Neither King Nor Kaiser' – were henceforward in the hands of an anti-British militant socialist and nationalist with a private army. Larkin's disappearance turned Connolly into a major player on the revolutionary scene. He set about 'shaping the "fermenting yeast"' of a 'disorganised, demoralised and ineffectual' ICA into a 'vanguard for revolution'.[38] Standing for the ownership of Ireland by the people and the unity of Irish nationhood, its members were given uniforms of dark green serge, with slouched hats like the Boers, and it flew the 'Starry Plough', a blue flag with seven gold stars shaped like the Plough constellation, designed by AE and woven by the Dun Emer Guild. Michael Mallin, a union activist, socialist and devout Catholic who had spent twelve years in the British Army, became Connolly's highly efficient chief of staff, and formed a good relationship with the equally devout Con Colbert, his opposite number in the Volunteers. Once the Volunteers had split, the previous animosity between both armies was giving way to co-operation, which sometimes included joint manoeuvres.

Suborning the other army, the Irish Volunteers, was a major undertaking for the IRB, but they set to it with a will. At a Convention at the end of October, MacNeill and O'Rahilly were re-elected president and treasurer of the Volunteers, and an IRB-inspired motion that members of the old Provisional Committee be re-elected meant the new Executive Committee was committed to the manifesto. Of the Central Executive of twelve, eight were IRB: Hobson was General Secretary, Ceannt was Financial Secretary, Pearse was Press Secretary and

Plunkett co-Treasurer. When in December it appointed Headquarters Staff, MacNeill was Chief of Staff, Hobson Quartermaster General and O'Rahilly director of arms, and Clarke placemen included Plunkett as Director of Military Operations, MacDonagh as Director of Training and Pearse as Director of Military Organisation, a job he lobbied for with his customary energy and with the help of a paper on how resistance to conscription could escalate into guerrilla warfare. This was the policy of Hobson, who as editor of the *Irish Volunteer* spread the message that the Volunteers could not defeat the British Army but should instead aim to dismantle its government in Ireland and withhold violence until conscription guaranteed public support. All the Volunteers paid lip-service to this policy, but it was being undermined covertly by the Clarke loyalists, who in turn were the objects of Hobson's suspicion. Clarke was the better conspirator: Liam Mellows, for instance, who was Hobson's protégée and confidant, was in fact spying for Clarke, with whom he had bonded when he found they were both the sons of British Army sergeants. At Mac Diarmada's suggestion, the Supreme Council appointed Mellows national organiser of the Fianna at the end of 1912, thus reducing Hobson's influence.

Pearse produced an organisational scheme that owed much to the British army. Companies consisted of a maximum of one hundred men under a commander; four to eight companies made a battalion under a commandant (chosen as a title rather than colonel as a nod to the German or French armies); and three to five battalions a brigade. Although they were still heavily outnumbered, when the appointments were made in March, IRB men were appointed to key positions throughout the country. Pearse, Plunkett and Hobson were commandants unattached to any battalion. Dublin was sewn up: MacDonagh, now sworn into the IRB, had turned out to be a gifted administrator and was made Dublin Brigadier and commandant of the 2nd Battalion. The 1st was commanded by Ned Daly, the 4th by Ceannt, and the 3rd by Eamon de Valera, who disliked secret societies but was talked into joining the IRB by MacDonagh. Summoning the battalion commanders, Pearse talked of the possibility of an insurrection in September 1915.

For Clarke and his allies, suborning the IRB itself was easier. In

October the IRB Supreme Council had set up an Advisory Committee of IRB Volunteers to plan for a rising: too big for Clarke's liking, it was allowed to lapse. Instead Clarke and Mac Diarmada established the Military Committee,* which would retrospectively be known as the Military Council. It consisted of Ceannt and Plunkett, who were interested in military strategy, and Pearse. Among Clarke's great strengths were his intuitiveness and his respect for people with complementary qualities. He had become utterly convinced of the commitment of Pearse and Plunkett to revolution and saw their brains, their eloquence in speech and on paper, as well as their social status, as incalculable advantages for acquiring recruits and for making a revolution acceptable to posterity.

The relationship with Germany was a matter of great importance to both Volunteers and the IRB. Convinced that war was inevitable, Hobson and Casement had been discussing the issue since 1910, their view being that if Ireland helped Britain it would share its defeat if it lost and gain nothing if it won, while if it helped Germany to win it might gain independence. In America, Devoy had been thinking along the same lines for almost as long, and when Hobson took the Casement memorandum to America in March 1914 Devoy agreed with it fully. Casement had travelled to America in July to fundraise for more arms and was acclaimed as a hero for his role in the gun-running until the outbreak of war turned attention elsewhere. Redmond's pledge that the Volunteers would defend Ireland had wrong-footed unionists and gone down well in America and Casement had proved to be a poor fundraiser. Convinced that the British and Russians were the aggressors in a war against German commerce and industry, he was now passionately pro-Germany: 'I pray for the salvation of Germany night and day – and God Save Ireland now is another form of God save Germany!'[39]

Devoy was purely pragmatic, bent on exploiting the war for the benefit of Ireland. He told the German Ambassador, Johann von Bernstorff, that the Clan's 'friends in Ireland' would rebel if they got the arms and trained officers Germany could supply, thus deflecting

---

* For the sake of simplicity, I will henceforth call it the Military Council.

British troops from Europe to Ireland. Because of the British blockade of Germany, censorship, spies and the severing of transatlantic cables between Germany and America, communications between the US, Germany and Ireland were very difficult. In August Devoy chose an envoy, John Kenny (who had sworn Tom Clarke into the Clan in the Napper Tandy club in 1880), to take documents to the German government from both Casement and himself and convince them of the potential of a rebellion. Much impressed by Germany, Kenny proceeded to Dublin, and in late September 1914 reported to Clarke (who was now between bouts of illness) that there was military stalemate, but that Germany would ultimately triumph, thus assuring Clarke that he had 'time to mature his plans for a rising, time to overcome the scepticism of Germany's political leaders, time for its General Staff to realise Ireland's strategic importance and time to edge the IRB into the victor's camp'.[40]

Devoy ran under the Clan's name a series of articles in the *Gaelic American* based on Casement memoranda under the title 'Ireland, England, Germany and the freedom of the seas'. Casement, who was having delusions about being a successor to other great Protestant leaders of Irish nationalism, wrote a perfervid letter to the *Irish Independent* appealing to Irishmen who cared about Irish freedom not to join 'the allied millions now attacking Germany in a war that, at best, concerned Ireland not at all'.[41] He was now appalled by American values, and, having made it too dangerous for himself to go back to Ireland, suggested to von Bernstorff that he should try to raise an Irish legion from among Irish prisoners in Germany. Devoy found Casement's reluctance to work only through the Clan a nuisance, but, although he doubted if he could succeed, McGarrity trusted him, so the Clan paid his expenses to Berlin and lent him money. Accompanied by his lover, a young Norwegian sailor, Adler Christensen, who claimed to be his servant, he sailed for Berlin in October as the Clan envoy.

In America, Devoy would henceforward use the resources of the Clan to oppose the allies in every way possible, including disseminating German propaganda and assisting spies. But in Berlin, Casement – who apart from his temperamental problems seemed to most Irish prisoners to resemble an aristocratic Englishman – was failing comprehensively in his mission, securing only 56 recruits to an 'Irish Brigade' from a total of around 2,300. He had little more success with the Germans, about whose commitment he became as disillusioned as he had over the years with every group with whom he worked. Concluding that Germany's motives were selfish, he would denounce them in 1916 as 'Cads' who were 'hated by the world and England will surely beat them'.[42]

It was against this background that in spring 1915 the Military Council sent Joe Plunkett to negotiate with Germany. Despite being often confined to bed with fever, Plunkett was still full of intellectual energy, and had turned the *Irish Review* into the mouthpiece of his wing of the Volunteers. From a change of visitors and frequent references to 'the organisation', Gerry – his messenger and agent – realised he had joined the IRB. She recorded that during the short-lived discussions over the abortive attack on the Mansion House Plunkett had had his first long conversation with Connolly and 'came home very excited, saying that Connolly was the most intellectual and the greatest man he knew in every way'. Larkfield – where Gerry and Joe had been allowed by Ma to use an empty cottage – was by now an invaluable centre for drilling and gun-practice, with more arms being acquired through a friendly gunsmith, and soldiers and others selling and stealing army supplies. Plunkett had acquired a Mauser automatic that he loved taking apart and putting back together.

For fear of the Defence of the Realm Act (DORA), which had come into operation four days after war broke out and included a prohibition against spreading 'reports likely to cause disaffection or alarm among any of His Majesty's forces or among the civilian population', newspapers did not publish the 'Manifesto to the Irish Volunteers'. It appeared in the *Irish Review*, which was being published less and less frequently, in November, with, for good measure, 'Twenty Plain Facts for Irishmen', which included a description of the Union Jack as 'the symbol of the Act of Union of 1800 by which the Irish nation was deprived of her last rights and liberties'. The censor would suppress it, Gerry told Plunkett. 'What harm?' he replied. 'We're broke anyway.' The copies were seized, though the magazine was not suppressed, but it died anyway. That same month, the IRB's *Irish Freedom* – which had accused Redmond of 'crawling imperialism' and of being a Judas – and Connolly's *Irish Worker* were closed down for sedition. For a short time Connolly published *The Worker*, which was also banned; its successor, *Workers' Republic*, survived until the Rising.

Plunkett had something else to occupy him: with MacDonagh, he had started the Irish Theatre in Hardwicke Hall, another property of Ma's that she was unsure what to do with. Although she was as parsimonious as ever about necessities, she was still generous when big ideas seized her imagination, and she provided a luxurious stage. The objective was to put on modern playwrights like Ibsen, Chekov and Strindberg; some regular funding was put up by Edward Martyn, an *Irish Review* contributor, political nationalist and donor to many cultural ventures including at times the Abbey Theatre and St Enda's. The producer was MacDonagh's brother John, who was also an actor; other actors included MacDonagh and another brother, Joseph, and Plunkett, his brother George and sister Philomena as well as Willie Pearse, the elusive Columba O'Carroll and G.N. Reddin, who had known Plunkett since Belvedere. He would describe the delight Plunkett had in controversy that extended to rushing away from people he was talking to 'in order to settle a point in dispute with a noisy group in the other corner, then rush back to the people he had forsaken, and, taking up the thread of conversation where he had left it, settle their difficulty to his perfect satisfaction'. Plunkett's mind was so restless, said Reddin, as to be 'a disease'. The Irish Theatre suffered from Martyn's insistence on having his own unimpressive plays produced, but it did succeed in staging a significant amount of modern European and Irish drama, including a play of Patrick Pearse's. The month before the insurrection – perhaps to protect it in future – an otherwise engaged Plunkett would sever his connection by making an unconvincing fuss about a Strindberg play.

Part of Plunkett's fertile mind had been focused for some time on devising a military plan for the Rising. Shortly after Christmas 1914, probably at his suggestion, the Military Council decided he should go to Germany, from where Casement was sending disturbing messages. He taught Gerry the cipher he would use, arranged for the routing of mail via a cousin to Mac Diarmada or Pearse, tore up all the photographs of himself that he could find, and told everyone that he was going to Jersey at Easter for his health. Leaving Dublin on 17 March, he kept a diary in a tiny notebook sprinkled with encrypted names and places and bits of uncertain Irish, along with literary quotations, the odd poem and short disquisitions on architecture and wine. He experienced occasional searches along the way including one from the French navy. He travelled to Germany via Liverpool, London, Paris and San Sebastian (where he was in bed with fever for a week), thence to Barcelona, Genoa, and Florence, where he was ill again. Travelling now as James Malcolm, after Milan and Lausanne, he spent two weeks in Berne growing a beard and waiting for papers, and then reached Basle, where he had immense problems at the German border with both Swiss and German officials. He later said he almost died on the twenty-three-hour subsequent train journey to Berlin, where he arrived on 20 April as Johann M. Peters from San Francisco and met up with Casement and innumerable German officials.

Plunkett's zeal for the drama now seems to have led him to replicate the spirit and style of Wolfe Tone's journal when seeking Revolutionary French aid in 1796–8. He seemed to take effortlessly to a cloak-and-dagger world that he often enjoyed, refusing to allow anyone under the rank of ambassador to know his real name. He banned Casement from giving it to Adler Christensen either, even though Casement said he was reliable. Plunkett's instincts were right: Christensen would betray his master.

Casement, who had wanted a large German force, was now convinced this would be a disaster and culminate in Ireland becoming part of the German Empire. Plunkett recognised that apart from the damage caused by Casement's hopeless performance in Berlin, there was in any case no German appetite for an invasion of Ireland, and so scaled down the demands: after weeks of on-and-off illness, frustrating hanging about and having inconclusive meetings, he finally reached an understanding in mid-May that if the Military Council named a date and convinced Berlin they were serious, Germany might send a cargo of arms, paid for by the IRB, possibly accompanied by a skeleton force of officers and trained men.

A newspaper report that 'a tall man with a black beard' had been with Casement and had made a recruitment speech to Irish prisoners frightened Gerry, who knew that if identified Plunkett would be jailed, which would probably kill him. She took one encrypted communication to Pearse, about which she later recalled:

> His sister Maggie kept hopping in and out of the room, madly trying to find out what was going on, but Pearse stopped speaking while she was in the room. She left the door open each time and each time he got up and closed it before speaking again. He was a most impressive person. I would have done whatever he told me to do because of his authority, not, as in Seán MacDiarmada's case, because I loved him.

While awaiting instructions from the Military Council that it was safe to go home, Plunkett had a month's holiday with Casement, who was desperate to go back to Ireland with him, but, being depressed, unrealistic and notorious, was a liability whom Plunkett succeeded in leaving behind in Germany. He was back in Dublin in mid-July, now based full time in Larkfield, where Gerry had moved them permanently, pretending to Hobson that there was no German interest whatsoever, reassuring him that the Military Council agreed with his decision about Casement, and content with the instruction to go to America in August to report to Devoy about Germany. He set off equipped with a hollow walking stick full of encrypted documents. He was refused admission at Ellis Island because of the tubercular gland on his right cheek, but on the grounds that Plunkett was dying anyway, with the help of a senator and a $1,000 deposit, Devoy got him admitted for two months for 'literary pursuits'. Plunkett saw Devoy and McGarrity, but was uneasy about the Clan's desire to be the decision-makers on the rebellion, while also being guilty in a spy-ridden New York of loose talk 'which could cause a man to be jailed in Ireland'.

Before leaving for America, Plunkett had had a painful interview with Columba O'Carroll, whose brother Frank, a good friend of Plunkett's, had been killed in early June at Gallipoli. She had told Plunkett earlier in the year that he must give up pursuing her; she was making changes in her life and the separation was to be total. In one of several unsent letters to her from New York in which he complained of the meaninglessness of her instruction to 'be myself', he asked what she wanted and offered a classified list of choices that no one else could have written:

> Badman, Adventurer, Softie, Greenhorn, Sleuth, Napoleon, Toots, George Washington, The Thin Woman's Husband, Micawber, Romeo, St Francis, Don Juan, Robert Emmet, Boss Croker, Cuchullin, Kaiser Bill, Don Quixote, The Virginian, Dante, Danton, Tomás, Sir Roger Casement, Fr Browne, Fool (various qualities all the one price . . .) Explorer, Navvy, Old Moore, Walt Whitman, Sophocles, or Endymion.*

In another unsent letter from America, he wrote:

> Is it not six months since I left my country, home, friends and you for your sake? Have I not even abstained from writing to you? What greater works could love have done than these? To have found what I did seek, honourable death would have been far easier to endure than the 'ordeal by life'.

Yet his sense of purpose remained. In New York Padraic Colum was 'impressed by the decision and command he had attained to', and he told Sydney Gifford 'I am a different man since I joined the Volunteers.' He also bonded with Joyce Kilmer, the mystic and Catholic poet who

---

* Owen Dudley Edwards provided the following elucidation of the more obscure references: 'Badman' from John Bunyan's *The Life and Death of Mr Badman*; 'Adventurer', probably from J.M. Barrie's *Peter Pan* (1904) with its all-too-appropriate 'To die will be an awfully big adventure'; 'Toots', a Royal Family nickname for recently widowed Princess Louise of Argyll; The Thin Woman's Husband is a character in James Stephens' *The Crock of Gold* (1912); Boss Croker of Tammany Hall's ill-gotten gains won him the Derby in 1907 when his horse beat King Edward VII's; *The Virginian* (1902) was Owen Wister's novel; Father Browne (misspelled) was Chesterton's priest–detective who first appeared in 1911; 'Navvy', Patrick MacGill's autobiographical *Children of the Dead End* (1914) on sometimes horrific conditions of Irish migrant labour in Scotland; Old Moore (of the prophesying *Almanac*); 'Endymion', John Keats's poem about the beautiful shepherd beloved by the moon goddess.

had just published 'Trees' ('Poems are made by fools like me, / But only God can make a tree'). Plunkett arrived home in late October carrying two swords, visited his trusted cousin and, in typically flamboyant mode, took a small red wafer out of the back of his gold hunter watch and threw it into the fire, saying 'There goes the seal of the German Foreign Office.'

In between Germany and America, on 1 August 1915 Plunkett had been at the funeral of the old dynamiter O'Donovan Rossa, the IRB's most potent piece of theatre ever, which lifted the separatist cause to a new high, established the reputations of Clarke and MacDonagh as organisers of military precision and was Pearse's apogee as a speaker.

Pearse had been in an increasingly insurrectionary mode, his rhetoric ever more incendiary. Like most of the IRB, the Volunteers and, indeed, Europe, the Seven had succumbed to war fever: even the poets now saw themselves as military strategists. In October 1914 Pearse had told McGarrity that the crisis the IRB craved would be precipitated by a German invasion, conscription, a food shortage, an attempt to disarm the Irish Volunteers, or an attempt to arrest its leaders. This was one of a sequence of letters talking up the bellicosity of the Volunteers and seeking to influence Clan policy that were essentially irrelevant since Clarke was the Clan's man and McGarrity was not telling Pearse what was going on with Casement and Germany.

Publicly, Pearse was becoming much better known, assisted by the Provost of Trinity, Professor Mahaffy, who in November 1914 had banned a Trinity College Gaelic Society meeting commemorating the birth of Thomas Davis because one of the speakers was 'a man called Pearse . . . a supporter of the anti-recruiting agitation'. Held outside Trinity on 20 November, the meeting received much press attention. Yeats was among the speakers, declaring himself 'not more vehemently opposed to the unionism of Professor Mahaffy' (whom he commended for his 'good service to English literature') 'than I am the pro-Germanism of Mr Pearse' (whom he commended for his 'good service to Irish literature'). Pearse's speech showed how his position was hardening and that physical force had become his religion, for he elevated the 'gospel' of John Mitchel, whom Yeats said 'taught hate of England', above that of Davis, who 'taught love of Ireland'. Yeats was becoming concerned about Pearse: he would tell Ezra Pound that 'Pearse was half-cracked and wanting to be hanged. He has Emmet delusions same as other lunatics think they are Napoleon or God.'[43]

Pearse continued to make speeches to largely appreciative crowds of the like-minded, which helped bolster his exaggerated view of how much the Irish population shared his attitudes. In May, after publishing in the *Irish Volunteer* an article called 'Why We Want Recruits', he visited Limerick on a recruiting mission with de Valera and other Volunteer leaders at the head of a parade of around 1,000 Volunteers from Dublin and Cork. They were jeered at and stoned by sections of the Limerick crowd, chiefly the families of British army men who relied on the separation allowance to keep them housed and fed. On being told that the Volunteers might have to fight an angry crowd to get to the train, one officer told his company to load their rifles, an order countermanded by Pearse as soon as he heard of it. He was, of course, terrified of a Volunteer equivalent of Bachelors Walk: in fact, the only casualty was one man wounded with a bayonet. The experience brought home to him that his hopes of rousing the country by these means were non-existent, and he swiftly issued an order to all Volunteers forbidding any unauthorised discharge of firearms on pain of suspension.

The doubts and contradictions that often plagued him were addressed that same month in *The Master*, a play staged by St Enda's in the Irish Theatre along with *Iosagán*. Ciaran (played by Willie), the master of a small forest school in Ireland who had abandoned his quest for earthly glory by giving up the world's temptations and becoming a Christian, is challenged by Daire, the King, to prove the efficacy of his new religion. Daire threatens to kill Ciaran's favourite pupil, little Iollan – who 'has a beautiful white body and therefore you all love him; aye, the Master and all' – unless Heaven intervenes. Ciaran will not fight and his faith is defective, but Iollan's is so strong that he successfully summons up the warrior Archangel Michael to defend him. Ciaran, while acknowledging this revelation and his own deficiency, dies of emotional shock. That faith was all was the message.

Pearse made this clear, too, in an article that month about the Volunteers.

We have no misgivings, no self-questionings. While others have been doubting, timorous, ill-at-ease, we have been serenely at peace with our consciences . . . We called upon the names of the great confessors of our national faith, and all was well with us. Whatever soul-searchings there may be among Irish political parties now or hereafter, we go on in the calm certitude of having done the clear, clean, sheer thing. We have the strength and peace of mind of those who never compromise.

Henceforward, Pearse's writings and speeches would show no doubts or hesitations, as he was to show to stunning effect when called on by Tom Clarke to be at the centre of his greatest stunt.

Devoy had become reconciled with his old enemy O'Donovan Rossa in his last years of anecdotage and lapses into senility and had made a useful ally of his wife. When Rossa died at the end of June 1915 at the age of eighty-three, his timing was perfect: in Devoy's words, 'he performed his last and perhaps greatest service to the Fenian cause'. Clarke's response to the news was to cable Devoy asking for the body to be sent home immediately.

Devoy and Clarke were set on using Rossa as a symbol of all suffering Fenians. As Devoy put it later, in terms that gave a slight hint of what an appalling nuisance Rossa had been to everyone, including the Clan, in

this predominant Fenian quality of self-sacrifice, O'Donovan Rossa was the most typical Fenian of them all. He began to sacrifice himself, his family, and his interests at the very inception of the movement and he continued it to his last conscious hour. Often the sacrifice was wholly unnecessary and even unwise, but Rossa believed it was called for and never hesitated or counted the cost.

Of course, everyone forgot that Rossa's final employment had been in an Irish government job obtained for him by John Redmond.

Clarke was uninterested in the truth about Rossa. He intended using the funeral to demonstrate that his ideals were alive and that a new generation of Fenians was ready to sacrifice themselves to complete his mission. To that end he wanted the funeral to be 'a drama, a pageant, a recruiting platform that would swell the ranks of separatism. It was also designed to be armed propaganda that would legitimise O'Donovan Rossa's political violence, ignore his conciliatory old age and make constitutional nationalism seem just a temporary aberration in the centuries of resistance to British rule in Ireland.'[44] The use of the dead to justify as well as dictate the policy of the living was a hallowed precedent that would be enthusiastically adopted by subsequent generations of violent republicans.*

Clarke, who was in increasingly poor health, bet his reputation and that of the Irish Volunteers and the IRB on making the Rossa funeral a separatist triumph, using every penny he could lay his hands on. He chaired the O'Donovan Rossa Committee, with eleven subcommittees covering everything from special trains to a souvenir booklet, including such prominent names as Griffith, MacNeill and Markievicz. Ceannt was on the publicity committee, as well as commanding the 4th Dublin Brigade, and Áine was a Cumann na mBan representative. Connolly, with whom Clarke was increasingly friendly, was put on the Guards and Procession subcommittee, which meant the ICA and Volunteers would form a joint guard of honour. Clarke was hampered by the absence of Seán Mac Diarmada, who in May had been sentenced to four months with hard labour after a particularly inflammatory anti-recruiting speech in County Galway, but MacDonagh took his place and acted as chief marshal in close consultation with Clarke. Obsequies included a Solemn Requiem High Mass in St Mary's Pro-Cathedral, after which the casket with a glass lid was escorted to the City Hall (beside Dublin Castle), which for four days thousands of mourners filed past. On Sunday 1 August, chosen because next day was a bank holiday, at 2:00 p.m., Clarke closed the lid and draped the coffin with a tricolour and Volunteers carried it into a hearse. The two-mile-long cortège was headed by an honour guard of (illegally) armed Volunteers, followed by 20,000

---

* The original Fenian and IRB movements had won their first public success in 1861 with the funeral of the Young Irelander Terence Bellew McManus, whose corpse was also transported across the Atlantic.

mourners, who included representatives of every nationalist organisation in Ireland including both lots of Volunteers, Cumann an
mBan, the ICA and the AOH, innumerable bands playing patriotic
songs, and many women and children. The sun was shining and there
was no police or army presence to challenge the procession on the
indirect route that took Rossa through five miles of Dublin to his
destination in Glasnevin Cemetery beside his old Fenian comrades
John O'Leary and James Stephens, where he was buried and prayed
over.

Clarke had chosen Pearse to give the panegyric with the instruction
'Make it hot as hell, throw all discretion to the winds.' As hundreds of
people laboured over funeral plans in Dublin, Pearse had spent days
polishing his words in his little Rosmuc cottage, where he could
rehearse before Willie and Desmond Ryan. In his Volunteer officer's
uniform, he delivered powerfully a speech that has never been
surpassed in republican history for its propagandistic brilliance. On
behalf of all the dead Fenians, Pearse pledged to Ireland 'our love and
we pledge to English rule in Ireland our hate': the seeds of the young
men of '65 and '67, he said, were now ripening in the young men of this
generation. Years later, Darrell Figgis, who had stood opposite him
across the grave listening to 'his slow passion and deliberate eloquence',
could 'see him yet as he flung back his head, and can hear him yet as his
voice rose to the close'.

> Life springs from death; and from the graves of patriot men
> and women spring living nations. The Defenders of this
> Realm have worked well in secret and in the open. They
> think that they have pacified Ireland. They think that they
> have purchased half of us and intimidated the other half.
> They think that they have foreseen everything, think that
> they have provided against everything; but, the fools, the
> fools, the fools! – they have left us our Fenian dead, and
> while Ireland holds these graves, Ireland unfree shall never
> be at peace.

Then Volunteers fired three volleys over the grave. 'After it was all over
I saw him', recalled Figgis,

with his curious heavy gait, in plain simple Volunteer uniform, without a single decoration of rank. Soon after a motor passed me, holding Tom MacDonagh, the Commandant-General for the day, surrounded by staff officers, smart and resplendent with yellow tabs. I little dreamed that I should never see them again.[45]

Éamonn Ceannt was not impressed. While he tried to keep his passions under control, he spoke to Figgis

with cold contempt of Padraic Pearse's slow and moving eloquence and appeal to sentiment as 'green-flaggery'. He would have none of it. It revolted his pride. The straight, nervous blow was, for him, its own jurisdiction, needing no other; and if defeat came, such as warriors could not prevent, it would at least not touch or tarnish his pride.[46]

Joe Plunkett had been present in uniform, but kept a low profile because of his imminent journey to America; his father had been at the grave saying goodbye to one of his old friends, Gerry had been in the crowd, and Jack, who had been a motorbike messenger for MacDonagh, described it as a 'perfect organisation with a completely successful scheme to prevent arrests'. Connolly's contribution to the Souvenir Handbook about the ICA's role ended with 'We are, therefore, present to honour O'Donovan Rossa by right of our faith in the separate destiny of our country, and our faith in the ability of the Irish workers to achieve that destiny.' MacDonagh would write a poetic eulogy, ending 'Him England for his love of Ireland hates; / This flesh we bury England's chains have bitten: / That is enough; for our deed he waits; / With Emmet's let his epitaph be written.'

The militarisation of MacDonagh was something that astonished many of his friends. He loved Volunteer work of all kinds, carried a revolver, stored weapons at home and even allowed the Volunteers to drill in the Irish Theatre. In May 1915 he wrote to his old friend Dominic Hackett of his sheer exhilaration in the job and of the forty boys from ten to sixteen 'who would do anything for the country at my bidding' he had training and drilling and studying Irish and Irish history. He was obsessed with military textbooks, and, according to his son Donagh, 'the official publications of the English War Office soon decorated the shelves which had held the works of English scholars'. He wrote notes and gave lectures and speeches on military themes. His interests were wide: he once told the Volunteers that 'one could live indefinitely and work hard on a diet of nothing but onions, and he urged all and sundry to sow plenty of onions without delay'. He also insisted on discipline, sobriety, punctuality and regular training, 'including drilling, scouting, ambushes and fieldwork, often involving two companies of Volunteers in war games, with skirmishing and the seizing of strategic points'. He also planned to set up instruction centres and rifle ranges and weekly training throughout the country and to have an engineering corps. Nationalism and militarism infused every-thing, even the poem he wrote for his daughter, Barbara, who was born in March 1915. The following month he joined his two great friends, Pearse and Plunkett, in the IRB.

Francis Sheehy-Skeffington attended a speech MacDonagh gave in full Volunteer uniform in May 1915 to a women's anti-war meeting. By now a fine speaker, he was enthusiastically received by many but not all for his support for women's movements and his attacks on Redmond. The Irish Volunteers were different, he was reported as saying, because they 'were not going to exploit their own people. He hoped – he knew – they would never be used against their fellow countrymen.' Still, the redoubtable chairwoman took exception to his rhetoric, and suggested that 'if the men of Ireland devoted more of their time to loving Ireland, and less to hating England, they would have built up a strong nation'. Like many in the audience, as Shane Kenna put it, Skeffington 'did not fail to see the irony of a senior Volunteer condemning violence in Europe while boasting of being one of the creators of a new militarism in Ireland'. He wrote MacDonagh an open letter begging him to rethink his membership of the Volunteers 'before the militaristic current draws you too far from your humanitarian anchorage' and challenged MacDonagh's assertion that the Volunteers were there to defend Irish rights and prevent civil war: they were being 'organised to kill', and eventually they would. But MacDonagh was beyond saving, telling Hackett that Irish independence could be won only by 'zealous peace I hope, but war if necessary'.

Reproduced in full in the Souvenir Handbook, Pearse's speech circulated around nationalist Ireland like samizdat. Like Emmet's speech from the dock, parts were learned off by heart and recited in homes and pubs and at GAA matches. When an exhausted Clarke arrived in Limerick to recuperate, his sister-in-law Madge recalled that 'He was wild with delight and believed that the effect would be splendid.'

The effect was almost undermined when a writ arrived at St Enda's demanding unpaid rent, which – though he was floundering in unpaid bills – Pearse thought with some justification was a plot to destroy his reputation as 'bankrupt and discredited'. He told McGarrity that without £300 St Enda's would go under and he would be unable 'to give the cause at this supreme moment any help. I am down and out.' Clarke telegraphed begging that McGarrity 'attend to Paddy's communication regarding school – it is both urgent and vital', and the school and Pearse were saved for the time being. Having rescued his invaluable chief propagandist, Clarke set about organising a revolution, moving the remainder of his pawns into place in the organisations where he needed them. His increasing influence was to be seen in the ruthless way he achieved the IRB takeover of the Gaelic League that August, forcing Douglas Hyde's resignation by committing this hitherto apolitical organisation to an Ireland free of British rule, installing the ever faithful Seán T. O'Kelly as general secretary and MacNeill – whom Clarke regarded as a handy ineffectual figurehead – as president. Ceannt had long ago decided that the League should become political; Pearse, however, regretted that the League had abandoned Hyde. Mac Diarmada, who had been elected to the Coisde Gnótha while in jail, had no such scruples: cultural organisations were as expendable as awkward people. He was released in September, rather stronger than when he went in, and he and Clarke joined Pearse, Plunkett and Ceannt on the Military Council.

The Volunteer leadership was split: MacNeill, Hobson and O'Rahilly stuck to the defensive position. In the IRB, the Supreme Council was also split between those who stuck to the IRB constitution's stipulation about public support and those who were determined on insurrection and who kept their plans secret from colleagues. While several of the Military Council fancied themselves as military strategists or tacticians, essentially, they adopted Plunkett's plan. No copy is available, but in Townshend's view it was based on 'a fusion of historical and theoretical thinking' with at root the belief that defenders were in a better position than attackers. J.J. 'Ginger' O'Connell, who had spent two years in the US army and was Hobson's right-hand man, watched the manoeuvres commanded by MacDonagh and Pearse at the Dublin Brigade's field day at Easter 1915 and found them minutely planned but unimpressive. The fundamental problem was their 'preconceived idea of an insurrection', which allowed Volunteers no flexibility. 'The fact is both Pearse and MacDonagh, and Plunkett also, believed that the art of war could be studied in books without any trouble being taken to fit the book theories to material facts.'[47] They were amateurs, whose articulacy and charisma persuaded others that they knew what they were talking about. Fixated on Dublin, they made virtually no plans for the rest of the country. But then the primary concern of the poets was to make a better showing than Robert Emmet.

In conversation with a friend, MacDonagh dismissed 'country fighting' and assured him that the British would not shell the city because they would injure their own supporters.

> It seemed to me that the British were at least convinced that they were now fighting for their existence as an Empire, while we should be fighting to drive them completely out of Ireland. To expect them to accept defeat rather than shell Dublin seemed to me fantastic. But MacDonagh smiled tolerantly at my objections and again reassured me that everything was quite all right, Dublin would not be bombarded. One could not stand up against his cheery optimism.[48]

Connolly would join the Military Council in January and reinforce these delusions, since he believed the British army would not use artillery in Dublin because that would damage capitalist interests. Hobson had 'hot arguments' about it with Pearse, arguing that guerrilla tactics had a better chance of success than gambling everything on one throw, but Pearse said what mattered was to have a sacrifice, and it had to be a sacrifice of high theatrical impact. As Conor Cruise O'Brien put it,

'What he was aiming at essentially was the staging in Dublin of a national Passion Play, but incorporating a real life-and-death blood sacrifice.'

Plunkett wore down opposition with his argument that marching out of Dublin to fight was what the British would expect them to do. He thought there was a chance that the Volunteers could hold out in Dublin for three months. As F.X. Martin summed it up, 'the insurgents had no intelligible, or militarily speaking intelligent, blueprint for an all-Ireland rising'.[49]

The choice of buildings to occupy was similarly capricious and paid little attention to such issues as vulnerability, communications or the availability of supplies. The GPO, cut off from the other chosen locations by the Liffey, was, for instance, a bizarre choice of headquarters. Was it simply, as Townshend suggests, 'its visually impressive location opposite Nelson's pillar on Lower Sackville Street, Dublin's widest thoroughfare'? Did no one, even Connolly, consider how vulnerable would be the inhabitants of the slums on which the GPO abutted?

Connolly's long-standing hope had been that 'Ireland may yet set the torch to a European conflagration that will not burn out until the last throw and the last capitalist bond and debenture will be shrivelled on the funeral pyre of the last warlord'.[50] In Hobson's view, his conversation

> was full of clichés derived from the earlier days of the Socialist movement in Europe. He told me that the working class was always revolutionary, that Ireland was a powder magazine and that what was necessary was for someone to apply the match. I replied that if he must talk in metaphors, Ireland was a wet bog and that the match would fall into a puddle.[51]

Connolly was as naïve as the Military Council when it came to planning, being convinced that in a city 'really determined civilian revolutionists' could defeat regular troops. Like the Military Council, he was fast seeing himself as a military expert: in the summer of 1915 he had written in the *Workers' Republic* a series of military studies that included the 1905 Moscow Insurrection and the Alamo.

In December, at a meeting to appoint a new President of the Supreme Council to replace the terrified and absent Deakin, Denis McCullough told Mac Diarmada that he intended to propose Pearse, who had joined in September.

> 'Oh, for the love of God, don't be stupid, don't be foolish,' he said.
> 'Why?' I said, 'he is an excellent man.'
> 'We couldn't control him,' he said.
> '"And who are you going to have?'
> 'Now leave that to Tom and myself. We will get all that fixed.'[52]

So Clarke and Mac Diarmada proposed McCullough, who did not realise his attraction was that he lived in Belfast and rarely came to Dublin. By Christmas, the Military Council had decided against their original date of Good Friday, and had chosen Easter Sunday, 23 April, as the date of the Rising, but no one told the Supreme Council at its January meeting. Instead, Mac Diarmada proposed a motion to rise 'at the earliest possible date'. Pat McCartan asked 'Who are we to call a rising?' but appeals to the IRB's constitution from him and Hobson carried no weight.

Through the Military Council, the IRB was firmly under Clarke's control, but, consumed with frustration at the failure of the anti-recruitment movement to make much headway, Connolly was becoming a loose cannon; he was as hostile towards ordinary army recruits as he was towards generals. Liberty Hall would give no help to the family of a soldier regardless of his membership of the union. He looked capable of snapping at any provocation, taking his tiny force on to the streets and starting a hopeless revolution that would bring the authorities down on everyone they thought potentially subversive. Larkin had left the ITCWU in a financial and administrative shambles, which Connolly was painfully sorting out, but Connolly was doing what Larkin would not have tolerated – turning Liberty Hall into what O'Casey described as 'the centre of Irish National disaffection', a revolutionary headquarters with a fully furnished arsenal. All his speeches and writings, lamented O'Casey,

proclaimed that Jim Connolly had stepped from the narrow
byway of Irish Socialism on to the broad and crowded
highway of Irish Nationalism . . . The high creed of Irish
Nationalism became his daily rosary, while the higher
creed of international humanity that had so long bubbled
from his eloquent lips was silent for ever, and Irish Labour
had lost a Leader.[53]

Relentlessly, he goaded the Volunteers in the *Workers' Republic*.
Volunteer-ICA and later IRB-ICA meetings merely reinforced
Connolly's impatience and IRB fears of his impetuosity. Around
Christmas 1915, Pearse told Desmond Ryan that

Connolly is most dishonest in his methods. He will never
be satisfied until he goads us into action, and then he will
think most of us too moderate, and want to guillotine half
of us. I can see him setting up a guillotine, can't you? For
Hobson and MacNeill in particular.[54]

Like MacDonagh and Plunkett, Pearse was now emotionally on the
side of workers against employers, and, though he was a long way
from being a socialist, he was making gestures towards Connolly's
thinking. However, there was a public row in December. In *The
Spark* (an anti-IPP, anti-Castle single-sheet the censor thought not
worth suppressing), Pearse had held out the hand of friendship to
Liberty Hall by writing of the 'exploitation of the English masses by
cruel plutocrats' and had expressed his hope that the war might
kindle 'in the slow breasts of the English toilers a wrath like the
wrath of the French in 1789'. This had been followed by a paean of
praise to the heroism of the European war that reflected the hysteria
of the times: 'It is good for the world that such things should be
done. The old heart of the earth needed to be warmed with the red
wine of the battlefields. Such august homage was never before
offered to God as this, the homage of millions of lives given gladly
for love of country.' Connolly's brutal response in the *Workers'
Republic* on Christmas Day 1915 was: 'No, we do not think that the
old heart of the earth needs to be warmed with the red wine of

millions of lives. We think anyone who does is a blithering idiot. We are sick of such teaching, and the world is sick of such teaching.' Pearse, who had read large quantities of Connolly's equally vehement prose, was deeply hurt, but the episode did not damage their growing mutual respect and he made an effort to moderate his language slightly.

Connolly did not. 'The time for Ireland's battle is NOW', he yelled in print in January: 'the place for Ireland's battle is HERE'. Tom Clarke was impatient himself, fearful that Germany might collapse, or else a peace conference might be arranged without Irish nationalist representation. What was more, the British authorities were no longer turning a blind eye at every turn, and there was a real fear of mass arrests, not least because the ICA were carrying out night-time mock attacks on Dublin Castle and other government buildings. 'Connolly is becoming impossible,' Mac Diarmada said at Christmas in Limerick with the Clarkes and Dalys. In January, after a particularly explosive issue of the *Workers' Republic*, Clarke and Mac Diarmada decided to act. On 19 January Connolly disappeared from Liberty Hall (coaxed, not kidnapped, as many people feared) and stayed away for three days, the first of which he spent in intense argument and then discussion with Mac Diarmada, Pearse and Plunkett, who had Clarke's imprimatur to tell him everything and offer a seat on the Military Council in exchange for his joining the IRB and agreeing co-operation between the ICA and the Volunteers. Over three days of conversation and walking and thinking, he decided to throw in his lot with the other six on the Military Council, which was now in sole charge of organising the insurrection. Mac Diarmada had been the most convincing voice.

The tone of the *Workers' Republic* on 29 January carried a clear message to his new allies.

> In solemn acceptance of our duty and the great responsibilities attached thereto, we have planted the seed in the hope and belief that ere many of us are much older, it will ripen and blossom into action. For the moment and hour of that ripening, that fruitful and blessed day of days, we are ready. Will it find you ready?

Clarke was not in a condition to celebrate that achievement, for his friend Seán McGarry had accidentally shot him in the right elbow. He was in acute pain for weeks and never recovered the full use of his arm, but he learned to shoot with his left hand. After some weeks recuperating in Limerick at Dalys' house, he was back in Dublin by mid-March.

Pearse had been very busy. Around him in St Enda's was a little hive of revolutionary activity. Con Colbert, a Gaelic League enthusiast and pious Catholic from a Fenian background, had enrolled in the Fianna in 1909 at the inaugural meeting when he was twenty-one. He became chief scout, refused to accept a salary as part-time drill-master at St Enda's from 1910 because he was working in the national interest, became head of the exclusively Fianna Mitchel IRB circle formed by Hobson in 1912, undertook the covert drilling of IRB members, and was a very practical member of the Irish Volunteers. A zealot without qualms, he recruited Desmond Ryan and several other St Enda's pupils into the IRB once they were seventeen, under the unsuspecting nose of the Pearse brothers. In addition to military manoeuvres, St Enda's hid weapons and had a bomb factory in the basement staffed by boys.

Pearse was uninvolved in all this, for, in addition to his Volunteer and IRB work and running St Enda's, he was sorting out his literary and political legacies. His second collection of Irish short stories was published in January, showing a move away from the sentimentality of his first. 'An Dearg-Daol' ('The Black Chafter'), which he thought the best he had ever written, dealt with death and disaster in a peasant family, for Pearse had grasped at last that the life of the poor was hard. His educational writings were collected in 'The Murder Machine' also in January and there were four more pamphlets that laid out his justifications for the revolution he now believed inevitable. As a lawyer, he had hated the profession and barely practised, but now, based on a brilliant, powerfully written, wholly partisan and unhistorical interpretation of the story of Ireland, he produced a book of law for future generations of Irish nationalists on to which was grafted his idiosyncratic Catholicism to make it also a holy book, a patriotic bible.

'Ghosts', finished on Christmas Day 1915, constructed a separatist tradition of unbroken nationalist heroism going back to those who resisted the Norman invasion in 1169. The Irish people were in 'the image and likeness of God' and like 'a divine religion, national freedom bears the marks of unity, of sanctity, of catholicity, of apostolic succession'. The four evangelists who had left behind them 'a body of teaching' that made them fathers of the nationalist religion were Wolfe Tone, Thomas Davis, John Mitchel and James Fintan Lalor, all of whom were presented as precursors of what was the political thinking of the mature Pearse. Their gospels were analysed and stitched together in the next three pamphlets. 'The Separatist Idea', written in January, examined Tone, 'the greatest man of our nation: the greatest-hearted and the greatest-minded' and the evangelist to whom the other three were subordinate, who emerged as a separatist with socialist inclinations through whom 'God spoke to Ireland'. February produced 'The Spiritual Nation', which dealt with Davis's contribution to the spiritual tradition 'which is the soul of Ireland' and justified Pearse's cultural nationalism. 'The Sovereign People', which was written in March, covered Lalor and Mitchel. Careful quotes from Lalor, a social-democrat and a revolutionary whose major concerns were with tenants of small farms rather than landless labourers or the urban poor, enabled Pearse to blend with nationalism his own new and rather incoherent version of socialism. And 'fiery-tongued' Mitchel, the prophet who 'did really hold converse with God', produced the 'apocalyptic wrath', the call for vengeance. Being by nature a bad hater, Pearse temporised by claiming that Mitchel's hatred was for English misgovernment rather than the English people.

In his summing up toward the end there was something for each of the Seven, and, indeed, anyone who would be going forth at Easter.

> Tone is the intellectual ancestor of the whole modern movement of Irish nationalism, of Davis, and Lalor, and Mitchel and all their followers; Davis is the immediate ancestor of the spiritual and imaginative part of that movement, embodied in our day in the Gaelic League; Lalor is the immediate ancestor of the specifically democratic part of the movement, embodied to-day in the more virile labour organisations; Mitchel is the immediate ancestor of Fenianism, the noblest and most terrible manifestation of this unconquered nation.

In the preface, written on 31 March, he wrote 'For my part, I have no
more to say,' after which he begged his publisher to rush the pamphlets
through by 17 April: 'you will later appreciate the reason and regard it
as sufficient'.

He hadn't confined himself to the evangelists, though. In the preceding months he had also produced in English a play and some political
poems. *The Singer*, which was not staged in his lifetime, represented
the culmination of his religious nationalism in its story of MacDara, a
poet, orator and revolutionary leader who wants to die for his people.
At the end he is grieved that sixteen other men, including his younger
brother, had gone out before him, for their sacrifice was unnecessary.
'One man can free a people as one Man redeemed the world. I will take
no pike, I will go into the battle with bare hands. I will stand up before
the Gall as Christ hung naked before men on the tree.' When he read it,
Joe Plunkett remarked that 'If Pearse were dead, this would cause a
sensation.'

The self-justification infused the poems. 'The Rebel' angrily warned
'my people's masters: Beware, / Beware of the thing that is coming,
beware / of the risen people, / Who shall take what ye would not give.'
'The Fool' asked all the wise men 'What if the dream come true? And
if millions unborn shall dwell / In the house that I shaped in my heart,
the noble house of my thought?' And 'The Mother' was a gift to Mrs
Pearse to help her bear her terrible future and be content with the lot
of most women in Pearse's imaginative writing.

> I do not grudge them: Lord, I do not grudge
> My two strong sons that I have seen go out
> To break their strength and die, they and a few,
> In bloody protest for a glorious thing,
> They shall be spoken of among their people,
> The generations shall remember them,
> And call them blessed;
> But I will speak their names to my own heart
> In the long nights;
> The little names that were familiar once
> Round my dead hearth.
> Lord, thou art hard on mothers:

We suffer in their coming and their going;
And tho' I grudge them not, I weary, weary
Of the long sorrow—And yet I have my joy:
My sons were faithful, and they fought.

Pearse was ready for revolution. So too was Joseph Plunkett, who in December had astounded Gerry by announcing his engagement to another good-looking MacDonagh sister-in-law, Grace Gifford, who according to Gerry MacDonagh thought little of and distrusted. 'Joe thought the same at the time. I do not think that I have ever met anyone who put on more airs and graces – she patronised all other women, she thought anything serious was stuffy and dull and then presumed that we were all like that. She was a dreadful bore.' He had met her at MacDonagh's flat and she had contributed cartoons to the *Irish Review*, and, though not really interested in politics, she was in favour of votes for women and nationalism and had helped distribute food during the lock-out. What drew them together, though, was her passionate desire to convert to Catholicism, about which they talked incessantly. It was also possible, Joe Plunkett being the kind of person he was, that since, as his biographer pointed out, 'the word "grace" is draped all over his poetry',[55] he was spiritually attracted by her Christian name.

He did not tell Grace about his revolutionary intentions and although he was mainly confined to bed, mysteriously she put this down to bronchitis. Nor does she seem to have believed him when he said he was penniless. When he was well enough, he was working on the plans, and often others of the Seven had to come to him for meetings. Ma had gone to America for months in September, and although she left utter financial chaos, her absence was a blessing to everyone.

My brother Owen had a memorable encounter with Gerry in 1966, after she was shown the commemorative TV programme *On Behalf of the Provisional Government* on which he had worked and to which she had been a key contributor. He said:

> I had begun it with Plunkett's poem 'When I am dead let
> not your murderous tears / Deface with their slow

dropping my sad tomb . . . They mourn the body whom
the spirit slay / And those that stab the living weep the
dead.' She [Gerry] fixed a terrible accusing eye on me when
it had finished, and said, "Did you choose that poem? Did
you know who he wrote it to? He wrote it to my mother.
She was a horrible woman. He hated her, we all hated her.
He wanted some money. She wouldn't give it to him. So he
went upstairs and wrote that. Would you have used it if you
had known that?' And then, looking at me, 'I suppose you
would.'

All the family except Moya, now a nun, were living in the armed camp
that Larkfield had become, as were the 'Liverpool Lambs', a few
hundred refugees from England avoiding conscription, who were
training as Volunteers and forming, under George Plunkett, the
Kimmage Garrison. Gerry's valiant attempts to sort out Ma's affairs as
well as look after Joe were made much easier when he provided her
with an able part-time and ex-post-office clerk called Michael Collins,
who also sometimes acted as his or Seán Mac Diarmada's bodyguard,
and would collect and deliver Plunkett's letters to and from members
of the Military Council. There was constant target practice and an
explosives factory in the outbuildings supervised by Gerry's fiancé
Tommy Dillon, Jack Plunkett was a full-time aide, mainly working on
wireless experiments, and Philomena operated as a transatlantic
courier.

Having read that Asquith had visited Pope Benedict XV, who had
denounced the war as futile and called for peace, Plunkett swore his
father into the IRB and dispatched him to the Vatican to claim his
right as a papal count to an audience with the pope and stop him
condemning the Rising. He bore with him a letter almost certainly
written by Joe himself or both of them, purporting to come from Eoin
MacNeill, 'President of the Supreme Council of the Irish Volunteers',
and told the pope in a two-hour meeting that there was now a chance
'to obtain the freedom of rights and worship for our Catholic country'
and, among a string of other impressive lies, that they had 80,000
trained men, that American and German assistance had been promised, that 'the people, the Catholic nation is with us' and that the

insurrection would be on Easter Sunday. He claimed to have secured a general blessing for the Volunteers as good Catholics, but not an endorsement of the Rising. Nonetheless, if true, as Townshend remarks, 'The Pope knew more about what was going on than did Eoin MacNeill.'

If Plunkett's story was true, he also knew more than the President of the IRB. Worried by rumours, Denis McCullough went down to Dublin to see Clarke.

> I said to Tom, 'What in the name of God is going to happen?' He said, 'I declare to God I know nothing more than you do. All I know is I have orders to report to Ned Daly on Sunday morning and have my arms and equipment and I have them ready.' He brought out an old revolver that would have killed him if he had fired it. And he said, 'I'm turning out.'[56]

McCullough went in search of Mac Diarmada, who dodged him for two days. Mac Diarmada then told McCullough a German submarine would come up the Liffey with 250 officers and more of what McCullough thought 'a cock and bull story'. Asked what he thought, McCullough said: 'Well, Seán, in truth,' I said, 'it looks to me like murder and suicide.' He promised, though, that if Dublin turned out, he and his men would do their best. '"But," said I, "if I live through this, Seán, I'll have something to say to you and Tom Clarke." And he laughed, and threw his head back and said, "I don't think you need bother about that because probably neither of us will live through it."'[57] Up to his death in 1968, McCullough still believed that Tom Clarke had been telling the truth, thus confirming the wisdom of Clarke and Mac Diarmada in choosing him as the President of the Supreme Council, a body they now completely ignored.

That Plunkett had only a few weeks to live became clear when his tubercular abscess was operated on, but with the help of Collins he kept going. Grace was baptised a Catholic early in April and thrown out by her mother, so it was strangely decided that she and Joe and Gerry and Tommy would have a double wedding on the morning of Easter Sunday.

Clarke and Mac Diarmada were obsessively secretive, while MacDonagh was trusting and notoriously indiscreet, which is presumably why, though he had the vital job of Dublin Brigade commandant, he was not co-opted on to the Military Council until April. He was behaving very erratically. One of his students, Austin Clarke, remembered him as tense and sometimes abstracted and worried. 'Suddenly, one day, during a lecture on the Young Ireland poets, he took a large revolver from his pocket and laid it on the desk. "Ireland can only win freedom by force," he remarked, as if to himself.'[58] Clearly, Plunkett had been telling him about the plans all along, for MacDonagh had been dropping hints everywhere, long before he joined the Military Council, including to a group of Volunteers that included a British spy codenamed 'Chalk'. On 16 April, he obligingly told much the same audience, 'we are not going out on Friday but on Sunday. Boys, some of us may never come back – mobilisation orders to be issued in due course.' A report went to Dublin Castle, and nothing happened. This was symptomatic of the chaos of the system.

There was ample evidence about the irredentist ambitions of advanced nationalists and most of the Seven's plans were known to one part of the government or another. Despite all Clarke's and Mac Diarmada's precautions against informers, there were plenty in the Volunteers and plenty more in Ireland and America as given to loose talk as MacDonagh, and Pearse and Connolly had been signalling their intentions at the top of their voices, even if they had toned down the language and turned down the volume after January. Yet the forces they were up against were almost incapable of dealing with the information served up to them. 'If the Irish system of government be regarded as a whole,' said the post-1916 Commission of Enquiry, 'it is anomalous in quiet times, and almost unworkable in times of crisis.' Intelligence-gathering involved the Admiralty, MI5, Irish Command, the RIC and the unreliable DMP, which produced institutional rivalry, crossed lines, poor co-ordination and an uncertain chain of command. Major Ivor Price, Irish Command's Intelligence Officer, who was in charge of censorship and surveillance, was ambitious and assiduous, but overloaded and understaffed. Augustine Birrell, Chief Secretary since 1908, a proponent of Home Rule, was friendly towards nationalism and tended towards appeasement of radicals, and he was disinclined to worry about – let alone prosecute or suppress – most of the newspapers Price thought dangerous. There was an increase in arrests and deportations that spring, including that of Liam Mellows, but mostly these involved small fry. Birrell's able Under-Secretary, Sir Matthew Nathan, was much more aware of the underlying revolutionary threat, noting correctly that 'Irishmen are affected by what they read and hear probably more than more phlegmatic peoples', but he followed Birrell's instructions and avoided provocation as much as possible.

The police were cautious too. A week before Easter, there was a DMP raid on the union shop that led into the machine room in Liberty Hall that housed the printing press. When the police had seized copies of a radical paper called *The Gael*, Connolly appeared with a gun and said, 'Drop those papers or I will drop you.' As a young policeman urged his comrades to rush him, Markievicz appeared behind them with her automatic. 'They beat a hasty retreat but it was clear that they would return with a larger force. Within an hour of this incident a large contingent of Citizen Army men were mobilised to defend Liberty Hall.'[59]

The objective, of course, was to stop the police seizing the printing press or discovering the stockpiles of grenades, bullets and bombs. Thenceforward, Connolly and a number of other ICA men slept on the premises, and he was allocated a full-time bodyguard. Two days later, for the first time he appeared in public in the ICA uniform, as in the presence of a large crowd a republican flag of gold harp on green was hoisted over Liberty Hall. 'He had banished the Committee, and now ruled alone,' wrote O'Casey; 'so, after being thoroughly rehearsed, the Citizen Army, numbering about one hundred and seventy men, paraded outside, and Connolly, followed a pace behind by Madame Markievicz, inspected them.'[60] That night he told the ICA that a rising was inevitable and would be fought on their terms. 'The odds are a thousand to one against us . . . If we win, we'll be great heroes; but if we lose, we will be the greatest scoundrels the country ever produced.' And then, more menacingly, 'In the event of victory, hold on to your rifles, as those with whom we are fighting may stop before our goal is reached. We are out for economic as well as political liberty. Hold on to your rifles!'

Connolly had not told his family about the date of the Rising, but Lillie was instructed to move from Dublin to Markievicz's cottage in the Dublin mountains. 'Sadly,' wrote Ina,

> mother looked around the home that she cherished; here she was leaving all the convenience of modern life and the work of the last five years which it took to build up, to go to an empty cottage on the hills of Dublin, miles away from anyone she knew. But she would carry out the wishes of her husband. She left Belfast very downhearted with the feeling that once again her hopes of a happy home had been dashed to the ground.'[61]

Nora and Ina, both members of Cumann na mBan, stayed behind to try to join what they thought would be the northern revolutionary force, who in fact had instructions from Pearse to abandon the hostile ground of Ulster to march south west to Galway. As F.X. Martin put it apropos the plans for the country at large, 'It was a Napoleonic plan, but there was no Napoleon to supervise it and no *Grande Armée* to execute it.'[62]

MacDonagh was important for the Military Council because of his friendship with his UCD colleague Eoin MacNeill, who was crucial to their plans. MacNeill had made it clear to James Connolly that if the ICA staged a revolution the Volunteers would stay well away. Having asked his Executive their views, he had discovered that MacDonagh, Pearse and Plunkett were in favour of insurrection, and had spelled out to them the familiar argument that it could be justified only if the government tried to introduce conscription, suppress the Volunteers or renege on Home Rule, and that in any case it had to have popular support. In early April he heard rumours about something being afoot, was assured by Pearse that neither he nor his friends 'contemplated insurrection or wanted to commit the Volunteers to any policy other than that to which they were publicly committed', and was rebuked by MacDonagh for a lack of trust. Pearse no longer lived up to his exhorations to his boys to be like Fianna, who 'never told a lie' nor had 'falsehood imputed to them'. MacNeill was promised that no order would be issued without his counter-signature.

On Sunday 16 April, at a Cumann na mBan concert featuring rebel songs and speeches glorifying an armed Rising, when asked to make an impromptu speech, Hobson took the opportunity to warn 'of the extreme danger of being drawn into precipitate action', as 'no man had a right to risk the fortunes of a country in order to create for himself a niche in history'. Some thought it 'a timely word of caution', commented one observer: others thought it 'black treachery'. Afterwards, Mac Diarmada assured MacCullough, 'We'll soon stop this bloody fellow.'[63]

Then came what was known as the Castle Document, listing 'precautionary measures sanctioned by the Irish Office on the recommendation of the General Officer Commanding the Forces in Ireland'. Those to be arrested included the key people in Sinn Féin, the Volunteers, the ICA and the Gaelic League. Among the premises to be occupied were Liberty Hall, Surrey House and Volunteer and Gaelic League headquarters; among those places to be 'isolated' were Larkfield, St Enda's, the houses of MacNeill and O'Rahilly, and, bizarrely, Archbishop's House, whose occupant was no revolutionary.

Historians have argued for years about the authenticity of this document. The most likely sequence is that in the second week of April a sympathiser in Dublin Castle smuggled out a genuine dispatch from General Friend detailing precautionary measures should conscription be imposed. At a time when the Military Council was preoccupied with how to bring MacNeill on board, this was a godsend. There were no plans for conscription, but, in Townshend's term, Plunkett 'sexed it up' so it was no longer evident that this was a contingency plan, nor that it had not been approved by Birrell. After a meeting of the Military Council it was printed on Plunkett's small handpress at Larkfield and sent on Saturday 15 and Sunday 16 April to newspapers and to prominent people. Only the editor of *New Ireland* was prepared to run the risk of printing it and the censors closed down the paper.

Shown it by a trusted friend, MacNeill saw the document as the justification for armed resistance, and cried 'the Lord has delivered them into our hands'. Mac Diarmada lied to an emergency meeting

of the Volunteer executive that the British parliament intended to
hold or had held a secret session to discuss peace terms with
Germany, which added to the pressure for immediate action. Dublin
Castle was dismissing the document as a fabrication and many scep-
tics thought it a forgery, but MacNeill was convinced. After another
meeting the following day, following instructions from MacNeill, on
Wednesday the still slightly sceptical Hobson circulated MacNeill's
orders for all units to be ready 'with defensive measures' to protect
the Volunteers' 'arms and organisation': it was a plan that reflected
Hobson's and O'Connell's belief in guerrilla warfare, or 'hedgefight-
ing', as its opponents disparagingly called it. The Military Council
met in the evening and sent messages to all its commandants that the
Rising would begin on Easter Sunday, 23 April, at 6:30 p.m. in Dublin
and 7:00 p.m. in the rest of the country. The mood was optimistic.
Clarke was euphoric, telling his sister-in-law Madge that the youth of
the country would flock to their standard and the English would be
too stretched to put down a general rising. Kathleen was sent on
Thursday to Limerick to leave the children with her mother, give
dispatches to Volunteer leaders and then return with their responses.
Mac Diarmada had persuaded the Supreme Council to appoint her
as custodian of its decisions and she had the names to contact if the
Council were arrested. Yet everything was unravelling, not least
because Hobson was suspicious that the Military Council was up to
something.

On Thursday night, Ginger O'Connell checked with Hobson suspicious orders supposedly signed by MacNeill, who now grasped the full
significance of Pearse's order in the *Irish Volunteer* for field manoeuvres
on Easter Sunday. They roused MacNeill from bed and the three went
to St Enda's to wake up Pearse. 'For the first time', wrote MacNeill, 'I
learned by Pearse's admission that the rising was intended. I told him
that I would use every means in my power except informing the govt.
to prevent the rising. He said I was powerless to do so, and that my
countermand would only create confusion.' Pearse also told Hobson
that as a sworn member of the IRB he was bound to help with the
insurrection, and was reminded of the IRB constitution.

Giving authority to his colleagues to cancel all orders for any
Volunteer activity over the weekend, MacNeill, with Hobson and

O'Connell, drafted a countermand of all Pearse's orders 'with regard to military movements of a definite kind'. At 8:00 a.m. Mac Diarmada, MacDonagh and Pearse arrived to see MacNeill, who on being told that an arms shipment was about to arrive said 'if that is the state of the case I'm with you'. His reasoning would seem to have been that now suppression was inevitable so guerrilla resistance should commence. MacNeill also believed insurrection was permitted by Catholic teaching only if there were a reasonable chance of success, which an arms landing put within the realm of the possible. Confusion reigned. MacDonagh thought MacNeill had transferred his authority as Chief of Staff to Pearse, while Mac Diarmada said MacNeill had recalled O'Connell and instructed commanders to 'proceed with the rising', which MacNeill remembered as an instruction to stand by to defend themselves. MacNeill recollected Plunkett arriving to ask him to sign a 'proclamation': when MacNeill asked what was in it, Plunkett would not tell him.

And then came the disaster in Kerry, where an arms shipment – which was all that the Germans were prepared to provide and which the Admiralty knew all about – was due at Fenit. Having given up hope of German help, in February the Military Council had asked Devoy to send a shipload of arms before Easter Sunday, but the Clan had been cleaned out of money, having sent $100,000 over the previous year to Clarke. But, having made a further plea to Germany, Devoy found a better response than before and an agreement was made to send arms to arrive on Good Friday.

Philomena Plunkett had delivered a message to Devoy on 14 April from the Military Council that vital arms must not be landed before midnight on Sunday 23rd and asking 'if submarine will come to Dublin Bay'. There was no radio contact with the captain of the German cargo ship, disguised as a Norwegian steamer, the *Aud*, which arrived on April 20 in Tralee Bay ready to rendezvous off Inishtooskert Island with a U-boat carrying Casement, whom Devoy had told not to come, whom no one wanted and who himself wanted to abort a rebellion he thought hopeless. They missed each other, Casement landed from a collapsed dingy on Good Friday morning on a beach at Banna Strand and was arrested, and the *Aud* drifted about waiting for the Volunteers to find it until, while being escorted towards the shore on Saturday

morning by British armed trawlers, the captain scuttled it. The local
Volunteers failed to rescue him and Casement the following day was
rushed to London.

Now the Military Council turned on its chief critic. 'Hobson is the
evil genius of the Volunteers,' MacDonagh had told Ceannt, 'and if
we could separate MacNeill from his influence, all would be well.'[64]
He 'has been an obstacle in our path,' Ceannt explained to an IRB
colleague that weekend. 'He is opposed to an insurrection. He is
perfectly honest, he is not a traitor, but it would be better that he
were as then we could shoot him.' Connolly had recommended
taking him to Larkfield and chloroforming him, but 'Pearse or
MacDiarmada or both . . . said "No" to that' and suggested arresting
him and imprisoning him in a house.[65] And so, on Good Friday, on
the orders of the Military Council, Hobson was kidnapped by the
IRB. (Claire Gregan, his fiancée, spent the weekend trying to find
him, and on Monday morning would confront Connolly, Pearse and
Mac Diarmada at Liberty Hall. Having been told the truth and
assured that he was safe, she got them to admit that he was 'a man of
integrity and sincerity'. She would later describe Connolly as surly,
Pearse as nice and Mac Diarmada as reassuring and sympathetic, but
'deadly sly'.[66] Hobson would not be released until Monday evening,
after which he would be shunned and airbrushed out of the nationalist narrative.)

Meeting on Friday afternoon, the Military Council was happy
and excited. Ceannt confided to a colleague that he was eating and
sleeping well and was hugely looking forward to the fight. 'We are
rising on Sunday and we are going to win. We are going to bring off
something unprecedented in the way of revolutions. We are going to
smash the bloody old empire.'[67] The assumption was that now
MacNeill would come into line. MacDonagh had the job of acting as
an intermediary between him and the Military Council but, as
events changed, so did MacNeill's mind. At one stage he set up a
meeting between MacDonagh and a group including Arthur Griffith
and O'Rahilly, but MacDonagh left when he realised they were all
against having an insurrection. There was a confrontation at St
Enda's late on Saturday afternoon, when a very excitable Pearse –
who, like everyone else, was exhausted – told MacNeill brutally:

'We have used your name and influence for what they were worth, but we have done with you now. It is no use trying to stop us: our plans are all made and will be carried out.' When MacNeill countered that he would forbid the mobilisation, Pearse said 'Our men will not obey you.'

MacNeill took some more hours to make a decision, but the news about Hobson, about events in Kerry and his dawning belief that the Castle Document was a forgery, made up his mind. A stream of messengers cycled, drove or took taxis throughout Saturday night to take to the country the message: 'Volunteers completely deceived. All orders for special action are hereby cancelled, and on no account will action be taken. Eoin MacNeill, Chief of Staff.' At 1:30 a.m., MacNeill cycled to the *Irish Independent* officers and had a countermanding order inserted in its Sunday edition.

All the Seven except Connolly, who was in Liberty Hall, were told on Saturday to hide in safe houses: Clarke's instructions were that Volunteer bodyguards should resist arrest parties to the death. Pearse and his brother Willie, who was a Volunteer captain on Patrick's staff, did not leave St Enda's until Saturday night. Desmond Ryan was there as their mother said goodbye: 'Now, Pat, above all, do nothing rash!' As usual, he had replied, 'No, mother.' Mac Diarmada had an emergency meeting that night attended by MacDonagh, Pearse and Plunkett at which 'physically worn out by the strenuous months of anxiety through which he had just passed' he 'writhed in anguish'.[68] Pearse and Plunkett wanted to stick to the timetable, but Mac Diarmada and MacDonagh voted for delay and a meeting of the Military Council was called for Sunday morning at Liberty Hall. Nora Connolly had seen her father crying when he heard of MacNeill's countermand: 'the only thing we can do is to pray for an earthquake to come and swallow us up and our shame.'[69] Sometime later, though, he told her that 'we have got another saviour now. That saviour is the sword.' Markievicz, 'in a raging temper', had told Connolly in the printing room that she would shoot Eoin MacNeill and was told not to hurt a hair on his head.

Clarke's reaction had been that it was 'the blackest and greatest treachery': Ceannt's had been that MacNeill should have been shot. Ceannt had broken the punctual habits of a lifetime by turning up late that morning because, since he had returned home at 5:00

a.m., Áine had left him to sleep despite a summons from Connolly. When a messenger arrived at 8:30, Ceannt leaped on his bicycle without a collar or tie and made for Liberty Hall. The *Sunday Independent* hit the newsstands as they signed the Proclamation of the Irish Republic,* drafted by Pearse and printed on the presses

---

* Irishmen and Irishwomen:

In the name of God and of the dead generations from which she receives her old tradition of nationhood, Ireland, through us, summons her children to her flag and strikes for her freedom.

Having organized and trained her manhood through her secret revolutionary organization, the Irish Republican Brotherhood, and through her open military organizations, the Irish Volunteers and the Irish Citizen Army, having patiently perfected her discipline, having resolutely waited for the right moment to reveal itself, she now seizes that moment, and, supported by her exiled children in America and by gallant allies in Europe, but relying in the first on her own strength, she strikes in full confidence of victory.

We declare the right of the people of Ireland to the ownership of Ireland, and to the unfettered control of Irish destinies, to be sovereign and indefeasible. The long usurpation of that right by a foreign people and government has not extinguished the right, nor can it ever be extinguished except by the destruction of the Irish people. In every generation the Irish people have asserted their right to national freedom and sovereignty; six times during the past three hundred years they have asserted it in arms. Standing on that fundamental right and again asserting it in arms in the face of the world, we hereby proclaim the Irish Republic as a Sovereign Independent State. And we pledge our lives and the lives of our comrades-in-arms to the cause of its freedom, of its welfare, and of its exaltation among the nations.

The Irish Republic is entitled to, and hereby claims, the allegiance of every Irishman and Irish woman. The Republic guarantees religious and civil liberty, equal rights and equal opportunities of all its citizens, and declares its resolve to pursue the happiness and prosperity of the whole nation and of all its parts, cherishing all the children of the nation equally, and oblivious of the differences carefully fostered by an alien government, which have divided a minority in the past.

Until our arms have brought the opportune moment for the establishment of a permanent National Government, representative of the whole people of Ireland

downstairs.* Markievicz – who had now been rampaging around threatening to kill Hobson – had grabbed a copy off the press and had rushed out to read it out to the passers-by in Lower Abbey Street.

At the Military Council on Tuesday 18 April, at which the Castle Document had been accepted, the Seven had also agreed the text of a proclamation that on the authority of God and various dead patriots had established a Provisional Government composed of the seven of them, which in the event of victory would conduct the Rising and administer Ireland. (Of course this information was not passed on to the Supreme Council, to which in theory they reported.) Clarke was offered and refused the presidency, which went to Pearse, who had the public profile, the rhetoric and the oratorical ability to create the right impression. Pearse had insisted that Clarke's name must lead the rest of the signatories of the Proclamation, but Clarke demurred. Then MacDonagh said that 'to his mind no other man was entitled to the

---

and elected by the suffrages of all her men and women, the Provisional Government, hereby constituted, will administer the civil and military affairs of the Republic in trust for the people.

We place the cause of the Irish Republic under the protection of the Most High God, Whose blessing we invoke upon our arms, and we pray that no one who serves that cause will dishonour it by cowardice, inhumanity, or rapine. In this supreme hour the Irish nation must, by its valour and discipline and by the readiness of its children to sacrifice themselves for the common good, prove itself worthy of the august destiny to which it is called.

Signed on behalf of the Provisional Government,

THOMAS J. CLARKE
SEAN MAC DIARMADA
THOMAS MACDONAGH
P.H. PEARSE
EAMONN CEANNT
JAMES CONNOLLY
JOSEPH PLUNKETT
* The printing press could not write Irish script, hence the absence of fadas (acute accents) on 'Sean' and 'Eamonn'.

honour. "You Sir, by your example, your courage, your enthusiasm, have led us younger men to where we are today . . . No man will precede you with my consent."[70] So Clarke agreed.

As President, Pearse was also to be what Townshend called 'a kind of generalissimo' – Commandant-General of the Army of the Irish Republic, composed of the ICA and the Volunteers, with Connolly Vice-President and Commandant-General of the Dublin division. 'In effect,' says Michael Foy of the treatment of the IRB,

> Tom and his colleagues were acting like a junta enacting a coup, one that overthrew the elected president and government, appointed themselves as their replacements, suspended the constitution and produced a Proclamation that in part resembled a new constitution. They had also empowered themselves to rule by decree. These were the boldest examples yet of Tom's lifelong conviction that constitutions were not worth the paper they were printed on. He had long sworn that nothing – and nobody – would stand in his way and he was as good as his word.[71]

Kathleen said of that Tuesday night that Clarke thought himself too old to do the necessary job of guiding the younger men, who would need 'a man of iron', someone with a touch of Cromwell in him for the first five years. "Would Pearse be suitable?" I asked. "God Almighty no," he said. "He is too Christ-like." Clarke's candidate was John Devoy, whom he believed had the necessary knowledge, experience, force of character and ruthlessness. 'Envisaging the return of a seventy-four-year-old autocrat after almost half a century's exile in America', commented Foy, 'raises the disturbing possibility that Clarke envisaged Devoy's iron hand ruling an independent Ireland on similar lines to the Clan and IRB.'

So in their four-hour meeting it was as the self-styled Provisional Government that the Seven considered their options. None of them could contemplate the humiliation of cancellation. Clarke, who was terrified of going back to prison, was insistent they should go ahead with the original plans, and to his shock was opposed by all the others, even Mac Diarmada, who on this occasion had not deferred to his old mentor. When he went home after the meeting, Seán McGarry thought him crushed and weary. 'We had a great opportunity. Now in a way we could never have foreseen all is spoiled.' Kathleen thought he looked like a broken man, 'old and bent', ill and silent. He opened up later to denounce MacNeill's actions as despicable and dishonourable.

Connolly had no countermanding orders to deal with as the ICA was unaffected, and would mobilise his men that evening and take them on a route march, after which they bedded down at Liberty Hall. Some of the others were involved in the weary work of confirming MacNeill's cancellation orders while drafting another set of orders for the next day. Mac Diarmada – who knew infinitely more than all the others put together about the disposition of the IRB and Volunteers around the country – was a key player in deciding what went to whom.

MacDonagh was optimistic, telling one of the compositors in Liberty Hall that Germany had promised Casement that if they could hold out for three days they would get to the peace conference, and if Germany won it would recognise the Irish Republic. But he was unhappy to be required to deceive MacNeill further by visiting him to tell him the Rising was off and that it had in any case been intended only to occupy a few buildings as barracks so the British would come to terms. He wrote a memorandum afterwards to assuage his guilty conscience, saying that his

> future conduct may be different from anything now antici-
> pated by MacNeill and Fitzgibbon,* two honest and sincere
> patriots, though I think wrong in their handling of the
> present situation ... I have guarded secrets which I am
> bound to keep. I have, I think, acted honourably and fairly
> by all my associates. I have had only one motive in all my
> actions, namely the good of my country. I now pray to God
> for the gifts of counsel and fortitude and his blessing for
> the cause of my country.

Significantly, under the pressure of the preparation for insurrection and the likelihood of death, MacDonagh had returned to the God he

---

* Seán Fitzgibbon, a senior Volunteer.

had discarded in more peaceful times. He had told Muriel on one of his visits that, if possible, he would be back to see her and the children in the morning. 'He did not say anything about the Revolution. I never saw him afterwards.'[72]

Plunkett, who had been managing to attend meetings while staying in a nursing home during that bewildering week as he recuperated from his latest operation, shared MacDonagh's hopes about a peace conference. He had called off his Easter Sunday wedding, promising Grace that if he were arrested they would marry in jail. Michael Collins helped him move on Friday evening to the Metropole Hotel, across from the GPO. On Saturday evening, Gerry and Tommy visited; he told them what he knew about the uncertain future and gave Tommy instructions to take over any chemical factory captured and organise the manufacture of munitions. The Military Council had done everything possible to ensure they had military status, he reassured them, having uniforms and officers. He did not, he told them, want to die.

As they left, news arrived of a fresh disaster. A friend of Plunkett's called Con Keating, who had worked with him on his wireless experiments at Larkfield, had been part of a group of five sent from Dublin to seize equipment from the wireless station at Cahirciveen so as to communicate with the Germans in the hope they might intervene if they knew there was a rising. At Ballykissane pier, a car took a wrong turning, and three of them, including Keating – the only one who knew what their orders were – had drowned, leaving the others no choice but to return to Dublin. Plunkett went on to a further meeting that night and later on was aroused by the porter on the insistence of Ina Connolly, whose father wanted her to tell him the bad news she and Nora brought from Belfast about the effect on Volunteers of the countermanding order. 'All at once there appeared a tall, thin man in a dressing gown coming slowly down the stairs. He had his neck wrapped in bandages or a white scarf . . . He made me feel at ease and talked to me just as my father did, asking questions, assuring me that he had plenty of time to listen to all my chatter.' He had then dressed and joined them at breakfast at Liberty Hall. Unable to go to his sister's wedding, he went back to the hotel in the evening, and at nine o'clock wrote to Grace to keep up her spirits and 'trust in Providence.

Everything is bully.' He was going to the nursing home to sleep and was 'keeping as well as anything but need a rest'. He added, 'Take care of your old cold, sweetheart.'

Éamonn Ceannt had gone back to a home full of people seeking information and instructions. He had already warned his men several times that someday 'they would go out not to return', but, as he had explained the day before to Áine, when he first told her about the Rising, they had not been told the exact day in case they 'thronged the Churches for confession'. His siblings Michael and Nell arrived to tell him that their sister-in-law, wife to the retired RIC constable J.P. Kent, had died that morning in childbirth. He had to refuse to go with them to condole with their brother, but he went with Áine to Howth to look at where the gun-running had happened. Áine and Lily were being visited by another Cumann na mBan stalwart, the actress Máire Nic Shiubhlaigh, and there were mobilisation orders to fill out.

> I stayed with the Ceannts all day. That evening at tea Éamonn, dark, quiet, reserved as he always was, seemed preoccupied with thoughts of his own. He seemed to have withdrawn into himself; he did not join to any great extent in the talk which went on during the meal. Afterwards he asked for a fire in a separate room and withdrew. Later Mrs. Ceannt joined him.

As she chatted to Lily about her acting plans,

> In the nearby room Ceannt and his wife wrote industriously. Occasionally a knock came to the front door and he rose and answered it himself. There were murmurs in the hallway and the rustling of papers as though documents were changing hands. Later on, Mrs. Ceannt joined us before the fire. She did not mention anything about what Éamonn was doing. We were an ordinary little party, passing what seemed a quiet, not very eventful, Sunday evening ... As I shook hands, Éamonn came out of the front room. He looked tired and strained. 'Good-bye, Máire,' he said. I never saw him again.[73]

That same evening, still clinging to their long-held obstinate misconception that Casement, 'that lunatic traitor',[74] was the leader of the conspirators, and believing that the German debacle had derailed the Rising, Birrell and General Friend left for London. Lord Wimborne, the Lord Lieutenant, was more clear-eyed, and persuaded Nathan to order the arrest of the Volunteer leaders, pending approval from Birrell, to whom he sent a telegram. Meanwhile, at 8:00 p.m., Pearse had finally dispatched the couriers bearing the message for delivery during the night. 'We start operations at noon to-day, Monday. Carry out your instructions. P.H. Pearse.'

Chapter Nine

LAST ACT[1]

'We were all making wonderful plans in those days about the kind of work we were going to do for Ireland, and once when some fantastic scheme was suggested that would have involved a lot of trouble, danger and hard work, MacDonagh asked the company: 'When this grand party's over, who'll wash up?'

Sydney Gifford Czira[2]

Rising

This story is about the Seven, so of the locations in the map on page viii of this book it will mainly concern only four: Liberty Hall, which had in the previous few days been their headquarters, the GPO, where Clarke, Connolly, Mac Diarmada, Pearse and Plunkett were stationed, and Jacob's Biscuit Factory and the South Dublin Union, which were occupied respectively by Thomas MacDonagh and his 2nd Battalion and Éamonn Ceannt and his 4th. Because of planning deficiencies, wishful thinking, the obsessive secrecy enjoined by Clarke and Mac Diarmada that deprived many men of essential information, and the communications chaos of the previous days, fewer than 2,000 insurgents – many of whom had no idea they were to participate in a revolution – were involved at any time in Dublin; skirmishes outside were confined to a few hundred men in the Counties of Dublin, Meath, Wexford and Galway.

Five of the Seven left from Liberty Hall that morning. What would be called the Headquarters Battalion was very much depleted, but there were only a few attempts to make any adjustment to plans. There was a pessimistic moment when Connolly said to William O'Brien

'Bill, we are going out to be slaughtered' and an embarrassing one for everyone when Pearse's younger sister, Mary Brigid, the sibling who did not live with the family, appeared and called to him 'Come home, Pat, and leave all this foolishness.'

MacDonagh had appointed William Brennan-Whitmore to help Michael Collins fetch Plunkett from the nursing home to Liberty Hall. When he saw Plunkett for the first time, Brennan-Whitmore said: 'If ever death had laid its mark openly on a man, it was here.' Helped at every stage to the Metropole Hotel, Plunkett had to rest again there, and then took maps, books and three revolvers from his trunk and told Collins that if the intelligence man in the vestibule tried to interfere he must be shot. He arrived at Liberty Hall 'beautifully dressed, having high tan leather boots, spurs, pince-nez',[3] in full dress uniform, his throat enveloped in bandages covered by a silk scarf, wearing his customary rings and finding the strength to brandish a sabre and walk unaided. Behind him were his brothers, twenty-two-year-old George and eighteen-year-old Jack, and the rest of the Kimmage Garrison.

There was a big welcome from Pearse and Connolly. Pearse, rather heavy and balding, was – like Willie, who accompanied him – turned out in his greatcoat, green Volunteer uniform, Sam Browne belt and matching slouch hat with Volunteer badge. According to O'Casey, Connolly did not look too well in his uniform, 'for he had a rather awkward carriage; and bow-legs, partly ensnared in rich, red-brown, leather leggings, added to the waddle in his walk'. He was by now also rather plump, having had for three years, at Constance Markievicz's home, enough to eat. Despite the pleadings of Lillie, Connolly had brought his fifteen-year-old son Roddy as an aide. He put an end to the sociable milling round with a shout of 'Form Fours' to the 150 from mixed ICA, Volunteer and Cumann na mBan units, and led the procession forward. Clarke and Mac Diarmada, both in civilian clothes though they were rank-and-file members of the Volunteers, had gone ahead by car and were waiting at the corner of the GPO.

When they reached the fine century-old and recently refurbished building, its classical-columned portico rising to the top of its three stories, the procession halted, Connolly shouted to wheel left and charge, and the troops poured in, scattering customers and staff alike. They would be there for most of a week, during which time Connolly acted like a military leader, Pearse and Plunkett mostly thought, wrote and talked, and Clarke and Mac Diarmada exulted and encouraged the young.

Collins took a British lieutenant and an elderly policeman prisoner, and a party sent upstairs by Pearse found an armed guard of seven soldiers, none of whom had ammunition. Connolly set men smashing and fortifying windows and barricading doors. Reinforcements kept arriving from Volunteers late for various units and looking for a base, the St Enda's boys, on whose chests Mrs Pearse had pinned miraculous medals, and the occasional on-looker who decided to join in. Clarke and Mac Diarmada sat back, 'beaming satisfaction and expressing congratulations'. The most famous unexpected arrival was O'Rahilly, who had been touring the country with MacNeill's cancellation, and though angry, that he had not been told about the insurrection, leaped out of his car and allegedly produced the first memorable line of the day's drama: 'Well, I've helped to wind up the clock – I might as well hear it strike.'

The flags had been left behind, but Connolly sent Seán T. O'Kelly to retrieve them, and two were unfurled on the GPO: a green, white and orange tricolour (first used by Young Irelanders in 1848) and Markievicz's creation, a coverlet dyed green adorned with a particular type of golden Irish harp of which Pearse approved. 'Irish Republic' was painted on it in gold. On the orders of Connolly, the Starry Plough banner was placed on the Imperial Hotel, which belonged to William Martin Murphy; Gerry and Tommy had spent their wedding night there and were watching the events from the window. Unbeknown to them, Grace was there too, but Plunkett sent a message to her to leave, which she did.

In song and legend, Pearse read the Proclamation 'from the steps of the GPO', but its only step was a doorstep. In fact, he walked out on to Sackville Street, where there was no sympathetic audience of the kind he was used to. He read to a few hundred random bystanders, among whom was a friend, Stephen McKenna:

> very pale he was, very cold of face, as he scanned the crowd,
> the indifferent-seeming crowd that at times and in places
> warmed only to show positive hostility. I saw him . . . read

the Proclamation of the Irish Republic: but for once his
magnetism had left him; the response was chilling; a few
thin, perfunctory cheers, no direct hostility just then; but
no enthusiasm whatever; the people were evidently quite
unprepared, quite unwilling to see in the uniformed figure,
whose burning words had thrilled them again and again
elsewhere, a person of significance to the country.

Connolly, however, moved forward, took Pearse's hand and said:
'Thanks be to God, Pearse, that we've lived to see this day.' And as the
men he had ordered to paste copies of the proclamation on the pillars
began their work, the two men walked inside. Gerry saw this, as she
saw her brother intervene after Volunteers had failed to blow up a tram
to create a barricade. 'Joe put another bomb in the tram and shot at it
with his Mauser from about thirty yards – he was a beautiful shot. The
shot exploded the bomb and smashed the chassis,' which did the job.
The explosion broke the windows of a sweet shop and a boy discovered he could help himself. 'An hour later there was not a window left
in the street.' Gerry enjoyed incidents like the dummies from dress
shops being 'taken dancing down the street', but in the GPO there was
horror at the looting. There seemed to be little understanding among
the leadership of how tempting free goods were for miserably poor
people, particularly those lining up outside the GPO to collect their
separation allowances, who had been told that with the establishment
of an Irish Republic these would no longer be available. Gerry sent a
message to Joe asking to come and help the other women with the
nursing and catering, but he sent her back to Larkfield where he
thought she would be more useful. The following day, when their
father arrived back from tying to persuade bishops not to condemn the
Rising on the grounds that the Pope had given it the nod, he wanted to
be taken on as a Volunteer, but he was sent home too.

Seán McGarry remembered:

We had with us five members of the Provisional
Government – Tom Clarke, his eyes sparkling with elation.
MacDermott in joyous mood, Connolly happy as a school-
boy at a picnic, Plunkett who was very ill on Sunday seemed

to have taken on a new life and Pearse quiet as usual but in high humour.[4]

Although Clarke was still furious with MacNeill, McGarry thought him cool and imperturbably calm. Another of his old circle thought him thirty years younger and so happy you could imagine you were talking to him in his old shop. Mac Diarmada was equally joyous, reporting 'Everything splendid' when he sent the order to release Hobson. Both would spend much of their time being father figures to the young, circulating, listening to and solving problems, and boosting morale. Clarke's main job was to look after the armoury, supervising the maintenance of guns and the making of grenades. He made a very political point of deferring to Pearse and Connolly as the figures in authority. He and everyone else also apologised for the way O'Rahilly – a man 'so devoted he was not only ready to give his life but to give it under the command of those whose action had imposed upon him a mortal insult' – had been treated .

In theory, in the ICA, women were on equal terms, but in practice few were allowed to fight. Connolly sent Nora and Ina north, where Pearse had ordered not a gun should be fired, rather than allow them to come into the GPO with him. And the Cumann na mBan women were swiftly assigned supportive tasks.

Min Ryan was the most important of the many girls to whom Mac Diarmada was charming but in whom he never confided and to whom he was never committed. He genuinely liked and respected women, though he had no qualms about lying to them and using even those of whom he was most fond as couriers in very perilous circumstances. Min described having 'a great laugh' with Mac Diarmada in the GPO on Tuesday night about her having been an unwitting bearer of the countermanding message; next day he sent her into the dangerous streets to carry orders from Pearse to command posts around the city. The following morning he could not resist taking her and her sister to where Pearse was sitting, saying 'Now, here are two nice girls to see you.' They were hastily passed over to O'Rahilly.

Clarke had a more serious conversation with Min, telling her at length in the kitchen where she was working that while the Irish people would condemn the Rising it had to be gone through as otherwise the

Volunteers would have been destroyed. Shedding blood, he explained, had always raised Irish spirits. '"Of course", he added, "we shall all be wiped out." He said this almost with gaiety. He had got into the one thing he had wanted to do during his whole lifetime.'[5]

In the GPO hospital that week, Min's brother James, a medical student, was joined by Clarke:

> sitting down quietly beside me he began to talk. For no apparent reason he launched into a full history of the I.R.B. from the time of his release from prison (1898) up to 1911. Then he gave me a detailed account of the events leading up to the Rising. This talk lasted for two hours and at the end I was aware of the reason for it. I was now Red Cross and so, he said, I might possibly be spared by the enemy in the final bayonet charge which was evidently expected by him as well as the rest of us. If, therefore, I should survive, he hoped I now understood and would make known the motives of those who signed the Proclamation. He enumerated carefully the arguments in favour of rising but, with characteristic chivalry, he gave the most telling points advocated by those against rising at this particular juncture.[6]

Connolly seemed transported back to the army days none of his companions knew about and had practical men like Collins and O'Rahilly to rely on. Collins would say later:

> Of Pearse and Connolly, I admire the latter most. Connolly was a realist, Pearse the direct opposite. There was an air of earthy directness about Connolly. It impressed me. I would have followed him through hell had such action been necessary. But I honestly doubt very much if I would have followed Pearse – not without some thought anyway.[7]

But while Connolly impressed the men by always being in the thick of it and showing decisiveness, he made some terrible decisions based on his utterly wrong premise that the British would always prefer to put their soldiers in peril by sending them in with small arms rather than use artillery and destroy property. It was 'a reading of British culture in which modern socialist thinking was compounded by traditional Irish nationalist assumptions'.[8] It also ignored the simple fact that in wartime the British could not afford to waste time and divert troops unnecessarily. Connolly dispatched men to set up outposts near the GPO, which involved hours and hours of tunnelling and 'really heartbreaking work' getting ready for the infantry attack that the British were never crazy enough to order. Foraging parties were sent out to offer receipts with a promise of later compensation for food, bedding and medical supplies, to the consternation of local shops and hotels.

Not that the insurgents knew it, but there were only 400 troops available for action in Dublin that day, General Friend was in London and many officers were at the Fairyhouse races. Before nightfall, though, the Viceroy Lord Wimborne had declared martial law. The first sign of action as far as the GPO was concerned was when just after one o'clock a company of Lancers on horseback who had been in the area charged down the street with their sabres drawn. Four were hit by fire from the GPO that had not been ordered; the rest fled. But by early Tuesday morning, General Lowe, the Curragh commander, and 1,600 of his troops were in Dublin with more to follow and a plan developing to cordon off the main rebel positions. In the GPO, they made ready for another attack like that of the Lancers.

Of all the observers in the GPO, Desmond FitzGerald, a London-born intellectual of Irish parentage, left the most illuminating record. A friend of many poets, including Ezra Pound, he had married Muriel, from a Presbyterian unionist background, who had converted him to Irish cultural and political nationalism; in 1913 they moved to Ireland where he became a Volunteer organiser. 'His English accent and literary pose did nothing for his popularity among men who immediately associated such traits with pretension, foppishness, and snobbery, and he could be pedantic and supercilious'[9] is one assessment, but it was precisely his perspective, which was often that of a slightly amused outsider, as well as his seriousness of mind in conversation with Pearse and Plunkett, that make his memoirs so valuable.

He arrived on Monday and was welcomed by Pearse, who he thought showed a mixture of elation and a heavy sense of responsibility, and was appointed adjutant to O'Rahilly, who was on the top storey. The two of them set about such basic tasks as seeing who was at which post where, and when they would be relieved, and then talked. O'Rahilly thought the Rising had been mistimed and that they would all be wiped out within a few hours. FitzGerald went downstairs and was told to report to Pearse, Connolly and Clarke. He observed Pearse looking around him deeply moved at the 'pitiful weapons' of the young men who 'had come out at his bidding to give their lives for Ireland'. Pearse asked no questions about the arrangements: 'I felt that he would hesitate to criticise any arrangement once we had come out in answer to the call.' He also spoke affectionately of O'Rahilly, whom he agreed had been very unjustly treated. Hearing rumours about German troops marching on Dublin, FitzGerald had complained to Pearse about having people under his orders given 'false hopes by false rumours'. He agreed. Then FitzGerald asked him for something hopeful and true and was told that smoke had been seen in the bay, so they believed there were submarines there. Later on Pearse sent FitzGerald out with the man who had done the commandeering of supplies to pay in cash.

When the looting had started, FitzGerald was standing in the street with Pearse feeling overwhelmed by the thought

> that the sacrifice he was making meant no more to them than that the sanctions of ordered society were toppling over and gave them a chance to enrich themselves with stolen goods. An eloquent plea to them from Mac Diarmada had had not the slightest effect. Pearse stood beside me looking down the street at them, and there was tragedy written on his face . . . I asked were those caught looting to be shot, and he answered 'yes'. But I knew that he said it without any conviction. And some time later a prisoner was actually handed over to me charged with looting. When I reported this to Pearse and asked what was to be done, he replied: 'Ah, poor man, just keep him with the others.'

O'Rahilly and FitzGerald both doubted if there was a real justification 'for leading those young men out to die', and FitzGerald was convinced that anyone not killed in the fight would be executed. He found Pearse a bewildering commander. To his amazement, when Pearse was told they had enough food to feed two hundred for three weeks if exercised with the most rigid economy, he said 'Then exercise the most rigid economy' since they might well be there that long. Perhaps he believed his own propaganda, for on Tuesday he had written an encouraging bulletin about Dublin being in Republican hands, the populace cheering them on and reports coming in of the country rising; later that day outside the GPO he had read a declaration to the citizens of Dublin calling on every Irishman and woman worthy of the name to assist the Provisional Government. Occasionally, he toured the building with Willie, reminding people that they had already put up a better show than Emmet.

FitzGerald regularly stopped to talk to Plunkett, who looked 'appallingly ill but at the same time very cheerful'. He was keeping a field notebook, dated in the manner of the French Revolutionaries according to the Days of the Republic. Probably desperate for intellectual company, he came upstairs to see FitzGerald the first evening, looking as if he were dying, and they talked about friends and Plunkett about his journey to Germany. They were joined by Pearse, who looked exhausted. 'He talked of the Rising as a glorious thing in itself, without reference to what it might or might not achieve in the light of the position at that moment.' Both spoke of how much bigger it would have been had its original plans not been scuppered, 'but they did not suggest that even in that case we might have expected a military victory. The very fact that the conversation returned so steadily to what might have been was an admission that there was no doubt now as to what was going to be.'

Discussing the arms from Germany, he found Pearse very anxious to make it clear that they had been paid for by Ireland or the Clan. They agreed that what was happening would make the Irish nation ready 'to spring into life'. Thinking about the apparent indifference of the Germans at a time when they might have helped the insurrection succeed, FitzGerald wondered why if they were victorious 'they would put themselves out to make the satisfaction of our demand for freedom a condition of the peace that was to follow the war'. He asked Pearse 'what interest the Germans would have in coupling our demands with their own when and if the hour of their victory came'. Both Pearse and Plunkett put forward the theory that a victorious Germany would not try to annex England because it would create for them a permanent source of weakness, nor to annex Ireland as that would 'merely make us a weakness to them as we were now to England'. But they would need to be sure that England was not a danger. Therefore, they believed, the sensible policy would be to establish an independent Ireland under Prince Joachim,* which would encourage de-anglicisation because Joachim would gravitate towards nationalists and would favour the Irish language over English, since making the country German-speaking would not be possible. After the first generation or so the ruler would have become completely Irish.

Over the ensuing days, FitzGerald gravitated towards Pearse and Plunkett at every opportunity, feeling that these talks gave them comfort. When alone with Plunkett, whom he pitied, they talked about literature and writers. But he could not look at Pearse's face without being moved. 'Its natural gravity now conveyed a sense of great tragedy. There was no doubt in my mind that when he looked round at all the men and the girls there, he was convinced that they must all perish in the Rising to which he had brought them.' And that he knew the people in the street were ready to attack them. Again and again in their conversations Pearse came back to his favourite topic:

> the moral rectitude of what we had undertaken. These can
> hardly be called discussions for only one side was taken.
> We each brought forward every theological argument and
> quotation that justified that Rising. And if one of us could
> adduce a point that the other two had not been aware of it
> was carefully noted.

FitzGerald used to ask for such points to be repeated and for exact references because they were comforting to the questioners, though he knew he as well as they were seeking reassurance. 'Certainly none of the three gave voice to any argument that might call the rightness of

* Prince Joachim Franz Humbert of Prussia (1890–1920) was the youngest son of the Kaiser. Suffering from acute depression at his commoner status after his father's abdication, he shot himself.

our action into question, unless it was that we had an immediate refutation ready for it.'

FitzGerald found Connolly intimidating and did not address difficult questions to him.

> I felt that it would take very little to make him angry . . . I had always felt when I went to talk to him that he was likely to round on me and rend me. I had gone to see him one time when he seemed to be in a furious temper. I gathered that he had given an order that someone was to lead out a body of men to bring something in, and it had not been done. He appeared to think that the man had been afraid to venture out, and shouted to the men to follow him.

FitzGerald had thought he was unwelcome because he was not a member of the ICA. Pearse got on Connolly's nerves too. Winifred Carney recorded that on Wednesday, Pearse

> standing with his usual sad demeanour annoyed J.C. Fearful of the effect he may have on the Volunteers J.C. remonstrates with him. Afterwards I ask Connolly how could he speak so to Pearse and wearily he replies 'it is so difficult to get these people to understand the sordidness of a revolution'.[10]

That morning HMS *Helga*, normally employed on fishery protection, came up the Liffey and pulverised Liberty Hall. This shook confidence in Connolly's thesis, but he came up with the explanation that this proved the British were expecting imminent German landings. Up to then, Sackville Street had had to suffer only snipers, but latterly artillery based in Trinity had begun lobbing incendiaries into buildings within range. That did not deter Pearse from writing more mendacious bulletins. Michael Collins would write later:

> I do not think the Rising week was an appropriate time for the issue of memoranda couched in poetic phrases, nor of actions worked out in a similar fashion. Looking at it from

> the inside . . . it had the air of a Greek tragedy about it, the
> illusion being more or less completed with the issue of the
> before mentioned memoranda.[11]

Outside, things was terrible too, as the locals were abruptly evacuated with nowhere to go, were cowering in their slums, or, if they dared to go out to find food, risking being caught in crossfire.

On Thursday, as the insurgents on the perimeter were no longer able to hold up the British advance, the cordon was tightening and rifle and artillery fire increased. Clarke took FitzGerald to a yard to show him a concrete opening like a room and tell him that he was promoted ('though I wasn't sure what rank the promotion gave me') and that when the end came I was to gather all the girls I could in the shelter and defend them to the last. 'It means that if you are not killed beforehand, that you will be taken by the enemy and probably executed.' FitzGerald, who after a nightmare had an obsessive horror of being hanged, asked if he would be shot or hanged. 'I should think they will probably shoot the men they take,' said Clarke, 'but they may keep to the hanging. The English love hanging.' 'But can't you say for certain?' 'No, but I should think it would be shooting after a Rising like this, and in the middle of a war.'

Plunkett and Pearse 'thought the worst would be shooting' but hanging was possible. The fires spread and the din of bombs, drums exploding in the oil works across the street, shells, sniper fire and breaking glass was incessant. Winifred Carney chided Connolly for exposing himself to British marksmen: he replied 'Do not blame me now, I must take risks like the others.'[12] As he tried to set up an outpost, his ankle was shattered by a ricocheting bullet. He fired his pistol a few times to attract attention in the GPO and was heard by George Plunkett, who found him and carried him into the GPO. Pearse was exhausted and was preparing another speech and declaration, so Clarke and Mac Diarmada, with the help of O'Rahilly, took overall control and began promoting officers, moving munitions and prisoners around the building and deciding about outposts. Plunkett got another burst of energy and, according to one of the Larkfield Lambs,

> moved amongst us all the time, his eloquent comforting
> words at odds with his bizarre, eccentric appearance, his

sabre and his jewelled fingers. We all, somehow, and in
many differing ways, responded to his gentle urgings and
praise. He was greatly loved. Most of us by now knew that
he'd risen from his deathbed to lead us.[13]

With a surge of excitement, Plunkett said to one of them: 'It's the first
time this has happened since Moscow! The first time a capital city has
burned since 1812.'

There was an operation to remove the bullet, during which
Connolly was heard to cry 'Oh, God, did ever a man suffer more for
his country!', but on Friday morning he insisted on being moved into
the front hall on a bed with castors from where he dictated a dispatch
'phrased in the most defiant and hopeful terms . . . at variance with
even the known facts'[14] and Pearse's more realistic offering. FitzGerald
suggested to Pearse the women should be sent away and, although
they almost staged a riot, they were persuaded by Mac Diarmada and
left on Friday morning. The flames were burning themselves out, but
the shelling of the GPO had begun in earnest, and fires were starting
inside. There were more corpses and wounded in the street and in the
GPO, as well as terrified men and prisoners. Clarke could see with his
own eyes that British soldiers had inflicted on his capital the kind of
destruction that he had tried to visit on theirs over thirty years
earlier.[15] But he was still indomitable, announcing as the evacuation
began: 'You can all go and leave me here. I'll go down with the
building.'

A priest who had been ministering to the insurgents had arranged
safe passage for the wounded, who were taken to hospital. A British
army doctor who had been captured on the first day and had worked in
the hospital was tending to Connolly (who had refused to leave) and
saw how Pearse (who was always good in a crisis) dealt with disaster
and managed to instil calm.

I could see no panic, no obvious signs of fear – and in the
circumstances that would have been excusable, for parts of
the building were already an inferno and the roof and ceil-
ings had already given way in places. To me, at that hasty
moment, it seemed to me that Pearse, in the way he held

them all together, was a gifted leader and a man supremely
fitted to command.[16]

There was a gradual assembling of men in the courtyard of the GPO
side gate on Henry Street. O'Rahilly had left with thirty men to see if it
would be possible to get across to Moore Street and find and occupy a
suitable building but was shot along with twenty of them within ten
minutes.

That news caused the men to scatter, as Clarke, Mac Diarmada and
a revitalised Plunkett shouted for order and courage. At one stage,
Plunkett ordered a van pulled across in Henry Street to form some sort
of barricade, and, 'as no-one wanted to cross under fire, he lined them
up, held up his sabre and each time he lowered it sent a batch across
shouting "On! On! Don't be afraid. Don't be cowards any of you."'
Connolly was carried into a stable where they found people who had
been shut in all week and 'were maddened by hunger and by the fire . . .
In no uncertain language Connolly told us to get him out of that.'[17]
Pearse, Willie, Connolly and his stretcher bearers were the last to leave
and were soon reunited with Clarke and Mac Diarmada in a grocery
shop in Moore Street with seventeen wounded, who included one
British soldier and two nurses.

During Friday night, Mac Diarmada, the ever-practical organiser,
took over effective leadership; the job of finding an escape route was
given to a talented and brave young Volunteer called Seán McLoughlin,
who was given the temporary rank of commandant general and devised
a plan involving a diversionary assault on the British troops in Moore
Street and the evacuation of the remainder of the republican forces to
the Four Courts, where Ned Daly's battalion was still fighting. Led by
Pearse, they moved through holes in the walls of adjoining houses
until Connolly could no longer be moved because of the terrible pain
from his gangrenous wound. Sitting on a bed in their new headquarters, No. 16 Moore Street, dating his letter the 6th Day of the Irish
Republic, Plunkett wrote to Grace to apologise for not having been
able to arrange their marriage, assuring her this was his only regret, telling her he wished everything he had to go to her, and saying that 'all
you do will please me'. He was sitting at the end of Connolly's bed
when Jack Good pointed out to him that he had lost one of his spurs.

He smiled, said '"The doctors give me six months to live," took off the other spur and kicked it under Connolly's bed.'

In the daylight, through a window Pearse saw three civilians – parents and their daughter – shot despite their white flag. Mac Diarmada went out to consult McLoughlin and saw many corpses, including that of O'Rahilly, who was lying on his back in a pool of blood. They knelt by his body and said an Act of Contrition and then returned to No. 16, where McLoughlin told them his plans. Not long afterwards, after seeing more dead civilians, although Clarke and Pearse were pleading for a shoot-out, the others decided on surrender and the majority prevailed. On a piece of cardboard, Pearse wrote:

> Believing that the glorious stand which has been made by the soldiers of Irish freedom during the last five days in Dublin has been sufficient to gain recognition of Ireland's national claim at an international peace conference, and desirous of preventing further slaughter of the civil population and to save the lives of as many as possible of our followers, the members of the Provisional Government here present have agreed by a majority to open negotiations with the British commander.

With the die cast and Nurse Elizabeth O'Farrell on her way with a verbal message for Brigadier-General Lowe, Pearse, Connolly and MacDermott chatted. Winifred Carney saw Clarke in anguish 'standing near the wall against the window. Suddenly he turns his face to the wall and breaks down. I go over to calm him only to break into an uncontrollable fit of weeping myself. It is so sad to see him cry. This steadies him and he begs me to control myself.'[18]

Escorted to Tom Clarke's shop by the nearest senior officer, O'Farrell eventually saw Lowe, who sent her back with a note to Pearse demanding unconditional surrender. A request for terms for his men and unconditional surrender for himself was rejected. Nonetheless, Pearse shook hands all round and left with O'Farrell, and after a short meeting with Lowe when he handed over his arms he was taken to meet General Sir John Maxwell, who had arrived that morning to assume the supreme command in Ireland. He wrote and signed a surrender order that said that 'the Commandants of the various districts in the City and Country will order their commands to lay down arms'.

The next problem was to persuade all the commanders to accept the terms.

Tom MacDonagh's orders to his Battalion on Easter Monday had been to assemble at St Stephen's Green by noon. He had been fortunate that as he addressed the men John MacBride, who had had plenty of military experience, happened by, offered to join in and was made second-in-command. MacBride had had a bad decade since the acrimonious split with Maud Gonne, the trashing of his reputation, financial troubles, alcoholism and being pushed off the Supreme Council in 1911 by his old friend Tom Clarke, but he was still an asset to an inexperienced young commandant. In his navy blue suit and grey hat, smoking cigars and carrying a Malacca walking stick, he would be a steadying influence throughout the week.

MacDonagh, his brother John and MacBride led the march to seize Jacob's Biscuit Factory, a huge building of considerable strategic importance and easy to defend. En route, separation-allowance women screamed and struck at Volunteers and when they got there tried to stop them breaking in or setting up outposts. When they were ensconced, the women tried to get inside to eject them. It being a bank holiday, there was no one to resist except a caretaker and some maintenance men. Outside was a rough and hostile area and MacDonagh eventually brought the men back into the building along with a few captured policemen. Depleted numbers made it impossible to carry out the plan to take over Trinity College. The only other main purpose of being in Jacob's was to prevent troops entering the city from the south, though in fact this devolved mainly on de Valera's men in Boland's Mills.

There was some fire directed at thirty or so soldiers who appeared nearby, wounding several, but otherwise there was no sight of the enemy, who were uninterested. The garrison consisted of 178 men, mostly Volunteers, but with a few from the ICA and the Fianna, and some Cumann na mBan cooks. They waited all week for an attack that never came, as General Lowe deliberately wore them down psychologically by using snipers and noisy armoured cars to keep them awake

day and night. One of them recalled 'the ear-splitting crash of all sorts
of arms gave the impression of being attacked front and rear . . . nerves
were as taut as a violin at pitch'.[19] They were exhausted, and sickened by
a diet of far too many biscuits and cakes.

MacDonagh put on the best face he could. Máire Nic Shiubhlaigh,
for instance, in command of the kitchen, thought he carried 'his usual
business-like air with him' and was 'an excellent leader who hid his
responsibilities and his worries behind his good humour, never allowing anyone to think other than that the fighting was going well'.[20] But
MacDonagh, who was getting no news other than the occasional
courier passing on unfounded heroic tales, overdid it with the optimism and the rousing speeches, assuring the men that the insurrection
was on its way to being victorious. Whereas in the GPO, the garrison
had the evidence of their own eyes to counteract at least some unrealistic propaganda, MacDonagh's men believed him and he believed
himself. Nic Shiubhlaigh wrote of rumours being the worst enemies
the garrison had:

> German troops had landed at Wexford and were striking
> inland in thousands, routing British garrisons as they drove
> towards Dublin in support of the Rising; it was said that
> the Volunteers were fighting bitterly along the coastline to
> Cork where the city was supposed to be out like Dublin . . .
> Dublin Castle was on fire; the British were using explosive
> bullets and shooting prisoners . . .[21]

Sometimes, for lack of anything else to do, MacDonagh sent out small
parties to reconnoitre or set up the odd outpost, but to little purpose.
Orders were often pointless and contradictory. He undertook one
mission when de Valera sent a message asking for arms and ammunition at Boland's Mill: MacDonagh went out with fifteen cyclists, who
shot a lone sentry outside a house with soldiers billeted in it, had a
brief fight, and then concluded they could not get to Boland's. On the
way back one of them was killed. And that was that.

'Overpromoted, separated from the Military Council's collective
strength and wisdom and lacking Plunkett's comforting presence,' say
Foy and Barton, 'MacDonagh surrendered completely to wishful

thinking.'[22] As the week went on, MacBride, who confessed to a Volunteer that he simply could not understand why Jacob's had been occupied, was calm and experiencing a rebirth by recovering his lapsed faith and confessing his sins. Religion was on the minds of all the men. So was diversion. A gramophone record of 'God Save the King' was played when MacDonagh inspected troops, the library was raided for books and there were reading circles.[23]

At the end of the week, though, the garrison had been able to see the burning of the GPO and they realised the climax was coming and began strengthening defences and firing on any British troops who passed by. Then, on Sunday morning, Nurse O'Farrell arrived with Pearse's surrender order and described what had happened. MacDonagh refused to accept instructions from a prisoner and said he was now de facto commander-in-chief and would talk only to the British General Officer Commanding. Two Capuchin priests, Fathers Aloysius and Augustine, who were acting as mediators, told him Lowe would demolish Jacob's if MacDonagh refused to talk, but he persisted in claiming to be in an excellent position to fight on and thus guarantee Irish representation at the peace conference.

He met Lowe and accepted the inevitable until he went back to Jacob's and met rage and threats to fight it out. MacDonagh eventually broke down, crying 'Boys, we must give in. We must leave some to carry on the struggle.' He called in Nic Shuibhlaigh, who fainted at the shock. Louise Gavan Duffy (daughter of Young Ireland leader Charles Gavan Duffy), who had been disapprovingly helping in the GPO all week, was with her, and told MacDonagh the Rising should never have happened as it was wrong and doomed to failure. He responded by telling her not to talk to his men, but he delegated the job of telling the rank-and-file downstairs. When they came to see him, he told them listlessly and sadly that he was just obeying orders, and fled as the arguments continued. A composed MacBride came in and persuaded those who could escape to escape; and at the appointed time a dishevelled MacDonagh led the remainder to the surrender point where he had a kind of breakdown and made wild accusations against the British military. He was in poor emotional condition to undertake his next duties of persuading Eamon de Valera and Éamonn Ceannt to surrender.

*   *   *

Ceannt had left home after a serious setback, for one of his senior officers, William O'Brien, had arrived at his house to say he would not be part of the Rising. 'At least', said Ceannt, 'he had the courage to come and tell me,' but O'Brien had kept important papers and maps, the lack of which would cause confusion. Before he left, Áine asked him how long the fight would continue, and he said 'If we last a month then they – the British – will come to terms.'[24]

Wearing an ordinary Volunteer uniform with an Australian bush ranger's hat, Ceannt arrived at the assembly point where there was a very low turnout of about a hundred, most of whom did not know the Rising was about to happen. Among them was Cathal Brugha, who 'knew nothing of fear and had little sympathy for anyone who did. He spoke little of his political views, but one gathered he regarded the gun as the only effective sound in Irish politics.' Ceannt led the men to the South Dublin Union.

This location was an extraordinary choice: covering fifty acres, it was an enormous poorhouse catering for three thousand inmates and included three hospitals, one for the mentally ill. It was a sprawling site that would have required many hundreds to man properly, and, being close to several British army barracks, a major railway station, and controlling an important approach to the city, it was potentially a serious threat to the British army, so it was attacked from the first day. According to one of the men:

> When the time came for dinner [midday] sentinels were posted and Commandant Ceannt addressed us. 'Men,' he said, 'you may have noticed that this is not an ordinary manoeuvres. We have been firing and our fire has been returned. Now, the reason for that is this. There has been a secret session of the House of Commons in London and it has been decided that the British will sue for an armistice. That will mean a peace conference but in order for Ireland to be represented at the peace conference we must be a belligerent. So long as we are in arms at the time of the armistice we will be able to go to the peace conference and get the freedom of Ireland. This has been decided under a treaty made by Sir Roger Casement acting for Ireland and the German Foreign minister Herr von Zimmerman.'[25]

If this is accurate, and it is in line with the information being given by other commanders, it is further evidence of how normally truthful men had become used to lying.

Over the ensuing week the Union administration, who concentrated the inmates into selected buildings, with the co-operation of both the Volunteers and the British tried to keep the inhabitants safe, but there were some casualties among them and widespread terror during the gun battles.

A small group posted at the western end of the grounds was quickly overwhelmed by 300 British soldiers, but Ceannt's men in the main buildings managed the extraordinary feat of hanging on all week to the Union and its outposts. He concentrated his forces in two buildings, which he held on a night of ferocious hand-to-hand fighting up and down long corridors, made possible by exceptional leadership from both him and Brugha: both of them were inspirational in their courage and for most of the time also were lucky. Ceannt, said one Volunteer, moved about 'as if he had an enchanted life'. As a result of their unexpected success, the British withdrew and did not return until Thursday, during which time the battalion was hard at work fortifying the nurses' home they had commandeered. Ceannt arranged for officers and men to eat together in the kitchen, where he chatted informally and was always 'cool and cheerful'. They also had regular conferences with everyone to keep them up to date with reality, not fantasy of the kind he had fed them with their first lunch. Ceannt planned too for daily confessions and led the men in the rosary during lulls in fighting.

The British were back on Thursday, needing to attack in order to allow a wagonload of ammunition to pass by free of sniper fire. They had reinforcements for a massive attack that involved rifles, machine guns and grenades, finally breaking into the nurses' home with high explosives. 'Everything was bizarre on that day,' wrote Dublin-born Major Francis Vane of the Munster Royal Fusiliers to his wife,

> for we advanced through a convent where the nuns were all praying and expecting to be shot, poor creatures, then through the wards of imbeciles who were all shrieking – and through to one of poor old people. To get from one

> door to another was a gymnastic feat because you had to
> run the gauntlet of the snipers.

When they began the assault, the Volunteers were so inspired that they fought like fanatical veterans for five hours. Cathal Brugha received twenty-five wounds but never complained and after months in hospital would be ready to fight again for his uncompromising vision of Ireland. Ceannt showed his hardness too. Having realised that a medical doctor in the Union was helping the British, he told Volunteers 'that if any of our men saw treason he would be hanged and hanged by our men'.[26] Later on, he shot dead a policeman wearing RIC trousers and a khaki tunic, thus becoming the only one of the Seven who other than unwittingly killed someone during the Rising. He was heard 'to refer to it afterwards with obvious satisfaction'.[27] On Friday, without Brugha, with constant snipers' fire and the prospect of another concerted attack, he was found by a Red Cross man 'in a small room by himself, his rosary beads in his hands, and big tears rolling down his cheeks and face'. Catching sight of the visitor, who began to back away, Ceannt 'called him in, buried his face in his handkerchief, and after about half a minute was again the leader'. He then showed his men where to dig trenches if the British began to use artillery. All went smoothly until Sunday, with maintenance and preparations for the next offensive, when two cars arrived outside with MacDonagh and the two priests and three British officers. MacDonagh 'looked old, weary and ill'.

A horrified Ceannt hated the idea of surrender, wanting instead to be involved in a guerrilla campaign, but he accepted collective responsibility and read Pearse's surrender order to his men. He told them, though, that if they refused, he would lead their continued fight. Asked his opinion, he reluctantly recommended surrender. If any men wished to escape, they could do so, he said, but he would prefer them to behave like soldiers to the end. 'You men will get a double journey,' he told them, 'but we, the leaders, will get a single journey.'

MacDonagh had left to negotiate with Lowe, and on the way with Father Augustine was fired upon by a British soldier who was immediately arrested by an officer, who apologised. After another meeting with Ceannt to tell him the timing of his surrender, MacDonagh was depressed and pointed out to the priest the place 'where the scaffold was erected on which Robert Emmet was hanged'. Ceannt organised his men and when the time came the relevant British officer attempted to shake hands, 'but Ceannt remained rigid. Then the British officer said "You had a fine position here." Ceannt replied "Yes, and made full use of it. Not alone did we hold your army for six days but shook it to its foundation."' After the men were mustered, Sir Francis Vane asked Ceannt if the main buildings had been held with only forty men; he replied quietly, 'No, forty-two.'[28] Marching at the head of the men with General Lowe, 'Eamon looked great; he had his shirt thrown open, his tunic thrown open and was swinging along at the head of his men. He looked a real soldier.'[29]

Retribution

Patrick Pearse was left under the supervision of Irishman Captain Harry de Courcy Wheeler, who was locked in the room alone with him, instructed to keep a loaded revolver pointed at him and to shoot if he tried to escape. He recalled that Pearse 'smiled at me across the table and did not seem in the least perturbed'.[30] Later he was transferred to Arbour Hill Detention Barracks. Richard Mulcahy, who had been fighting in Ashbourne with the 5th Dublin Battalion, was brought to him to verify the orders, and found him in a cell lying on bare trestle boards with beside him a glass of water and some biscuits. Pearse moved towards him, and Mulcahy asked him if the order applied to the whole of Ireland. '"Would it be of any use," I asked, "if a small band of men were to hold out any longer?" And Pearse replied "No." My lips moved to frame a "Beannacht Dé agat" [God bless you] but the sound was stifled, absorbed in the solemnity of my salute which closed the scene.'[31]

Two emissaries from Wexford arrived later. 'He rose up and advanced to meet us; it seemed to us that he was physically exhausted but spiritually exultant ... The Dublin Brigade, he said, had done splendidly – "five days and nights of almost continuous fighting" ... "No," he was not aware that we in Wexford were out."' The order to lay down arms was written, but as the military guard showed it to the officer outside, 'Pearse whispered to us to hide our arms in safe places. "They will be needed later," he said.'

Lowe had ordered that Connolly be taken by stretcher from Moore Street to the military hospital at Dublin Castle, where he was carried to a small ward in the Officers' Quarters. 'The nurses in charge of him acknowledged, without exception, that no one could have been more considerate, or have given less trouble.'[32] At his request, Father Aloysius visited him on Monday 1 May, and claimed that Connolly spoke of the brave conduct of priests and nuns during the week, described them (startlingly) as 'the best friends of the workers', made his confession and the following day took communion. It is more probable that Connolly made a pragmatic decision to neutralise religious opposition to the insurrection. Nora saw him there too, and saw the gangrene was beginning to affect his whole body; he could do little more than lift his head from the pillow.

When Pearse and Connolly had both left, 'we kneel down', said Carney, 'and say the rosary in Irish, Seán MacDermott giving it out while we respond. It is tragedy in the extreme.' Clarke was not part of that, and not just because he was a non-believer, but because he was in the basement recovering his equilibrium, something this man did best alone. Then, weeping, Mac Diarmada called McGarry and said 'we are going to ask the lads to surrender. It would have been far better to go down in a good fight but it is too late now.' Clarke and Mac Diarmada had to deal with a threatened mutiny from some of the men in Moore Street and even Plunkett could not convince the Kimmage Garrison to surrender, but Clarke reminded them of his own life-long struggle for Irish independence and said if he was satisfied so should they be. Mac Diarmada was eloquent in reassuring them that the surrender was to save the city and its people from destruction; that though the Seven would be shot, the rest would get no more than a few years in jail, and that they then would be around to finish the job. He then read them the surrender instructions from Lowe.

Before they left, some of the men knelt to say the rosary, and then, with the wounded in front, they were led by Willie Pearse, waving the white flag like a banner of victory, and Plunkett, Mac Diarmada and Clarke, who had his hands in his pockets and his cap on the back of his head. About 320 of them marched towards the Parnell Monument where they were disarmed, taken to the forecourt of the Rotunda Hospital and told to lie down. Some Volunteers expected summary execution or worse, but others showed defiance by smoking, smashing surrendered weapons to the ground and generally behaving as if they had won, which annoyed some of their captors, particularly those of the Royal Irish Regiment from Belfast.

There were occasional exhibitions of bad behaviour. One officer said to Mac Diarmada: 'You have cripples in your army.' 'You have your place, sir,' he replied, 'and I have mine, and you had better mind your place, sir.' Another kicked Plunkett on the shiny soles of his shoes. But the prize went to Captain Lea Wilson, the commanding officer who came on duty drunk at midnight, who strode around roaring conflicting orders at soldiers and prisoners alike. 'He bends over Plunkett,' observed Desmond Ryan, 'and snatches a document from an inner pocket: "Ah, his will! Knew what he was coming out to get."' Then 'he yells at Tom Clarke: "That old b----- is the Commander-in-Chief. He keeps a tobacco shop across the street. Nice General for your f------- army!" He has Tom Clarke searched and snatches scarfs from men here and there. A police inspector arrives and eyes him coldly. The Volunteers are marched away.'[33]

It had been a cold, miserable and squalid night in a place with no sanitary facilities. On Sunday morning they were taken to Richmond Barracks, two miles away, enduring on the way a barrage of abuse and rotten vegetables from people angry at the destruction of their city: many, but by no means all, were separation-allowance wives. Mac Diarmada, who had had his stick confiscated, limped there with the help of Carney and Julia Grenan, arriving forty-five minutes after everyone else, 'pale as death'.

Clarke, who believed he would be summarily executed, slipped a large wad of money to a Volunteer and scribbled a note to Kathleen:

> Dear K, I am in better health and more satisfied than for many a day – all will be well eventually – but this is my good-bye and now you are ever before me to cheer me – God bless you and the boys. Let them be proud to follow same path – Seán is with me and McG[arry], all well – they are all heroes. I'm full of pride my love, Yours Tom.

On the other side, Mac Diarmada, who had never dared call her by her first name, wrote to her as 'Dear Cáit, I never felt so proud of the boys. Tis worth a life of suffering to be with them for one hour. God bless you all, Seán.'[34] Clarke gave his watch to a British soldier to have the letter delivered. Kathleen got it three weeks later.

With around six hundred prisoners and hundreds more troops, the barracks were at bursting point: the prisoners were parked in bare rooms with blankets, buckets and meagre rations. During the day, they were joined by men from other companies, including Ceannt and MacDonagh. At one stage prime suspects had been separated from the rank-and-file, and about twenty of them, including Clarke, Mac Diarmada, MacDonagh and MacBride, sat with their backs to the wall, while Ceannt 'defiantly strode up and down in front of them, arms folded, looking very much like a caged lion.'[35]

One of those prisoners was Liam Ó Briain, a UCD lecturer and Volunteer who had been in St Stephen's Green with Markievicz. There is evidence that she had taken literally Connolly's advice to remember what the police did during the Lockout and 'how they treated you in 1913' and had shot dead an unarmed policeman, crying 'I got him.'[36] 'My best friend, Seán MacDermott, was there,' he recalled, 'poor, lame Seán, affectionate, gay, handsome and warm hearted.' Mac Diarmada had asked Ó Briain to give the old quilt he had brought with him to Plunkett, who was

> very sick. For a couple of days following he had the old quilt, sometimes under him as a bed, sometimes under his head as a pillow . . . Tom Clarke was sitting there just as we had seen him twenty times in his shop in Parnell Street, with the same clothes, the same look, quiet, silent, with the suspicion of a smile on his lips now and then. Tom was very satisfied with himself and the situation.

He saw 'a dreamy-eyed young man with rather long hair who looked like an artist and was wearing a Volunteer uniform: he was Willie Pearse'. Sleep did not guarantee rest.

> Seán fell asleep with his head on Tom's chest. Young Pearse was turning from side to side on my left, very disturbed

though he was fast asleep. I don't think Tom slept at all – nor did I for a long while. It was clear that the other two, in their dreams, were back in the G.P.O. Seán would start a little and we would hear a mutter from him saying 'The fire! The fire! Get the men out!' Then you would hear Tom's quiet voice saying gently, 'Quietly, Seán! We're in the barracks now. We're prisoners now, Seán.' In the same way, Pearse would utter a little moan 'The fire! The fire!' now and again.

On Tuesday morning, Seán Murphy

left the yard to go to the Wash House and Seán McDermott who accompanied me across was leaning on me, having being [sic] relieved of a stick he carried on account of his infirmity. I said: 'We will walk together, Seán.' On the way over by way of conversation I said: 'Well, that's all, Seán. I wonder what's next?' and in reply he said to me, 'Seán, the cause is lost if some of us are not shot.' Those words seemed to have burned themselves on my mind and I seemed never to have forgotten them and never will. 'Surely to God you do not mean that, Seán. Aren't things bad enough?' I replied. 'They are', he said, 'so bad that if what I say does not come true they will be very much worse.'[37]

General Maxwell had a straightforward view of what had to be done. He believed that Britain's back was to the wall, and had German arms landed there could have been a serious rebellion that could have led to its defeat. On the Western Front, men who had been fighting in the most terrible circumstances were being executed for losing their nerve and running from enemy gunfire. The ordinary British soldier would not understand if the men responsible for the Dublin insurrection got away with it. There had not been political executions since those of 1883 related to the Phoenix Park murders, but in these circumstances, in Maxwell's view, when dealing with traitors, deterrence was essential. There was therefore no question in his mind but that the leaders should be executed and the rest interned in Great Britain. The job of the military police and G-men was to identify prominent suspects who would quickly be tried.

Around 3,500 had been arrested (of whom 79 were women), but within a short time close on half were released, and most of the rest sent across the Irish Sea. There would be court martial trials of Constance Markievicz and 186 men. They appeared in front of a panel of three officer judges; death sentences had to be unanimous and approved by Maxwell.

The first to be tried was the self-identified President of the Provisional Government and Commandant-General of the Army of the Irish Republic. Realising this, on Monday Pearse had thrown himself into a frenzy of creation. There were three poems to the two people he had loved inarticulately but devotedly all his life. 'To My Mother' was full of self-revelation. In return for her rich gifts of life, love, pity, sanity and the strong faith on which his was founded, he said all he had given her was sorrow / 'O Mother (for you know me) / You must have known, when I was silent, / That some strange thing within me kept me dumb, / I have sobbed in secret / For that reserve which yet I could not master.' Still, 'I have brought you something else besides – / The memory of my deed and of my name / A splendid thing which shall not pass away.' For Willie, there was 'To My Brother':

> O faithful!
> Moulded in one womb,
> We two have stood together all the years,
> All the glad years and all the sorrowful years,
> Own brothers: through good repute and ill,
> In direst peril true to me,
> Leaving all things for me, spending yourself
> In the hard service that I taught to you
> Of all the men that I have known on earth,
> You only have been my familiar friend,
> Nor needed I another.

His mother had asked him for a little poem 'which would seem to be said by you about me' and he composed 'A Mother Speaks', a prayer to Mary ('that didst see thy first-born Son / Go forth to die amid the scorn of men / For whom He died') asking her to receive Patrick ('Who also hath gone out to die for men') and keep him safe. There were instructions about his literary and complicated financial affairs, which expressed his regret that he would be unable to pay his many friends and creditors the 75 per cent still outstanding, and included a request to the Clan to look after a friend who had signed a large bill for him. There was a hastily written letter to his mother explaining how the surrender had come about, telling her Willie and the St Enda's boys were well and no longer in danger, but expressing the readiness of the leaders to die 'cheerfully *and proudly*. Personally I do not hope or even desire to live, but I do hope and desire and believe that the lives of all our followers will be saved including the lives dear to you and me (my own excepted) and this will be a great consolation to me when dying'. She should not grieve. 'We have preserved Ireland's honour and our own. *Our deeds of last week are the most splendid things in Irish history.* People will say hard things of us now, *but we shall be remembered by posterity and blessed by unborn generations.* You too will be blessed because you were my mother.' There was a PS: 'I understand *that the German expedition which I was counting on actually set sail but was defeated by the British*.' It was nicely ambiguous, suggesting that he had thought the ship had troops on board. Apart from 'A Mother Speaks', which he gave to a Capuchin who gave it to Mrs Pearse next day, everything else was sent to Maxwell with a request to send the lot to her. The business letters were sent on and the rest, which Maxwell thought seditious, were sent to Asquith, but a copy of his letter to his mother was typed up and used as evidence next day in Richmond Barracks, where all the trials were heard and all in private. As Judge Seán Enright shows,[38] proceedings were a legal travesty even by the standards of courts martial. None of the defendants was allowed legal support.

Had the prisoners been in civil courts they would have been charged with treason, rebellion or murder, for all of which the death penalty was available. But the Proclamation of 25 April revoked the right to trial by jury and under DORA a court martial could impose the death penalty only where the breach of regulations was carried out 'with the intention of assisting the enemy'. So they all faced the same charge: 'Did take part in an armed rebellion and in the waging of war against His Majesty the King, such an act being of such a nature as to be calculated to be prejudicial to the Defence of the Realm and being done with the intention and purpose of assisting the enemy.' Pearse's thoughtfully added postscript about German aid ensured there could be no doubt about the death penalty. As Enright put it, 'it is unlikely that Pearse believed his mother was remotely interested in whether the German fleet had sailed or not'. He was a barrister who knew what he was doing, as several Volunteers had been tried under the DORA regime. He was ensuring he was given the death penalty he craved and deliberately put the postscript at the top of the first page. And, in his closing address in his trial, he emphasised German involvement.

Unfortunately for some of his co-revolutionaries who might have preferred to survive, this helped sink them by association in the minds of the judges. The army had looked for proof that Pearse had acted with the intention of assisting the enemy, but, said Enright,

> this requirement was simply overlooked or ignored in rela-
> tion to many of the trials that followed. Both standing
> courts at Richmond Barracks took the same approach.
> There is no record of their deliberations, only the results of
> their discussions and it is therefore a question of inference.
> It seems likely that the courts took the view that if it was
> proved against Pearse that he had acted with the intention
> and for the purpose of assisting the enemy, that could be
> inferred in respect of the other prisoners.

Pearse did not defend himself in his short trial. When asked if he had been well treated, he confirmed he had. Sergeant Goodman gave evidence that he had been on duty at Arbour Hill and had seen Pearse writing the letter now produced in court. The person writing the trial record included a note quoting the 'short crucial postscript'. He made a speech, freely admitting responsibility, acknowledging and implicitly justifying the request for foreign aid, and claimed a dedication since childhood to free Ireland. It was a very eloquent speech, said William Wylie, the Crown Prosecutor, 'what I always call a Robert Emmet type'. (Actually, it was closely modelled on Tone's from the dock.) Pearse spoke and held himself well; Colonel Blackader, who chaired Pearse's and several other courts martial, told Elizabeth, Countess of

Fingall at dinner that he had 'just done one of the hardest things I have ever had to do. I have had to condemn to death one of the finest characters I have ever come across. There must be something very wrong in the state of things that makes a man like that a rebel. I don't wonder his pupils adored him.'[39]

Maxwell confirmed the verdict, highlighting Pearse's contact with Germany and referring to the Proclamation as 'the Declaration of Independence', which contained 'the following passage: "She (viz. Ireland) now seizes that moment and supported by her exiled children in America and by gallant allies in Europe . . . she strikes in the full confidence of victory"'. He mentioned the postscript and that Pearse 'stated at his trial that he was in communication with Germany and that his object was to defeat England'. MacDonagh and Clarke were tried immediately after Pearse and afterwards were briefly reunited in the Barracks gymnasium as they waited to hear the verdicts.

In Kilmainham Jail, where Pearse was told he would be executed next day at dawn, in his cell he wrote a longer and more polished version of his speech, amplifying Germany's role in the Rising and pleading that what he had said 'must not be used against anyone who acted with me'. He ended: 'You cannot extinguish the Irish passion for freedom. If our deed has not been sufficient to win freedom, then our children will win it by a better deed.' He also wrote 'The Wayfarer', which began 'The beauty of the world hath made me sad, / The beauty that will pass,' described his delight in 'things young and happy' and ended it 'sorrowful', because they would 'change and die.' Father Aloysius arrived without Mrs Pearse, whom he could not collect because of some persistent snipers, but gladdened Pearse's heart by telling him he had given Holy Communion that morning to Connolly. 'Thank God,"' he replied, 'It is one thing I was anxious about.' He took communion himself, wrote a little note thanking Willie ('No one can ever have had so true a brother as you'), a letter to his mother with familiar sentiments ('This is the death I should have asked for if God had given me the choice of all deaths, – to die a soldier's death for Ireland and for freedom. We have done right.') And he urged her to see it as 'a sacrifice which God asked of me and of you.' He thanked her for her 'great love for me and for your great faith . . . I hope soon to see Papa, and in a little while we shall all be together again.' He would, he said, call to all his family 'in my heart at the last moment'.

Willie was being taken to see him at 3:30 on the morning of 3 May when he heard a volley of shots. One of the guards looked at the others and said 'Too late.' MacDonagh and Clarke were shot that morning too. MacDonagh had said nothing at his trial except to plead not guilty and at the end tell Blackader that 'I did everything I could to assist the officers in the matter of the surrender, telling them where the arms and ammunition were after the surrender was decided upon.' There had been no conclusive evidence at his trial, but in confirming his sentence Maxwell referred to a letter found on MacBride's person signed by MacDonagh in his capacity as a member of the Provisional Government and of the Irish Republican Army. After his execution, a long and eloquent statement justifying the Rising was widely circulated in the press, which was full of fine and stirring rhetoric. His family and the world in general believed it to be authentic until his son Donagh was convinced otherwise in adulthood and dismissed it as a forgery. Wylie regretted his execution: 'It was particularly unnecessary in his case.'

He was visited in Kilmainham by Father Aloysius and by his sister Mary (Sister Francesca), whom he assured that Muriel would become a Catholic. He asked her to look after her and the two little children, accepted rosary beads to take to his execution and took communion. On her way to see him, Muriel was stopped by a roadblock. Worried about the family's financial future, MacDonagh wrote to her making suggestions for the publication of his *Literature in Ireland*, and predicting that there would be a large demand for his work when he died. He included messages and blessings to his darling little boy and daughter, whom he had 'loved more than ever a child has been loved'. He thanked Muriel, his dearest love, 'for all you have been to me . . . Goodbye, my love, till we meet again in Heaven.' He also wrote anxiously that his statement about the surrender might sound like an appeal, which it was not. 'I make no appeal, no recantation, no apology, for my acts . . . It is a great and glorious thing to die for Ireland and I can well forget all petty annoyances in the splendour of this.'

Taken to the exercise yard, he was affected by the youth of some of the twelve-man firing squad and their nervousness. He gave them cigarettes, and handed the officer in charge his silver case: 'I won't be needing this, would you like to have it?' He was then reported to have said 'I know this is a lousy job, but you're doing your duty – I do not hold this against you.' A British officer was reported to have said afterwards, 'they all died well, but MacDonagh died like a Prince'.

As Tom Clarke had told his fellow prisoners, he would plead not guilty for the sake of the record on the grounds that what he had done was for Ireland, not 'with the intention and purpose of assisting the enemy'. His only intervention was to ask the officer who had been a prisoner in the GPO and identified him as a person in authority there if he had been well treated, which he agreed he had. Kathleen Clarke had to be brought from Dublin Castle to see him in Kilmainham, for she had been arrested on suspicion of having been involved in the Rising and taken there with Arthur Griffith, whom she embarrassed by shouting encouragement at Volunteer prisoners as they passed them in the streets. Father Aloysius, who was hovering, asked her to intercede with Clarke to see him. She refused. Clarke told her the priest had wanted him to say he was sorry for what he had done: 'unless I did he could not give me absolution. I told him to clear out of my cell quickly. I was not sorry for what I had done. I gloried in it and the men who had been with me. To say I was sorry would be a lie, and I was not going to face my God with a lie on my tongue.' That was consistent. He had upset the Sister of Mercy nurses in January when he refused the sacraments before being operated on for the bullet in his elbow.[40]

Kathleen found him in a 'very exalted' frame of mind, full of hope for the future of Ireland. He begged her not to let his death 'shadow' their happy children's lives but to 'train them to follow in my footsteps'. Kathleen replied tartly that 'his death would shadow their lives no matter what I did and I thought it was a hard road he had picked for them, to follow in his footsteps: children did not always carry out their parents' wishes.' He told her that her twenty-five-year-old brother Ned, who had commanded the Four Courts, had proved himself a hero and a fine soldier who would certainly be shot.

He instructed her to do two things. First was to refute any notion that the Germans had let them down. They had 'carried out their promise to us, to the last letter . . . What help they could give us would entirely depend on their progress in the war; they had promised that if they won out, they would free Ireland.'

Second was to ensure that 'our people' knew Eoin MacNeill's 'treachery to us. He must never be allowed back into the National life of the country, for so sure as he is, so sure will he act treacherously in a crisis. He is a weak man, but I know every effort will be made to white-wash him.' Clarke made Kathleen memorise his last message to the Irish people:

> My comrades and I believe we have struck the first success-ful blow for freedom, and so sure as we are going out this morning, so sure will freedom come as a direct result of our action. It will not come today or tomorrow, and between this and freedom Ireland will go through Hell, but she will never lie down again until she has attained full free-dom. With this belief, we die happy. I am happy and satis-fied at what we have accomplished.[41]

Kathleen kept her head up and did not break down. She did not tell him that she was pregnant because she thought it would sadden him to know he would never see the baby. He was shot shortly after she left.

Willie Pearse was the only defendant to plead guilty, yet insisted he had had only a minor supporting role as his brother's aide. He was shot on the fourth along with Ned Daly, a friend of MacDonagh's (and author of the Jacobite story for boys *A Swordsman of the Brigade*) called Michael O'Hanrahan, and Joe Plunkett. The evidence against Plunkett had been thin, and, unusually – for they had no signed copy – rested mainly on his name having appeared on the 'Proclamation issued by the Irish Volunteers'. Plunkett's questioning and address to the court was designed to protect the Irish Volunteers: 'I have nothing to say in my defence but desire to state that the Proclamation . . . is signed by persons who are not connected with the Irish Volunteers and the proc-lamation was not issued by the Irish Volunteers.' Maxwell gave several reasons for confirming the sentence, including that he 'being of good education, exercised great influence for evil over the other members' and that 'his residence was a training ground and arsenal for the rebels'.

He ended his life as flamboyantly as he had lived it, being married to Grace by candlelight in his cell that evening with two soldiers as witness. She had to leave immediately, but was allowed back at 2:00

for ten minutes. 'We who had never had enough time to say what we wanted to each other found that in that last ten minutes we couldn't talk at all.' His parents, who were imprisoned in Richmond Barracks, had been brought to the jail separately but were not told why and did not see their son. It may be that, facing death, he really did not want to see Ma. Father Sebastian said that while Plunkett waited to be called to the exercise yard he said: 'Father, I am very happy. I am dying for the glory of God and the honour of Ireland.' At the end, according to Father Augustine, he was calm, cool and self-possessed. 'No fine talk. No heroics. A distinguished tranquillity.' There is a story that the officer in charge of the firing squad was his old friend, Kenneth O'Morchoe, from Kilternan, and that he asked to be replaced by someone else.

MacBride was shot alone on the fifth, and Con Colbert, Michael Mallin and Seán Heuston along with Éamonn Ceannt, were shot the following day. Tried on 3 and 4 May, Ceannt had fought for his life. He had done his homework meticulously; among his notes was 'shall not deny anything proven or admit what is not proven'. He had reason to think he had a chance, for he was being accused of being at Jacob's Factory, not the South Dublin Union, and he cross-examined vigorously and cleverly as he challenged this technicality. He called MacBride, who testified that Ceannt had not been in Jacob's, and then tried to call MacDonagh, whom he probably knew was dead, only, as the court record put it, to find he 'was not available as he was shot this morning'. The case was adjourned and resumed the next day. Ceannt's closing address, said Seán Enright, 'was remarkable in its clarity, although he made minor evidential concessions which were unnecessary'. He denied 'assisting the enemy' and said the prosecution had not attempted to substantiate that portion of the charge. Maxwell was in London, but Ceannt wrote to Áine to say he expected the death sentence, 'which better men have already suffered . . . I shall die like a man for Ireland's sake.' She had had hope for a while, for a newspaper report on Wednesday said Asquith had said in the House of Commons that he had been sentenced to three years' penal servitude. 'For the time being our hearts bounded with joy,' wrote Michael Kent in his diary. And happy though Áine was then, she thought that very tough on MacDonagh, 'who to my mind had not been so deeply involved until the last moment'. She found her house trashed, but succeeded in getting permission to visit her husband on Saturday and asked him if the Rising had been 'an awful fiasco'. 'No,' he said, 'it was the biggest thing since '98.'

Ceannt's defence had cut no ice with Maxwell, who ruled he had signed the Proclamation and was identified 'with all pro-German movements'. Ceannt wasted no time in his cell. There was a will, a list of practical notes for Áine about insurance policies, a possible grant from the union, potential dependants' funds and a request that small tokens be given to his brothers, including Bill in the British Army. A letter to the Commandant of the gaol listed the possessions to be given to his wife. There was a letter

> for the guidance of other Irish Revolutionaries who may tread the path which I have trod this advice, never to treat with the enemy, never to surrender at *his* mercy, but to fight to a finish. I see nothing gained but grave disaster caused, by the surrender which has marked the end of the Irish Insurrection of 1916 – so far at least as Dublin is concerned.

The enemy had shown no generosity towards those who had 'withstood his forces for one glorious week'. He bore no ill will towards those 'against whom I have fought. I have found the common soldiers and the higher officers human and companionable, even the English who were actually in the fight against us'. He paid tribute to the 'magnificent gallantry and fearless, calm determination of the men who fought with me . . . Even I knew no fear nor panic and shrink from no risk even as I shrink not now from the death which faces me at daybreak. I hope to see God's face even for a moment in the morning.'

He was allowed a visit from his sister, his wife and his brothers Michael and Dick late on Sunday night. 'He received us and shook hands quite calmly,' wrote Michael, 'and after a word or two, put his arm around Áine, bent down with a sweet smile and kissed her lovingly. They were lovers again.' After the two had had ten minutes alone talking in the corner, the group met together and sent for Father Augustine. After he had had communion again, he wrote Áine a love letter, promising her she would be 'the wife of one of the leaders of the Revolution' who should accept 'the little attentions which in due time will be showered upon you'.

His last hour was spent praying with the priest and invoking Irish saints; Augustine lent him his crucifix and he held it while he was being executed. Augustine would tell that story in a speech in America three years later, referring to 'the poor, sweet, gentle soul, the dying saint'. Ceannt deserved better.

He was shot on 8 May and Thomas Kent the following day, also the day of Mac Diarmada's and Connolly's trials. By now, there was enormous pressure on Maxwell to halt the executions, but he was determined not let the remaining two of the Seven, Mac Diarmada and Connolly, survive. By now, Mac Diarmada was in no doubt that, as signatories, he and Connolly would be shot. The day before his trial, he insisted on having a concert, and he gave a recitation of 'Brian Boy Magee', a favourite of his about the brutal 1641 rebellion. Apparently, the last verse would upset him so much he used to tear open his shirt collar.

> I am Brian Boy Magee!
> And my creed is a creed of hate;
> Love, Peace, I have cast aside –
> But Vengeance, *Vengeance* I wait!
> Till I pay back the four-fold debt
> For the horrors I witnessed there,
> When my brothers moaned in their blood,
> And my mother swung by her hair.

On the morning of the trial, he borrowed a razor from a guard, and said to his comrades with a smile: 'I have to make a nice corpse, you know.'

There were problems with the Mac Diarmada case, for he had no rank in the Volunteers, was disabled, in civilian clothing and unarmed, but there were several witnesses who knew him well, and, though Mac Diarmada cross-examined some of them, he was inevitably found guilty. Because of howls of outrage from the Irish party about the flawed legal proceedings, there was more of an effort to make the proceedings resemble a proper trial. Afterwards, he was sitting with some other captives on the lawn when MacNeill arrived under military escort: he tried to shake hands with Mac Diarmada and was rebuffed. The Proclamation was the clincher for Maxwell, even if he hadn't had access to mobilisation orders found in Mac Diarmada's house.

Connolly, who was tried in the Dublin Castle hospital propped up in bed, made no defence except against an unfounded allegation that there had been wanton cruelty to prisoners. He did, however, read into proceedings a document justifying what he had achieved in proving that Irishmen were ready to die trying to win for Ireland their national rights, which later he managed to pass covertly to Nora.

Maxwell confirmed both death sentences, but there was a delay while Asquith considered them. In the House of Commons he said that he hoped and believed there would be no more executions beyond the two persons already sentenced who had 'signed the Proclamation'. 'If it was justifiable, as we think it was, in the case of the five other persons who signed the Proclamation, it would be extremely difficult, on any ground of justice or of fairness, to discriminate between them and these two others simply for the reason that they happen to have been tried a little later in point of date.' Their executions were fixed for the twelfth.

Mac Diarmada used his time to write two letters, one to John Daly and the other to his siblings. He told Daly that he was to have a soldier's death and would be 'joining Tom and the others in a better world . . . We die that the Irish nation may live. Our blood will rebaptise and reinvigorate the old land . . . Let present-day place-hunters condemn our action as they will, posterity will judge us aright from the effects of our action.' Among the messages he sent was one asking to be remembered 'specially to Mrs. Clarke and tell her I am the same Seán she always knew'.

The message to his brothers and sisters was much the same, though the organiser's mind was evident in the chat about practicalities and the future careers of nieces and nephews and many protestations about how happy and proud he was and how even now he could 'enjoy a laugh a d a joke as good as ever'. He reported having had a priest with him almost constantly, including his dear old friend Father Patrick Browne, Professor of Mathematics in Maynooth. He would be seeing 'Miss Ryan, she who in all probability, had I lived, would have been my wife.'

Mac Diarmada had become so secretive that he not only kept things sometimes from Clarke but had not told Min Ryan how he felt about her. In response to his request, she was brought to see him late on the night of 11 May, along with his accountant and his landlady. In a three-hour visit, he made his will, and tried to make keepsakes for various female friends by scratching his name and the date on his few coins and on the buttons he cut from his clothes. It was clear he very much wanted to be left alone with Min, and she with him, but the other two failed utterly to get the hint. When the chaplain arrived at 3:00 a.m. they all stood up promptly and left together, allowing the two of them just time for him to kiss her and say: 'We never thought that it would end like this, that this would be the end.' Although, of course, they had. He had been carefully rationing his cigarettes, so had two left to see him through till his execution at 3:45. He gave the chaplain a message for his 'fellow-countrymen', which said he was going to his death 'for my love of country and hatred of her slavery . . . as fearlessly as I have worked for that sacred cause during all my short life'.

Lillie had been allowed to visit Connolly at the Castle on Monday and she and Nora saw him again in the early morning of the twelfth. They were warned to discuss only personal matters. 'Papa was mainly concerned with leaving us; what would happen to a family of mainly girls and Mother. He was thinking of the old days and all the misery we had been through and that it would be no life for us at all. So he was advising us to go to the States.' He asked Nora to arrange for Francis Sheehy-Skeffington to arrange publication of some of his songs and give the proceeds to Lillie. Nora blurted out 'Skeffington* is gone,' and

---

* In one of the most appalling events of Easter Week, Skeffington, who was trying to stop the looting by organising a civilian defence force, was murdered by firing squad in Portobello Barracks with two other civilians on the orders of Captain John Bowen-Colthurst. His superiors covered it up, but Sir Francis Vane (who had fought against Ceannt) took the case to Kitchener and the

then could tell him no more. She told him that Roddy – whom Connolly had sent away from the GPO on the third day – had been in prison. '"How long?" "Eight days," I said. "He fought for his country, and has been in prison for his country," said Papa, "and he's not sixteen. He has had a great start in life, hasn't he, Nora?"' Nora asked if he might avoid execution because of his wound, but he said no. 'Mama was very upset . . . but Papa was very calm and cool.'

That afternoon, Father Aloysius gave him communion, heard his confession and gave him last rites. Lillie was still upset when in the middle of the night they were taken to see him again.

> 'Well, Lillie, I suppose you know what this means?' he said. She said: 'Oh, no, Jim. Oh no!' and he said: 'Yes, lovie,' and then Mama broke down sobbing, with her head on the bed. Papa said: 'I fell asleep for the first time tonight and they wakened me up at eleven and told me I was to die at dawn.' Mama said: 'Oh, no!' again, and then crying bitterly, 'But your beautiful life, Jim, your beautiful life!' and he said: 'Wasn't it a full life, Lillie, and isn't this a good end?' And she still cried and he said: 'Look, Lillie, please don't cry. You will unman me.'

The women tried to control themselves. He said to Lillie: 'The Socialists will never understand why I am here. They will all forget I am an Irishman.' He also asked her to become a Catholic. Then they were told that the time was up and the nurse had to come and take Lillie away.

Injected with morphine, he was taken to Kilmainham by ambulance in his pyjamas, taken by stretcher to the exercise yard and placed in a chair. The surgeon who attended him claimed that before the execution he asked Connolly if he would pray for him and for those about to shoot him and that Connolly replied: 'Yes, Sir. I'll pray for all brave men who do their duty according to their lights.'

Prime Minister's Principal Private Secretary. A closed military court martial found Bowen-Colthurst guilty of three murders but declared him unsound of mind.

Fearing that 'Irish sentimentality will turn those graves into martyrs' shrines to which annual processions etc. will be made,'[42] General Maxwell decreed that the bodies of the executed should not be returned to their families. All were taken to Arbour Hill military cemetery, buried in the exercise yard in unmarked graves and the bodies covered in quicklime before the graves were filled in.

Chapter Ten[1]

LEGACIES

In the commonly accepted view of Irish history the Irishman of today is asked to disown his own past. He is expected to censure as unpatriotic the common Irishmen who were not attracted by the new revolutionary ideas, but who adhered to an ancient tradition. Irishmen of today are invited at least implicitly to apologise for their fellow-countrymen who accepted loyally the serious guidance of the Church to which they belonged. Irishmen of today must despise as unmanly those of their own country who preferred to solve problems, if possible, by peaceful rather than by violent means.

Father Francis Shaw, SJ*

In 1910, in *Labour in Irish History*, Connolly tried to persuade nationalists that Irish independence would do little or no good for most Irish people unless it brought about profound changes in society, including the destruction of capitalism. The book looked at the failed revolutions from the time of the United Irishmen that were regularly being eulogised in the songs, speeches and commemorations of one kind or another that had been popularised by the IRB and had obtained a grip on the Irish nationalist imagination.

'The Irish are not philosophers as a rule,' he wrote; 'they proceed too rapidly from thought to action.'

In November 1915, in his *Workers' Republic*, it was clear that Connolly could not wait to replace thought with action. Marking the

---

* Father Shaw intended his essay 'The Canon of Irish History – A Challenge' to appear in the Jesuit journal *Studies* in 1966 as a counterpoint to the celebrations of the fiftieth anniversary of 1916. It was 1974 before the editorial board had the nerve to publish it.

forty-eighth anniversary of the execution of the Manchester Martyrs, he wrote:

> This week our Anniversary is not of thinkers, but of doers, of men who when a duty was to be done did not stop to think, but acted, and by their action violated every rule of prudence, sanity, and caution, and in violating them all obeyed the highest dictates of wisdom and achieved immortality.

As Maureen Wall pointed out in the 1960s, looking at the effect on public opinion of the execution of those three men there was 'no reason to be surprised at the effect produced by the executions in 1916', and she quoted the prophetic words of James Connolly's account of the incident.[2] Aching to take his tiny army onto the streets of Dublin, Connolly thundered:

> We honour them because of their heroic souls. Let us remember that by every test by which parties in Ireland today measure political wisdom, or personal prudence, the act of these men ought to be condemned. They were in a hostile city, surrounded by a hostile population; they were playing into the hands of the government by bringing all the Fenians out in broad daylight to be spotted and remembered; they were discouraging the Irish people by giving them another failure to record; they had no hopes of foreign help even if their brothers in Ireland took the field spurred by their action; at the most their action would only be an Irish riot in an English city; and finally, they were imperilling the whole organisation for the sake of two men. These were the sound sensible arguments of the prudent, practical politicians and theoretic revolutionists. But 'how beggarly appear words before a defiant deed!'[3]

He had bought fully into Fenianism. The Proclamation he signed tipped its cap to him by mentioning the ICA and making a glancing reference to 'the right of the people of Ireland to the ownership of

Ireland', but otherwise it was straight from the Fenian hymnbook with its genuflection to 'the dead generations from which she receives her old tradition of nationhood' and the six occasions during the previous three hundred years that they had 'asserted it in arms'.

Did the Seven ever have a conversation as a group about the kind of Ireland they wanted if they won? Not long before Easter, Ceannt told Áine they had allocated posts they would hold 'when the fight was over', that either Pearse or MacDonagh had been chosen for Education and that he would be Minister for War, but there was no suggestion that fundamentals were addressed. They might all agree about the need for de-anglicisation, but Joe Plunkett would have had no sympathy with Tom Clarke's Anglophobia. Clarke and Seán Mac Diarmada might have much in common with Connolly's contempt for parliamentary democracy, but how could their tunnel-visioned insular nationalism have lived with his internationalism? How could the Marxism Connolly wanted his men to fight for be reconciled with the German monarchy favoured by Plunkett and Pearse? And how would that have worked with Clarke's republicanism? Could MacDonagh's and Plunkett's intellectual cosmopolitanism have sat easily with Éamonn Ceannt's rigid Irish-Irelandism? Or Clarke's and Connolly's rejection of religion with Ceannt's devotionalism? And could any of them have taken at all seriously the prelapsarian innocence of Pearse's fantasy of a Celtic Utopia? In 1916 he wrote:

> In a free Ireland there will be work for all the men and women of the nation. Gracious and useful rural industries will supplement an improved agriculture. The population will expand in a century to twenty millions; it may even in time go up to thirty millions. Towns will be spacious and beautiful . . . but, since the country will chiefly rely on its wealth and agriculture and rural industry, there will be no Glasgows or Pittsburghs.
>
> Literature and art will flourish. The Tain and the Fionn-story will come again in mighty dramas. The voice of a people that has been dumb for many centuries will be heard anew; and it will make such music as has not been heard since Greece spoke the morning song of the free people.[4]

What many of them had in common were early problems of identity, loss or displacement. Tom Clarke was born out of wedlock to a Catholic mother; his father was a Protestant and a soldier in the British army; as a child he took sides in the turbulent politics of South Africa; at eight was moved to a hotbed of Ulster sectarianism; at twenty-one he fled to the embrace of Irish-American Fenianism.

Seán Mac Diarmada's mother was ill for years and died when he was only nine; he spent several teenage years failing to pass the exams to qualify as a teacher; he had menial jobs in Edinburgh and Belfast and then was rapidly converted from being a faithful and pious member of the AOH to radical republicanism.

Éamonn Ceannt's mother died suddenly when he was thirteen and though his father was an RIC sergeant he was sent to an intensely nationalistic school. Thomas MacDonagh's mother was half-English and an enthusiastic convert from Unitarianism and he had a profound crisis of faith in his early twenties. Joe Plunkett had appalling health, a crazy mother and a consistently disrupted childhood. From the time Connolly went to Ireland in 1896 he felt obliged to conceal his Scottish birth, his seven years in the British Army and his atheism.

And then there was Pearse, whose father was an Englishman, a Freethinker and a rationalist who for business reasons had pretended to convert to Catholicism, while his mother was an emotional, unthinking, Catholic Irish nationalist who so over-mothered her four children that three of them never left home, none of them had a normal sexual relationship, and Pearse was a tormented, repressed paedophile.

Clarke, Mac Diarmada and Connolly wouldn't have cared, but Ceannt, MacDonagh, Pearse and Plunkett were as well aware as Eoin MacNeill that what they were precipitating did not meet their church's criteria for a just war, which of course is why Count Plunkett had lied so resoundingly to the Pope about the reasons for revolution and the prospects of success. Whatever their current religious beliefs, they were all of Catholic birth and transferred their initial religious conviction to their ultimate nationalism. But they were consumed with the belief in their own rightness that was one of the hallmarks of the Irish physical force nationalism that had been popularly lauded during many decades of IRB propaganda.

It was such thinking that would cause tiny groups to keep violence going for another century, in what were known as the war of independence, the civil war, the border campaign, the Troubles and nowadays the sporadic dissident attacks. What they, their supporters and what are known in Ireland as their 'sneaking regarders' saw and used as justification were the actions of the Seven, men who began a revolution for which there was little popular support, and went on – as they had predicted – to be retrospectively legitimised and elevated to the status of founding fathers of the new state.

Few people had known about the tobacconist, the political organiser, the head-teacher, the clerk, the academic, the dying polymath and the trade union leader, but within a very short time they had become nationalist icons. There was plenty of material with which clever nationalist propagandists would mould public opinion over the next few years. A distinguished practitioner was J.J. O'Kelly, a bitter member of the bitter Keating branch of the Gaelic League who had been a vicious critic of Pearse in his *Claidheamh* days, but as editor of the *Catholic Bulletin*, which had a large circulation and a very substantial readership, relentlessly promoted the Rising and its 'martyrs'. (The *Bulletin*'s brand of Catholicism can be gauged from the title of an article by an Irish priest that found space in the middle of all the hagiography: 'Ritual Murder among the Jews'.) Censorship, explained O'Kelly, required him to overlook 'the political and controversial features of the upheaval', so he would confine himself to 'Catholic and social aspects of the lives and last moments of those who died either in action or as a result of trial by court-martial'. He was helped by the Capuchin priests, who anonymously fed him pious recollections.

Patrick Pearse was the *Bulletin*'s first subject, his published words described as

> permeated, for the most part, with the Catholic idealism of Gaelic Ireland and that trust in God and His Virgin Mother which is characteristic of the Irish-speaking peasantry. His exquisite letter from his prison cell to his aged mother has already found its way round the world. The lines he wrote in his last moments, at her request, as if addressed by mother to son, may appropriately close this brief notice.

There was plenty about Éamonn Ceannt and Pope Pius X: 'On the day of surrender, I saw him lead his men to the place where they laid down their arms,' said an eye-witness. 'His bearing was noble, magnificent. I felt proud of him in my heart, and the soldiers looked on in wonder. Some day I hope to tell much that is inspiring of his last moments and his glorious death, with my own crucifix in his grasp.'

Thomas MacDonagh, in a 'most touching letter' to his wife, had 'expressed his confidence that his country would take his children in its hands: "I devoted myself too much to national work and too little to money-making to leave them a competence".' He 'died as he had lived, with no rancour in his heart, with his courage high and unshaken, and with a firm faith in the Saviour by whose Precious Blood we are redeemed'.

Joe Plunkett's marriage was featured: his wife's 'tragic lot recalls Sarah Curran ... and other heroines of '48 and '67'. He had died happily for God and Ireland. 'His gentle but dauntless mother suffered all the hardships and indignities of the Dublin prison for weeks after the Rising, and shares reluctant exile from Erin, since their mutual release, with her distinguished husband, perhaps the best honoured Catholic layman in Europe.'

Socialism was anathema to the Irish Catholic Church, but while James Connolly's entry mentioned that he had founded the Irish Socialist Republic Party, it explained that he was basing 'his propaganda largely on the teachings of Fintan Lalor and the Irish clan system'. Attributing many talents to him, including 'undoubted military genius', the story of his words to the surgeon before being shot was retailed with a quote from 'a distinguished Capuchin Father, on the occasion of his Requiem Mass, "that those who differed from him in life will remember his dying words and recognise that he was actuated by the most Christian and Catholic spirit of forgiveness even at the very last".'

Tom Clarke 'had interested himself actively in nationalist journals and in kindred propagandist work' and had been considerate to prisoners. They got round the embarrassing problem of his refusal of sacraments with 'He was attended before his execution by Fr. Tom O'Ryan of Inchicore.'

Seán Mac Diarmada, 'most lovable, perhaps, of all that earnest band', had his health 'shattered' by his 'unselfish work for Irish-Ireland' but in his last letter had expressed his happiness: 'Before God, let me again assure you how proud and happy I feel . . . Arrange for Fr. Foy and Fr. MacLoughlin to offer Masses for me.'

The result of all this was to make the Rising seem even more exclusively Catholic than it had been, which of course was exacerbated by the expulsion from public life of Bulmer Hobson. A lengthy article on Casement after his execution adjudged that although he had been Protestant all his life, in Pentonville he had come to realise that 'there was no choice for him, as he put it, "between the Catholic Church and religious anarchy, between the infallibility of the Pope and religious chaos"'. He had gone to Heaven 'with all the faith and piety of an Irish Catholic as if he had been brought up to it from his youth'. (The following year, Constance Markievicz would enthusiastically climb aboard the Catholic bandwagon, although she never came to grips with its theology.)

Small wonder that when Joyce Kilmer, who would die in France in 1918 as an American soldier, wrote 'Easter Week' in memory of Joe Plunkett his last verse was:

> Romantic Ireland is not old.
> For years untold her youth shall shine.
> Her heart is fed on Heavenly bread,
> The blood of martyrs is her wine.

With material like this circulating at home and abroad, the reputations of the Seven in nationalist Ireland were soaring. Better poets than Kilmer had contributed their share to the business of ensuring their immortality in lines that still resonate. Even if they thought the insurrection wrong or foolish, the heroism and the theatricality of it moved them deeply. Yeats sought to explain events that sorely confused and distressed him. His 'Easter 1916', speaking of those he knew, ended with

> We know their dream; enough
> To know they dreamed and are dead;
> And what if excess of love
> Bewildered them till they died?

MacDonagh and MacBride
And Connolly and Pearse
Now and in time to be,
Wherever green is worn,
Are changed, changed utterly:
A terrible beauty is born.

AE wrote of those he knew:

Their dream had left me numb and cold,
  But yet my spirit rose in pride,
Refashioning in burnished gold
  The images of those who died,
Or were shut in the penal cell.
  Here's to you, Pearse, your dream not mine,
But yet the thought, for this you fell,
  Has turned life's water into wine.

I listened to high talk from you.
  Thomas McDonagh, and it seemed
The words were idle, but they grew
  To nobleness by death redeemed.
Life cannot utter words more great
  That life may meet by sacrifice,
High words were equalled by high fate,
  You paid the price. You paid the price.

The hope lives on age after age,
  Earth with its beauty might be won
For labour as a heritage,
  For this has Ireland lost a son.
This hope unto a flame to fan
  Men have put life by with a smile,
Here's to you, Connolly, my man,
  Who cast the last torch on the pile.

And while the poets mostly confined their elegies to dead poets, one of them, Seamus O'Sullivan, provided 'A Lament for Seán MacDermott', which began:

> They have slain you, Seán MacDermott; never more these
> eyes will greet
> The eyes beloved by women, and the smile that true men
> loved;
> Never more I'll hear the stick-tap, and the gay and limping
> feet,
> They have slain you, Seán the Gentle, Seán the valiant,
> Seán the proved.

There were no distinguished ballads, the most notable being 'Erin go Bragh' [Ireland forever] by Peadar Kearney (composer in 1907 of 'A Soldier's Song', which in the 1920s was translated into Irish as 'Amhrán na bhFiann' and became the national anthem). Kearney name-checked those he knew best: 'Now here's to brave Pearse and his comrades who died/ Tom Clarke, MacDonagh, MacDermott, MacBride, / And here's to Jim Connolly who gave one last hurrah, / And placed the machine guns for Erin Go Bragh.'

Kearney had served under MacDonagh in Jacob's Factory and paid tribute to the warriors in the South Dublin Union. 'Old Ceannt and his comrades like lions at bay, / From the South Dublin Union poured death and dismay, / And what was their horror when the Englishmen saw / All the dead khaki soldiers in Erin Go Bragh.'

But Ceannt, like Clarke, never seized the public imagination. These two self-effacing men would be the least well known of the Seven: Éamonn Ceannt, the only successful soldier among them, and Tom Clarke, without whom the insurrection would not have happened. Their redoubtable wives, however, did not stay in obscurity.

Kathleen Clarke was devastated by the deaths of her husband and brother, a subsequent raid on her house and the ransacking and looting of the shop, and the building's permanent repossession by the landlady. She went most weekends to Limerick to see her children, but otherwise there was little comfort there, for her mother was focused on mourning her only son, Ned Daly, who as a commandant had taken the Four Courts and was shot on 4 May. Uncle John was devastated by the loss of his nephew and two of his closest friends. He died at the end of June.

Within days Kathleen had established the Volunteer Dependants' Fund, was distributing assistance from the £3,100 Clarke had given her, and liaising with John Devoy, to whom she passed on the confidences meant for him. Her house became the first port of call for women looking for their menfolk or for aid. When the money ran out she became involved in fundraising, and helped amalgamate her fund with one supported by the IPP, creating the National Aid and Volunteer Dependants' Fund. (When Michael Collins came out of jail, she supported his appointment as Secretary, a job that gave him the opportunity to move freely around the country in his capacity as an operator in Sinn Féin, a party that had nothing to do with the Rising but was blamed for it and subsequently tried to claim the credit.)

Kathleen miscarried a few weeks after the Rising and almost died, but returned to active life not long afterwards. As a vice-president of Cumann na mBan and a member of Sinn Féin's executive, she was co-presenter of a successful motion during Sinn Féin's 1917 convention ensuring that equal rights for women became party policy. Arrested in May 1918 on an unconvincing charge of conspiracy with Germany, she was in Holloway prison with Maud Gonne MacBride* and Constance Markievicz, both of whom she thought thundering snobs, and while there followed in her uncle's and husband's footsteps by being granted the freedom of Limerick City.

Released in February 1919 on the grounds of ill-health, she became a member of Dublin corporation and campaigned for the official recognition of the Sinn Féin government that was set up in opposition to Westminster and created Dáil Éireann. She sat on various committees and was appointed to Sinn Féin courts. She was also a founder member of the Irish White Cross (1920), which distributed American aid, and was elected to the Dáil in 1921. Despite her relationship with the pro-Treaty Michael Collins, like all the 1916 relatives she vehemently opposed this.

* After her estranged husband's execution, she wore widow's weeds and went back to calling herself Maud Gonne MacBride. By his death, she said, he had left a name for their son to be proud of: 'Those who die for Ireland are sacred.'

In her public life, Clarke for a time supported de Valera and his Fianna Fail party, but she lost trust in him during her eight years as a senator and clashed with his government over what she saw as its betrayal on the women's rights promised in the 1916 proclamation. Close relatives of signatories of the Proclamation were given privileges, obeisance and state funerals, but on the whole conservative, bourgeois, Catholic post-independence Ireland was a cold place for women, who rapidly found themselves back in the metaphorical kitchen, as it was for many of the vibrant revolutionary generation who had been working for a high-minded, pluralist Utopia. As Bulmer Hobson put it in a private letter to Denis McCullough in 1956, 'the phoenix of our youth has fluttered to earth such a miserable old hen I have no heart for it'.[5]

Not that Kathleen Clarke ever gave in. In 1939–1941 she became the first woman lord mayor of Dublin, promptly removed all British symbols from the office and had the portraits of British monarchs taken down from the Mansion House. She flew flags at half-mast on the Mansion House and City Hall when an IRA man was executed for shooting a policeman, broke with Fianna Fail in 1941, lost her seat on the corporation, stood unsuccessfully for the militantly republican Clann na Poblachta and thereafter devoted herself to humanitarian work, the Wolfe Tone Memorial Fund and the National Graves Association. She never felt Tom Clarke got the recognition he deserved and said 'Pearse had no more right to sign himself President than I had . . . and . . . was very ambitious and vain as a peacock.'

The Clarke children were largely raised in Limerick by their aunts and grandmother and went to school locally. Whether in Dublin or Limerick, their childhood was disrupted by raids by the British Army and later that of the Free State. Daly Clarke, whose wife's father had been in the RIC, worked with the Irish Hospitals Sweepstakes and died childless in 1971, the year before Kathleen. Tom managed Daly's Bakery for many years, fell out with his mother when he stood unsuccessfully for Fianna Fail in the 1940s, also had a childless marriage and was left out of his mother's will. Emmet became a psychiatrist and emigrated to England and had two sons, Tom and Emmet. His mother lived with him in Liverpool from 1965 and had a state funeral in Dublin.

On the day after Éamonn Ceannt's execution, his brother Michael accompanied Áine and Ronan to the office of City Treasurer to collect a cheque for four pounds and fourteen shillings for outstanding pay. The Scottish Amicable Life Assurance Society refused to pay up and the union, for which he had done so much, declined to establish a general fund for the relief of dependents, though at the December AGM some help was given her. Ceannt's last letter to her had been as protective as ever of his 'little child, my dearest pet, my sweetheart of the hawthorn hedges', but though Áine had little experience of work she proved to be formidably effective. Like her husband, she was an ideal committee member and was a leading light in aid work, Cumann na mBan and Sinn Féin. Appointed to Sinn Féin courts, including to the labour court, she investigated industrial disputes. Travel was difficult and dangerous in these years and, lacking legal training, she often found the work daunting. When the Irish White Cross was established in 1920 to assist the civilian population during the war of independence, she was appointed to its general council, and in 1922 she became its secretary. It would be dissolved in 1928, but from the formation of the Irish Red Cross in 1939 she would be active there too. For a quarter of a century, she worked indefatigably for orphans, widows and the needy in general.

A committed republican, during the war of independence her house was raided eleven times by troops and police, with serious damage on at least three occasions. She took the anti-treaty side in the civil war but from December 1922 to April 1923 was a member of a Sinn Féin peace committee that attempted to bring the conflict to an end. Her home was also regularly raided by Free State troops, and so frequent and severe were the raids in the early months of 1923 that it was left largely uninhabitable. She abandoned politics, but maintained her interest in the Gaelic League, serving on its Coiste Gnótha until in 1925 she accepted the post of honorary treasurer; she served on its executive committee, participated in the management of its junior branch, and, as a government nominee, was a member of its central council.

Ronan became a solicitor and obeyed his father's wish that he look after his mother by living (unmarried) with Áine (and Lily) until she died in 1954 – sometimes wondering, as he wrote to Máire Nic

Shiubhlaigh, if Áine was disappointed in him 'for not having shown myself as fine a man as my father was . . . It might have seemed to her that my lack of forcefulness etc., as compared with my father's courage was a bit of a "let-down".'

It was Mrs Pearse and Margaret, though, who had in Patrick the most famous and recognisable brand among the signatories. Broken-hearted but proud, they struggled desperately with his chaotic finances, and with a lot of help from friends settled with creditors and kept St Enda's going, with Thomas MacDonagh's brother Joseph as headmaster until he was arrested in 1917; as a TD* he opposed the Treaty. In America, with the help of what she called her 'Pat and Willie' speech, Mrs Pearse raised much more money than her son had, but both women fought with the fundraising committee. Pearse's inspirational style was replaced by endless teaching of cate-chism, and, always operating at a loss, St Enda's declined steadily until it died in 1935.

Mrs Pearse reacted furiously if anyone questioned the pre-eminence of her sons and denounced John Devoy for daring to claim that Clarke was the most important of the 1916 men. She threw herself into poli-tics, which she did not understand: elected to the Dáil in 1921, she opposed the Treaty on the grounds that 'Pat and Willie' would have, and lost her seat in 1922; her home was also raided during the civil war. Eamon de Valera found her a valuable figurehead, manipulated her skilfully, put her on the executive of Fianna Fail when it was founded in 1926, and, as Taoiseach, organised for her in 1932 an enor-mous state funeral, where he made a graveside oration.

Her daughter Margaret inherited the Pearsean mantle, was elected to the Dáil in 1933, lost in 1937, but was appointed to the Senate in 1938, where she remained until her death in 1968. She and her sister had financial arguments about royalties on Mary Brigid's use of Patrick's fragment of autobiography in her mawkish *The Home Life of Patrick Pearse*, which in the interests of respectability omitted what Patrick had written about his more humble origins.

Utterly devastated by her husband's execution, estranged from

---

* Teachta Dála, a member of Dáil Éireann, the lower house of the Irish Parliament.

her parents because of the manner of his death, and with two small children, Muriel MacDonagh struggled with depression. As MacDonagh had requested, she converted to Catholicism. She lived for a time with the Plunketts at Larkfield, with MacDonagh relatives in Tipperary and then in a Plunkett property in Marlborough Road, where she was supported by the Irish Volunteers Dependents' Fund, of which she was an officer and committee member. Her financial pressures were lessened by the income from Thomas's collected poems and *Literature in Ireland*. In 1917, swimming alone in the sea while on holiday with other 1916 widows, she drowned. There was a vast crowd at her IRB-organised funeral, but her son could not attend because of ill health. He and his sister would be caught in childhood in rows over their upbringing between the Protestant Giffords and the Catholic MacDonaghs. MacDonagh's brother John, a singer and the actor-manager of the Irish Theatre, had been in Jacob's with Thomas during the Rising, after which he was imprisoned in England.

The grief of MacDonagh's many friends at his death was exacerbated by a feeling that he had not wanted to die. 'I do not think he had any other ambition than to write good verse and to love his friends,' wrote James Stephens. 'I think that when he faced the guns which ended life and poetry and all else for him, he said in his half humorous, half tragic way, "Ah me!" and left the whole business at that. Poor MacDonagh! There went a good man down when you went down.'

'Oh Grace', wrote an anonymous balladeer writing in the persona of Joe Plunkett, 'Just hold me in your arms and let this moment linger / They'll take me out at dawn and I will die / With all my love I place this wedding ring upon your finger / There won't be time to share our love for we must say goodbye.'

The coy implication that their relationship was unconsummated is challenged by Gerry's testimony that she had uncontrovertible evidence that Grace had a miscarriage shortly after Easter while staying at Larkfield. As a member of the Sinn Féin executive with little understanding of politics, she designed banners and posters. She opposed the Treaty, was imprisoned for a while, and then mostly gave up politics. Always in financial difficulties, she was given a pension by the Fianna Fáil government in 1932, and a couple of years later took a lawsuit against the Plunkett family for her husband's share in an uncle's estate; they settled out of court. She died in 1955, in Gerry's words, 'a loner and often very difficult' to the end.

Count Plunkett lost his job and with Ma was imprisoned after the Rising and deported to Oxford for nine months. He won a parliamentary seat for Sinn Féin in 1917, opposed the Treaty and later the foundation of Fianna Fail, considering the Dáil illegitimate. Jack fought in the civil war and continued to help the IRA with his engineering and wireless skills; in 1939, interned in the Curragh, he went on hunger strike for forty days. George, who had commanded the Kimmage Garrison, also fought in the war of independence and the civil war, stayed in the IRA and was on its Army Council when it launched the 1939 British bombing campaign, after which he was arrested and interned. There was a scene after his funeral in 1944, when Ma screamed at one of Gerry's daughters to get out of the house with her mother and never to return. As they left, Gerry said to her daughter, 'She'll be dead of bad temper in a month.' She died six weeks later.

James Connolly's instruction to his wife to become a Catholic was probably intended to protect her. She obeyed his wishes but was unable to take the family to America as he and she had wished as she was denied a visa. Roddy Connolly became President of the first Communist Party of Ireland in October 1921, opposed the Treaty and fought in the civil war. He joined the Labour Party and was a TD for a few years, had a period in the Senate and mellowed into being a supporter of a Labour Party coalition with Fine Gael in the 1970s. Nora Connolly O'Brien had three terms as a Senator from 1957. All her life she would stay a hardline Irish republican and a Trotskyite.

Seán Mac Diarmada's relatives were not prominent in politics, but they were as implacably opposed as all the other 1916 relatives to the Treaty. The message emanating from the latest dead generation was not one of compromise. In Irish-America, there was a split. John Devoy accepted the Treaty, was a welcome guest of the Free State government and was given a state funeral in 1929. Joe McGarrity refused to recognise any Irish government, supported the IRA bombing campaign in England in 1939 and died the following year after assisting its Chief of Staff, Seán Russell, in his attempts to secure support from Nazi Germany.

*   *   *

The rebellion, insurgency, Rising, would achieve a measure of international fame especially among Anglophobes, and would be lauded by many abroad. Patrick Pearse would be the poster-boy for Catholic nationalists: James Connolly for communists and socialists. To this day Connolly societies flourish in Britain. But looking back across the century, the 1916 revolution was really a violent attack on constitutionalism. In a democracy, a seven-man secret clique (the Military Council) within a secret clique (the IRB) within a clique (the 10,000 Irish Volunteers) determined to ignore the electorate's endorsement of the IPP and of Home Rule and instead to start a war for their conception of Irish freedom. Many of their followers did not even know they were going into danger.

There were fewer than 1,800 involved at any one time in Dublin and a handful outside. Around 200,000 uniformed Irishmen served the state in the army during the Great War. Yet the tiny group had decided to ally themselves with their enemies.

In October 1915 the nurse Edith Cavell was shot by a German firing squad. The night before she was killed, she said: 'Patriotism is not enough. I must have no hatred or bitterness towards anyone.' Her execution happened at a time when the IRB and Clan na Gael were secretly begging Germany to send an invasion force as well as arms. Cavell's death did not seem to bother the Irish or Irish-American conspirators, even though there was a big international outcry. The German Under-Secretary for Foreign Affairs issued a statement saying it was a pity Miss Cavell had to be executed, but it was necessary. 'She was judged justly . . . It is undoubtedly a terrible thing the woman has been executed; but consider what would happen to a State, particularly in war, if it left crimes aimed at the safety of its armies to go unpunished because committed by women.' Cavell had helped allied prisoners escape from occupied Belgium. Constance Markievicz, who been involved in a revolution that left hundreds dead and Dublin in ruins, was granted a recommendation for mercy 'solely and only on account of her sex'.

Pearse didn't think of killing for Ireland, but of dying for it. But the reality was different. The immediate casualties were 450 dead and 2,600 injured, of whom 116 were soldiers, 16 policemen and 242 civilians (of whom 28 children were from the slums). During that same week, more than 500 Irishmen were killed by a German gas attack on Irish lines. Only 76 rebels died, of whom 15 were executed between 3 and 12 May, but, along with Roger Casement, who was hanged in August, they would become the only deaths that mattered in the national narrative of martyrdom. (Sheehy-Skeffington's death was an exception, as the IRA found it useful ammunition.)

As far as the British military authorities were concerned, they were being exceptionally restrained in their response. But they were, of course, falling into the familiar trap of veering between coercion and conciliation. Had they done what liberal onlookers wanted them to do and executed no one, latent Irish Anglophobia would probably have remained buried. Had they done what the Germans would have done and executed everyone in a position of authority, they could have wiped out the opposition for a long time to come. Yet the first option was impossible in wartime and the second would never have been countenanced by the British parliament. So they shot those they considered ringleaders *pour encourager les autres*, released most of those they had captured within a month and had a general amnesty in 1917 for those sentenced to long prison terms, who came back rested, prepared and ready for rebellion if conscription was imposed.

There was no perception in nationalist Ireland that the authorities had shown restraint. In such a small country, the way in which the executions had been dragged out was, in a famous phrase, 'as though they watched a stream of blood coming from beneath a closed door'.[6] There was intense curiosity about the dead and the telling and retelling of real and imagined poignant detail which stoked up the culture of martyrdom and victimhood, turning nationalist opinion pro-rebel in a very short time. On 11 May, the IPP MP John Dillon made a famous emotional speech about the dead. 'I admit they were wrong; I know they were wrong; but they fought a clean fight, and they fought with superb bravery and skill, and no act of savagery or act against the usual customs of war that I know of has been brought home to any leader or any organised body of insurgents.' He was, he said, 'proud of these men'.

Calling for an absolute stop in the executions, he said, 'You are letting loose a river of blood, and, make no mistake about it, between two races who, after three hundred years of hatred and of strife, we had nearly succeeded in bringing together.' So because Maxwell was not prepared to tolerate the anomaly of letting off Connolly and Mac Diarmada, whom he thought 'the worst of the lot', to the toxic martyr-dom narrative was added the story of the heartless shooting of a hand-some young polio victim and a man who had to be carried on a stretcher to the place of execution.

To the British and to Irish unionists, who saw the revolution as a murderous stab in the back when the United Kingdom was in grave peril, this was hard to swallow. The trouble was that both sides were right. Like it or not, the British government was the legitimate author-ity and helping its enemy was treachery of the highest order. Yet, the rebels were brave, and though the Seven had no conceivable justifica-tion for taking it upon themselves to bring death and destruction on their country, there was no denying their many fine qualities. Culturally, Irish nationalists were romantically conditioned to revere and love young, attractive men who threw away their lives on hopeless causes, whatever the collateral damage, which was in any case always the fault of the British oppressor. The desire to be posthumously famous was regarded as a perfectly good reason to be a revolutionary rather than as dangerous egocentricity and narcissism.

Writing in December 1917, AE was unhappy about what was happening to the Irishmen on the wrong side of history, those who had been fighting in the British army, so he added new verses to 'Salutation', his poem in memory of Pearse, MacDonagh and Connolly, commem-orating three who died fighting in the army, including Tom Kettle, who had died in France in September 1916.

> You who have fought on fields afar,
>   That other Ireland did you wrong
> Who said you shadowed Ireland's star,
>   Nor gave you laurel wreath nor song.
> You proved by death as true as they,
>   In mightier conflicts played your part,
> Equal your sacrifice may weigh,
>   Dear Kettle, of the generous heart.

That was a forlorn hope. The treatment of men coming back from France or of the widows of those who did not make it was despicable. They learned to keep their heads down. Around 30,000 Irish were killed during World War I, but, like the 8,000 or so in World War II, they were ignored by nationalists and republican memorials continued to proliferate all around the country.

The sanctified Seven were the role models and they were very clear in their intransigence. In the statement Connolly had presented at his court-martial, he had said: 'Believing that the British Government has no right in Ireland, never had any right in Ireland, and never can have any right in Ireland, the presence in any one generation of even a respectable minority of Irishmen ready to die to affirm that truth makes that Government for ever a usurpation, and a crime against human progress.'

In the 1918 general election, Sinn Fein won 73 seats out of 105, though less than half the popular vote. While there would have been widespread support had the British persisted in their insane plan to impose conscription, there was little clamour for more violence except from those who had developed a taste for it. Dan Breen was one of those who took the instructions of the dead generations seriously and in January 1919 started a war after a colloquy with a few friends. Recalling why he had launched an ambush on policemen in January 1919, he explained:

> We took the action deliberately, having thought over the matter and talked it over between us. Seán Treacy had stated to me that the only way of starting a war was to kill someone, and we wanted to start a war, so we intended to kill some of the police whom we looked upon as the foremost and most important branch of the enemy forces . . . The only regret that we had following the ambush was that there were only two policemen in it, instead of the six we had expected.

The main targets in this war were Protestants (being presumed to be unionists) and police. Sporadic murders led in 1920 to the arrival of badly trained ex-servicemen – Black and Tans and Auxiliaries – and terror being met with counter-terror, violence and an escalation in brutality. The mostly Catholic police bore the brunt of casualties: there were around 1,400 dead, of whom about 550 were IRA.

It ended with a peace settlement, a treaty that gave twenty-six of the thirty-two counties of Ireland dominion status, while, ironically, giving Home Rule to that part of Ireland that had been prepared to fight to resist it but which now accepted it as a lesser evil. But though it was accepted by a majority of the Dáil and then by a majority of the electorate, its uncompromising opponents – including many relatives of the signatories – instigated another civil war, mainly on the issue of the oath of allegiance, that was even more brutal than that which preceded it. 'The people', said de Valera, 'had no right to do wrong.' The casualties this time were between 1,500 and 2,000. In a successful war against Protestants between 1920 and 1925, 50,000 were driven out of the 26 counties or elected to drift away.

The Seven had known little of Ulster, but had come to realise that any kind of insurrection there would be a catastrophe. Insofar as Ulster had been addressed in the Proclamation, it was in the oblique phrase committing the Irish Republic to 'cherishing all the children of the nation equally', which most people don't realise was a gesture to Ulster Protestants and had nothing to do with rich and poor. Pearse had ordered that no shots should be fired there and the instructions to the Volunteers had been to take the weapons and men to the west of Ireland. The main result of violence from 1916 was to exacerbate tribal hatred on the island and leave it with two confessional and mutually hostile bourgeois states with many tens of thousands of refugees, isolationism, poverty, bigotry and philistinism.

Irish democracy survived because first the Free State and then de Valera's Fianna Fail suppressed the irreconcilables. Whatever the limitations of successive governments, they did succeed in imposing peace and they were brutal in protecting it. The Free State had executed seventy-seven rebels: De Valera dealt with the recalcitrant members of the IRA with internment and the imprisonment of hundreds; three were allowed to die on hunger strike; six were hanged.

Still, the Easter Rising had become sacred, the Proclamation was Holy Writ and popular narrative was that, as the men of 1916 insisted, the Irish Republic was entitled 'to the allegiance of every Irishman and

Irishwoman'. Unionists and constitutionalists, like it or not, you were Irish republicans. To challenge the morality of the Rising or criticise those who fought in it was to be denounced as unpatriotic, to risk social and professional suicide, and to make a political career an almost impossible ambition. The many constitutional achievements of Irish parliamentarians were downgraded contemptuously.

Many of the schools – particularly those of the Christian Brothers – gave children a message that would have gladdened Tom Clarke's heart. Paddy McEvoy, the author of *A Disobedient Irish History*, collated examples of the songs – good, bad, indifferent and ghastly – which expeditiously advanced the nationalist cause and were taught in the schools:

> 'Roddy McCorley' ('For young Roddy McCorley goes to die on the Bridge of Toome today'); 'The Bold Fenian Men' ('Heads erect, eyes to front, stepping proudly together – out and make way for the Bold Fenian Men') . . . 'Kevin Barry' ('. . . gave his young life for the cause of liberty') . . . Robert Emmet ('Bold Robert Emmet, he died with a smile') . . . 'A Nation Once Again ('For freedom comes from God's right hand') . . . 'The Boys of Wexford' ('To free my land I'd gladly give the red drops of my heart'); Boolavogue ('Twas at Slieve Coillte our pikes were reeking with the crimson stream of the beaten foes'); The Wearing of the Green ('For they're hanging men and women for the Wearing of the Green') . . .

'To ask a young person to swim against this propaganda-stream is wrong,' he added, 'and those who were responsible, state and church, should be aware of the harm they did.' In 1966, the fiftieth anniversary, there was a great outpouring of emotion that would scare unionists and embolden republicans. Railway stations were named after signatories and relatives were given honorary degrees, except for the irreconcilable Margaret and Rose MacDermott. The Taoiseach, Seán Lemass, was anxious that there should be no dangerous glorification of violence, but the messages were too nuanced. As Paddy McEvoy puts it 'almost every pub in the country became the equivalent of an open-mike venue where every would-be performer, dreamer, wannabe-patriot and activist stood up and emoted passionately about the troubles and glories of Erin.

By the 1960s and onwards, the great ballad boom had taken off, and a new crop of troubadours had come of age and songs like 'Me Ould Alarm Clock' (about the IRA bombings in England in 1939: 'It ticks away politely, 'til you get an awful shock' – hilarious stuff); 'Seán South of Garryowen' (about the IRA attacks on border police stations in 1966 . . . and with Sten guns and with rifle a hail of death did pour'); 'The Patriot Game' ('I learned all my life cruel England to blame . . . I don't mind a bit if I shoot down police, they're lackeys for war, never guardians of peace'); 'The Boys of Kilmichael' ('The boys of the column, who made a clean sweep of the lot' – there was another more unsubtle version of this line) . . . 'James Connolly' ('God's curse on you England, you cruel-hearted monster').

And then, in 1969, came the fourth civil war, and this time it was even more sectarian. It would last until 1998 and kill over 3,700, 56 per cent of them civilians. Romantic Irish-American enthusiasts for physical force kept up the Fenian tradition by contributing arms and money to help young people ignore the will of the Irish people and once again kill and die for Ireland because they believed themselves commanded to do so by 'the dead generations'. Its major consequence was to make partition even more desirable for the people of the whole island, but since its end there has been a sustained effort by Sinn Féin to substitute a self-serving narrative. The IRA fought in pursuit of a United Ireland but their apologists claim the issue was civil rights. The new narrative is as much as ever involved in political necrophilia and bone-rattling, with much energy being expended on proving that people like Bobby Sands and several of their other assassins should be beside the Seven in the pantheon of Irish heroes. Were they, after all, not heroically dying for their country? Were their intentions not good?

The IRA were beaten to a standstill, the republican leadership opted for a political deal, and the gap between north and south is wider than ever, but there are still irreconcilables at work, focusing on what they see as the unfinished business of a United Ireland. Their position is perfectly logical and absolutely in line with Pearse's words:

> I make the contention that the national demand of Ireland is fixed and determined; that that demand has been made by every generation; that we of this generation receive it as a trust from our fathers; that we have not the right to alter it or to abate it by one jot or tittle; and that any undertaking made in the name of Ireland to accept in full satisfaction of Ireland's claim anything less than the generations of Ireland have stood for is null and void, binding on Ireland neither by the law of God nor by the law of the nations.

Very few politicians have been prepared to speak out for those who believe the Rising to have been a catastrophe that poisoned Irish veins with the toxin of political violence. Conor Cruise O'Brien was a remarkable exception: his political career was destroyed by it. John Bruton, who was Taoiseach from 1994–7, is open about his support for John Redmond and his opposition to the Rising. Most members of Bruton's party, Fine Gael (whose parent party won the civil war and governed from 1923–1932), approve of 1916 and the War of Independence, but think all violence after that lacked legitimacy. Fianna Fail, who opposed the Treaty and whose parent had been on the losing side of the civil war, think all violence after 1923 is illegitimate. Sinn Féin view as true patriots everyone ever involved in republican violence until 1998, when they accepted the 1998 Belfast Good Friday Agreement and the Provisional IRA agreed to go out of business.

Sinn Féin denounce the so-called dissidents (Continuity and Real IRAs and other fringe groups) who regard themselves as the true heirs of the men of 1916. If a century ago it was legitimate in a democracy for a tiny cabal to kill people in the name of Irish freedom, they point out, the Provisionals – who fought for decades for a United Ireland by seeking to destroy Northern Ireland but ended up participating in a British administration in Stormont – have no right to prevent another generation following in their bloody footsteps.

As one dissident spokesman put it apropos the Sinn Féin condemnation of the Real IRA's Omagh bomb in 1998, 'If we were wrong now, then they were wrong for all them years: and if we are right now then they are wrong.' The same, surely, applies to the seven.

By courting death for a cause that had no popular support, were the Seven different from Bobby Sands and his comrades who committed suicide by starvation? Or from the jihadis who these days joyously sacrifice themselves in suicide bombings? They shared a sense of their own absolute moral superiority as well as an ambition to achieve some kind of immortality.

Ireland has had a surfeit of brave young idealists who in their desire to make things better made everything much, much worse. Tom Clarke and his generation of IRB irreconcilables turned the futile political violence of Wolfe Tone, Robert Emmet, the Fenians and the Manchester Martyrs into a cult to inspire more gullible young people to tread the same paths.

At the time of the national celebrations of the fiftieth anniversary of 1916, the Taoiseach, Seán Lemass, tried to send out the message that the young should live rather than die for Ireland. He had been sixteen when he fought in the General Post Office. His older brother, who like him had been on the anti-Treaty side of the Civil War, was abducted, tortured and murdered after it ended. Lemass was trying to form a constructive relationship with Captain Terence O'Neill, the Prime Minister of Northern Ireland, but the republican propaganda emanating from 1966 triumphalism alienated unionists and re-inspired physical force nationalism of increasing brutality. In what were euphemistically called The Troubles, there were innumerable instances of the cowardice, inhumanity and rapine that in the Proclamation the Seven had prayed would not dishonour their cause.

Pillars of Irish society who had encouraged worship of dead patriots would queue up to condemn violence over the next fifty years. Yet as Yeats had shown bleakly in 1939, the influence of the Seven seemed as immutable as ever:

> Some had no thought of victory
> But had gone out to die
> That Ireland's mind be greater,

Her heart mount up on high;
And yet who knows what's yet to come?
For Patrick Pearse had said
That in every generation
Must Ireland's blood be shed.

The Christmas before his death, having finished 'Ghosts', the pamphlet in which he created a mythological unbroken separatist tradition, Patrick Pearse explained blithely: 'There is only one way to appease a ghost. You must do the thing it asks you. The ghosts of a nation sometimes ask very big things; and they must be appeased, whatever the cost.'

The costs to the Irish people have been enormous.

After a century of being haunted, is Irish nationalism finally ready to contemplate exorcism?

ACKNOWLEDGEMENTS

In recent times an immense amount of material on the Seven has become available, including the evidence of witnesses in the Bureau of Military History. It would have taken me years to go through everything, but because of the centenary of 1916, armies of scholars have mined the archives assiduously and have published the key documents as well as writing excellent books based on them. I owe them all a debt of gratitude. I've also benefitted over many decades in my thinking about Irish history from many kind, knowledgeable and inspirational friends. I've also gained from many arguments with people who completely disagreed with me, not all of whom were well disposed. But I'll confine myself here to mentioning those whose help on this book was above and beyond the call of duty or normal friendship.

The name of Owen Dudley Edwards, my brother, who has an exceptionally well-stocked mind and an elephantine memory, leads all the rest. Always incredibly generous with his time and his money, he sent me countless books of his own that were hard to get hold of, photocopied and dispatched to me reams of material, and gave me excellent information, leads and advice. He then read the entire typescript, picked up all sorts of errors and made invaluable observations and suggestions. Owen is a long-time student, admirer, biographer and interpreter of James Connolly, so it was perhaps inevitable that he hated some of what I wrote about him. It is a tribute to our deep mutual affection that our relationship has survived intact.

I'm very grateful also to Liam Kennedy, who read and most helpfully commented on all of my manuscript, as did Máirín Carter. Among the many others with whom I've talked over the theme of the book are Roy Foster, James McGuire and Seán O'Callaghan. I also had much moral support from such good and kind friends as Colm and Alva de Barra, Nina

Clarke, Jo Cohen-Jones, Jane Conway-Gordon, Emily Dyer, Barbara Sweetman FitzGerald, Kathryn Kennison, Jim and Lindy McDowell, John and Mindy Fransen Phelan, Henry and Lorraine Reid, and David Taylor.

As she has done for twenty-five years, my assistant Carol Scott has calmly picked up the pieces and sorted me out at every stage in the proceedings. London Library staff have been as helpful and efficient as ever.

My agent, Peter Robinson, found me Sam Carter of Oneworld, who immediately got the point of what I wanted to do and has been wise in his advice, patient at the difficult times and a pleasure to work with, as have the other members of the firm involved with this book. Special thanks are due to Jon Bentley-Smith, who has undertaken innumerable wearisome tasks uncomplainingly and efficiently, Paul Nash, the "Yes-We-Can" Production Director and Margot Weale, who is the kind of Publicity Director authors dream of. Jill Morris, the copy-editor, has been indefatigable in hunting out and correcting infelicities and errors.

A Note on Photographs

Photos of the young Tom Clarke (1), Éamonn Ceannt (4), Patrick and Willie Pearse (7), Tom MacDonagh (9), MacDonagh and Muriel (10) and the handbill advertising Connolly's farewell dinner (13) were provided courtesy of the National Library of Ireland (references TC 31, NPA POLF 8, R16760, NPA POLF 116, NPA TMD 52, LO P 113).

Photos of Seán Mac Diarmada (2), the proclamation (15), Kilmainham Gaol (18) and Connolly's statue (21) courtesy of Wikimedia Images; photos of Daly, Clarke and Mac Diarmada (3) and 'The Last Stand' (14) courtesy of the Waterford County Museum; photo of Áine and Rónán Ceannt (5) courtesy of Dublin City Library and Archive; photo of Kathleen Clarke and her children (6) courtesy of Helen Litton; the Pearse family portrait (8) courtesy of the Pearse Museum; the Plunkett family portrait (11) courtesy of Ciaran O'Donnell (private collection); Joe Plunkett's passport photo (12) courtesy of Honor O Brolchain; photos of Hobson and McGarrity (16) and Sir Roger Casement and Devoy (17) courtesy of Villanova Digital Library; and the portrait of W. B. Yeats (20) © Pictorial Press/Alamy.

ABBREVIATIONS

AOH	Ancient Order of Hibernians
DMP	Dublin Metropolitan Police
DORA	Defence of the Realm Act
GAA	Gaelic Athletic Association
GPO	General Post Office
ILP	Independent Labour Party
INL	Irish National League
IPP	Irish Parliamentary Party
IRB	Irish Republican Brotherhood
ISRP	Irish Socialist Republican Party
ITGWU	Irish Transport and General Workers' Union
ITUC	Irish Trades Union Congress
IWFL	Irish Women's Franchise League
IWW	Industrial Workers of the World
NEC	National Executive Committee (of the SLP)
RIC	Royal Irish Constabulary
SPA	Socialist Party of America
SPI	Socialist Pary of Ireland
SSF	Scottish Socialist Federation
UCD	University College Dublin
UIL	United Irish League
UVF	Ulster Volunteer Force

SELECT BIBLIOGRAPHY

The utterly invaluable *Dictionary of Irish Biography*, Cambridge University Press, Cambridge, 2009 (*DIB*)
Oxford Dictionary of National Biography, Oxford University Press, Oxford, 2004 (*DNB*)

Augusteijn, Joost, *Patrick Pearse: The Making of a Revolutionary*, Palgrave Macmillan, Basingstoke, 2010
Barton, Brian, *From Behind a Closed Door: Secret Court Martial Records of the 1916 Rising*, The Blackstaff Press, Belfast, 2002
Clarke, Kathleen, *Kathleen Clarke: Revolutionary Woman*, ed. Helen Litton, O'Brien Press, Dublin, 2008
Clarke, Thomas James, *Glimpses of an Irish Felon's Prison Life*, Maunsell & Roberts, Dublin and London, 1922 (reproduced by BiblioLife)
Collins, Lorcan, *James Connolly*, The O'Brien Press, Dublin, 2013
Colum, Padraic and O'Brien, Edward J. (eds), *Poems of the Irish Revolutionary Brotherhood*, Small, Maynard & Company, Boston, 1916
Conyngham, D.P., *The History of Ireland from the Treaty of Limerick to the Year 1868, Being a Continuation of the History of the Abbé Mac-Geoghegan, by John Mitchel, Revised and Continued to the Present Time*, D&J Sadlier, Montreal, 1889
Cronin, Seán (ed.), *The McGarrity Papers*, Anvil, Tralee, 1972
D'Arcy, Fergus A., 'James Connolly' in *DIB*
Devoy, John, *Recollections of an Irish Rebel*, Irish University Press, Shannon, 1969
Dillon, Geraldine Plunkett, *All in the Blood: A Memoir*, ed. Honor O Brolchain, A. & A. Farmer, Dublin, 2006
Edwards, Owen Dudley, *The Mind of an Activist: James Connolly*, Gill & Macmillan, Dublin, 1971

Edwards, Owen Dudley and Ransom, Bernard (eds), *James Connolly: Selected Political Writings*, Jonathan Cape, London, 1973

Edwards, Ruth Dudley, *James Connolly*, Gill & Macmillan, Dublin, 1980

Edwards, Ruth Dudley, *Patrick Pearse: The Triumph of Failure*, Poolbeg, Dublin, 1990

Edwards, Ruth Dudley, 'James Connolly' in *DNB*

Edwards, Ruth Dudley, 'Patrick Henry Pearse' in *DNB*

Elliott, Marianne, *Robert Emmet: The Making of a Legend*, Profile, London, 2003

Enright, Seán, *Easter Rising 1916: The Trial*, Merrion, Kildare, 2014

Feeney, Brian, *Seán MacDiarmada*, The O'Brien Press, Dublin, 2014

Figgis, Darrell, *Recollections of The Irish War*, Ernest Benn, London, 1927, https://archive.org/stream/recollectionsofi00figg/recollectionsofi00figg_djvu.txt

FitzGerald, Desmond, *Memoirs of Desmond FitzGerald 1913–1916*, Routledge & Kegan Paul, London, 1968

Foster, R.F., *W.B. Yeats: A Life I – The Apprentice Mage 1865–1914*, Oxford University Press, Oxford, 1997

Foster, R.F., *W.B. Yeats: A Life II – The Arch-Poet 1915–1939*, Oxford University Press, Oxford, 2003

Foster, R.F., *Vivid Faces: The Revolutionary Generation in Ireland, 1890–1923*, Penguin, New York, 2015

Foy, Michael, *Tom Clarke: The True Leader of the Easter Rising*, The History Press Ireland, Dublin, 2014

Foy, Michael T. and Barton, Brian, *The Easter Rising*, The History Press, Stroud, 2011

Gallagher, Mary, *Éamonn Ceannt*, The O'Brien Press, Dublin, 2014

Geoghegan, Patrick M., *Robert Emmet: A Life*, Gill & Macmillan, Dublin, 2004

Ghairbhí, Róisín Ní, *Willie Pearse*, The O'Brien Press, Dublin, 2015

Greaves, C. Desmond, *The Life and Times of James Connelly*, Lawrence & Wishart, London, 1961

Hay, Marnie, *Bulmer Hobson and the Nationalist Movement in Twentieth-Century Ireland*, Manchester University Press, Manchester, 2009

Heartfield, James, and Rooney, Kevin, *Who's Afraid of the Easter Rising? 1916–2016*, Zero Books, Winchester, 2015

Henry, William, *Éamonn Ceannt: Signatory of the 1916 Proclamation*, Mercier Press, Blackrock, 2012

Higgins, Roisín, *Transforming 1916: Meaning, Memory and the Fiftieth Anniversary of the Easter Rising*, Cork University Press, Cork, 2012

Higgins, Roisín and Uí Chollatáin, Regina (eds), *The Life and After-Life of P.H. Pearse/Pádraic Mac Piarais: Saol and Oidhreacht*, Irish Academic Press, Dublin, 2009

Hobson, Bulmer, *Yesterday, Today and Tomorrow*, Anvil, Tralee, 1968

Hughes, Brian, *Michael Mallin: 16 Lives*, The O'Brien Press, Dublin, 2013

Inglis, Brian, *Roger Casement*, Hodder & Stoughton, London, 1973

Kenna, Shane, *War in the Shadows: The Irish-American Fenians Who Bombed Victorian Britain*, Merrion, Kildare, 2013

Kenna, Shane, *Thomas MacDonagh: 16 Lives*, The O'Brien Press, Dublin, 2014

Kennedy, Liam: *Unhappy the Land: The Most Oppressed People Ever, the Irish?* Irish Academic Press, Dublin, 2015

Kibler, M. Alison, 'Pigs, Green Whiskers, and Drunken Widows: Irish Nationalists and the "Practical Censorship" of McFadden's Row of Flats in 1902 and 1903,' *Journal of American Studies*, 42, 3 (2008), pp. 489–514

Larkin, Emmet, *James Larkin*, Routledge & Kegan Paul, London, 1965

Le Caron, Henri, *Twenty-Five Years in the Secret Service: The Recollections of a Spy*, William Heinemann, London, 1892

Le Roux, Louis N., *Tom Clarke and the Irish Freedom Movement*, Talbot Press, Dublin, 1936

Lee, J.J., 'Patrick Henry Pearse' in *DIB*

Leveson, Samuel, *James Connolly: A Biography*, Martin Brian & O'Keefe, London, 1973

Litton, Helen, *Thomas Clarke: 16 Lives*, The O'Brien Press, Dublin, 2014

MacAtasney, Gerard, *Seán MacDiarmada: The Mind of the Revolution*, Drumlin, Leitrim, 2004

MacAtasney, Gerard, *Tom Clarke: Life, Liberty, Revolution*, Merrion, Kildare, 2013

MacDonagh, Thomas, 'The Art and the Craft,' *Irish Review*, I, January 1912, pp. 557–9

MacDonagh, Thomas, *The Poetical Works of Thomas MacDonagh*, The Talbot Press, Dublin, 1919

MacDonagh, D., 'Plunkett and MacDonagh,' in F.X. Martin (ed.), *Leaders and Men of the Easter Rising: Dublin 1916*, Methuen, London, 1967, pp. 165–76.

MacDonagh, Thomas, *When the Dawn is Come*, De Paul University, Chicago, 1973

MacDonagh, Thomas, *Literature in Ireland: Studies Irish and Anglo-Irish*, Relay, Nenagh, 1996

MacLochlainn, Piaras F., *Last Words: Letters and Statements of the Leaders Executed After the Rising at Easter 1916*, Kilmainham Jail Restoration Society, Dublin, 1971

Martin, F.X. (ed.), *Leaders and Men of the Easter Rising: Dublin 1916*, Methuen, London, 1967

Matthews, Ann, *Renegades: Irish Republican Women 1900–1922*, Mercier Press, Cork, 2010

McEvoy, Paddy, *A Disobedient History of Ireland: Awkward Questions and Divergent Answers*, Book 1, TTG Publications, Dublin, 2013 (Kindle edition only)

McBrien, Peter, 'Poets of the Insurrection III: Joseph Plunkett', in *Studies: An Irish Quarterly Review* 5, 20 (December 1916), pp. 536–49.

McConville, Seán, *Irish Political Prisoners, 1848–1922: Theatres of War*, Routledge, London and New York, 2003

McCoole, Sinéad, *Easter Widows: Seven Irish Women Who Lived in the Shadow of the 1916 Rising*, Doubleday Ireland, Dublin, 2014

McGarry, Fearghal, *The Rising: Easter 1916*, Oxford University Press, Oxford, 2011

McGarry, Fearghal, *Rebels: Voices from the Easter Rising*, London, Penguin, 2012

Moran, Séan Farrell, *Patrick Pearse and the Politics of Redemption: The Mind of the Easter Rising*, Catholic University of America Press, Washington, 1994

Nevin, Donal, *James Connolly: 'A Full Life'*, Gill & Macmillan, Dublin, 2005

Nic Shiubhlaigh, Máire, *The Splendid Years*, J. Duffy, Dublin, 1995

Norstedt, Johann A., *Thomas MacDonagh: A Critical Biography*, University of Virginia Press, Charlottesville, 1980

Nowlan, Kevin B., *The Making of 1916: Studies in the History of the Rising*, Stationery Office, Dublin, 1969

O'Braonain, Cathaoir, 'Patrick H. Pearse', in *Studies: An Irish Quarterly Review*, 5, 19 (September 1916), pp. 339–50

O'Brien, Conor Cruise (ed.), *The Shaping of Modern Ireland*, Routledge & Kegan Paul, London, 1960

O'Brien, Conor Cruise, *States of Ireland*, Hutchinson, 1972

O'Brien, William and Ryan, Desmond (eds), *Devoy's Post Bag*, vol. II, 1871–1928, C.J. Fallon, Dublin, 1953

O'Brien, Nora Connolly, *James Connolly: Portrait of a Rebel Father*, Four Masters, Dublin, 1975

O Brolchain, Honor, *Joseph Plunkett*, The O'Brien Press, Dublin, 2012

Ó Buachalla, Seamus, *The Letters of P.H. Pearse*, Colin Smythe, Gerrards Cross, 1980

O'Callaghan, Sean, *James Connolly: My Search for the man, the myth and his legacy*, Century, London, 2015

O'Casey, Seán, *Autobiograpies I*, Macmillan, London, 1972

Pašeta, Senia, *Irish Nationalist Women, 1900–1918*, Cambridge University Press, Cambridge, 2014

Pearse, P.H., *The Story of a Success*, ed. Desmond Ryan, Maunsell, Dublin, 1918

Pearse, P.H., *Collected Works of Pádraic H. Pearse*, four volumes, Phoenix Dublin, n.d.

Plunkett, Geraldine, 'The Insurrection of 1916: II. Joseph Plunkett: Origin and Background', *University Review*, 1, 12 (Spring 1957), pp. 35–46

Plunkett, Joseph Mary, *Poems*, The Talbot Press, Dublin, 1916

Quinn, James, 'Éamonn Ceannt' in *DIB*

Quinn, James, 'Thomas James Clarke ('Tom')' in *DIB*

Ryan, Desmond, *The Man Called Pearse*, Maunsel & Roberts, Dublin, 1923

Ryan, Desmond, *Remembering Sion: A Chronicle of Storm and Quiet*, Arthur Barker, London, 1934

Ryan, Desmond, *The Rising: The Complete Story of Easter Week*, Golden Eagle, Dublin, 1949

Ryan, Desmond, 'Stephens, Devoy and Tom Clarke', in Conor Cruise O'Brien (ed.), *The Shaping of Modern Ireland*, Routledge & Kegan Paul, London, 1960

Ryan, Desmond (ed.), *The 1916 Poets*, Allen Figgis, Dublin, 1963

Sisson, Elaine, *Pearse's Patriots: St Enda's and the Cult of Boyhood*, Cork University Press, Cork, 2004

Stephen, James, *The Insurrection in Dublin*, Colin Smythe, Gerrards Cross, 1978

Sullivan, T.D., Sullivan, A.M. and Sullivan, D.B. (eds), *Speeches from the Dock, Or, Protests of Irish Patriotism*, A. M. Sullivan, Dublin, 1868

Thompson, William Irwin, *The Imagination of an Insurrection: Dublin, Easter 1916 – A Study of an Ideological Movement*, Harper Colophon, New York, 1972

Tierney, Michael, *Eoin MacNeill: Scholar and Man of Action, 1867–1945*, ed. F.X. Martin, Clarendon Press, Oxford, 1980

Townshend, Charles, *Easter 1916: The Irish Rebellion*, Penguin, London, 2006

White, Lawrence William, 'Joseph Mary Plunkett' in *DIB*

White, Lawrence William, 'Seán' Mac Diarmada (MacDermott)' *DIB*

White, Lawrence William, 'Thomas MacDonagh' in *DIB*

Yeates, Padraig, *Lockout Dublin 1913*, Gill & Macmillan, Dublin, 2000

Yeats, W.B., *Autobiographies*, Scribner, New York, 1999

NOTES

1 Thomas J. Clarke

1. Michael Foy's *Tom Clarke: The True Leader of the Easter Rising*, The History Press Ireland, Dublin, 2014, is my default source for this chapter and is therefore rarely cited.
2. Desmond Ryan, 'Stephens, Devoy and Tom Clarke', in Conor Cruise O'Brien (ed.), *The Shaping of Modern Ireland*, Routledge & Kegan Paul, London, 1960, pp. 36–7.
3. Helen Litton, *Thomas Clarke: 16 Lives*, The O'Brien Press, Dublin, 2014 has a detailed account of James Clarke's career.
4. There are no records to back up the belief that Clarke was born in 1858 in Hampshire or the Isle of Wight and Kathleen Clarke was unequivocal that he was born in 1857. See Michael Foy, *Tom Clarke*, pp. 7–8.
5. Sinéad McCoole, *Easter Widows: Seven Irish Women Who Lived in the Shadow of the 1916 Rising*, Doubleday Ireland, Dublin, 2014, p. 13.
6. Gerard MacAtasney, *Tom Clarke: Life, Liberty, Revolution*, Merrion, Kildare, 2013, p. 33.
7. Louis N. Le Roux, *Tom Clarke and the Irish Freedom Movement*, Talbot Press, Dublin, 1936, p. 13.
8. Thomas Bartlett, 'Theobald Wolfe Tone', *DIB*.
9. Henri Le Roux, *Tom Clarke*, p. 15
10. Henri Le Caron, *Twenty-Five Years in the Secret Service: The Recollections of a Spy*, William Heinemann, London, 1892, pp. 102–3.
11. Ibid., p. 279.
12. Letter to *The Irish Times*, 4 August 2015.
13. Foy, *Tom Clarke*, p. 16.
14. Le Caron, *Twenty-Five Years*, p. 280.
15. Shane Kenna, *War in the Shadows: The Irish–American Fenians Who Bombed Victorian Britain*, Merrion, Kildare, 2013, p. 137.
16. Litton, *Thomas Clarke*, p. 36.

17. Quoted in Seán McConville, *Irish Political Prisoners, 1848–1922: Theatres of War*, Routledge, London and New York, 2003, p. 359.
18. Le Roux, *Tom Clarke*, p. 33.
19. Ibid., p. 34.
20. Foy, *Tom Clarke*, p. 23.
21. Thomas James Clarke, *Glimpses of an Irish Felon's Prison Life*, Maunsell & Roberts, Dublin and London, 1922, pp. 21–2.
22. McConville, *Irish Political Prisoners*, p. 361.
23. T.D. Sullivan, A.M. Sullivan and D.B. Sullivan (eds), *Speeches from the Dock, Or, Protests of Irish Patriotism*, A. M. Sullivan, Dublin, 1868, p. xx, online at http://www.gutenberg.org/files/13112/13112-h/13112-h. htm.
24. Quoted in Owen Dudley Edwards, 'Forward from Death', *The Drouth* (Winter 2014/15), p. 110.
25. McConville, *Irish Political Prisoners*, p. 369.
26. Litton, *Thomas Clarke*, p. 22.
27. McConville, *Irish Political Prisoners*, p. 379, note 29.
28. Ibid., p. 372.
29. Ibid., p. 365.
30. Foy, *Tom Clarke*, p. 35.
31. McConville, *Irish Political Prisoners*, p. 364.
32. Clarke, *Glimpses*, p. 55.
33. Le Caron, *Twenty-Five Years*, p. 244.
34. For the 'Record of Prison Offences of J464 Henry Hammond Wilson' see MacAtasney, *Tom Clarke*, pp. 16–17; in Clarke's *Glimpses*, p. 33, he gives the combined period as forty rather than thirty-six.
35. Clarke, *Glimpses*, p. 67.
36. http://www.bureauofmilitaryhistory.ie/reels/bmh/BMH.WS0226.pdf.
37. McConville, *Irish Political Prisoners*, p. 375.
38. Litton, *Thomas Clarke*, p. 42.
39. Ibid., p. 44.
40. MacAtasney, *Tom Clarke*, p. 24.
41. Quoted in McConville, *Irish Political Prisoners*, p. 384.
42. Clarke, *Glimpses*, p. 43.
43. Hansard, HC Deb 29 August 1893, vol. 16 c1357.
44. 18 June 1895; MacAtasney, *Tom Clarke*, pp. 125–6.
45. 27 August 1899 to Kathleen Clarke; ibid., p. 140.
46. Ibid., p. 34.
47. McConville, *Irish Political Prisoners*, p. 397.
48. Ibid., p. 401.
49. Hansard, HC Deb 29 June 1896, vol. 42 c270.
50. MacAtasney, *Tom Clarke*, p. 27.

51. Ibid., pp. 36–7.
52. To Patrick Jordan, 21 December 1897, ibid., p. 127.
53. Ibid., pp. 127–8.
54. Ibid., p. 46.
55. 26 March 1999 to Kathleen Daly; ibid., p. 133.
56. Kathleen Clarke, *Kathleen Clarke: Revolutionary Woman*, ed. Helen Litton, O'Brien Press, Dublin, 2008, p. 28.
57. Ibid., p. 13.
58. McCoole, *Easter Widows*, p. 10.
59. 22 January 1901 to Kathleen Clarke; Foy, *Tom Clarke*, p. 80.
60. MacAtasney, *Tom Clarke*, p. 50; 4 May 1899 to Kathleen Clarke; MacAtasney, *Tom Clarke*, p. 131.
61. Ibid., p.51.
62. Ryan, 'Stephens, Devoy and Tom Clarke,' p. 25.
63. John Devoy, *Recollections of an Irish Rebel*, Irish University Press, Shannon, 1969, p. 392.
64. N.d., but September 1899; MacAtasney, *Tom Clarke*, pp. 144–5.
65. Kathleen Clarke to Clarke, quoted in ibid., p. 290.
66. Kathleen Clarke, 30 October 1899; ibid.
67. 5 November 1899 to Kathleen Clarke; ibid., p.147.
68. Christmas Eve 1899 to Kathleen Clarke; ibid., p. 153.
69. 27 August 1899 to Kathleen Clarke; ibid., p. 140.
70. 11 March 1900 to Kathleen Clarke; ibid., p. 157.
71. To Tom Clarke, 28 March 1900; ibid., p. 290.
72. Foy, *Tom Clarke*, p. 76.
73. Kathleen to Clarke, 18 March 1901, quoted in MacAtasney, *Tom Clarke*, p. 291.
74. Tom Clarke to Kathleen Clarke, June 1904; ibid., p. 181.
75. William O'Brien and Desmond Ryan (eds), *Devoy's Post Bag*, vol. II, 1871–1928, C.J. Fallon, Dublin, 1953, pp. 349–50.
76. Clarke, *Kathleen Clarke*, p. 39.
77. Kathleen Clarke, quoted in Foy, *Tom Clarke*, p. 41.
78. Clarke, *Kathleen Clarke*, p. 43.
79. Litton, *Thomas Clarke*, p. 82.
80. Le Caron, *Twenty-Five Years*, p. 103.
81. Clarke, *Kathleen Clarke*, p. 44.
82. Ibid., p. 43.
83. M. Alison Kibler, *Censoring Racial Ridicule: Irish, Jewish, and African American Struggles Over Race and Representation, 1890–1930*, University of North Carolina Press, Chapell Hill, 2015, p. 79.
84. For an account of this see M. Alison Kibler, 'Pigs, Green Whiskers, and Drunken Widows: Irish Nationalists and the "Practical Censorship" of

McFadden's Row of Flats in 1902 and 1903,' *Journal of American Studies*, 42, 3 (2008), pp. 489–514.

85. Foy, *Tom Clarke*, p. 83.
86. Clarke, *Kathleen Clarke*, p, 48.
87. Denis McCullough in Fearghal Garry, *Rebels: Voices from the Easter Rising*, London, Penguin, 2012, p. 21.
88. Clarke, *Kathleen Clarke*, p. 50.
89. MacAtasney, *Tom Clarke*, p. 60.
90. Ibid., p. 60.
91. Foy, *Tom Clarke*, p. 94.

2 Seán Mac Diarmada

1. Brian Feeney's *Seán MacDiarmada*, The O'Brien Press, Dublin, 2014, is my default source, and is therefore rarely cited.
2. His birth certificate said 29 March 1883, but his baptismal certificate had him christened on 29 January. The consensus is that he was probably born on 27 January 1883.
3. Feeney, *Seán MacDiarmada*, discusses this background at length.
4. Gerard MacAtasney, *Seán MacDiarmada: The Mind of the Revolution*, Drumlin, Leitrim, 2004, p. 7.
5. *Irish Freedom*, August 1913; quoted in Feeney, *Seán MacDiarmada*, p. 36.
6. Quoted in MacAtasney, *Seán MacDiarmada*, p. 9, from D.P. Conyngham, *The History of Ireland from the Treaty of Limerick to the Year 1868, Being a Continuation of the History of the Abbé Mac-Geoghegan, by John Mitchel, Revised and Continued to the Present Time*, D&J Sadlier, Montreal, 1889.
7. MacAtasney, *Seán MacDiarmada*, p. 9.
8. Ibid., p. 10.
9. It was published in *The Nation* in 1854.
10. The friend was Sarah Curran's father, John Philpot Curran, Patrick M. Geoghegan, *Robert Emmet: A Life*, Gill & Macmillan, Dublin, 2004, p. 55.
11. Sullivan, *Speeches from the Dock*, 1868, online at http://www.gutenberg.org/files/13112/13112-h/13112-h.htm#THEOBALD_WOLFE_TONE.
12. Marianne Elliott, *Robert Emmet: The Making of a Legend*, Profile, London, 2003, pp. 138–9.
13. Ibid., pp., 113–14.
14. Ibid., pp. 116–18.
15. MacAtasney, *Seán MacDiarmada*, p. 16.
16. Seán Cronin (ed.), *The McGarrity Papers*, Anvil, Tralee, 1972, p. 23.
17. MacAtasney, *Seán MacDiarmada*, p. 15.

18. Ibid., p. 16.
19. Ibid., p. 19
20. Marnie Hay, *Bulmer Hobson and the Nationalist Movement in Twentieth-Century Ireland*, Manchester University Press, Manchester, 2009, p. 51.
21. MacAtasney, *Seán MacDiarmada*, p. 21.
22. Ibid., p. 20.
23. Hay, *Bulmer Hobson*, p. 53.
24. MacAtasney, *Seán MacDiarmada*, pp. 21–2.
25. Hay, *Bulmer Hobson*, p. 52.
26. MacAtasney, *Seán MacDiarmada*, p. 17.
27. Michael Laffan, 'Arthur Griffith', *DIB*.
28. Hay, *Bulmer Hobson*, p. 73.
29. MacAtasney, *Seán MacDiarmada*, p. 34.
30. Ibid., p. 31.
31. Cronin (ed.), *The McGarrity Papers*, p. 25.
32. MacAtasney, *Seán MacDiarmada*, p. 35.
33. Ibid., p. 37.
34. Foy, *Tom Clarke*, p. 97.
35. Clarke, *Kathleen Clarke*, p. 55.
36. Piaras Béaslaí, quoted in Foy, *Tom Clarke*, p. 98.
37. MacAtasney, *Seán MacDiarmada*, p. 44.
38. Ibid., p. 45.
39. Ibid., p. 44.
40. Ibid., pp. 43–4.
41. Ibid., p. 45; Feeney, *Seán MacDiarmada*, p. 200.
42. MacAtasney, *Seán MacDiarmada*, p. 48.
43. Ibid.,, p. 43.
44. Foy, *Tom Clarke*, p. 109.
45. Ibid., p.100.
46. Preface to Clarke, *Glimpses*, pp. xiv–xv.
47. Foy, *Tom Clarke*, p. 105.
48. Ibid., p. 106.
49. MacAtasney, *Seán MacDiarmada*, p. 53.
50. Clarke, *Kathleen Clarke*, p. 58.
51. Foy, *Tom Clarke*, p. 108; MacAtasney, *Seán MacDiarmada*, p. 58.
52. Foy, *Tom Clarke*, p. 108.
53. MacAtasney, *Seán MacDiarmada*, p. 55.
54. Mary Gallagher, *Éamonn Ceannt*, The O'Brien Press, Dublin, 2014.

3 Éamonn Ceannt

1. Mary Gallagher's *Éamonn Ceannt*, The O'Brien Press, Dublin, 2014, is my default source for this chapter and is therefore rarely cited.
2. William Henry, *Éamonn Ceannt: Signatory of the 1916 Proclamation*, Mercier Press, Blackrock, 2012, p. 28.
3. Martin Daly quoted in Henry, *Éamonn Ceannt*, p. 39.
4. Ibid., p. 44.
5. Ibid., p. 39.
6. Ruth Dudley Edwards, *Patrick Pearse: The Triumph of Failure*, Poolbeg, Dublin, 1990, p. 82.
7. Quoted from Áine Ceannt, in Henry, *Éamonn Ceannt*, p. 42.
8. Gallagher, *Éamonn Ceannt*, p. 47.
9. Henry, *Éamonn Ceannt*, p. 44.
10. Based on accounts of this visit from the MS by P.J. Daniels, 'Éamonn Ceannt's Visit to Rome' (NLI Ceannt Papers MS 41,479/8); there are accounts of this visit by both Gallagher and Henry.
11. Edwards, *Patrick Pearse*, p. 83.
12. Ibid., p. 89.
13. *An Barr Buadh*, 18 May 1912.
14. Feeney, *Seán MacDiarmada*, pp.114–5.
15. Edwards, *Patrick Pearse*, p. 182.
16. *An Barr Buadh*, 19 April 1912, quoted in Gallagher, *Éamonn Ceannt*, p. 111.
17. Peadar Ó Cearnaigh, quoted in Edwards, *Patrick Pearse*, p. 154.

4 Patrick H. Pearse

1. Among the many examinations of the life and legacy of Patrick Pearse are several biographies. In addition to my own, I have drawn most heavily on that of Joost Augusteijn, who has a great deal of new information on Pearse's youth and family background. He had access to the large cache of papers of Judge Michael Lennon, who in the 1940s collected information and reminiscences about Pearse from relatives, family friends and contemporaries. I will rarely cite either book.
2. Edwards, *Patrick Pearse*, p. 164.
3. *An Barr Buadh*, 11 May 1912, translated in Edwards, *Patrick Pearse*, p. 175.
4. Cook in Roisín Higgins and Regina Uí Chollatáin (eds), *The Life and After-Life of P.H. Pearse/Pádraic Mac Piarais: Saol and Oidhreacht*, Irish Academic Press, Dublin, 2009, p. 62.

5. Fragment of autobiography, quoted in Joost Augusteijn, *Patrick Pearse: The Making of a Revolutionary*, Palgrave Macmillan, Basingstoke, 2010, p. 7.
6. Brian Crowley, "I am the son of a good father': James and Patrick Pearse', in Higgins and Uí Chollatáin (eds), *The Life and After-Life of P.H. Pearse*, p. 31.
7. Mary Brigid Pearse (ed.), *The Home-Life of Patrick Pearse*, Mercier Press, Dublin, 1935.
8. Crowley, 'I am the son of a good father', pp. 21–2.
9. Ibid., pp. 26–7; see also Augusteijn, *Patrick Pearse*, pp. 15–16.
10. Liam O'Donnell quoted in Augusteijn, *Patrick Pearse*, p. 37.
11. Veale quoted by Augusteijn in Higgins and Uí Chollatáin (eds), *The Life and After-Life of P.H. Pearse*, p. 4.
12. Éamonn O'Neill quoted by Augusteijn in ibid, p. 46.
13. Veale quoted by Augusteijn in ibid., p. 5.
14. Augusteijn, *Patrick Pearse*, p. 45.
15. J.A. Duffy quoted by Augusteijn in Higgins and Uí Chollatáin (eds), *The Life and After-Life of P.H. Pearse*, p. 9.
16. Jimmy Whelan, quoted in Augusteijn, *Patrick Pearse*, p. 1.
17. Máire Nic Shiubhlaigh, *The Splendid Years*, J. Duffy, Dublin, 1995, p. 150.
18. Thomas Flannery, *For the Tongue of the Gael*, City of London Book Depot, 1896.
19. William Jackson quoted in Augusteijn, *Patrick Pearse*, pp. 63–4.
20. Gallagher, *Éamonn Ceannt*, p. 36.
21. Nic Shiubhlaigh, *The Splendid Years*, p. 148.
22. Augusteijn, *Patrick Pearse*, 137
23. P.H. Pearse, *The Story of a Success*, ed. Desmond Ryan, Maunsell, Dublin, 1918, pp. 4–5.
24. Ibid., pp. 90–92.
25. Elaine Sisson, *Pearse's Patriots: St Enda's and the Cult of Boyhood*, Cork University Press, Cork, 2004, *passim*.
26. Patrick Maume, 'Standish O'Grady,' in *DIB*.
27. R.F. Foster, *W.B. Yeats: A Life I – The Apprentice Mage 1865–1914*, Oxford University Press, Oxford, 1997, p. 399.
28. Seán Farrell Moran, *Patrick Pearse and the Politics of Redemption: The Mind of the Easter Rising*, Catholic University of America Press, Washington, 1994, pp. 123–4.
29. 'In First Century Ireland', Sisson, *Pearse's Patriots*, pp. 135–7.
30. Augusteijn, *Patrick Pearse*, p. 60.
31. Pearse, *The Story of a Success*, p. 22.
32. Edwards, *Patrick Pearse*, pp. 124–6.
33. Shane Kenna, *Thomas MacDonagh: 16 Lives*, O'Brien Press, Dublin, 2014, p. 80.
34. Augusteijn, *Patrick Pearse*, p. 48.

35. Desmond Ryan, *Remembering Sion: A Chronicle of Storm and Quiet*, Arthur Barker, London, 1934, p. 114.
36. http://www.bureauofmilitaryhistory.ie/reels/bmh/BMH.WS0909.pdf#page=2 (accessed 30 October 2015).
37. Seamus Ó Buachalla, *The Letters of P.H. Pearse*, Colin Smythe, Gerrards Cross, 1980, pp. 266–7.
38. Ryan, *Remembering Sion*, pp. 111–12.
39. Ó Buachalla, *Letters*, p. 253.
40. *An Barr Buadh*, 16 March 1912, translated in Edwards, *Patrick Pearse*, pp. 161–2.
41. Liam Kennedy, *Unhappy the Land*, pp. 128–90.

5 Thomas MacDonagh

1. Kenna's *Thomas MacDonagh* is my default source and hence will be rarely cited.
2. Padraic Colum and E.J. O'Brien (eds), *Poems of the Irish Republican Brotherhood*, Small, Maynard & Company, Boston, 1916, p. xxxi.
3. Colum quoted in Kenna, *Thomas MacDonagh*, p. 22
4. Lawrence White, 'Thomas MacDonagh', *DIB*.
5. Thomas MacDonagh, *Literature in Ireland: Studies Irish and Anglo-Irish*, Relay, Neagh, 1996, p. 181.
6. Yeats, *Autobiographies*, Scribner, New York, 1999, pp. 373–4.
7. Nancy Murphy, 'A Profile of Thomas MacDonagh', in MacDonagh, *Literature in Ireland*, p. 182.
8. Johann A. Norstedt, *Thomas MacDonagh: A Critical Biography*, University of Virginia Press, Charlottesville, 1980, p. 32.
9. White, 'Thomas MacDonagh', *DIB*.
10. Gallagher, *Éamonn Ceannt*, p. 42.
11. Norstedt, *Thomas MacDonagh*, pp. 35–6.
12. Yeats, *Autobiographies*, p. 360.
13. Donagh MacDonagh, 'Plunkett and MacDonagh,' in F.X. Martin (ed.), *Leaders and Men of the Easter Rising: Dublin 1916*, Methuen, London, 1967, pp. 172
14. Desmond Ryan, *The Man Called Pearse*, Maunsel & Roberts, Dublin, 1923, p. 56.
15. Ryan, *Remembering Sion*, p. 95.
16. 26 January 1909, in Foster, *W.B. Yeats*, I, p. 604.
17. Pearse, *The Story of a Success*, p. 79.
18. Edwards, *Patrick Pearse*, p. 133.

19. Ryan, *Remembering Sion*, p. 87.
20. Foster, *W.B. Yeats*, I, p. 392.
21. Yeats, *Autobiographies*, p. 373.
22. 'In Paris'.
23. Foster, *W.B. Yeats*, I, p. 418.
24. William Irwin Thompson, *The Imagination of an Insurrection: Dublin, Easter 1916 – A Study of an Ideological Movement*, Harper Colophon, New York, 1972, p. 130.
25. MacDonagh, *Literature in Ireland*, p. 181.
26. Ryan, *Remembering Sion*, pp. 114–15.
27. Ibid., p. 115.
28. Norstadt, *Thomas MacDonagh*, p. 152.
29. Thomas MacDonagh, *The Poetical Works of Thomas MacDonagh*, The Talbot Press, Dublin, 1919, p. ix.
30. Pearse, *The Story of a Success*, p. 81.
31. Patrick Maume, 'William Martin Murphy', *DIB*.
32. Padraig Yeates, *Lockout Dublin 1913*, Gill & Macmillan, Dublin, 2000, p. xi.
33. Ibid., p. 66.
34. Geraldine Plunkett Dillon, *All in the Blood: A Memoir*, ed. Honor O Brolchain, A. & A. Farmer, Dublin, 2006, p.143.

6 Joseph Plunkett

1. Honor O Brolchain's *Joseph Plunkett*, The O'Brien Press, Dublin, 2012, and Geraldine Plunkett Dillon's *All in the Blood* are my default sources and hence will be rarely cited.
2. Thompson, *The Imagination*, pp. 138–9.
3. 'Our Note Book', 30 November 1907; published as 'A Dead Poet' in G.K. Chesterton, *All Things Considered*, Methuen, London, 1908.
4. 'Francis Thompson', published in *The Irish Monthly*, 37, December 1909.
5. Geraldine Plunkett, 'The Insurrection of 1916: II. Joseph Plunkett: Origin and Background', *University Review*, Vol. 1, No. 12 (Spring 1957), p. 40.
6. Geraldine Plunkett's forword to Joseph Mary Plunkett, *Poems*, The Talbot Press, Dublin, 1916, quotes this line. At the time it was thought to be by St John of the Cross, though later it was attributed to Tomás de Jesús.
7. 4 May 1909 to Dominic Hackett, O Brolchain, *Joseph Plunkett*, p. 80.
8. Padraic Colum, letter to the editor, *Poetry*, 8, August 1916, pp. 268–73.
9. Peter McBrien, 'Poets of the Insurrection III: Joseph Plunkett', in *Studies: An Irish Quarterly Review*, Vol. 5, No. 20 (Dec. 1916), p. 548.
10. Ibid., p. 537.

11. Foreword by Geraldine Plunkett in Plunkett, *Poems*, xii–xiii.
12. Thomas MacDonagh, 'The Art and the Craft,' *Irish Review*, I, January 1912, pp. 557–9.
13. Joseph Plunkett, 'Obscurity and Poetry', *Irish Review*, 3, February 1914.
14. Kenna, *Thomas MacDonagh*, p. 109.
15. Brendan Kennelly, 'The Poetry of Joseph Plunkett', *Dublin Magazine*, Spring 1966.
16. Thompson, *The Imagination*, p. 133.
17. Thomas MacDonagh, 'Criticism and Irish Poetry', *The Irish Review*, 4, May 14, incorporated in MacDonagh, *Literature in Ireland*.
18. Sisson, *Pearse's Patriots*, p. 142.
19. Pat Cooke, in Higgins and Uí Chollatáin, *The Life and After-Life of P.H. Pearse*, p. 61.
20. *An Macaomh*, May 1913, quoted by Cook in ibid., p. 43.
21. MacDonagh, *Literature in Ireland*, p. 151.
22. Edwards, *Patrick Pearse*, p. 334.
23. Thompson, *The Imagination*, pp. 123–4.
24. *Irish Times*, 14 November 1964, referred to in ibid., p. 125.
25. Yeats, *Autobiographies*, p. 360.
26. *The Irish Review*, 3, October 1913.
27. Padraig Yeates, *Lockout Dublin 1913*, Gill & Macmillan, Dublin, 2000, p. 271.
28. Ibid., p. 278.

7 James Connolly

1. Of the many biographies of James Connolly, those on which I have drawn most heavily and rarely cite are by Donal Nevin (*James Connolly: 'A Full Life'*, Gill & Macmillan, Dublin, 2005), Samuel Leveson (*James Connolly: A Biography*, Martin Brian & O'Keefe, London, 1973), and myself (Ruth Dudley Edwards, *James Connolly*, Gill & Macmillan, Dublin, 1980).
2. Letter to Lillie Reynolds in Nevin, *James Connolly*, p. 721.
3. All the surviving letters to Lillie are in Nevin, *James Connolly*, pp. 719–25.
4. Ibid., p. 724.
5. Lorcan Collins, *James Connolly*, The O'Brien Press, Dublin, 2013, p. 41.
6. Ryan, *Remembering Sion*, pp. 57–8.
7. Nora Connolly O'Brien, *James Connolly: Portrait of a Rebel Father*, Four Masters, Dublin, 1975, p. 22.
8. Leveson, *James Connolly*, p. 41.
9. Quote from Ina Connolly Heron in McCoole, *Easter Widows*, p. 79.

10. Yeats, *Autobiographies*, p. 276.
11. Ibid., p. 277.
12. Leveson, *James Connolly*, p. 68.
13. Edwards, *James Connolly*, p. 46.
14. McCoole, *Easter Widows*, p. 80.
15. November 1902, Collins, *James Connolly*, p. 110.
16. Leveson, *James Connolly*, p. 103.
17. To John Carstairs Matheson.
18. C. Desmond Greaves, *The Life and Times of James Connelly*, Lawrence & Wishart, London, 1961, p. 154.
19. Leveson, *James Connolly*, pp. 125–6.
20. Ibid., p. 145.
21. Ryan, *Remembering Sion*, p. 57.
22. Yeates, *Lockout Dublin*, p. xxvii.
23. Darrell Figgis, *Recollections of The Irish War*, Ernest Benn, London, 1927, p. 87.
24. Quoted in Leveson, *James Connolly*, pp. 211–12.
25. Jack Carney quoted in Yeates, *Lockout Dublin*, p. 399.
26. A contemporary, James Doherty, in conversation with Owen Dudley Edwards, quoted in Edwards, *James Connolly*, p. 83.
27. Emmet Larkin, *James Larkin*, Routledge & Kegan Paul, London, 1965, p. 77.
28. Quote from Ina Connolly Heron, in Collins, *James Connolly*, p. 180.

8 No Turning Back

1. There are several excellent books on this period, but Charles Townshend's brilliant *Easter 1916; The Irish Rebellion* is the one I have used most here and therefore rarely cite. On individuals, the main sources are as I have given them in the earlier chapters.
2. Figgis, *Recollections*. This was published in 1927 but thought to have been written in 1921–2.
3. Seán O'Casey, *Autobiographies I*, Macmillan, London, 1972, p. 616.
4. Cathal O'Shannon, quoted in Hay, *Bulmer Hobson*, p. 75.
5. Foy, *Tom Clarke*, p. 111.
6. Feeney, *MacDiarmada*, p. 306.
7. Cronin, *The McGarrity Papers*, pp. 32–3.
8. Feeney, *MacDiarmada*, pp. 144–5.
9. Henry, *Éamonn Ceannt*, p. 54.
10. Foy, *Tom Clarke*, p. 112.
11. Charles Townshend, *Easter 1916: The Irish Rebellion*, Penguin, London, 2006, p. 40.

12. Brian Inglis, *Roger Casement*, p. 243.
13. Kenna, *MacDonagh*, p. 146.
14. MacAtasney, *Tom Clarke*, pp. 270–71.
15. Martin, *Leaders and Men*, pp.167–8.
16. Michael Laffan, 'Roger Casement', DIB.
17. Moran, *Patrick Pearse*, p. 141.
18. Ibid., p. 143.
19. Piaras Béaslaí, *Irish Independent*, 6 January 1953, quoted in Foy, *Tom Clarke*, p. 121.
20. Hay, *Bulmer Hobson*, p. 136.
21. Ibid., p. 140.
22. Ibid., p. 141.
23. Ibid., p. 160.
24. Ibid., pp. 161–2.
25. Foy, *Tom Clarke*, p. 136.
26. Ibid.
27. Feeney, *MacDiarmada*, p. 156
28. Ibid., p. 178.
29. Larkin, *James Larkin*, p. 160.
30. Joe McGowan, *Constance Markievicz: The People's Countess*, Constance Markievicz Millennium Committee, Sligo, 2003.
31. McCoole, *Easter Widows*, p. 95.
32. Maume, 'Bulmer Holson', DIB.
33. Canon Hannay, quoted in Townshend, *Easter 1916*, p. 75.
34. Foy, *Tom Clarke*, p. 138.
35. Edwards, *Patrick Pearse*, p. 218.
36. Foy, *Tom Clarke*, p. 138.
37. Ibid., p. 145.
38. Brian Hughes, *Michael Mallin: 16 Lives*, The O'Brien Press, Dublin, 2013, p. 90.
39. Inglis, *Roger Casement*, p. 266.
40. Foy, *Tom Clarke*, p. 150.
41. Inglis, *Roger Casement*, p. 268.
42. Townshend, *Easter 1916*, p. 106.
43. R. F. Foster, *W.B. Yeats: A Life II – The Arch-Poet 1915–1939*, Oxford University Press, Oxford, 2003, p. 62.
44. Foy, *Tom Clarke*, p. 166.
45. Figgis, *Recollections*, p. 103.
46. Ibid., p. 86.
47. Quoted in Townshend, *Easter 1916*, p. 371.
48. The friend was Desmond FitzGerald, *Memoirs of Desmond FitzGerald 1913–1916*, Routledge & Kegan Paul, London, 1968, pp. 79–80.
49. Quoted in Townshend, *Easter 1916*, p. 111,

50. Quoted in ibid., p. 112.

51. Edwards, *Patrick Pearse*, p. 250.

52. Ibid., p. 241.

53. Seán O'Casey, *The Story of the Irish Citizen Army*, The Journeyman Press, London, 1980, p. 52.

54. Ryan, *The Rising*, p. 49.

55. O Brolchain, *Joseph Plunkett*, p. 272.

56. Edwards, *Patrick Pearse*, p. 265.

57. Ibid., p. 268.

58. Brian Barton, *From Behind a Closed Door: Secret Court Martial Records of the 1916 Rising*, The Blackstaff Press, Belfast, 2002, p. 121.

59. Collins, *James Connolly*, pp.262–30.

60. O'Casey, *Autobiographies*, p. 647.

61. Ina Connolly Heron quoted in Collins, *James Connolly*, p. 270.

62. Martin, *Leaders and Men*, p. 251.

63. Hay, *Bulmer Hobson*, p. 186.

64. Kenna, *Thomas MacDonagh*, p. 194.

65. Hay, *Bulmer Hobson*, p. 194.

66. Ibid., pp. 195–6.

67. Foy, *Tom Clarke*, p. 202.

68. Diarmuid Lynch, quoted in ibid., p. 205.

69. Foy, *Tom Clarke*, p. 206.

70. Clarke, *Kathleen Clarke*, p. 69.

71. Foy, *Tom Clarke*, p. 198.

72. McCoole, *Easter Widows*, p. 225.

73. Nic Shiubhlaigh, *The Splendid Years*, pp. 162–4.

74. Nathan quoted in Leon Ó Broin, 'Birrell, Nathan, and the Men of Dublin Castle,' in Martin, *Leaders and Men*, p. 6.

9 Last Act

1. Apart from Charles Townshend's, among the excellent books I have drawn on for the Rising are those by Michael Foy and Brian Barton and two by Fearghal McGarry. Barton, *From Behind a Closed Door*, Seán Enright, *Easter Rising 1916: The Trial*, Merrion, Kildare, 2014, and Piaras F. MacLochlainn, *Last Words: Letters and Statements of the Leaders Executed After the Rising at Easter 1916*, Kilmainham Jail Restoration Society, Dublin, 1971, are the main sources for the retribution section.

2. Sydney Gifford Czira, *The Years Flew By*, Gifford & Craven, Dublin, 1974, pp. 20–22.

3. Joe Good quoted in Fearghal McGarry, *The Rising: Easter 1916*, Oxford University Press, Oxford, 2011, p. 131.
4. Foy, *Tom Clarke*, p. 215.
5. Ibid., p. 220.
6. Dr James Ryan quoted in MacLochlainn, *Last Words*, p. 39.
7. Thompson, *The Imagination*, p. 107.
8. Townshend, *Easter 1916*, p. 209.
9. William Murphy, 'Desmond FitzGerald', DIB.
10. Foy, *Tom Clarke*, p. 222.
11. Edwards, *Patrick Pearse*, p. 296.
12. Foy, *Tom Clarke*, p. 221.
13. Joe Good quoted in O Brolchain, *Joseph Plunkett*, pp. 387–8.
14. Desmond Ryan, *The Rising: The Complete Story of Easter Week*, Golden Eagle, Dublin, 1949, pp. 147–8.
15. Foy, *Tom Clarke*, p. 224.
16. Edwards, *Pearse*, p. 302
17. MacLochlainn, *Last Words*, p. 183.
18. Winifred Carney memoir, quoted in Foy, *Tom Clarke*, p. 232.
19. Michael T. Foy and Brian Barton, *The Easter Rising*, The History Press, Stroud, 2011, p. 122.
20. Nic Shiubhlaigh, *The Splendid Years*, p. 176.
21. Ibid., p. 179.
22. Foy and Barton, *The Easter Rising*, p. 123.
23. McGarry, *The Rising*, pp. 156–7.
24. Foy and Barton, *The Easter Rising*, p. 129.
25. Evidence of a survivor to Owen Dudley Edwards, 1966.
26. Ibid., p. 136.
27. Ibid., p. 137.
28. Ryan, *The Rising*, p. 172.
29. Fearghal McGarry, *Rebels: Voices from the Easter Rising*, London, Penguin, 2012, p. 251.
30. Edwards, *Patrick Pearse*, p. 308.
31. Ibid., p. 310.
32. McLoughlin, *Last Words*, 185
33. Ryan, *Remembering Sion*, p. 207. There are more colourful accounts of what happened, including the allegation that Clarke was stripped naked, but Ryan is a reliable witness who had no reason to censor the story.
34. Litton, *Thomas Clarke*, p. 202.
35. Foy and Barton, *The Easter Rising*, p. 291.
36. The evidence is from Geraldine Fitzgerald, ibid, pp 80–81.
37. John J. (Seán) Murphy, BMH WS 204.
38. Enright, *Easter Rising, passim*.

39. Elizabeth, Countess of Fingall, *Seventy Years Young*, Collins, London, 1937, p. 375.
40. Foy, *Tom Clarke*, p. 185.
41. Clarke, *Kathleen Clarke*, pp. 135–40.
42. Foy, *Tom Clarke*, p. 244.

10 Legacies

1. My main sources for this final chapter are fifty years of reading and writing about Irish history and following its politics closely, and, for more than twenty years, reporting and commentating on it week by week.
2. Kevin B. Nowlan, *The Making of 1916: Studies in the History of the Rising*, Stationery Office, Dublin, 1969, p. 236.
3. *Workers' Republic*, 20 November 1915.
4. Edwards, *Pearse*, p. 338.
5. R.F. Foster, *The Revolutionary Generation in Ireland, 1890–1923*, Penguin, New York, 2015, p. 289.
6. Countess of Fingall, quoted in Edwards, *Patrick Pearse*, p. 325.

INDEX